Creed and Culture

Paula Marrutto

McGill-Queen's Studies in the History of Religion
G.A. Rawlyk, Editor

Volumes in this series have been supported by the
Jackman Foundation of Toronto.

1 Small Differences
   Irish Catholics and Irish Protestants, 1815–1922
   An International Perspective
   Donald Harman Akenson
2 Two Worlds
   The Protestant Culture of Nineteenth-Century Ontario
   William Westfall
3 An Evangelical Mind
   Nathanael Burwash and the Methodist Tradition in
   Canada, 1839–1918
   Marguerite Van Die
4 The Dévotes
   Women and Church in Seventeenth-Century France
   Elizabeth Rapley
5 The Evangelical Century
   College and Creed in English Canada from the Great
   Revival to the Great Depression
   Michael Gauvreau
6 The German Peasants' War and Anabaptist Commu-
   nity of Goods
   James M. Stayer
7 A World Mission
   Canadian Protestantism and the Quest for a New Inter-
   national Order, 1918–1939
   Robert Wright
8 Serving the Present Age
   Revivalism, Progressivism, and the Methodist
   Tradition in Canada
   Phyllis D. Airhart
9 A Sensitive Independence
   Canadian Methodist Women Missionaries in Canada
   and the Orient, 1881–1925
   Rosemary R. Gagan
10 God's Peoples
   Covenant and Land in South Africa, Israel, and Ulster
   Donald Harman Akenson
11 Creed and Culture
   The Place of English-Speaking Catholics in Canadian
   Society, 1750–1930
   Terrence Murphy and Gerald Stortz, editors

Creed and Culture

The Place of English-Speaking Catholics in Canadian Society, 1750–1930

Edited by

TERRENCE MURPHY

and

GERALD STORTZ

McGill-Queen's University Press
Montreal & Kingston • London • Buffalo

© McGill-Queen's University Press 1993
ISBN 0-7735-0954-2

Legal deposit first quarter 1993
Bibliothèque nationale du Québec

Printed in Canada on acid-free paper

This book has been published with the help of a grant
from the Social Science Federation of Canada, using
funds provided by the Social Sciences and Humanities
Research Council of Canada.

Canadian Cataloguing in Publication Data

Main entry under title:
  Creed and culture: the place of English-speaking
  Catholics in Canadian society, 1750–1930
  (McGill-Queen's studies in the history of religion)
  ISBN 0-7735-0954-2
  1. Catholics – Canada – Social life and customs.
  2. Catholic Church – Canada – History. I. Murphy,
  Terrence. II. Stortz, Gerald J. (Gerald John). III. Series.
  FC141.C74 1993   282'.71   C92-090716-4
  F1035.E53C74 1993

Typeset in Palatino 10/12 by
Caractéra production graphique inc., Quebec City.

Contents

Illustrations follow page xl

Acknowledgments / vii

Contributors / ix

Glossary / xi

Introduction / xvii
TERRENCE MURPHY

1 English-French Relations in the Canadian Catholic
Community / 3
ROBERT CHOQUETTE

2 Anti-Catholicism in Canada: From the British Conquest
to the Great War / 25
J.R. MILLER

3 Catholicism and Colonial Policy in Newfoundland, 1779–
1845 / 49
RAYMOND J. LAHEY

4 Scottish Catholicism in Canada, 1770–1830 / 79
J.M. BUMSTED

5 The Policy of Rome towards the English-Speaking
Catholics in British North America, 1750–1830 / 100
LUCA CODIGNOLA

6 Trusteeism in Atlantic Canada: The Struggle for
Leadership among the Irish Catholics of Halifax,
St John's, and Saint John, 1780–1850 / 126
TERRENCE MURPHY

7 The Growth of Roman Catholic Institutions in the
Archdiocese of Toronto, 1841–90 / 152
MURRAY NICOLSON

8 "Improvident Emigrants": John Joseph Lynch and Irish
Immigration to British North America, 1860–88 / 171
GERALD STORTZ

9 The Parish and the Hearth: Women's Confraternities and
the Devotional Revolution among the Irish Catholics of
Toronto, 1850–85 / 185
BRIAN CLARKE

10 Toronto's English-Speaking Catholics, Immigration, and
the Making of a Canadian Catholic Identity, 1900–30 /
204
MARK McGOWAN

Index / 247

Acknowledgments

We should like to acknowledge the assistance we have received from various people in the preparation of this volume. Among those to whom we are especially grateful are Philip Cercone and Joan McGilvray of McGill-Queen's University Press; Mary Walsh, secretary of the Department of Religious Studies, Memorial University of Newfoundland; and Rosemary Shipton, who edited the text.

We also acknowledge with thanks permission to reprint portions of the article by Gerald J. Stortz, "Archbishop Lynch and New Ireland: An Unfulfilled Dream for Canada's Northwest," *Catholic Historical Review* 68, 4 (Oct. 1982), which are incorporated in chapter 8 of this volume.

Terrence Murphy and Gerald Stortz

Contributors

J.M. BUMSTED is a fellow of St John's College and professor of history at the University of Manitoba. His many published works include *The People's Clearance: Highland Emigration to British North America 1770–1815* (Edinburgh and Winnipeg 1982) and *Land, Settlement and Politics in Eighteenth-Century Prince Edward Island* (Kingston, Ont. 1987).

ROBERT CHOQUETTE is a professor in the Department of Religious Studies of the University of Ottawa. He is the author of more than ten books, including *Language and Religion: A History of English-French Conflict in Ontario* (Ottawa 1975) and *Christianity Comes to the Americas* (New York 1992), the latter in cooperation with Charles Lippy and Stafford Poole.

BRIAN CLARKE is a research associate at the Centre for the Study of Religion in Canada, Emmanuel College, and he teaches at York University. He is completing a study on Irish Catholic voluntary associations in Victorian Toronto.

LUCA CODIGNOLA is an associate professor of history at the Università di Genova. He is the author of *Guerra e guerriglia nell'America coloniale, 1754–1759* (Venice 1977), *The Coldest Harbour of the Land: Simon Stock and Lord Baltimore's Colony in Newfoundland, 1621–1649* (Montreal 1988), and *Guide to the Documents Relating to French and British North America in Propaganda, Rome, 1622–1799* (Ottawa 1991).

RAYMOND J. LAHEY, formerly head of the Department of Religious Studies, Memorial University of Newfoundland, is bishop of St George's, Newfoundland. His publications on the religious history of Newfoundland include *James Louis O'Donel in Newfoundland, 1784–1807: The Establishment of the Roman Catholic Church* (St John's 1984) and "The Role of Religion in Lord Baltimore's Colonial Enterprise," *Maryland Historical Magazine* 72, 4 (1977).

MARK G. MCGOWAN teaches history at St Michael's College at the University of Toronto, and he is currently president-general of the Canadian Catholic Historical Association. He is co-editor of *Prophets, Priests, and Prodigals: Readings in Canadian Religious History* (Toronto 1992).

J.R. MILLER is a professor of history at the University of Saskatchewan. His scholarly publications include *Equal Rights: The Jesuits' Estates Act Controversy* (Montreal 1979), "Anti-Catholic Thought in Victorian Canada," *Canadian Historical Review* 66, 4 (1985), and *Skyscrapers Hide the Heavens: A History of Indian-White Relations in Canada*, rev. ed. (Toronto 1991; first published 1989).

TERRENCE MURPHY is a professor in the Department of Religious Studies, Memorial University of Newfoundland. He is co-editor of *Religion and Identity: The Experience of Irish and Scottish Catholics in Atlantic Canada* (St John's 1987) and the author of "The Emergence of Maritime Catholicism, 1781–1830," *Acadiensis* 13, 2 (1984).

MURRAY NICOLSON is a sessional lecturer at Sir Wilfrid Laurier University. His publications on the Irish Catholic community in Toronto include "Irish Catholic Education in Victorian Toronto: An Ethnic Response to Urban Conformity," *Histoire Sociale/Social History* 17, 34 (1984), and "Peasants in an Urban Society: The Irish Catholics in Victorian Toronto," in Robert F. Harney, ed., *Gathering Place: Peoples and Neighbourhoods of Toronto, 1834–1945* (Toronto 1985).

GERALD STORTZ is an associate professor of history, St Jerome's College, University of Waterloo. He has published a number of articles on the religious history of Ontario, including "Archbishop John Joseph Lynch and the Anglicans of Toronto, 1860–1888," *Journal of the Canadian Church Historical Society* 27, 1 (April 1985), and "Twenty-Eight Years of Commitment: The Episcopacy of John Joseph Lynch," *Canadian Catholic Historical Association, Study Sessions* 49 (1982).

Glossary

CATHOLIC EMANCIPATION The removal of the legal penalties and civil disabilities that had been imposed on Roman Catholics in England, Ireland, and Scotland by a series of enactments between 1559 and 1772. The move towards Catholic Emancipation began with the first Catholic Relief Act of 1778 and culminated in the Catholic Emancipation Act of 1829.

CHAPTER The body of clergy attached to a collegiate church, often the cathedral church of a bishop.

CLEAR GRITS Political party founded in Canada West in the 1840s to promote reforms such as representation by population, free trade, and separation of church and state. The Clear Grits were strongly influenced by anti-Catholic sentiment.

DENOMINATIONALISM The organization of social institutions and/or the distribution of political power and patronage along denominational lines.

DEVOTIONAL CATHOLICISM A type of Roman Catholicism, associated with the Ultramontane revival, in which popular piety was characterized by the performance of devotions and paraliturgical rituals, often involving the use of sacred objects such as rosaries and scapulars. Such devotions were frequently promoted by lay voluntary associations.

DISSENTER Term used in England to describe people who separated themselves from the Established Church. The most common usage refers to Protestant dissenters, also known as nonconformists, but strictly speaking the term may also apply to Roman Catholic dissenters.

ESTABLISHED CHURCH A church that is officially recognized by the state and, as a result, enjoys exclusive legal privileges and special provisions for its material support; for example, the Church of England and the Church of Scotland.

EUCHARISTIC CONGRESSES Series of large gatherings of Roman Catholic laity and clergy on a local, national, or international level to explore Eucharistic worship and its relevance to modern life.

GREAT DISRUPTION The separation in 1843 of a large segment of the Church of Scotland to form the Free Church in protest over control of the church by lay patrons and civil authorities.

HENRICIAN REVOLUTION The reordering of church-state relations in England during the reign of Henry VIII, by which papal authority in England was overturned and the English church was brought more decisively under the control of the crown. The centrepiece of this revolution was the First Act of Supremacy (1534), by which Parliament declared the monarch supreme head of the Church of England.

HUGUENOTS Nickname given to the Protestant minority in France, possibly derived from the German *eidgenosse*, meaning "confederate," or more specifically from its dialectal form *eidgnoss*.

INDULGENCE The Roman Catholic practice of remitting all or part of the temporal punishment due to sins that have already been forgiven through the sacrament of penance. Indulgences are granted in recognition of the performance of a specified good work or act of piety, such as the making of a pilgrimage or the giving of alms.

NATIVISM Opposition to a religious or ethnic minority on the grounds that it is considered "foreign." Some manifestations of anti-Catholicism are nativistic in character.

OATH OF ABJURATION An oath imposed on Roman Catholics by an act of the English Parliament in 1643, which required the renunciation of papal supremacy and other Roman Catholic doctrines.

OATH OF SUPREMACY An oath acknowledging the supremacy of the English monarch over the Church of England. Required by the Second Act of Supremacy (1559) of all ecclesiastical and civil officials, the oath contributed to the exclusion of Roman Catholics from Parliament and public office until it was removed by the Catholic Emancipation Act.

PAPAL AGGRESSION Anti-Catholic term used to describe Pope Pius IX's restoration of a regular Roman Catholic hierarchy in England in 1850.

PENAL LAWS or PENAL CODE A body of anti-Catholic laws enacted in England, Scotland, and Ireland between 1559 and 1772 that imposed legal penalties and civil disabilities on Roman Catholics. The penal laws were repealed between 1778 and 1829, final relief coming with the Catholic Emancipation Act of 1829.

PREFECT APOSTOLIC A priest appointed under the immediate jurisdiction of the Holy See to oversee the Roman Catholic church in a mission territory. Unlike a vicar apostolic, a prefect apostolic is not a bishop.

PROPAGANDA (SACRED CONGREGATION *DE PROPAGANDA FIDE*) A branch of the Roman Curia, established in 1622, to oversee the affairs of the Roman Catholic church in mission territories or countries where Catholics lived alongside Protestant or Orthodox Christians. Canada came under the jurisdiction of Propaganda until 1908.

RITUALISM A controversial movement, beginning around 1840, to introduce more elaborate rites and ceremonies, many of which were associated with Roman Catholic practice, into the Church of England. Ritualism has strong links with but is not identical to Tractarianism.

ROMAN CURIA The papal bureaucracy, divided for the most part into departments called "congregations," also includes offices, secretariats, and permanent commissions. Congregations, such as the Sacred Congregation *de Propaganda Fide*, are usually under the direction of a cardinal prefect.

SECULAR CLERGY Term used to describe clergy who live "in the world" as opposed to regular clergy who, as members of monastic or other religious orders, are subject to a rule that requires some measure of withdrawal from the world. The secular clergy make up the bulk of parish ministers in the Roman Catholic church and are normally organized under the direct authority of a diocesan bishop.

SOCIETY FOR THE PROPAGATION OF THE GOSPEL Anglican missionary society founded in 1701, largely through the efforts of the Rev. Thomas Bray. Commonly known as the SPG, it was largely responsible for the appointment and support of Anglican clergy in the British colonies.

SUFFRAGAN BISHOP In Roman Catholicism, a bishop who is under the authority of a metropolitan or archbishop. Despite this subordination to an archbishop, a suffragan bishop is independent of archiepiscopal interference in the government of his own diocese.

TEST ACT An act of the English Parliament passed in 1673 that required all holders of office under the crown to receive the Eucharist according to the rites of the Church of England, to take both the Oath of Supremacy and the Oath of Allegiance to the monarch, and to make a Declaration against Transubstantiation. The Test Act contributed to the exclusion of Roman Catholics from public office until the passage of the Catholic Emancipation Act of 1829.

TITULAR BISHOP A bishop who is appointed to a diocese that was once under effective Roman Catholic ecclesiastical government but has since fallen under the control of non-Catholic authorities (eg, Islam). Titular bishops have full episcopal authority but cannot exercise it in the diocese to which they hold title. Prelates chosen to oversee mission territories were often appointed titular bishops if the erection of a regular hierarchy was legally impossible or politically disadvantageous in the country to which they were assigned.

TRACTARIANS Members of the Oxford Movement within the Church of England, including among others John Keble, John Henry Newman, and E.B. Pusey. From its inception in 1833, the movement worked for the recognition of the divine authority of the Church of England as a branch of the Catholic church, the upholding of the authority of bishops as the successors of the apostles, the independence of the church from government control, and the restoration of Anglo-Catholic traditions of worship and piety. Some of the Tractarians, notably Newman, were eventually converted to Roman Catholicism.

TRANSUBSTANTIATION The official explanation among Roman Catholics of how the Eucharistic elements of bread and wine are actually changed into the body and blood of Jesus Christ. Conceived in terms of Aristotelian philosophy, the doctrine of transubstantiation states that the accidents (ie, the outward appearances) of the bread and wine remain the same while the substance (ie, the underlying reality) changes.

TREATY OF UTRECHT The treaty of 1713 at the conclusion of the War of the Spanish Succession that established Newfoundland and Nova Scotia under British as opposed to French rule.

ULTRAMONTANISM The tendency in Roman Catholicism to exalt the authority of the pope and to centralize power in his hands, especially at the expense of national hierarchies or governments. This conception of the church enjoyed an international resurgence in the early decades of the nineteenth century and gained predominance by the middle of that century. Ultramontanes held that the state should be subordinate to the church, especially in matters of education and social welfare. They also promoted the spread of papally approved devotional practices.

VICAR APOSTOLIC A Roman Catholic titular bishop who is appointed under the immediate jurisdiction of the Holy See to oversee a mission territory. A vicar apostolic, unlike a prefect apostolic, enjoys full episcopal authority, including the power to ordain clergy.

VICAR FORANE A priest appointed by a bishop to assist in the administration of a specific portion of his diocese.

VICAR-GENERAL A priest appointed by a bishop to assist in the administration of his diocese by exercising jurisdiction in his name.

Introduction

In 1986, in the wake of the fiftieth anniversary celebrations of the Canadian Catholic Historical Association, Professor George Rawlyk complained that little had been accomplished in Canadian Catholic historiography. Roman Catholic historical writing in Canada, he said, was still "bogged down in a form of safe, parochial antiquarianism." Whereas Catholic scholarship ought to be the engine of religious historiography in Canada, it had in fact been the caboose.[1]

It is difficult to quarrel with Rawlyk's stringent judgment. Research into Canadian Catholicism has come mainly from within the Canadian Catholic community, and any frank assessment of this work would have to acknowledge that most of it has been narrow in focus and filiopietistic in spirit. One might suggest, however, that Rawlyk's criticism could have been more precise. It is the study of Catholicism in English-speaking Canada that has suffered most from parochialism and lack of imagination. By contrast, French-speaking Catholic historiography has been vital and creative.[2] A rapidly growing body of outstanding works, many employing innovative methodologies, has added considerably to our understanding of popular religion, religious thought, spirituality, religious art, pastoral care, and catechetical instruction in French Canada.[3] The stimulus for this work came largely from a renewed desire, associated with the "Quiet Revolution," to understand the French fact in North America. It was further enriched by the influence of European scholarship, including that of the *Annales* school of historiography. English-speaking Catholic historians, however, have been more insular, failing to benefit as much as they might have done from the example of American, English, and Irish Catholic historiography. Without any dramatic turning-point in their history to stimulate and enliven their efforts, they have until recently been inward-looking and unimaginative. While establishing the broad narrative framework of English-speaking Catholicism in Canada, they have provided little in the way of critical analysis.

The failure to cultivate English-speaking Catholicism properly as a field of inquiry has been exacerbated by the fact that Catholicism in Canada has been closely identified with French language and culture, while the ethos of English-speaking Canada has been firmly associated with evangelical Protestantism. To the extent that religion is taken into account in general interpretations of Canadian history, its influence is associated almost exclusively with French-Canadian Catholicism or Anglo-Saxon Protestantism. English-speaking Catholics, if mentioned at all, are identified with the Irish immigrants who poured into the country in the wake of the Great Famine. Any serious effort to understand their history must begin by overcoming this cliché. While the famine migration increased the numbers of English-speaking Catholics dramatically and gave them an importance in some parts of the country they had previously lacked, the roots of the English-speaking Catholic population in Canada reach back much further than the mid nineteenth century.

In the last decade or so, the quality of research on English-speaking Catholicism has been steadily improving. Major advances in our understanding of Irish and Scottish immigration to British North America,[4] a radically revised interpretation of Irish Catholicism in the nineteenth century,[5] a more critical spirit among Canadian Catholic scholars, and a new awareness on their part of the direction of scholarship in other countries have all contributed to this change. Some of the best new work has yet to appear in print, however, and even the portion that has been published has often represented only preliminary results.

In the pages that follow, we have gathered together the work of ten scholars engaged in ongoing research on Catholicism in English Canada. The first two essays, by Robert Choquette and J.R. Miller, are broader in scope than the others, for they deal with the basic realities that have conditioned every aspect of English Catholic life in this country: its relationship with French-Canadian Catholics on the one hand and with English-Canadian Protestants on the other. All ten contributions are alike, however, in that they seek to place English-speaking Catholicism in context by relating it to broader Canadian developments and by viewing it as part of the larger story of Catholicism in the English-speaking world. They also overlap in more concrete ways, complementing one another in their treatment of specific themes and pointing the way towards a fully integrated interpretation of the topic. In our view, a full narrative survey of English-speaking Catholicism in Canada would be premature at this stage. Before such an overview can be undertaken, research has to be extended beyond its current foci in Atlantic Canada and Toronto to include other regions of Ontario, the anglophone Catholic population of Quebec, and the West, and more up-to-date work has to appear on such crucial topics as Catholic education and social Catholicism. Nevertheless, we believe that the work collected here marks a new research plateau, the significance of which is fully apparent only when it is taken as a whole. This volume aims to be more than a random collection of essays loosely organized around a broad theme. Our intention is to furnish, so far as the current state of research allows, a coherent overview of the English-speaking Catholic community in Canada. We trace the development of Catholicism in English Canada from an almost sectarian status in eighteenth-century British North America, through its formation in the nineteenth century of a major ethno-religious subculture, to its final integration into the mainstream of Canadian life at the beginning of the twentieth century.

The earliest census returns from the British North American colonies are too fragmentary to provide an accurate indication of the size of the Catholic population. It is clear, however, that before 1815 the number of Irish and Scottish Catholics was small, both in absolute terms and as a percentage of the total population. After 1815 one can begin to discern a pattern of growth. For example, in 1827 the Catholic population of Nova Scotia was a little over 20,000; by 1851 it had increased to nearly 70,000, in large measure because of immigration from the British Isles.[6] Similar increases occurred (though at varying rates) in other colonies. By mid century, Catholics made up nearly a fifth of the population in Upper Canada, more than a quarter in Nova Scotia, approximately a third in New Brunswick, and almost half in Newfoundland and Prince Edward Island.[7] Even allowing for the substantial contingent of French-speaking Catholics in provinces such as New Brunswick, it is still obvious that the English-speaking Catholic population had grown substantially. In 1881 the total Catholic population of Canada, including Quebec, was approximately 1.8 million. Of this number, nearly 600,000, or 33 per cent, were English-speaking.[8] The percentage of anglophones among Catholics in predominantly English-speaking provinces was, of course, much higher: 77 per cent in Prince Edward Island, 65 per cent in Nova Scotia, 68 per cent in Ontario, and 91 per cent in British Columbia. The Catholic population of New Brunswick in 1881 was divided almost equally between anglophones and francophones. Manitoba's Catholic population was still overwhelming French-speaking. After 1896 the influx of Roman Catholic immigrants from central and Eastern Europe makes it harder to deduce from census returns the size of the specifically English-speaking Catholic population, because it is no longer possible to assume that nonfrancophone Catholics are anglophones. The Roman Catholic population of the country more than doubled between 1881 and 1931, reaching a new total of 4,289,839,[9] but it is impossible to say precisely what proportion of this growth occurred within the English-speaking portion of the population. In any case, growth in numbers was less important after the turn of the century than the integration of Catholics of British origin into the charter population of English Canada.

The expression "English-speaking Catholic" is not a residual term, signifying any Canadian Catholic whose mother tongue is not French. Rather, it refers to a specific historical community, over-whelmingly Irish and Scottish by origin, who were either English-speaking on their arrival in Canada or who became English-speaking when British North American society was still in its formative stages. Despite some significant differences among Catholics from the British Isles, they soon formed a cohesive and self-conscious community, distinguished from other English-speaking settlers by religion and from their French-speaking fellow Catholics by language. They not only spoke English as their first language, but came increasingly to identify the fortunes of Catholicism in this country with the spread of English-speaking civilization. At the end of nineteenth and beginning of the twentieth century, by which time English-speaking Catholics had already emerged as a major force in Canadian life, the new Catholic immigrants began to arrive from Eastern and central Europe. Most of these newcomers, whether German, Italian, Polish, or Ukrainian, adopted English as their second language. As we shall see, English-speaking Catholics actively promoted this process of anglicization but failed to assimilate the immigrants. Adhering to their distinctly ethnic forms of Catholicism, they formed not an additional ingredient in the English-speaking Catholic population but a third ethno-religious constellation within Canadian Catholicism, demanding and in many cases obtaining their own clergy, parishes, schools, and voluntary associations.[10] Indeed, in the case of the Ukrainian Catholics of the Eastern rite, they secured their own church with the appointment of Bishop Nykyta Budka in 1912. Even after the immigration of these European Catholics, therefore, the expression "English-speaking Catholics" applies mainly to Catholics of British origin.

The migration of Catholics from the British Isles to British North America began in the second half of the eighteenth century and gathered momentum after the Napoleonic Wars. Initially, the flow of immigrants was heaviest to the Atlantic colonies, where the English-speaking Catholic community, consisting of pre-famine Irish and Highland Scots, was well established by the middle of the nineteenth century. The second main centre of English-speaking Catholic settlement was Upper Canada. Scottish Catholics had established themselves in Glengarry and Stormont counties in the early part of the century, but it was the famine migration of the 1840s and 1850s that raised the Catholic population of Upper Canada to an unprecedented level. In 1842 the Catholic population of Upper Canada was 65,203, or approximately 13 per cent of the total polulation; by 1848 it had risen to 118,810 and to 16 per cent; by 1860–1 it had further increased to 258,151 and to 19 per cent. The greatest concentration of Irish and Scottish Catholics in British North America in absolute terms was in Upper Canada, though they never formed as high a percentage of the population as they did in other English-speaking colonies.

When the West was opened for settlement, English-speaking Catholics also made their way to the Prairies. Atlantic Canada and Ontario remained their centres of influence, however, whereas in the West they found themselves sharing the terrain with the French-speaking Catholics who had preceded them to the region as well as with the growing number of European Catholic immigrants. For English-speaking Catholics, the West long retained the character of a mission field, and it was only at the end of the period covered by this volume that they obtained a large measure of direct control over the region through the appointment of Irish and Scottish prelates to newly formed Prairie dioceses. The first English-speaking candidate to be named to a western diocese was Alfred Sinnott, installed as bishop of Winnipeg in 1915. (There had been French-speaking bishops in the West since 1819.) By 1930, however, after bitter quarrels with their French-speaking co-religionists, English-speaking Catholics had gained control of a majority of western sees.

Virtually from the outset, the relationship of English-speaking to French-speaking Catholics in Canada had been problematic and fraught with the potential for controversy. Catholic immigrants from the British Isles came initially under the jurisdiction of the Diocese of Quebec, which until 1817 encompassed all of British North America except Newfoundland. This meant that the bishops and clergy of Canada were suddenly faced with the task of providing spiritual care for the newcomers, a task made more difficult by the remote locations of their settlements. The resources of the Quebec church had already been sorely taxed as a result of the British Conquest, and the bishop was finding it problematic to provide sufficient clergy even for the centre of the diocese. Moreover, the problem was not merely one of human and material resources. The Quebec church had mature institutions and deeply entrenched traditions, both of which were rooted in experiences quite unlike those of the Irish and Scots. It had been for many decades the established church of New France, and its liturgical practices and disciplinary standards reflected its hitherto privileged and official status. The religious customs and attitudes of the immigrants, in contrast, had been shaped in the atmosphere of the British penal code, and often seemed strange, indeed reprehensible, to the Canadian clergy. The Irish and Scots faced the challenge of finding their place in a predominantly French-speaking church that did not always appear receptive to their ways or sensitive to their needs. It was a matter not only of overcoming language barriers but also of bridging a culture gap.

This encounter between Catholics of very different backgrounds led to more than a century of conflict, followed only gradually by a period of greater harmony and reconciliation. Broadly speaking, the troubled relationship can be divided into three phases. The first occurred in the Maritimes, where the initial expansion of the English-speaking Catholic population took place. After a brief period of cooperation, the Irish and Scottish clergy in the region began to feel unfairly neglected by their ecclesiastical superiors in Quebec, which caused them to press for separation from the diocese. By 1829 they had achieved their objective, but in lobbying for their cause at Rome they had painted a very unfavourable picture of their treatment by the French-Canadian clergy. Their accusations of neglect, some of which found their way back to Quebec, left a legacy of resentment. Furthermore, the changes in ecclesiastical jurisdiction that followed from the creation of independent dioceses in the Maritimes suddenly left the Acadians as a disadvantaged minority in a regional church controlled by anglophones. French-speaking candidates for the episcopate were systematically excluded in the Maritimes for nearly a century. Only after the Acadian renaissance of the late nineteenth and early twentieth centuries did Acadians begin to achieve a measure of equality with their English-speaking fellow Catholics. The first significant change was the appointment in 1912 of the Acadian Edouard LeBlanc as bishop of Saint John, followed by the nomination in 1920 of Patrice-Alexandre Chiasson as bishop of Chatham.

Ontario
French
+
English
Catholic
tensions

In Upper Canada, where the English-speaking Catholic population
grew more slowly, relations with Quebec remained harmonious until
the 1840s. The influx of Irish Catholics after the famine, however,
combined with such developments as the union of the two Canadas
in 1841 to inaugurate a second and far worse period of ethnic and
linguistic rivalry within the Canadian Catholic church. Matters were
brought to the breaking-point by the migration of French Canadians
to Ontario after 1860. Many of these Franco-Ontarians lived in the
Diocese of Ottawa, which straddled the civil boundary between
Canada East and Canada West but which was included in the ecclesiastical province of Quebec. Under the leadership of Archbishop
John Joseph Lynch, the English-speaking bishops of Ontario
launched a vigorous campaign to have the Ottawa diocese transferred
to the metropolitan jurisdiction of Toronto. This battle took place
against a background of rising tensions between French Canadians
and English Canadians generally, occasioned by such incidents as
the hanging of Louis Riel (1885) and the settlement of the Jesuit
Estates question (1888). Ethnic strife in Ontario's Catholic church
reached its high point between 1890 and 1930, with bitter conflicts
over diocesan boundaries, episcopal appointments, and bilingualism
in education. English-speaking Catholics were in theory well placed
to bridge the gap between Canada's two founding nations, but in
practice they identified more and more closely with the anglophone
majority and with the view that Canada was essentially an English-
speaking country.

con't

During this same general period, ethno-linguistic rivalries were
also extended to the West. Until the late nineteenth century, the
Catholic church in the sparsely settled West was essentially a French-
speaking institution largely under the direction of Oblate fathers
from Quebec or from France. When the Liberal government of Wilfrid
Laurier encouraged massive immigration to the West in the post-
1896 era, however, English Canadians responded to the opportunity
while French Canadians did not. This created a situation in which
francophones formed a declining (though still significant) portion of
the population, including the Catholic population. English-speaking
Catholic settlers refused to accept the services of clergy of French
ethnic origin and began to demand their own parishes, clergy, and
bishops. Matters were further complicated by the arrival in the West
of Polish and Ukrainian Catholics as part of the broader tide of
European immigration to Canada. English-speaking Catholics
insisted that these newcomers must be assimilated to English-Canadian culture, a view that was resisted by the immigrants and by
French Canadians alike. Catholics of Irish and Scottish origin,

supported by their confreres in Ontario and the Maritimes, were becoming a steadily more important element in an increasingly diverse and divided western Canadian church. Meanwhile, French-speaking Catholics, who resented this aggressive attitude, fought an embittered rearguard action in an effort to preserve their customary position of dominance.

The final phase in the relationship between French-speaking and English-speaking Catholics in Canada, which is one of increasing cooperation, falls outside the period covered by this book. It begins in the 1930s, with the first signs of more equitable treatment for francophone populations outside Quebec, and reaches its high point in the 1960s, when a new openness developed both in the Roman Catholic church and in Canadian society. Up until that time, however, language did more to divide than religion did to unite the Catholic inhabitants of Canada.

At the same time that English-speaking Catholics were working out their troubled relationship with their French-speaking co-religionists, they were also trying to adjust to an anglophone society dominated by Protestants. Anti-Catholicism was an important force in Canadian life from the British Conquest to the Great War, and, like ethnic rivalries within the Canadian Catholic church, it developed through three phases. During the first phase, which lasted from the Conquest until 1830, anti-Catholicism was an official policy of the government, expressed in legal restrictions on the religious and political freedom of Catholics. Official anti-Catholicism was a reflection of the British constitutional tradition. In some measure, it was part of a broader pattern of disabilities imposed not only on Catholics but also on Protestant dissenters as a way of preserving the privileged position of the established Church of England and Church of Scotland. But Catholics, whose loyalty to the pope rendered them suspect in the eyes of the crown, were subject to specific legal restraints incorporated in the penal code. In their most rigorous form, these anti-Catholic laws not only discriminated against Catholics but effectively denied them freedom of worship.

The penal code, however, was not always strictly enforced, and, by the time of the conquest of Quebec and the settlement of the English-speaking colonies, the anti-Catholicism of the British government was beginning to weaken. This circumstance, combined with hard political realities, promoted greater tolerance in the colonies. Catholics were simply too numerous to suppress, and as the tide of rebellion rose to the south it became an urgent necessity to foster loyalty in British North America. Catholics in the province of Canada were never subjected to anti-Catholic legislation. A promise of religious liberty was included in the Treaty of Paris in 1763 and reaffirmed and strengthened by the Quebec Act of 1774. This guarantee, intended originally for the French-speaking Catholics of Quebec, applied automatically to the English-speaking Catholics of Upper Canada. In other parts of British North America, the situation was more complex, for disabilities and penalties had been imposed on Catholics through royal prerogative or local statute. Emancipation could take place only by gradually reversing such provisions. Catholic relief proceeded at a slow but steady pace, and, by 1830, the process was complete in every colony except Newfoundland, which was exceptional in a number of ways.

When official anti-Catholicism came to an end in British North America, it was replaced by a more specifically theological variety of religious bigotry. In the middle decades of the nineteenth century, Protestant spokesmen launched a massive assault on the doctrines and practices of the Catholic church. Through newspapers, pamphlets, and public addresses, they attacked Catholic beliefs about the authority of tradition, the doctrine of transubstantiation, the veneration of Mary, the papacy, and auricular confession. At the same time, they argued that "popish" tyranny and superstition had deleterious effects on society, undermining individual liberty and stifling initiative. Catholics were depicted as slavishly submissive to clerical authority, politically disloyal, and economically backward. Such prejudices and stereotypes, derived for the most part from British and American sources, were reinforced by the migration to British North America of the famine Irish. The arrival of these destitute refugees, poverty-stricken, disease-ridden, and beset with social problems, seemed to confirm everything that the critics of Romanism had said about its harmful social consequences. The distress of the immigrants, which might have evoked compassion from fellow Christians, was used instead as an additional weapon in the war against "popery."

The third and final phase of anti-Catholicism began as the Irish Catholics were gradually integrated into Canadian society and as the Canadian West was opened up for settlement. Protestant concern over the assimilation of indigenous peoples and European immigrants to the West led to aggressive (though not very successful) missionary campaigns. Assimilation into Canadian society was equated by the evangelists with anglicization and conversion to Protestantism. This shift to nationalistic concerns meant that anti-Catholicism, previously a highly imitative phenomenon, was taking on a distinctive Canadian colouring. Religious bigotry was in fact being replaced by ethnic and linguistic prejudice, although the outward appearance of religious motivation was maintained. The position of English-speaking Catholics at this juncture was highly ambiguous. They competed directly with Protestant missionaries in order to preserve the Catholic faith of native groups and immigrants, yet they participated directly or indirectly in attempts to anglicize the West. The home missionary effort in the Prairie provinces marked the end of an era for English-speaking Catholics, bringing to a close their history as an immigrant community and signalling their integration into the mainstream of Canadian society.

Meanwhile, in studying the process by which English-speaking Catholics reached a *modus vivendi* with the civil authorities and with their Protestant neighbours, Newfoundland presents an especially interesting case. On the one hand, its experience was typical of all colonies where substantial numbers of Catholics had to secure their rights in the face of official intolerance and the jealously guarded privileges of the Church of England. On the other hand, its problems were intensified by the fact that Newfoundland was the only British North American colony apart from Quebec where Catholics formed a majority (or near majority) of the population. Newfoundland was also unique in that it lacked a local government. Regarded for many years as a fishing station rather than a settled colony, it was without a sovereign council and an assembly until 1825 and 1832, respectively, and even the governors of Newfoundland did not reside year round on the island until 1817. The absence of a local government meant there was no established political means by which Catholics could express their grievances or seek an improvement in their circumstances, and this deficiency tended in the long run to heighten sectarian resentment.

For a brief time, it appeared as though Catholic relief would be achieved in Newfoundland without undue controversy. Legal restrictions on the practice of Roman Catholicism were removed from the royal instructions as early as 1779, and this new policy of toleration was put into practice in 1783 and 1784 by Governor John Campbell. Catholics lived on essentially good terms with Protestants and the government for the next generation. After 1815, however, the growing size and influence of the Catholic population, together with the rising importance of Protestant dissent, made the Church of England more militant in asserting its rights. Although there was no legal basis for the establishment of the Church of England in Newfoundland, the Anglican minority sought and obtained increased financial assistance for clergy and schools, while the Catholic majority was denied such aid. The Anglicans also nearly succeeded in depriving Catholic priests of their traditional right to perform marriages in Newfoundland.

At the same time as sectarian resentment was being aroused in this way, new restrictions were placed on Catholics in the political sphere. In 1825, under a revised commission to the governor, they were excluded from public office and specifically from the newly created sovereign council. In the absence of a representative assembly, no action could be taken on the local scene to redress this injustice. When such an assembly was finally established in 1832, Catholics were included in the franchise, but they approached the first election feeling deeply aggrieved over their treatment in recent years. The fact that the political means for addressing Catholic grievances had been totally lacking before 1832 largely accounts for the acrimonious, sectarian spirit in which the election was conducted. Nevertheless, the election was a turning-point, for sectarianism thereafter affected every aspect of Newfoundland political and social life, differing not in nature but in intensity from religious bigotry elsewhere. The eventual solution to the problem, which emerged after the 1865 election, was a unique system of proportionate denominationalism, in which all forms of public support and recognition – including political appointments and school funding and items such as government contracts – were distributed to the various denominations on the basis of their share of the population.

While Irish Catholics were finding their place in the evolving society of Newfoundland, Catholic immigrants from the Scottish Highlands were establishing strongholds on the Island of St John (Prince Edward Island), Cape Breton and eastern Nova Scotia, and the southeastern district of Upper Canada (Glengarry and Stormont counties). More prone to group migration than the Irish, the Scots settled in precisely defined areas. At the time of their arrival, many were still primarily Gaelic-speaking, although like their fellow Catholics from Ireland they were destined to become anglicized. The process of anglicization led eventually to their absorption in the broader English-speaking Catholic population, but initially they stood as a group unto themselves. They were a minority within a minority within a minority – Gaelic-speakers among Catholics from the British Isles in a church dominated by Catholics of French origin living in a predominantly Protestant society. They struggled with astonishing determination to maintain their identity, but the difficulty of doing so was increased by the poverty of their mother church, which (quite unlike the Irish Catholic church) had survived for centuries as a loosely organized underground community. Scottish Catholic authorities were hard-pressed to provide Highland emigrants with priests, especially as their own limited resources were sorely taxed by Irish immigration into Scotland. One might have thought that Irish and Scottish Catholics would readily cooperate in the New World, but in fact traditional resentments and prejudices, exacerbated by recent contacts between Irish and Scots, made this sort of collaboration nearly impossible at first. Scottish Catholics in British North America therefore found themselves poorly supported from home and caught between the established francophone Catholicism of Quebec and the rising tide of anglophone Irish Catholic immigration.

In spite of the difficulties they faced, Scottish Catholics not only survived but managed to play a crucial role in the transformation of British North American Catholicism. One key to their success was the mutually supportive relationship they maintained with the civil authorities. In the late eighteenth century, Catholics in Scotland had forged a working alliance with the British government, and this partnership was something they carried with them to the colonies, where their clergy became trusted and well-rewarded defenders of the status quo. While traditional and conservative in their outlook, however, Scottish Catholics were forced by the exigencies of their situation to adapt. Senior Scottish clergymen played a leading role in the campaign to end Quebec's control of British North American Catholicism by lobbying in Rome for revised diocesan boundaries. Moreover, as the Diocese of Quebec was gradually dismembered, these same Scottish clergymen were appointed to the new bishoprics that were created in outlying regions. Of the first four nonfrancophone bishops appointed in North America, three were Scots – Alexander Macdonell, Angus MacEachern, and William Fraser. Authority over their own ecclesiastical jurisdictions, though fraught with difficulties of its own, paved the way to independence. The top priority of all three Scottish bishops was to establish diocesan seminaries where they could train their own priests, thus ending their reliance on Scotland and Quebec alike.

Scottish Catholics reached the height of their power in the British North American church around 1830. At that time, they controlled the three ecclesiastical jurisdictions mentioned above, the Dioceses of Kingston and Charlottetown and the Vicariate Apostolic of Nova Scotia. Not only had three of their clergymen achieved episcopal rank but, dissatisfied with their initial status as auxiliary bishops, Macdonell and MacEachern had successfully demanded complete independence from Quebec. This gave them an exhilarating sense of

accomplishment, enhanced by early success in their educational ventures and by the support they continued to receive from the (mostly
Scottish) colonial governors. The relative influence of Scots declined
over time, however, with shifting patterns of immigration. Irish Catholic settlers eventually outnumbered Scots by a vast majority, and
their superior numbers meant that they dominated the developing
Roman Catholic community in English Canada. Furthermore, Irish
Catholics were more closely attuned to changing political realities in
British North America. Nurtured in the spirit of Daniel O'Connell,
they supported for the most part the cause of reform, whereas their
conservative Scottish counterparts were identified with the established order. Nevertheless, while the future lay with Catholics of Irish
origin, Scottish Catholics had made a crucial and lasting contribution.
As the largest group of non-French Catholics in British North
America at the end of the eighteenth and beginning of the nineteenth
centuries, they were instrumental in the transition from a monolithic
to a diverse and pluralistic Canadian Catholic church. Their continued presence, and their concentration in specific geographical
areas, lent Canadian Catholicism a dimension not found elsewhere
in the English-speaking world.

The influx of Irish and Scots to British North America required
major adjustments not only on the part of the immigrants themselves
and of the French-speaking clergy of Quebec but also on the part of
the ecclesiastical authorities in Rome. This meant in practice that
fundamental changes had to take place in the perspective and policy
of the Sacred Congregation for the Propagation of the Faith (known
as Propaganda), the branch of the Roman Curia charged with responsibility for mission fields and for countries where Catholics lived
under a Protestant government. After the British Conquest, Propaganda had left the whole of British North America, except Newfoundland, in the care of the bishop of Quebec, on the mistaken
assumption that the Catholic population would continue to be
French-speaking. Even when large numbers of Catholic immigrants
began to arrive from the British Isles, Rome was slow to adjust. For
information on British North America, the cardinals of Propaganda
depended initially on correspondence with Quebec, forwarded
through an agent in Paris, and as long as this remained the principal
source they had at best an imperfect understanding of the situation.
In particular, they failed to appreciate the urgent need for Gaelic-
speaking and English-speaking clergy.

Their perception of British North America began to change in the
1780s, but the real turning-point was the French Revolution, which

threw the operations of the Holy See into disarray and severely curtailed its communication with the outside world. In the process, the role of Paris as a link between Rome and North America effectively came to an end. When regular correspondence resumed after 1815, the old Quebec-Paris-Rome network was replaced by separate channels of information between Propaganda and the various ethnic constituencies among British North American Catholics. Quebec affairs were handled through London and the English College, while Catholics in the English-speaking colonies preferred intermediaries in Ireland and Scotland, or Irish and Scottish agents in Rome. Sometimes representatives were sent directly to Rome from North America. These included bishops and senior clergy, such as Joseph-Octave Plessis of Quebec, Edmund Burke of Nova Scotia, and Alexander Macdonell of Upper Canada.

English-speaking clergy who communicated with or visited Rome campaigned with growing urgency for the creation of separate ecclesiastical jurisdictions in the Maritime colonies and Upper Canada. In their view, the creation of such jurisdictions was the only way to ensure Irish and Scottish Catholic settlers a supply of clergy appropriate to their needs. The manner in which they stated their case, however, often betrayed their mistrust of the Quebec bishops, who in turn resented them for their explicit or implicit accusations of neglect. Nevertheless, between 1815 and 1829, the Vicariate Apostolic of Nova Scotia and the Dioceses of Kingston (for Upper Canada) and Charlottetown (embracing Prince Edward Island, Cape Breton, and New Brunswick) were erected. Newfoundland had been an independent jurisdiction since 1784.

The immediate effect of these developments was a certain fragmentation of the British North American Catholic community, the inevitable result of growth in size and ethnic diversity. In the long run, however, they had the unforeseen result of increasing the real power of Rome over the North American church. For Roman Catholics everywhere, the nineteenth century was above all a time of centralization. The papacy, in conscious opposition to modern ideas of liberty, vigorously asserted its authority over every aspect of church life – administrative, theological, and devotional. This mounting authoritarianism, known as Ultramontanism (more precisely neo-Ultramontanism), found its ultimate doctrinal expression in the definition of the dogma of papal infallibility at the first Vatican Council (1869–70); equally important were the proliferation of Roman devotions and liturgical practices and the assertion, through the Roman Curia, of papal jurisdiction. The efforts of Propaganda in British North America ultimately became part of this much broader trend.

In its role of final arbiter between ethnic groups and regional interests, it was able to assert in practice the authority it had always possessed in theory. Not content any longer to respond piecemeal to individual pleas and petitions, Propaganda developed an autonomous policy for North America against which it could assess appeals from various interest groups. This policy appears to have applied equally to Catholics in the United States, who were undergoing a similar process of growth and diversification, and to have amounted to a master plan for North America, involving the erection of a metropolitan see on either side of the border, with a number of local dioceses under each. In the end, the scheme proved too rigid and simplistic to be neatly or completely implemented, but its very existence reflects a new directness and determination in Rome's exercise of authority. Fragmentation and diversity not only changed the nature of the North American Catholic community; they also fostered the growth of Ultramontanism.

In the early stages of Catholic immigration from the British Isles, when English-speaking Catholics still lacked religious institutions of their own, laymen often took the initiative in establishing parishes and recruiting priests. This was especially true among the Irish who settled in towns. In the three principal centres of Irish settlement in Atlantic Canada, for example – St John's, Halifax, and Saint John – the Catholic population included a small but dynamic middling class of merchants, professionals, and independent artisans. In each case, the first Catholic parish owes its origins largely to their efforts, as they obtained land, built chapels, and enlisted the services of a priest. Eager for social acceptance, these Catholic spokesmen adopted an accommodating attitude towards the dominant Protestant culture. Their role as the founders and benefactors of the new urban churches, however, quickly led them into controversy with their fellow Catholics. Claiming proprietorial rights over their parishes, they organized themselves into committees of management, in which capacity they attempted to control the temporal and even the spiritual affairs of local congregations. In the process, they antagonized both pastors and fellow parishioners. Episcopal authority eventually prevailed over the power of these lay trustees, but not before they had played a crucial role in founding Roman Catholic institutions and congregations had been torn asunder by their divisive policies.

The trustee controversies in Atlantic Canada closely resemble contemporary developments in the United States. Lay involvement in ecclesiastical affairs was so much a feature of American Catholicism in its formative stage that "trusteeism" is usually regarded as a distinctly American phenomenon. This interpretation has recently been restated forcefully by Patrick Carey, who sees trusteeism as essentially an attempt to adapt European Catholic institutions to the republican environment of the United States by democratizing church government.[11] The existence of trusteeism in the anti-republican environment of Atlantic Canada calls this American exceptionalism into question. Although the activities of trustees in the United States took on at times a peculiar American colouring, trusteeism as such is a broader phenomenon, a product of time and circumstance as much as place.

Once stable missions with resident priests had been established in the principal centres of English-speaking Catholic population, the next phase of institutional development was the creation of local dioceses. This development took place between 1817 and 1829, as leading Irish and Scottish clergy campaigned successfully at Rome for the division of the Diocese of Quebec. The bishops of Quebec acquiesced in and even encouraged this development, although not without misgivings about the ability of the new dioceses to support themselves. In the 1840s the new Dioceses of Kingston and Charlottetown were themselves divided with the creation of the Dioceses of Toronto (1841) and Saint John (1842). In 1844 Quebec was recognized as an archdiocese, the centre of an ecclesiastical province encompassing Kingston, Toronto, and a second French-speaking diocese in Montreal (1836).

By the middle of the nineteenth century, therefore, British North America possessed all the essential ingredients of traditional, metropolitan Roman Catholic church government. The appointment of local bishops vastly strengthened episcopal authority, and the creation of an ecclesiastical province facilitated the exchange of ideas between one region and another. New religious currents flowed easily from Europe to British North America and were effectively disseminated through the metropolitan network of communication. The church in British North America began to reflect more clearly the spirit and substance of the European Catholic revival, including the centralizing and homogenizing tendencies associated with Ultramontanism. A period of rapid institutional expansion ensued, during which simple, parochial institutions developed into complex diocesan structures. The effects of this growth are well illustrated by events in the Diocese of Toronto. Beginning with Bishop Michael Power (1842–7), but especially under his successor Bishop Armand de Charbonnel (1850–60), an elaborate system of Catholic philanthropic, educational, and pastoral agencies was established in the city, made possible partly by the introduction to the diocese of religious orders of men and women such as the Redemptorists and the Sisters of

Loretto. The influx of nuns, brothers, and regular clergy allowed for the development of educational and charitable programs that touched on nearly every aspect of a Catholic's life. At the same time, lay organizations, such as the philanthropic St Vincent de Paul Society, also played a crucial role. The interlocking network of diocesan institutions not only tended to the material and spiritual needs of Catholic immigrants but also provided them with a comprehensive alternative to Protestant social agencies. In this sense, it protected them against the dangers of conversion and assimilation, allowing them to preserve their identity in a predominantly Protestant culture.

Bishop Charbonnel's work in developing diocesan institutions in Toronto was carried on by his successor, John Joseph Lynch. Lynch, a native of Ulster, came to Toronto via the United States, where he had already established a record of service to Irish Catholic immigrants. In Toronto he continued his efforts to alleviate their social and economic problems through philanthropic and cooperative ventures. In spite of these supportive measures, however, Lynch was fundamentally opposed to large-scale Irish immigration to North American cities. So far from seeing emigration as a solution to the endemic poverty of the Irish countryside, he believed that it thrust penniless Irish peasants into a hostile urban environment where little else awaited them save a life of unemployment, drunkenness, violence, and crime. By settling in North American cities they faced not only material hardship but also loss of faith. Lynch was less convinced than some of his episcopal colleagues, such as Thomas Connolly of Halifax, that Catholic institutions could effectively shield immigrants against the assimilative pressures of urban life, although his pessimism stands in paradoxical contrast to his vigorous efforts to build up these institutions. His outspoken comments concerning the evils that beset Catholic immigrants earned him a mild rebuke from Propaganda, apparently because it played into the hands of anti-Catholic crusaders who relished further evidence of anti-social behaviour among Catholic immigrants. Nevertheless, Lynch remained firm in his views, insisting that the solution to the Irish problem was not the depopulation of the country but just treatment at the hands of the British government.

On only one significant occasion did Lynch relent in his opposition to Irish immigration. In the 1880s, against the background of Sir John A. Macdonald's National Policy, he endorsed a proposal for an Irish Catholic settlement in the Canadian West. This scheme for a New Ireland in Manitoba held out the prospect of a carefully planned, idyllic rural colony with Catholic priests living among a community of prosperous immigrant farmers. It differed dramatically from the familiar pattern of destitute Irishmen crowded into urban ghettoes. Lynch, whose enthusiasm for the proposal mounted steadily after 1880, cooperated closely with Archbishop Alexandre-Antonin Taché of Saint-Boniface, who, having despaired of attracting French-Canadian settlers to the West, believed that Irish Catholic colonists were better than no Catholic colonists at all. Lynch also travelled to Ireland and obtained support for the project from the Irish hierarchy. The plan began to falter, however, when the British government, in the midst of an anti-Irish backlash precipitated by the Phoenix Park murders, refused to endorse it. The Canadian government continued for a time to promise assistance, but when Lynch fell out with his long-time allies in the Conservative party, they too withdrew support. The scheme collapsed, and Lynch reverted to his former position as an opponent of Irish immigration. While opposing immigration in principle, however, Lynch maintained an unwavering practical commitment to the relief of those immigrants who did enter his diocese. By the time he died in 1888, he had made considerable strides towards expanding and refining the charitable network established by Bishop Charbonnel. Its success in promoting the well-being and preserving the faith of the growing Catholic population far exceeded his expectations.

At the same time that philanthropic institutions were being developed in Toronto and other major centres of Catholic immigration, Catholic spirituality was being transformed by the proliferation of new devotional practices. The new devotions – which were often medieval practices given new life – established rituals such as the recitation of the rosary and veneration of the Sacred Heart of Jesus as cornerstones of Catholic piety. Emanating from Rome, these new devotions were closely associated with the Ultramontane tendencies sweeping the church, and they fit together in a coherent pattern of emotional, demonstrative piety sometimes labelled "devotionalism." In this country as elsewhere they were sponsored chiefly by pious confraternities such as the Sodality of the Blessed Virgin Mary and the Archconfraternity of the Holy Family. Widespread lay participation was the key to their significance, because they not only transformed popular piety but also had the effect of increasing conformity among the Catholic population to clerical standards of observance.

The changes in popular practice that occurred in British North America can only be understood against the Irish background. Recent scholarship has shown that in pre-famine Ireland, church attendance was surprisingly low, especially among the less affluent classes in Gaelic-speaking rural districts. This fact is especially significant for those parts of North America, such as Upper Canada, where famine migrants had a major impact. The type of immigrant who poured into Upper Canada in the 1840s and 1850s had probably not formed the habit of weekly church attendance or of regular participation in the sacraments before leaving Ireland, if only because the resources of the church in his or her place of origin were so inadequate. High rates of conformity to clerical norms were achieved in Ireland as well as in the Irish diaspora only after the massive institutional expansion described above. The multiplication of pious confraternities was one aspect of this broader pattern of growth, but they promoted a "devotional revolution" that drew a large portion of the laity into the orbit of normative Catholicism.

The new devotions appealed especially to women. Associated with a carefully cultivated "cult of domesticity," they sacralized the role of women in the family and enhanced their moral authority in the home. In the process, the Irish Catholic household was transformed (at least according to the ideal) into a moral haven, where men could spend their leisure time innocently, safe from occasions of sin, and where women could comfort their husbands and at the same time encourage them in the habit of regular religious observance. Catholic devotionalism also gave women increased opportunities for leadership in the parish. In Toronto, whose experience in this respect was probably typical of other centres, membership in pious confraternities was almost exclusively female, although many were officially open to men. Female officers administered their affairs, and through the confraternities women were also able to play an important part in fund-raising for the parish and for charitable work among the sick and indigent. Ultimately the confraternities were subject to the paternalistic authority of the parish priest, yet they did provide women with a chance to engage in a form of corporate activity outside the home that was otherwise denied them. The initiative women displayed as a result proved decisive in reshaping religious practice among the Catholic laity.

By the latter half of the nineteenth century, Roman Catholicism in English-speaking Canada was clearly coming of age. The assertion of Catholic rights in the political sphere, the proliferation and integration of ecclesiastical institutions, effective lobbying in Rome, educational and philanthropic ventures, and the popularization of Ultramontane devotions had transformed an assortment of isolated, struggling missions into a flourishing and cohesive national community. The strength of this community, composed almost entirely of people of Celtic background, derived initially from its close identification of religion with ethnicity. Catholicism provided not only the framework for the religious life of its adherents but also the basis for their social identity. The very institutions that shielded them from the pressures of assimilation, however, also facilitated efforts at collective self-improvement and thus led eventually to integration into the dominant society. This process was reflected partly in the socio-economic mobility that English-speaking Catholics had achieved by the turn of the century but also in the fading of Irish nationalism as a driving force in the community. The rising generation of clergy, much more likely than their predecessors to be native-born Canadians, preached loyalty to the British empire, and their patriotic message struck a responsive chord among members of their flock. As anglophone Catholics entered into the mainstream of English-Canadian life, they embraced not only British imperialism but also its ideological counterpart, belief in the superiority of English-speaking civilization. The adoption of this mentality put an unprecedented strain on their relations with French-Canadian Catholics, but it was decisive for the process by which English-speaking Catholics became self-consciously Canadian.

An expansive, missionary spirit accompanied this change in outlook. Inspired by an address of Archbishop John Bourne, archbishop of Westminster, delivered in Montreal on the occasion of a Eucharistic Congress in 1910, English-speaking Catholics became convinced that Catholicism would be spread across the land through the medium of the English language. Moreover, the emergence of this view coincided with the arrival in Canada of the Catholic immigrants from Northern and Eastern Europe. English-speaking Catholics, already engaged in a struggle with their French-Canadian co-religionists for control of newly created dioceses outside Quebec, now began to vie with Protestants in their attempts to evangelize and assimilate their new countrymen. A vigorous home missionary developed among Italians, Ukrainians, and Poles in Ontario but soon expanded into a nationwide movement with Toronto as its nerve centre. Through organizations such as the Catholic Church Extension Society, supported by donors and members in the Maritimes as well as Ontario, English-speaking Catholics struggled to preserve the faith while transforming the culture of the newcomers. They faced their greatest challenge in the West, where Catholic institutions and clergy were most scarce but Catholic immigrants most numerous. Their anglicizing agenda was resisted both by the immigrants, many of whom were Eastern-rite Catholics, and by French Canadians. In the end, their attempt to assimilate Catholics of European origin failed, with the result that Canadian Catholicism took on an even more pluralistic character. The enduring symbol of this pluralism is the city of

Winnipeg, the only one in the world where three Catholic archdio-
ceses exist side by side: the French-speaking Archdiocese of Saint-
Boniface, the English-speaking Archdiocese of Winnipeg, and the
Ukrainian Archeparchy and Metropolitan See of Winnipeg.

While not successful in overturning the distinctive traditions of
immigrants, however, the home missionary movement was both a
reflection of and a further stimulus to the integration of English-
speaking Catholics into Canadian society. For more than a century
after their emergence as a significant group in British North America,
they had defended their integrity as a community largely by fusing
ethnic with religious consciousness. The challenge posed by the
influx of Catholic immigrants from Italy, Poland, Hungary, and
Ukraine forced them into the role of a host rather than an immigrant
society. The way had been prepared for this new self-definition by
social, economic, and religious developments, but it was in the context of missionary efforts among newcomers to Ontario and the West
that they finally identified themselves totally and clearly as Canadians. This fundamental transformation of their self-understanding,
linked to profound changes in the nation, marked the end of an era.
In the post-1930 era, English-speaking Catholics continued to occupy
a special place in Canadian society, blending as they did their Catholic heritage with the traditions of anglophone culture. This unique
combination, however, was no longer an obstacle to their social integration, nor was their Catholicism associated as before with a specifically ethnic consciousness. Integration did not lead to total
assimilation, but it did bring greater confidence about their place in
Canadian life. English-speaking Catholics now saw themselves, and
were seen by others, as members of the charter population. It was
from this vantage point, rather than that of an ethno-religious subculture, that they faced the challenges of the new age.

NOTES

1 G.A. Rawlyk, review of *Study Sessions/Sessions d'études 1983*, vols I and
  II, in *Canadian Historical Review* 67, 2 (1986): 269–70.
2 For a similar comment on Rawlyk's review see the untitled editorial by
  Brian P. Clarke and Mark G. McGowan in the *Bulletin of the Canadian
  Catholic Historical Association* 3, 2 (1988–9): 1–2.
3 For a valuable review of contributions to Catholic historiography in
  French Canada see Louis Rousseau, "Religion in French America,"
  Religious Studies Review 10, 1 (1984): 33–46. See also Guy Laperrière,

"L'histoire religieuse du Québec: principaux courants, 1978–1988," *Revue d'histoire de l'Amérique française* 42, 4 (1989): 563–78, which brings the topic up to date.

4 Among the most significant works on Irish and Scottish immigration are John J. Mannion, "The Irish Migration to Newfoundland," unpublished lecture, Memorial University of Newfoundland, St John's, 1973; Mannion, *Irish Settlements in Eastern Canada: A Study of Cultural Transfer and Adaptation* (Toronto: University of Toronto Press 1974); Mannion, ed., *The Peopling of Newfoundland: Essays in Historical Geography* (St John's: Institute for Social and Economic Research, Memorial University of Newfoundland 1977); Terrence Punch, *Irish Halifax: The Immigrant Generation, 1815–1859* (Halifax: International Education Centre, Saint Mary's University 1981); Peter Toner, "The Origins of the New Brunswick Irish, 1851," *Journal of Canadian Studies* 23, 1–2 (1988): 104–9; Toner, "The Irish of New Brunswick at Mid-Century: The 1851 Census," in P.M. Toner, ed., *New Ireland Remembered: Historical Essays on the Irish in New Brunswick*, 2nd ed. (Fredericton: New Ireland Press 1989); J.M. Bumsted, *The Scots in Canada* (Ottawa: Canadian Catholic Historical Association 1982); Bumsted, *The People's Clearance: Highland Emigration to British North America, 1770–1815* (Edinburgh and Winnipeg: Edinburgh University Press and University of Manitoba Press 1982); Bumsted, *Land, Settlement, and Politics on Eighteenth-Century Prince Edward Island* (Montreal and Kingston: McGill-Queen's University Press 1987); Donald H. Akenson, *The Irish in Ontario: A Study in Rural History* (Montreal and Kingston: McGill-Queen's University Press 1984)); Akenson, *Being Had: Historians, Evidence, and the Irish in North America* (Port Credit, Ont.: P.D. Meany 1985); Akenson, *Small Differences: Irish Catholics and Irish Protestants, 1815–1922* (Kingston and Montreal: McGill-Queen's University Press 1988).

5 The seminal work here is Emmet Larkin, "The Devotional Revolution in Ireland: 1850–75," *American Historical Review* 77 (June 1972): 625–52, reprinted in Emmet Larkin, *The Historical Dimensions of Irish Catholicism* (Washington: Catholic University of America Press 1976); but see also David Miller, "Irish Catholicism and the Great Famine," *Journal of Social History* 9 (fall 1975): 81–98; S.J. Connolly, *Priests and People in Pre-Famine Ireland* (New York: St Martin's Press 1982); Patrick Corish, *The Irish Catholic Experience: A Historical Survey* (Wilmington, Delaware: Michael Glazier 1985); Desmond J. Keenan, *The Catholic Church in Nineteenth-Century Ireland* (Dublin: Gill and Macmillan 1983); Eugene Hynes, "The Great Hunger and Irish Catholicism," *Societas* 8, 2 (1978): 137–56.

6 For the 1827 and 1851 Nova Scotia census returns see *Censuses of Canada, 1665–1871* (Ottawa 1876).

7 Ibid.

8 *Census of Canada, 1880–81*, vol. 1 (Ottawa 1882), 202 and 309. One arrives at this number by assuming that virtually all francophones were Roman Catholic and subtracting the total number of francophones from the total number of Catholics.

9 *Census of Canada, 1931*, vol. 1 (Ottawa 1936), 239.

10 For example, the founding of ethnic parishes in Toronto was begun by Archbishop McEvay in 1908; by 1920 the Italians had three such parishes, the Poles two, and the Ukrainians one. Meanwhile, ethnic parishes were established in other parts of Ontario, including Hamilton, Guelph, Kitchener, Coppercliff, Port Arthur, Sudbury, and Fort William, and also at Sydney, Nova Scotia. Across the country, the Poles alone had by 1929 established a network of thirty-three ethnic parishes and 157 missions. They operated bilingual Polish-English schools in Manitoba and Sakatchewan between 1897 and 1918, and in 1902 they established the Holy Ghost Fraternal Society of Winnipeg, their own Catholic mutual aid society. National religio-ethnic organizations, such as the Association of German Canadian Catholics and the Association of Poles in Canada, were also founded. For more information on these topics see Mark George McGowan, "We Are All Canadians: A Social, Religious, and Cultural Portrait of Toronto's English-speaking Roman Catholics, 1890–1920" (PhD dissertation, University of Toronto 1988); John E. Zucchi, *Italians in Toronto: Development of a National Identity, 1875–1935* (Kingston and Montreal: McGill-Queen's University Press 1988): D.H. Avery and J.K. Fedorowicz, *The Poles in Canada* (Ottawa: Canadian Historical Association 1982); and K.M. McLaughlin, *The Germans in Canada* (Ottawa: Canadian Historical Association 1985).

11 Patrick Carey, *People, Priests and Prelates: Ecclesiastical Democracy and the Tensions of Trusteeism* (Notre Dame: University of Notre Dame Press 1987).

John Joseph Lynch, cm, bishop (1860–9), archbishop (1869–88) of Toronto. The original of this photograph is reputed to have been taken by famed portrait photographer E.R. Notman. Archives of the Roman Catholic Archdiocese of Toronto

Nineteenth-century marian artifact. From the private collection of Ray Mitchell, Guelph, Ontario. Photography by Michael Kane, Toronto

Postcard portraying "The Glorious Twelfth," the anniversary of the defeat of the Catholic King James II at the Battle of the Boyne by Prince William of Orange. From the private collection of Andrew Thomson, Guelph, Ontario. Pen and ink reproduction by Michael Clifton, Kitchener, Ontario

Edmund Burke, Roman Catholic missionary and vicar-general of the Bishop of Quebec in Upper Canada, 1794–1801, and in Nova Scotia, 1801–17. Burke was appointed bishop of Sion and vicar apostolic of Nova Scotia in 1817, a position he held until his death in 1820.

The Right Reverend William Dollard, missionary in the Maritime colonies, 1817–42, and Roman Catholic bishop of Fredericton, 1843–51. The see of Fredericton was translated to Saint John in 1857.

Bishop Michael Fallon of London, Ontario, 1909–31. Although raised in Ottawa and himself fluently bilingual, Fallon opposed any extension of the French language in Ontario and was one of the main supporters of the infamous Regulation 17. From Mother St. Paul OSU, *From Desenzano to "the Pines"* (Toronto: Macmillan 1941)

GUIBORDISM REVERSED--CIVIL LAW MUST TRIUMPH!

The Ontario reaction to the refusal by Bishop Ignace Bourget to grant burial in consecrated ground to Joseph Guibord because of his association with the banned Institut Canadien. From *Grip*, 9 October 1875. J.W. Bengough Papers, William Ready Division of Archives and Research Collections, McMaster University, Hamilton, Ontario

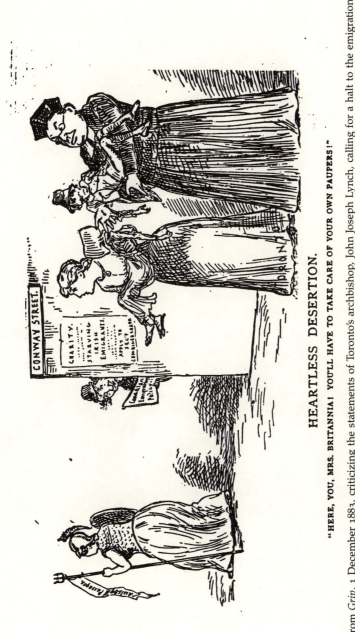

HEARTLESS DESERTION.

"HERE, YOU, MRS. BRITANNIA! YOU'LL HAVE TO TAKE CARE OF YOUR OWN PAUPERS!"

Cartoon from *Grip*, 1 December 1883, criticizing the statements of Toronto's archbishop, John Joseph Lynch, calling for a halt to the emigration of impoverished Irish servant girls. J.W. Bengough Papers, William Ready Division of Archives and Research Collections, McMaster University, Hamilton, Ontario

John Kent, Newfoundland merchant, political reformer, and brother-in-law of Bishop Michael Anthony Fleming. With Fleming's support, Kent was elected to the first Newfoundland House of Assembly in 1832. He served as Speaker of the House in 1849 and as premier from 1858 to 1861.

The Right Reverend Alexander Macdonell, first Roman Catholic bishop in Upper Canada, by an anonymous artist. National Archives of Canada, c-11059

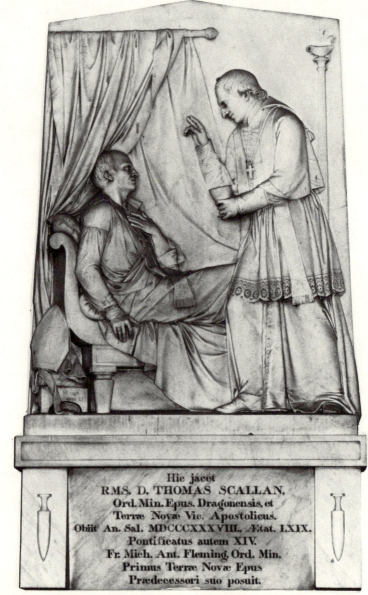

Hic jacet
RMS. D. THOMAS SCALLAN,
Ord. Min. Epus. Dragonensis, et
Terræ Novæ Vic. Apostolicus.
Obiit An. Sal. MDCCCXXXVIII, Ætat. LXIX.
Pontificatus autem XIV.
Fr. Mich. Ant. Fleming, Ord. Min.
Primus Terræ Novæ Epus
Prædecessori suo posuit.

Memorial to Thomas Scallan, vicar apostolic of Newfoundland, 1816–30, who is shown on his deathbed receiving anointing from his successor, Michael Anthony Fleming. The two men were deeply divided during Scallan's life over the latter's liberal and accommodating policies; local tradition interpreted this memorial as showing Scallan's reconciliation to Fleming and to the official church.

Creed and Culture

1 English-French Relations in the Canadian Catholic Community

ROBERT CHOQUETTE

Nearly half of Canada's population is Roman Catholic, and slightly more than half of the Catholic community are of French ethnic extraction. Relations between French-speaking and English-speaking Catholics have frequently proved to be problematical, erupting at times into open confrontation. The Canadian Catholic church, endeavouring to become a community of peace and brotherhood according to the dictates of the Master, has all too often been a hotbed of dissent and fratricidal bickering in a country torn asunder by political, regional, religious, and ethnic disagreements. A number of international, national, and regional factors must be invoked to explain this frequent bitter dissension.

Beginning with the capitulation of Canada to British forces in 1760 and the subsequent Treaty of Paris (1763), Canadian Catholics, French- or English-speaking, were always faced with two principal adversaries: the Protestants and the Catholics of the other linguistic group. From the early nineteenth to the mid-twentieth century, crusading Protestant evangelicalism saw its arch-enemy to be the "Antichrist," or the Romish idolatry of the papacy. As the nineteenth century wore on, this perfervid Protestant no-popery[1] fused with the increasingly arrogant white Anglo-Saxonism prevalent in both Great Britain and the United States. The related dogmas of progress and racial superiority inherent in this ideology served throughout English Canada as a basic plank in the social program of governments and Protestant churches well into the twentieth century.[2]

The other principal adversary of Catholics were the coreligionists of the "other" linguistic group, French or English. Among the English-speaking settlers who entered Canada in the wake of the British Conquest and the American War of Independence were large numbers of Irish and Scottish Catholics. These Catholics needed to adjust to a church dominated by French Canadians while frequently competing for the same jobs offered to both groups as "hewers of wood and drawers of water." Catholics of Irish lineage, whose numbers increased dramatically after the Great Famine of 1846, often perceived the preponderance of French-Catholic clergy as a conspiracy to "keep the Irish in their place" (see tables 1 and 2).

French-English relations within the Canadian Catholic community evolved through three distinct periods: the pre-1840 era, the period from 1840 to 1930, and the years from around 1930 to the present. The first of these phases was a time of relative peace, with the partial exception of the Maritime colonies; the third was one in which peace was gradually restored; but the second witnessed bitter ethno-linguistic rivalries within the Canadian Catholic church. In these years the country was rocked by the abolition of New Brunswick's confessional schools (1871), the Métis insurrections led by Louis Riel at Red River (1869–70) and the Saskatchewan River (1885), the abolition by Manitoba of both confessional schools and the official status of French (1890), the debate over the autonomy bills relating to the creation of the new provinces of Saskatchewan and Alberta (1905), the Ontario schools crisis centring on Regulation 17 (1912–27), and the conscription debates of the two world wars. The Catholic church was usually a key player in these issues, its attitude proving crucial to their outcome, for the church was frequently the only important national institution with deep roots in all parts of the country and enjoying the trust of its diverse members. Some Catholic leaders tried to effect rapprochement between apparently irreconcilable opposites, while others fanned the flames of French-Canadian or Irish-Canadian nationalism and bigotry.

Until the mid nineteenth century, however, the Catholic church in Canada was primarily a French-Canadian phenomenon. Only small pockets of Scots or Irish Catholics were found in southeastern Ontario (Glengarry County) and in the Northwest, that "Great Lone Land" encompassing the Hudson Bay, Arctic Ocean, and Pacific Ocean hinterland. The Atlantic region was, however, an exception to this rule. Significant immigration of English-speaking Catholics began there as early as the 1780s, and the main influx of Irish immigrants to Nova Scotia and Newfoundland was over by the time of the Great Famine. In Newfoundland the Catholic population was

Table 1
Catholic Population of Canada by Linguistic Affiliation

Year	Total Population	Total Catholic Population	Percentage of Catholics in Canada	Total French-Speaking Catholics	Percentage of French-Speaking Catholics
1881	4,324,810	1,791,982	41.4	1,208,929	67.0
1911	7,206,643	2,841,881	39.4	2,054,890	72.3
1951*	14,009,429	6,069,496	43.3	4,068,850	67.0
1981*	24,343,180	11,402,605	47.8	6,249,000	54.8

* The 1951 and 1981 data are based on mother tongue rather than on ethnic origin.

almost exclusively Irish, and had its own bishop as early as 1794; but in Nova Scotia, New Brunswick, and Prince Edward Island Irish and Scottish Catholics lived side by side with Acadians and fell initially under the jurisdiction of the bishop of Quebec. These newcomers had soon relegated the French-speaking population to the status of a minority. It is not surprising, therefore, that Atlantic Canada was the scene of the earliest difficulties between French- and English-speaking Catholics.

In 1758, three years after the order for the deportation of the Acadians, the newly established legislature of Nova Scotia officially outlawed the Catholic clergy.[3] While fugitive Acadians were being hunted down in rocky coves and inlets of the Atlantic shore, their principal missionary, Pierre-A.-S. Maillard, died in Halifax in 1762. No other Catholic priest set foot in Nova Scotia until 1768, when, notwithstanding the anti-Catholic laws, Bishop Jean-Olivier Briand appointed Father Charles-François Bailly de Messein as missionary to the region. Thereafter, the Catholics of Atlantic Canada always had priests, both French- and English-speaking. A Gaelic-speaking priest, James MacDonald, served in Prince Edward Island from 1770 to 1785, and in 1785 the first truly English-speaking clergyman, James Jones of Cork, arrived at Halifax. The behaviour of the Scottish and Irish priests who followed in their wake often left much to be desired, as was frequently the case in frontier regions, and this misconduct placed an additional strain on their relations with the Acadians.

The gradual emancipation of Catholics in Atlantic Canada began in the 1780s and was completed by 1830. During this half century, clergy of Canadian or French origin continued to be sent by the bishops of Quebec, but Irish and Scots Catholics also imported clergy from Scotland and Ireland. The result was a Catholic clerical establishment just as diverse and fractious as the ethnically fragmented flock it aspired to lead. With the rapid growth of the English-

Table 2
French-Speaking and English-Speaking Catholics in Select Provinces and Regions

Year and Province	Total Population	Total Catholic Population	Percentage of Catholics in Total Population	Total French-Speaking Catholics	Percentage of French-Speaking Catholics
1881					
New Brunswick	321,233	109,091	34.0	56,635	51.9
Ontario	1,926,922	320,839	16.7	102,743	32.0
Prairies	118,706	16,689	14.0	12,845	77.0
1911					
New Brunswick	351,889	144,889	41.2	98,611	68.1
Ontario	2,523,274	484,997	19.2	202,457	41.7
Prairies	1,322,709	226,279	17.1	73,995	32.7
1951*					
New Brunswick	515,697	260,742	50.6	148,760	57.0
Ontario	4,597,542	1,142,140	24.8	258,957	22.7
Prairies	2,547,770	542,119	21.3	88,454	16.3
1981					
New Brunswick	689,375	371,245	53.9	180,617	48.7
Ontario	8,534,265	3,036,245	35.6	522,770	17.2
Prairies	4,183,795	1,242,755	29.7	140,082	11.3

* The assumption here is that virtually all Canadians of French origin are Roman Catholic by religious affiliation or tradition.

speaking Catholic population, the feeling increased among Irish and Scottish people that French-speaking priests and bishops were insensitive to their needs.

In the early nineteenth century, the Irish Catholics of Nova Scotia were centred in Halifax. They provided the first English-speaking episcopal leader of the Maritime colonies in the person of Edmund Burke. Burke, a native of Ireland, was consecrated vicar apostolic of Nova Scotia in 1818. His appointment was followed by the naming of the Scot, Angus Bernard MacEachern, as vicar-general with episcopal powers (1819) and eventually as bishop of Charlottetown (1829). In 1842 New Brunswick got its own English-speaking bishop whem William Dollard, an Irishman, was named bishop of Saint John. The Irish of Halifax, who had spearheaded this movement towards ecclesiastical independence, never abandoned their control over the Halifax church. The earliest challenge to this leadership came from the Scot, William Fraser, second vicar apostolic of Nova Scotia (1827–42) and first bishop of Halifax (1842–4). It was a fight between Irish and

Scots, compounded by a strong current of lay independence as well as by personal rivalries and peculiarities.[4] Since both ethnic groups were anglicized or in the process of becoming anglicized, linguistic antipathy was actually a diminishing factor in their relations.

Things were not so simple with the Acadians. If ever Canada had an oppressed people, they were these refugees from British persecution. After 1766 the Acadians drifted back to their homes in Maritime Canada from their exile along the Atlantic seaboard, Europe, and Canada. They found their rich alluvial homelands of the Minas basin and the Chignecto peninsula occupied by the New England immigrants brought in by the British after 1760. Pushed out again, the Acadians were driven to settle in southwestern Nova Scotia or to join those already resettled in southern New Brunswick, in the Memramcook area, and along the more northerly coast around the Madawaska River and the Baie des Chaleurs. Those who chose to rebuild in the lower St John River valley were pushed further upriver by the arrival of thirty thousand Loyalists during the American War of Independence. The province of New Brunswick (1784) sheltered the greatest number of Acadians in its northern and eastern districts.

In the early nineteenth century, *Evangeline's* people[5] were a poor, downtrodden, and broken lot, unable to compete in a world of injustice and oppression. Like their Micmac and Abenaki co-religionists, the Acadians clung tenaciously to their faith. Wealth and education eluded them. Catholic clergy eventually provided a leadership capable of propelling the lethargic Acadians into a more confident and aggressive mood, but in the late eighteenth century few French-speaking priests came to Acadia. Nevertheless, from 1785 to 1800 the number of clerics grew from three to ten in the Maritimes. All the newcomers came from Scotland, Ireland, or France (royalist émigrés). During Edmund Burke's administration (1801–20) the Canadian connection revived with thirteen new appointments, leaving a solid contingent of eight Canadian missionaries in the Maritimes in 1820. These, added to the dozen French émigré clerics who came to the Maritimes in the 1790s, meant that French-speaking clergy, while not abundant, were now providing basic church services to the Acadians. This group would not be able to provide clergy of their own until they were equipped with an adequate education system in the late nineteenth century.

The number of Acadian Catholics was growing rapidly. By 1900 they represented two out of every three Catholics in New Brunswick, yet there had never been a French-speaking bishop anywhere in the Maritimes. The leaders of the growing Acadian renaissance[6] undertook to change this state of affairs. In fact, Acadians had been held back from advancement in the ranks of the hierarchy not only by their poor education system but also by the influence of the English-speaking clergy in the Maritimes, a group that reflected, somewhat earlier than elsewhere in Canada, the widespread bigotry prevalent in the English-speaking world after the mid nineteenth century. Archbishop Thomas Louis Connolly of Saint John (1852–9) and Halifax (1859–76), leader of this biased hierarchy, was profoundly detested by the Acadians. One breakthrough in this episcopal guer-rilla warfare was the appointment, in 1912, of Edouard LeBlanc as bishop of St John. In 1920 a second Acadian, Patrice-Alexandre Chiasson, was appointed to Chatham, and eighteen years later this diocese was transferred to the predominantly French-speaking town of Bathurst.[7]

Closely related to the influence of church and clergy was the influence of the schools, which proved to be a favourite arena for the wars of English- and French-speaking Catholics in the Maritimes as elsewhere. Although some private Catholic schools existed as early as the seventeenth century, in Port-Royal (Annapolis Royal), for example, education became a major social concern only in the mid nineteenth century. As elsewhere in the Western world, this interest resulted in a series of governmental measures designed to provide all citizens with educational services. The battle was joined between the advocates of "nonsectarian" public education and those of confessional schools. Acadians joined in the fray, insisting not only on Catholic schools but also on French Catholic schools because, in their eyes, the basic values of language and faith were inseparable. This policy put the Acadians at odds with their English-speaking co-religionists, who were concerned only with repelling the Protestant incursion and who took it for granted that the English language must prevail in British colonies. They could not understand why the Acadians felt they needed to fend off both Protestants and English-speaking Catholics.

The struggle for Acadian emancipation characterized the history of elementary education in New Brunswick, Nova Scotia, and Prince Edward Island. The hierarchy and clergy were always deeply involved in these struggles on both the French and English sides because, to most people, church and school were one. They were seen to be the primary instruments for the preservation of cherished values. Throughout this century of conflict, from the mid nineteenth to the mid twentieth century, English-speaking Catholics came to feel that the Acadians were more interested in language than in faith and accused them of "nationalism," by which they meant placing ethnic and linguistic considerations above religious concerns. Acadians, for their part, felt that their foremost oppressors were not Protestants but Irish Catholics.

Similar tensions arose in the field of higher education. For example, when the Collège Saint-Joseph, a small Catholic college established by Father François-Xavier Lafrance in Memramcook in 1854, was forced to close in 1862, only to reopen in 1864 with the fathers of the Holy Cross at the helm, some Acadians were unhappy because it was bilingual, in fact primarily English. The pastor of Saint-Louis de Kent therefore opened the competing Collège Saint-Louis in 1874. He was forced to close his school in 1882, however, owing to pressure exerted by his Irish bishop, James Rogers of Chatham, who contended that the English were ill served in the Collège Saint-Louis.

In Ontario, where Irish immigration did not reach its peak until the mid nineteenth century, the estrangement between French- and English-speaking Catholics developed later than in the Maritimes. Once ethnic rivalries took shape, however, their consequences were especially serious, not only for Ontario itself but also for the rest of the country. As the home of more than one-third of Canada's people, Ontario frequently exported its views and prejudices to other parts of the country, notably the West.

During the seventeenth and eighteenth centuries, Ontario was part of the vast *pays-d'en-haut* criss-crossed by voyageurs and *coureurs de bois*. Military and fur-trading posts ensured France's control over the land, and after 1760 the British posts in the western portion of the province of Quebec served the same purpose for the new rulers. When Upper Canada was separated from Lower Canada in 1791, its 10,000 white inhabitants included several hundred French-speaking Catholics located in Ontario's oldest parish, L'Assomption (Windsor), on the southern shore of the Detroit River. In addition, several hundred more Scottish Catholics were established in Glengarry County at the southeastern extremity of Ontario. Both colonies enjoyed the services of a priest at the turn of the nineteenth century, the eve of the tidal wave of immigration that transformed the wilds of Upper Canada into the nation's industrial heartland. Thus when Father Alexander Macdonell arrived in Upper Canada from Scotland in 1804, French- and English-speaking Catholics each occupied distinct and distant parts of the province, and ethnic conflict was not a serious problem. Macdonell soon became vicar-general (1807) to the bishop of Quebec, then auxiliary bishop to the bishop of Quebec (1820), and finally first bishop of the new Diocese of Kingston (1826), the mother see of all Ontario Catholic churches.[8]

Macdonell managed to survive in his new frontier church with the assistance of the older churches of the lower St Lawrence valley, particularly that of Montreal. The bishop maintained regular and friendly correspondence with Bishops Jean-Jacques Lartigue and Ignace Bourget of Montreal as well as with the superiors of the Montreal Sulpicians. He obtained modest gifts (chalices, vestments, money) for his new churches and new clergy for the pioneer districts of Upper Canada. Macdonell's correspondence reveals few traces of ethnic or linguistic prejudice in spite of the fact that he sought administrative autonomy for his diocese. He worked hand in hand with his French-speaking colleagues. Indeed, when his first coadjutor bishop, the Englishman Thomas Weld, resigned without having set foot in Canada, he recommended Father Joseph Quiblier, French superior of the Montreal Sulpicians, to succeed him. Quiblier refused the appointment. Macdonell thereupon approached another Sulpician, the Irishman John Larkin, who also refused the appointment in 1832. Despairing of finding the appropriate candidate for his diocese, Macdonell asked Weld to help him find a candidate who was neither Scottish nor Irish, the two major ethnic groups in his diocese. At this stage, he thought the candidate should be either English or Canadian. Nevertheless, when Lartigue responded to an inquiry from Macdonell by recommending the appointment of Rémi Gaulin, a trilingual (French, English, Gaelic) Canadian priest, Macdonell was overjoyed. Gaulin was consecrated coadjutor bishop in 1833 and succeeded Macdonell upon the latter's death in 1840.

Thus, before 1840, Catholic church leaders in Upper Canada were not particularly infected with ethno-linguistic bias. During the next twenty years, however, several factors began working to exacerbate French-English relations. The rebellions in Upper and Lower Canada in 1837–8, followed by Lord Durham's Report, prepared the union of the Canadas. This new constitutional structure brought a number of injustices upon Catholics and French-speaking Canadians, not to mention upon Lower Canada as a whole. Furthermore, the Catholic population of Upper Canada (now Canada West) rose sharply in the 1840s, 1850s, and 1860s owing to the arrival of large numbers of Irish Catholics.

The dioceses and parishes created to accommodate the newcomers were more often than not directed by bishops of French ethnic origin. The Canadian Rémi Gaulin followed Macdonell in the historic see of Kingston (1840), and Michael Power, a "frenchified" pastor of Irish lineage, became first bishop of Toronto (1841), only to be followed upon his premature death in 1847 by Bishop Armand de Charbonnel (1850), a French aristocrat. Meanwhile, the new Diocese of Bytown (Ottawa) was given the Frenchman Joseph Guigues as founding bishop (1847), while the see of London was established in 1856 with the Canadian Pierre-Adolphe Pinsoneault as first bishop. Thus, in

1856, four of Ontario's six bishops were of French origin (two Canadians and two Frenchmen). The growing majority of Irish faithful began to be restive in the face of this apparent domination of their church by the French. A similar phenomenon was apparent among the members of various religious orders now moving into Ontario as they established schools, hospitals, colleges, and missions. Jesuits, Oblates, Basilians, and Grey Nuns were among the legions of priests, brothers, and sisters active in Ontario in the expanding Catholic church. The ethnic composition of the hierarchy and clergy was out of proportion to that of its flock.[9]

The tensions between French and English Catholics were further exacerbated by a series of international, national, and regional factors over the next seventy-five years. English-speaking Catholics were people of their times and, despite their growing alienation from Protestant Ontario, they were nearly as prone as Protestants to consume the heady wine of progressivism, British imperialism, English-language superiority, and related racist doctrines. When French Canadians began migrating in ever-increasing numbers to Ontario after 1860, the sentinels of Orange Protestantism were alarmed. Eastern, southwestern, and subsequently northeastern Ontario began to put on a French-Canadian face. A growing number of schools used French as a language of instruction and communication. New French parishes sprang up. There was no shortage of Quebec clergy ready to staff these churches and schools. The result was a growing estrangement between English- and French-speaking bishops and clergy, as English Catholics saw that these new migrants insisted on preserving their language in church and school. While French schools had existed since the earliest days of Ontario settlement (1786), they had never provoked any opposition because they were few in number. After 1880, however, the former peaceful coexistence of a bilingual Quebec and an English Ontario was threatened by the ambition of these new Ontarians to make Ontario into another Quebec. The Quebec "reservation" was threatening to become an expansive empire.

The man who inherited the mantle of leadership of the newly confident Irish Catholics was John Lynch, third bishop of Toronto (1860–88). In concert with his colleagues in the Ontario episcopate, he led a running battle against the bishops of Ottawa. Beginning in 1874, this campaign aimed at cutting the ties of the Ottawa see with the ecclesiastical province of Quebec. Lynch and his colleagues were determined to have all the civil province of Ontario under their sway. To accomplish this goal, they wanted to realign the boundaries of the Diocese of Ottawa, which at that time straddled the Ontario-

Quebec boundary, to the boundaries of the new province of Ontario, created in 1867. The resulting truncated Diocese of Ottawa could then be brought under the jurisdiction of the ecclesiastical province of Toronto (1870).

Bishops Guigues and Joseph-Thomas Duhamel of Ottawa opposed the concerted attack of the Ontario prelates and marshalled the support of the French-Canadian hierarchy. After 1873, all of French Canada's bishops stood shoulder to shoulder to counter their opponents' moves in Rome. Throughout the 1870s, 1880s, and 1890s, increasing tension and harsh words characterized the relations between Canada's French and English bishops.

Moreover, although conflicts within clerical ranks are usually withheld from public view, a series of national and provincial factors coalesced after 1885 to push ethno-linguistic rivalries into the open. The hanging of Louis Riel in Regina was the opening shot in a protracted struggle between French and English Canadians. Along with its industrial vocation, Ontario had become the cultural centre of English Canada. While Ontario public opinion demanded the hanging of Riel, French Canada just as resolutely opposed it. Reaction to the hanging of Riel on 16 November 1885 facilitated the election of Honoré Mercier's nationalist government in Quebec the following year, a régime that adopted legislation (1888) compensating the Society of Jesus for property losses dating back to the previous century. In turn, D'Alton McCarthy founded the Equal Rights Association (1889), a militantly anti-Catholic and anti-French movement that prefigured Manitoba's 1890 legislation abolishing confessional schools and the official status of French. The fat was now in the fire right across the country, as French and English struggled to determine the future shape of Canada. Was it to be a bilingual entity where French and English citizens were equal in all regions, or a binational state consisting of a French Quebec and an English Canada?

The Catholic church was intimately involved in all these disputes, not only because nearly all French Canadians were Catholic but also because English-speaking Catholics were becoming more militant. Moreover, in both the French and English Catholic communities, the clergy's role in community leadership increased as each group felt more alienated from Protestant Ontario. The struggle over diocesan boundaries was soon compounded by regular confrontations over the ethno-linguistic affiliation of individual candidates for bishoprics.

Indeed, in 1889 it was rumoured in the press that Archbishop Duhamel of Ottawa was seeking the creation of a new diocese in eastern Ontario, centred in Hawkesbury and encompassing Prescott

County. Although the report was groundless, it was sufficient to provoke Ontario's English-speaking bishops into petitioning the Holy See in Rome for the erection of a new diocese in eastern Ontario. Rome promptly responded by creating the Diocese of Alexandria, a division of the Diocese of Kingston covering Glengarry and Stormont counties. The intention of Ontario's bishops was subsequently to solicit the annexation of Prescott and Russell counties (part of the Diocese of Ottawa) on the grounds that the resources in Glengarry and Stormont were inadequate to support a diocese. Meanwhile, Ottawa, a metropolitan see since 1886, objected once more to the ecclesiastical imperialism of Ontario's English-speaking prelates. These quarrels over ethnic and linguistic affiliation of prospective bishops have continued until the present day in all bilingual areas of Ontario.

The most virulent controversies within Ontario's Catholic church erupted between 1890 and 1930. Successive episcopal nominations in the Dioceses of London, Alexandria, Ottawa, and Sault Ste Marie provoked a barrage of petitions, counter-petitions, grievances, and protests from clergy and laity. Franco-Ontarians demanded the appointment of French-speaking priests and bishops sympathetic to their aspirations and willing to conduct church services in French. With few exceptions, the English-speaking prelates and clergy who occasioned criticism from Franco-Ontarians were of Irish lineage.

The most noisy and troublesome controversies centred on the schools, where French-Canadian and Irish-Canadian clerics contended for control. The rapid increase in the number of Franco-Ontarians between Confederation and the Second World War led to a rapid growth in the number of French schools. Before 1885 most Franco-Ontarians established their schools within the public school system rather than in the separate school system. The rise of an Ontarian and Canadian francophobia, however, was reflected in progressively more restrictive school legislation after 1885, and this caused a shift of allegiance. Thereafter, French schools were usually established within the separate school system because the Franco-Ontarian ratepayers felt the Catholic church's moral influence helped to protect them from provincial government oppression. The Catholic bishops also worked towards a similar end. Yet this required French-English cooperation within numerous separate school boards. In other words, the French and Irish Catholics, well used to locking horns in the ecclesiastical arena, now had to learn to coexist within school boards. Harmony did not come easily. To this day Franco-Ontarians have been determined to maintain and develop their French Catholic schools, while English-speaking Catholics still consider religion and language as separate issues in education. Faced with Ontario governments and public opinion increasingly hostile to other-than-English schooling, English-speaking Catholics have proved willing to sacrifice French schools in order to preserve separate schools. English-speaking Catholics, as the Irish Catholic leader Bishop Michael Fallon (1910–31) would have said, felt trapped between the upper millstone of French-Canadian nationalism and the lower millstone of Protestant bigotry.

The saddest chapter in the fight between Ontario's French and English (Protestant and Catholic) people was the period from 1912 to 1927, which saw the battle over Regulation 17. This controversy was provoked by the 1912 ruling of the Ontario Department of Education that aimed to ban the use of French as a language of communication and instruction in all Ontario schools. Franco-Ontarians, bishops and priests included, rose as one to fight a policy endorsed by most English-speaking Ontarians, Catholic as well as Protestant. The province of Quebec supported the fight of their "front-line" French-Canadian brothers in the "trenches" of Ontario. The First World War and the conscription crisis of 1917–18 exacerbated feelings even more, so that the unity of Canada was in peril. Finally, the government of Ontario amended its controversial Regulation 17 in 1927, acknowledging that its effort had not succeeded in enforcing the law.

While controversy and mistrust were woven into the fabric of English-French relations in Ontario from the mid nineteenth until nearly the mid twentieth century, some Catholic leaders did manage to stand out by preaching a gospel of peace, reconciliation, and harmony based on the frank acknowledgment and acceptance of diversity. They dreamed of unity in diversity, a view consistent with the broad Catholic tradition throughout the centuries. Most Franco-Ontarian leaders were of this persuasion, for few of them ever considered trying to limit the rights of some 90 per cent of the Ontario population. Among English-speaking Catholics, an honour roll for agents of harmony would include the names of Father Edmund Cornell, omi, and Archbishops Charles Hugh Gauthier of Kingston and Ottawa and Neil McNeil of Toronto. In the thick of the fight, and in spite of tremendous pressures by their own linguistic group, they consistently managed to steer a course based on justice and respect for all.[10]

Canada's vast Northwest also experienced difficulties in French-English relations similar to those of Ontario and the Maritimes. The Rupert's Land of the Hudson's Bay Company (fd 1670) was dotted with the trading posts of either the British fur merchants or of the rival North West Company (fd 1775) centred in Montreal; the two companies merged in 1821, creating a rejuvenated Hudson's Bay Company with a string of trading posts that stretched to the Mackenzie Delta on the Arctic Ocean and to the shores of the Pacific. Although most of the officers and gentlemen engaged in this huge fur-trade monopoly were Englishmen, Scotsmen, or Orkneymen, the voyageurs and interpreters criss-crossing the northern continent were mostly French Canadians. These Canadiens mated with native women to produce western Canada's considerable Métis population. Native, French, and English languages were all used throughout the vast hinterland.

In 1812 the establishment of the Red River colony in what is now Manitoba gave birth to a bilingual society where a French-speaking, primarily Métis, majority coexisted with an English-speaking, fur-trading elite imported from Great Britain. A number of English-speaking Métis also lived in Red River.[11] Resident Catholic clergymen were present from 1818, the year Fathers Joseph-Norbert Provencher and Sévère Dumoulin arrived from Canada. Until 1845, when the Oblates arrived, Bishop Provencher never had more than four or five priests at one time to assist him in evangelizing the Red River colony. Nor did this French-Canadian Catholic clergy range far from Red River. Father Georges Belcourt (1831) was the only exception. He attempted to establish permanent missions for the Indians at Rainy Lake, Wabassimong at the mouth of the Winnipeg River, and St Paul's on the Assiniboine River, but failed.

In 1838 two Canadian priests, Norbert Blanchet and Modeste Demers, left Red River to start missions in Oregon. The expansion of Catholic missions along the North Saskatchewan River can be dated to 1842, when Father Jean-Baptiste Thibault journeyed to Fort Edmonton. By 1844 he had established a permanent mission station at Lake St Anne, west of Edmonton. This served as a springboard for further Catholic missionary expansion into northern Alberta. In 1846, when Father Alexandre Taché, omi, and Father Louis-François Laflèche put down roots at Ile-à-la-Crosse in northern Saskatchewan, the Oblate saga was well underway. In 1847 Taché journeyed to Lake Athabaska, where the new mission station allowed Father Henri Faraud, omi, to reach Great Slave Lake in 1852, awaiting Father Henri Grollier, omi, who went down the Mackenzie River in 1858, 1859, and 1860 to establish mission stations at Fort Norman, Fort Simpson, Fort Good Hope, and Fort McPherson on the Peel River. By this time the Oblates were also encamped on the Pacific coast, thus spanning the continent in an apostolic monopoly as impressive as the commercial empire of the Hudson's Bay Company. In short order a growing list of Oblate bishops led a missionary phalanx that ranged throughout all western and northern Canada, including Hudson Bay and Labrador. With few exceptions, these Catholic missionaries and bishops were French-speaking and of French or Canadian birth.[12]

As was the case elsewhere, education was a basic concern for Catholic as well as Protestant missionaries.[13] Both established schools alongside their churches as fast as possible. Throughout the nineteenth century, western and northern Canada's Catholic clergy usually established bilingual (French/English) schools, although they also established a few English schools, primarily in British Columbia. Until the early twentieth century there was little evidence of ethnolinguistic bickering within this western Catholic community despite the predominant numbers of French-speaking Oblates, if only because English-speaking Catholics were a rare commodity. Catholicism was so totally identified with the French language that the Indians, in fact, referred to the "English religion" or the "French religion" in order to distinguish Protestant from Catholic.

The massive immigration into western Canada, facilitated by the completion of the Canadian Pacific Railway (1885) and the policies of Clifford Sifton in the Laurier government (1896ff), changed everything. English-speaking Catholics grew in number, while French Canadians from Quebec refused to go west.[14] Moreover, most immigrants of whatever ethno-linguistic origin adopted English upon settling in western Canada. Within the Catholic church, this resulted in a growing estrangement between English-speaking communities and their French-speaking clergy. The problem was compounded by the fact that most French-speaking western Catholics lived in relatively homogeneous rural areas, whereas the English-speaking Catholic newcomers settled in pluralistic cities. This made for different needs. For example, the controversial Manitoba schools legislation of 1890 and the subsequent Laurier-Greenway compromise agreement of 1896 providing religious instruction where the numbers of Catholics were sufficient to warrant it satisfied most Franco-Manitobans; they lived in homogeneous rural areas and their schools were supervised by tolerant inspectors.[15] The opposite was true for English-speaking Catholics. They found themselves in urban centres like Winnipeg and Brandon, unable to maintain Catholic schools because they were compelled to pay taxes to non-denominational public (in fact Protestant) schools.[16]

When these same English-speaking Catholics went to worship, more often than not they were served by French-speaking but bilingual clergy. English-speaking Catholics began to demonstrate in order to obtain English parishes, English clergy, English Catholic schools, and English bishops. This growing francophobia across English Canada put the French-speaking clergy of western Canada on the defensive. Controversy erupted in Winnipeg over the erection of French or English parishes and led ultimately to the division of the Diocese of Saint-Boniface to create the English Diocese of Winnipeg (1915).[17] Meanwhile, the newly erected Diocese of Calgary (1913) had its rounds when its first bishop, John Thomas McNally, undertook to put the French clergy (80 per cent of the clergy) in their place.[18] Similar quarrels also occurred in Regina and Edmonton.[19] French and English parties both appealed for support to prominent churchmen, politicians, and diplomats in centres such as Ottawa, London, Paris, and Rome. The English-speaking Catholic crusade to obtain anglophone priests and bishops escalated into a campaign for the virtual elimination of French. Obviously, the leaders of the English Catholic party were infected with the same "English-only" virus as their white Anglo-Saxon Protestant (wasp) fellow citizens.

English-speaking Catholics emerged victorious from this battle. A growing list of English-speaking bishops acceded to the new sees (Winnipeg and Calgary, for example) or followed French predecessors into episcopal office (Edmonton, Regina, Victoria, and Vancouver, for example). It could hardly have been otherwise, given the growing disproportion in the numbers of English and French Catholics in twentieth-century western Canada, a phenomenon reinforced by the nativist mood in the Prairies[20] and its associated repressive school legislation.[21] Indeed, in 1916 Manitoba rescinded its 1897 legislation authorizing bilingual schools. Saskatchewan attained the same objective in 1918 and 1931.

Although this review of English-French relations in the Canadian Catholic community inevitably highlights conflict and disagreement, it does not mean that French-English relations have not had their good moments in Canadian Catholic history. Some of the faithful and clergy did manage to overcome the prejudice of their milieu, even during the difficult years of the late nineteenth and early twentieth centuries. Credit for the ultimate resolution of conflict belongs to them. Nevertheless, the squabblers, the bigots, and the clerical powermongers set their stamp upon French-English relations in the Canadian Catholic community for many decades.

The basic fact that emerges from this history is that the fighting and mistrust between French and English Catholics was continuous from the mid nineteenth to the mid twentieth century. With the exception of Quebec, where little evidence exists of ethno-linguistic wrangling within the Catholic church, the rest of Canada witnessed many eruptions of ethno-linguistic fighting, both within the church and in society as a whole. At the turn of the twentieth century, in New Brunswick, the contenders were a majority Acadian community set against an exclusively English-speaking hierarchy; in western Canada the growing English-speaking Catholic majority challenged an exclusively French-speaking hierarchy.

In Ontario the situation was not as clear cut. The province's first bishop, Alexander Macdonell, was succeeded mostly by French-speaking bishops, but not because the Canadian hierarchy favoured French. Through no fault of its own, it had simply failed on many occasions to secure the episcopal appointments of clerics of Irish origin. The bishops did succeed in appointing Michael Power to the see of Toronto, Patrick Phelan to that of Kingston, and John Farrell to that of Hamilton, but they were unsuccessful, as was Macdonell, in securing a native English-speaker to succeed Macdonell in King-ston. They also failed, in spite of papal intervention, to secure an English-speaking successor to Power in Toronto. The difficult situa-tion of these pioneer churches of Upper Canada and the resulting refusal of several prominent English-speaking priests to accept the episcopal burden led to the appointment of a higher-than-normal proportion of French-speaking (but bilingual) bishops: hence the appointment of Gaulin in Kingston, Charbonnel in Toronto, and Pinsoneault in London. When Lynch took on the mantle of English-speaking Catholic emancipation after 1860, he faced no opposition from the hierarchy of French Canada. The bishops acknowledged that Toronto should become an autonomous ecclesiastical province (1870) and that most of its bishops should be English-speaking, indeed Irish. The English-French fight in Ontario Catholicism did not result, as in the Maritimes and the West, from a unilingual hierarchy fending off a majority of faithful and clergy of the other language group. In Ontario, the fight resulted from the policy of appointing English-speaking prelates in majority-French dioceses. This was the case in Ottawa, Alexandria, and Sault Ste Marie, not to mention London. There, a strong French-speaking contingent engaged the bigoted Bishop Michael Fallon (1910–31).

The fact that French- and English-speaking Catholics fought in the Maritimes, the West, and Ontario during the late nineteenth and early twentieth centuries is incontrovertible. The question worth asking, however, is why these two ethnic groups, bound together by a common religion, fought so bitterly.

A metropolitan thesis might explain this fratricidal war, if researchers found that one or several ecclesiastical metropolises exploited their hinterland. But the history of this ethno-linguistic fight across Canada cannot support this view. In the Maritimes, the Acadians were not rebelling against the metropolitan authority of Halifax but against the refusal of English-speaking bishops, be they residents of Halifax like T.L. Connolly, or of Saint John like John Sweeney, or of Bathurst like James Rogers, to allow Acadians to rise to positions of influence within the church. The same was true in Ontario, where the Toronto ecclesiastical metropolis had little control over the Franco-Ontarians of the province. Franco-Ontarians were not fighting the English to keep Toronto at bay but to control their own church destiny and preserve their language. To them, their faith was the guardian of their language and their culture. The conflict, then, was primarily a way to affirm a group's full and equal rights as Canadians. This interpretation is corroborated by the earlier history of the church in Upper Canada, when Bishop Macdonell's Upper Canadian hinterland managed to get along well with the Montreal metropolis. Some tensions resulted from their unequal status, but they never took on a particularly ethno-linguistic colouring.

The crux of the fight on both the ecclesiastical and the secular stage was what vision of Canada and of the Catholic church would prevail. Were Canada and the Catholic church to be officially bilingual entities acknowledging both linguistic groups as equals? Or were they to become a binational state and church comprising of a French Quebec and an English Canada? On the one hand, English-speaking Canadians, Protestant and Catholic alike, favoured a homogeneous British English-speaking nation with allowance for a bilingual French Quebec "reservation." On the other hand, the Acadians and French Canadians of Ontario and the West, nurtured by their vision of a bilingual Canada, fought for equal rights in their respective regions. Each group, English or French, adamantly insisted that its view must prevail.

This story of conflict reveals that English-speaking Catholics (largely of Irish origin) and French-speaking Catholics (mostly French Canadian) have not trusted one another. Both ethno-linguistic groups have competed for control of church and school. While engaged in this ongoing power struggle, each has felt that the surrounding wider society is hostile. English-speaking Canadian Catholics have accepted more readily a number of adjustments and compromises occasioned by their North American secular society. Even apparently trivial concessions, such as the decision not to wear cassocks in the streets or the willingness to allow dancing in parish halls, show that English-speaking priests felt more comfortable in a Protestant-dominated English Canada than did their French-speaking colleagues.[22]

Canada's English-speaking Catholics were not threatened in language or culture, only in religion, by the militantly aggressive Protestantism of the period.

The French-speaking Catholic is threatened not only in his religious faith but also in his language and culture. The threat to his identity is therefore much more profound. Protestants, English Catholics, and French Catholics all have a distinct identity centring on which ethnic group constitutes their heritage. Because ethnicity is an amalgam of religion, language, and culture, French Canadians outside Quebec are threatened on all fronts. Consequently, they are traditionally less accepting of the secularizing customs of English Canada.

For both English and French parties, language has proven more important than religion. In the protracted Ontario squabble, Bishop Fallon and his supporters were the foremost apostles of French repression in Ontario schools. Their policies were interchangeable with those of the Orange francophobes. The partisans of each group have always chosen sides according to linguistic and cultural criteria. Religious considerations were secondary.

The long fratricidal war within the Canadian Catholic community continued for more than a century and the legacy of bitterness it left is sometimes evident today. By the middle and the later decades of the twentieth century, however, the Canadian Catholic church was embarking on a new era in which the rights of francophones outside Quebec received increasing recognition. The appointment of francophone bishops in New Brunswick in 1912 and 1920 was followed by the creation of an Acadian diocese at Moncton in 1936 and another at Yarmouth, Nova Scotia, in 1953. By the same token, the Collège Saint-Joseph joined with other institutions in 1972 to become a key part of the new French university in Moncton, the Université de Moncton. Meanwhile, in Ontario, following the amendment of Regulation 17, Franco-Ontarians gradually obtained greater recognition of their rights in church, school, and society. This culminated in a series of legislative enactments between 1968 and 1988. The policies of men such as Cornell, Gauthier, and McNeil bore fruit, especially after the Second World War. The deep social revolution that occurred in Canada and in the Catholic church in the 1960s included, as a basic premise, greater respect for minority groups. As the governments of Canada and Ontario acknowledged and gradually implemented a policy of bilingualism, the Ontario bishops moved down a parallel path. In a series of public statements they took clear stands in favour of bilingualism in Canada and Ontario. They asked the province of Ontario to become officially bilingual, no doubt causing Bishop Fallon to roll over in his grave. Finally, the western provinces of Manitoba and Saskatchewan began in 1968 to dismantle their francophobe legislation.

In reflecting on these English-French troubles in Canadian Catholicism, it is worth noting that both parties shared a common Rome-centred theology, both invoked the authority of Rome as final arbiter of these differences, and both then ignored the spirit of papal directives. Two papal encyclicals[23] urged Canada's and Ontario's bishops to compromise, but they fell on deaf ears.

Intervention by external ecclesiastical authority could not by itself resolve the conflicts. In the end, the French-English conflict within the Canadian Catholic community could only be resolved when it was addressed by the broader Canadian society in the twentieth century, especially after 1960.

NOTES

1 A substantial body of literature documents this no-popery. One example is Le Roy Edwin Froom, *The Prophetic Faith of Our Fathers: The Historical Development of Prophetic Interpretation*, 4 vols. (Washington: Review and Herald Publishing Association 1950). See also J.R. Miller, "Anti-Catholic Thought in Victorian Canada," *Canadian Historical Review* 66, 4 (1985): 474–94, and "Anti-Catholicism in Canada: From the British Conquest to the Great War," in this volume. For the American phase of the story see Ray Allen Billington, *The Protestant Crusade 1800–1860: A Study of the Origins of American Nativism* (Chicago: Quadrangle Books 1938, 1964).

2 N. Keith Clifford, "His Dominion: A Vision in Crisis," in *Studies in Religion* 2, 4 (1973): 315–26.

3 John Moir, *The Church in the British Era: From the British Conquest to Confederation* (Toronto: McGraw-Hill Ryerson 1972).

4 Terrence Murphy, "The Emergence of Maritime Catholicism, 1781–1830," *Acadiensis* 13, 2 (1984): 29–49; Mason Wade, "Relations between the French, Irish and Scottish Clergy in the Maritime Provinces, 1774–1836," Canadian Catholic Historical Association, *Study Sessions*, 1972: 9–33; Ronnie Gilles Le Blanc, "Antoine Gagnon and the Mitre: A Model of Relations between *Canadien*, Scottish, and Irish Clergy in the Early Maritime Church," in Terrence Murphy and Cyril J. Byrne, eds., *Religion and Identity: The Experience of Irish and Scottish Catholics in Atlantic Canada* (St John's: Jesperson Press 1987), 98–113.

5 In 1847 the American William W. Longfellow published his poem *Evangeline*, a literary piece that made the Acadian epic known throughout the world.

6 The Acadian renaissance is usually dated from the early 1880s. George
F.G. Stanley, "The Flowering of the Acadian Renaissance," in David Jay
Bercuson and Phillip A. Buckner, *Eastern and Western Perspectives*
(Toronto: University of Toronto Press 1981), 19–46.

7 Anselme Chiasson, "Le clergé et le réveil acadien (1864–1960)," *Revue de
l'Université de Moncton* (fév. 1978): 29–46; Jeffrey Brian Hanington, *Every
Popish Person: The Story of Roman Catholicism in Nova Scotia and the Church
of Halifax, 1604–1984* (Halifax: Archdiocese of Halifax 1984); Martin S.
Spigelman, "Race et religion: les Acadiens et le hiérarchie catholique
irlandaise du Nouveau-Brunswick," in *Revue d'histoire de l'Amérique française* 29, 1 (1975): 69–85; Léon Thériault, "L'Acadianisation de l'Eglise
catholique en Acadie, 1763–1953," in Jean Daigle, *Les Acadiens des Maritimes: études thématique* (Moncton: Centre d'études acadiennes 1980),
293–369; Thériault, "Les origines de l'archevêché de Moncton: 1835–
1936," *La Société historique acadienne, Les Cahiers* (oct.–déc. 1986): 111–32;
Fay K. Trombley, "Thomas Louis Connolly (1815–1876)" (PhD dissertation, Université de Louvain 1983).

8 For a detailed discussion of the ecclesiastical negotiations associated
with the development of Catholic church structures in early nineteenth-
century Canada see Lucien Lemieux, *L'établissement de la première province ecclésiastique au Canada, 1783–1844* (Montréal: Fides 1968).

9 Robert Choquette, *L'Église catholique dans l'Ontario français du dix-neuvième siècle* (Ottawa: Editions de l'Université d'Ottawa 1984).

10 Robert Choquette, *Language and Religion: A History of English-French Conflict in Ontario* (Ottawa: University of Ottawa Press 1975); Choquette, *La
foi gardienne de la langue en Ontario: 1900–1950* (Montréal: Bellarmin
1987).

11 On the historiography of Red River before 1870 see Frits Pannekoek,
"The Historiography of the Red River Settlement, 1830–1868," *Prairie
Forum* 6, 1 (1981): 75–85.

12 A summary treatment of this missionary expansion is in Lionel Groulx,
Le Canada français missionnaire (Montréal: Fides 1962). A much more
detailed presentation of western Catholic history is A.-G. Morice, *Histoire de l'Eglise catholique dans l'ouest canadien (1859–1915)*, 4 vols. (Saint-
Boniface and Montréal: Author and Granger Frères 1921).

13 An original and scholarly treatment of the Anglican church in Red
River is in Frits Pannekoek, "The Churches and the Social Structure of
the Pre-1870 Canadian West" (PhD dissertation, Queen's University
1973). An abridged version of the same argument is in Pannekoek,
"The Anglican Church and the Disintegration of Red River Society,
1818–1870," in Douglas R. Francis and Howard Palmer, eds., *The Prairie
West: Historical Readings* (Edmonton: Pica Pica Press 1985), 100–15.

14 A.I. Silver, "French Canada and the Prairie Frontier, 1770–1890," in Francis and Palmer, eds., *The Prairie West*, 140–62; Robert Painchaud, "The Catholic Church and the Movement of Francophones to the Canadian Prairies 1870–1915" (PhD dissertation, University of Ottawa 1976); Painchaud, *Un rêve français dans le peuplement de la Prairie* (Saint-Boniface: Editions des Plaines 1986).

15 Cornelius J. Jaenen, "The Manitoba School Question: An Ethnic Interpretation," in Martin L. Kovacs, ed., *Ethnic Canadians: Culture and Education* (Regina: Canadian Plains Research Center 1978), 317–32.

16 Archbishops A. Taché and A. Langevin opposed the Manitoba legislation and the Laurier-Greenway agreement of 1896. In fact they were primarily defending the English-speaking Catholics of their diocese. The literature on the Manitoba school question is extensive. For a recent assessment of the question see Gilbert L. Comeault, "La question des écoles du Manitoba – Un nouvel éclairage," *Revue d'histoire de l'Amérique française* 33, 1 (1979): 3–24.

17 Robert Choquette, "Adélard Langevin et l'érection de l'archidiocèse de Winnipeg," *Revue d'histoire de l'Amérique française* 28, 2 (1974): 187–207.

18 Robert Choquette, "John Thomas McNally et l'érection du diocèse de Calgary," *Revue de l'Université d'Ottawa* 45, 4 (1985): 401–16.

19 Robert Choquette, "Olivier-Elzéar Mathieu et l'érection du diocèse de Régina, Saskatchewan," *Revue de l'Université d'Ottawa* 45, 1 (1975): 101–16; Raymond Huel, "The Irish French Conflict in Catholic Episcopal Nominations: The Western Sees and the Struggle for Domination within the Church," Canadian Catholic Historical Association, *Study Sessions*, 1975: 51–70.

20 On the broad question of nativism in western Canada see Howard Palmer, *Patterns of Prejudice: A History of Nativism in Alberta* (Toronto: McClelland and Stewart 1982); Palmer, "Strangers and Stereotypes: The Rise of Nativism, 1880–1920," in Francis and Palmer, eds., *The Prairie West*, 309–33.

21 Wilfrid Denis, "Les lois et la langue: l'oppression des Fransaskois de 1875 à 1983," in P.-Y. Mocquais et al., *La langue, la culture et la société des francophones de l'Ouest* (Regina: University of Regina 1983), 75–110; Manoly R. Lupul, *The Roman Catholic Church and the North-West School Question: 1875–1905* (Toronto: University of Toronto Press 1974); Raymond Huel, "Gestae Dei Per Francos: The French Canadian Experience in Western Canada," in Benjamin G. Smillie, ed., *Visions of the New Jerusalem* (Edmonton: NeWest Press 1983), 39–53; Huel, "J.J. Maloney: How the West was Saved from Rome, Quebec and the Liberals," in John Foster, ed., *The Developing West* (Edmonton: University of Alberta Press 1983); Huel, "L'Association catholique Franco-Canadienne de la

Saskatchewan: A Response to Cultural Assimilation, 1912–1934" (M.A. thesis, University of Saskatchewan 1969); Huel, *"La Survivance* in Saskatchewan: Schools, Politics and the Nativist Crusade for Cultural Conformity" (PhD dissertation, University of Alberta 1975); Huel, "Mgr Olivier-Elzéar Mathieu: Guardian of French Catholic Interests in Saskatchewan," *Revue de l'Université d'Ottawa* 42, 3 (1972): 384–407; Huel, "The French Canadians and the Language Question, 1918," *Saskatchewan History* 23, 1 (1970): 1–15; Huel, "The Teaching of French in Saskatchewan Public Schools," *Saskatchewan History* 24, 1 (1971); Huel, "The Public School as a Guardian of Anglo-Saxon Traditions: The Saskatchewan Experience, 1913–1918," in Kovacs, ed., *Ethnic Canadians*, 295–304.

22 Robert Choquette, "Problèmes de moeurs et de discipline ecclésiastique: les catholiques des Prairies canadiennes de 1900 à 1930," *Histoire sociale / Social History* 8, 15 (1975): 102–19.

23 *Commisso Divinitus* (1916) and *Litteris Apostolicis* (1918).

2 Anti-Catholicism in Canada: From the British Conquest to the Great War

J. R. MILLER

Anti-Catholicism has gone through several phases and has appeared in three distinct forms since the arrival of Europeans in Canada. During the earliest decades of the European's presence, anti-Catholicism was an external threat. With the imposition of British rule it assumed the form of an official posture. After the phase of official anti-Catholicism, a theologically based version took root and dominated. In the late nineteenth century the emphasis on theological disputation gave way to a nationalistic preoccupation with the social and political implications of Catholicism for a country such as Canada. Throughout these various phases, opposition to Roman Catholicism has been both an ideology informing individuals and a movement of people organized to resist Rome. In other words, anti-Catholicism in Canada has been an analytical tool and an instrument for combatting what the analysis revealed to be the problem. Whatever its precise preoccupation and form, anti-Catholicism has played a lively, if often disruptive, role in the history of Canada.

Thanks to the timing of French colonization efforts and to royal policy, however, anti-Catholicism did not exist within Canada for the first century and a half of European settlement. France's seventeenth-century efforts to establish permanent settlements in North America followed wars of religion that had pitted Huguenots against Catholics, and these attempts coincided with the period of intense religious feeling known as the Catholic or Counter Reformation. Not surprisingly, then, the French crown early decreed that New France should be closed to the people who followed the reformed Christian religion.

If the official policy did not absolutely prevent the entry of Huguenots, it did discourage their open involvement in public affairs and prevent their challenging Catholicism.

Since many New Englanders were nonconformist Protestants with a healthy dislike of popery, it was natural for them to couch their unease about French commercial and military presence in the language of religious militancy. While such rhetoric was more an exercise in self-justification than a reason for American hostility to New France, it did serve to reinforce the identification of Catholicism and French, both to the Canadiens and to some of their allies. As a result, anti-Catholicism was perceived by many of the peoples who later formed the Canadian populace as an external threat to their identity, security, and well-being.

The fall of New France brought a new, official form of anti-Catholicism. The United Kingdom had been legally and aggressively Protestant since the Henrician revolution of the sixteenth century. The crown was officially Protestant, the succession could go only to a Protestant, and there were statutory prohibitions on Catholicism and restrictions on its followers. The presence of Catholic priests and the observance of their rituals in Britain had been illegal since Elizabeth's day. Catholics could not harbour priests or attend mass, nor had they the right to hold or acquire land except from the crown. Political rights were rendered nugatory by laws that required electors and elected representatives to swear oaths denying the temporal authority of the pope and foreswearing allegiance to the Stuart line, as well as an "Act for preventing Dangers which may happen from Popish Recusants" that required them to make a declaration against transubstantiation.[1]

This well-entrenched English tradition of official anti-Catholicism was beginning to weaken by the 1760s. The union of Scotland, containing many Highland Catholics as well as Lowland Presbyterians, added a significant Romish element to the population. The 1800 Act of Union joining Ireland to this United Kingdom would add a further complication. But Britain was still, officially, a Protestant state. In North America it had already had the unhappy experience of trying to incorporate a Catholic population in Nova Scotia after 1713. With the acquisition of Quebec, it would have to grapple with the same problem of integrating a Catholic population into the laws of a Protestant state. And the colony of Newfoundland, whose heavily Irish population was moving towards Catholic numerical dominance in the later eighteenth century, was a further challenge.

Although the battle against the anti-Catholicism of the penal laws would take more than six decades, the result was never in doubt.

The sheer force of Catholic numbers, the influence of British North America's geographical remoteness from Whitehall, and the proximity of a strategic threat to the south all meant that British planners sooner or later would have to accommodate the empire to the Catholics of North America, rather than seeking to force them to adjust their beliefs to the empire.

The colony of Quebec quickly established a pattern that would be replicated elsewhere. The Treaty of Paris (1763) had promised that the "new Roman Catholick subjects may profess the worship of their religion according to the rites of the Romish church, as far as the laws of Great Britain permit," even if this leniency was not extended to the male religious orders, the Jesuits and Sulpicians.[2] Although the Jesuits were gradually choked off and extinguished by 1800, secular clergy and religious orders of women were left to their own devices. The issue of consecration of a new bishop was a ticklish one, but in the mid 1760s Britain acquiesced to pressure for this appointment, too.[3] Imperial authorities in both Quebec and London conveniently ignored Vicar-General Jean-Olivier Briand's trip to France, where he was consecrated bishop of Quebec in 1766, subsequently glossing over his episcopal status by referring to him as "superintendent of the Romish Clergy." The main reason for Britain's tacit approval of Briand's elevation was London's growing recognition of the impossibility of governing the "new subjects" against their will and an imperial desire to win Catholic support for Britain at a time of growing restiveness in the Thirteen Colonies.

Catholic political rights also emerged as a matter to test the official anti-Catholicism of Britain. The Royal Proclamation of 1763 held out the promise of a representative assembly, but in the face of the penal laws it would have been impossible for the great majority of Canadiens to vote for an assemblyman or hold a seat in the chamber. That, in part, is why the governor refused the importunate demands of the Anglo-Canadian merchants for the immediate grant of an assembly. During the incessant petitioning and reporting on the question in the 1760s at least one important point was established: in 1765 the law officers of the crown ruled that the penal laws did not have force in the Province of Quebec.[4] That concession was followed in 1774 by the Quebec Act, which not only reconfirmed that "His Majesty's Subjects, professing the Religion of the Church of *Rome* of and in the said Province of *Quebec*, may have, hold, and enjoy, the free Exercise of the Religion of the Church of *Rome*, subject to the King's Supremacy," but provided a statutory basis for the collection of tithes by their priests.[5] The latitudinarianism of the Quebec Act was not the expression of a sudden British tolerance;

rather, it was a response to the worsening conditions in the Thirteen Colonies. (Proof that Britain continued to hope for the extirpation of popery could be found in secret instructions of 1775 to the governor of Quebec that encouraged him to interfere with and work against the Catholic bishop.)[6] Nonetheless, Catholics were appointed to the Council in 1775. Finally, in 1791 the Canada or Constitutional Act confirmed these political gains by granting Lower Canada a representative Legislative Assembly for which Canadiens could vote and in which they could sit.

Since it was also the Constitutional Act that established Upper Canada as a separate colony with its own assembly, Roman Catholics in this predominantly English-speaking region enjoyed full political rights from the outset. The number of Catholic inhabitants was initially very small, consisting mostly of Scots in Glengarry and French-speaking Catholics in the vicinity of Fort Sandwich. As the Catholic population increased as a result of Irish immigration, however, it was spared the necessity of struggling to overcome legal restrictions on its civil and religious freedom. Anti-Catholic sentiment existed as elsewhere, but official anti-Catholicism was something against which the Catholics of Upper Canada never had to contend.

In the other English-speaking colonies, the situation was different. Nova Scotia, an advanced colony with relatively mature institutions even in the eighteenth century, followed the pattern established in Quebec. Official anti-Catholicism there, too, ran head-on into hard colonial realities. In the 1760s, for example, even though "popish priests" were supposedly outlawed by Nova Scotian law, a Father Pierre Maillard was permitted to say mass and received a government salary of £100 for missionary work to the Micmac and Acadians. The council of Nova Scotia ruled in 1757 that "popish recusants" would not be allowed to vote in assembly elections, but by 1789 the assembly itself had passed a Catholic enfranchisement bill.[7] A 1783 Nova Scotian act removed the prohibition against priests and extended the right to hold land to Catholics. The first elected Catholic, a Cape Bretoner who became a Nova Scotian after the annexation of the island in 1820, was allowed in 1823 to take only the oath of loyalty, London having agreed that he need not make the offensive declaration against transubstantiation.[8] A bill passed by the local assembly in 1827 sought to repeal all limitations on Catholic political rights by dispensing with state oaths. This bill was reserved by Britain, which doubted its constitutionality, but the passage in 1829 of Britain's own Catholic emancipation legislation settled the issue finally in Nova Scotia and all other British North American colonies.[9]

The other Atlantic colonies followed the same pattern as Nova Scotia. New Brunswick, previously included in Nova Scotia, began life as a separate colony in 1784 with toleration of Catholics' right to buy, inherit, and hold land. By executive decision, New Brunswick Catholics were allowed to vote in the first assembly election the next year. The assembly, however, subsequently unseated a candidate who won the riding of Westmorland by means of the Acadian vote on the grounds that the laws of England barred the Catholics who had provided the margin of victory from exercising the franchise. In the 1790s the assembly passed legislation that imposed the oaths of abjuration and supremacy, though not the declaration against transubstantiation, on all electors and members of their house. It was only in 1810 that new legislation was passed that made the Catholic right to vote meaningful by substituting a simple oath of allegiance for the obnoxious state oaths. Even then, the Catholics in New Brunswick were still effectively excluded from holding office by the requirement that assemblymen swear some of the objectionable oaths before taking their seats. They would not receive full political rights until the question was settled elsewhere.[10] Following the passage of the Catholic Emancipation Act in Britain, the secretary of state ordered New Brunswick, as he did other British North American colonies, to implement its provisions. This the assembly did by passing an enabling act making the imperial statute applicable to New Brunswick.[11]

In Prince Edward Island, which was conceived as a plantation for "foreign Protestants," Catholics faced their most difficult struggle against official anti-Catholicism. Limitations similar to the Nova Scotian council's were applied to Prince Edward Island in 1773, and the gains of Catholics in Nova Scotia and Quebec failed to persuade the authorities to remove the restrictions. The growth of the Catholic population from the 1780s onward only hardened resistance to conceding Catholic rights, for the Catholics tended to support the anti-landlord faction in the assembly.[12] It was not until 1830 that a statute extended to Catholics the right to vote and hold public office, and that occurred only after the franchise qualification was raised to prevent the poorest landholders from voting.[13]

In many ways Newfoundland was the most interesting example of the colonists' struggle against official anti-Catholicism. In Newfoundland as in Quebec, the dominating realities were demographic and strategic. By the late eighteenth century Catholics were approaching half the total population, a proportion far too large to ignore indefinitely.[14] Moreover, from the 1780s onward Britain had to consider the potential for disaffection among Newfoundlanders, as earlier they had worried over potential restiveness of the "new subjects" of Quebec on the eve of the American Revolution. In the case of Newfoundland the factors were the war with France and Irish disaffection. The possibility of the heavily Irish-origin populace turning against Britain's military interests lay behind London's decision to extend political rights to Newfoundland Catholics.[15] What distinguished Newfoundland, however, was the fact that it had no representative assembly, and the absence allowed a governor in 1779 not to act on a change in his instructions that had been instituted by imperial authorities. Before that time governors had been instructed to extend "a liberty of conscience to all persons, except Papists."[16] The 1779 alteration in effect dropped the words "except Papists." Since the governor ignored the alteration, it was not till 1784, amid the changed conditions that the peace had ushered in for relations with the Americans and French, that a new governor proclaimed the existence of political rights for "papists."

That the initiative of 1784 did not solve Newfoundland Catholics' problems, religious and otherwise, was illustrated by some of the events between the proclamation of religious liberty and the granting of a representative assembly. The first bishop, the Franciscan James Louis O'Donel, was falsely accused of pro-French sympathies and attacked physically by Prince William Henry, the future William IV.[17] Later a succession of governors granted greater revenues to the Anglican clergy in an effort to help them resist the Catholics.[18] A sign of worsening relations with officialdom was the termination of a small stipend that the Catholic bishop had received. Similarly, growing tension over denial to Catholics of access to funds for schooling began to trouble relations in the 1820s. And disputation over the right to solemnize marriage also pitted the Catholics, often allied on this issue with dissenters, against the Anglicans' pretensions. Finally, contention over political rights resumed in the later 1820s, at first over membership on the appointed Executive Council that was instituted in 1825, and later over appointments to public office.[19] The Catholics' admission to Newfoundland's House of Assembly in 1832 ended the long phase of official anti-Catholicism that had begun in the 1760s.

The struggle against official anti-Catholicism had enduring consequences. In the first place, the fact that the early efforts to secure civil and political rights for Catholics occurred within the framework of an authoritarian government enhanced the role of the clergy. Though British North America did not develop anything analogous to Ireland's "castle bishops," the North American colonies did produce generations of prelates who saw their role as representing the faithful politically to alien authorities. The habits of mind that this formative process encouraged would be hard to break, even after representative and responsible government led to the emergence of strong lay politicians. Second, the lasting preoccupation of both the legal and political worlds with the rights of Catholics meant that the definition of civil liberties in Canada at first revolved mainly around religious identity. Unlike the United States, where the campaign of black Americans ensured that civil rights were discussed largely in racial terms, in Canada civil rights issues long remained oriented to sectarian matters.[20]

A third consequence of the manner in which Catholics won political rights under British rule was that the notion of "the Protestant constitution"[21] did not take root in Canada to the extent it had in the United Kingdom. Since Catholics had won full political rights before the idea that Catholicism was a danger to the state became entrenched, it would be much more difficult to argue in Canada than it was in Britain that Catholicism was of itself a menace to the state. Finally, the political triumph of Catholics ensured that, when the mid nineteenth-century battles over church-state relations broke out, the forces that opposed a rigidly voluntarist separation of church and state would be numerically (and hence politically) dominant. The Catholics' winning of political rights, in other words, helped to ensure that British North America would not develop the rigid constitutional separation of church and state that was found in the American republic. The relatively quick victory over official anti-Catholicism helped to ensure that Canada's political culture, insofar as it involved the role and rights of organized religion, would differ markedly from both the United States and the United Kingdom.

The official or legal phase of anti-Catholicism gave way in the nineteenth century to a preoccupation on the part of critics of Romanism with theology. Of course, differences in theology had never been absent from the strictures that anti-Catholics levelled. In the nineteenth century, however, the extent and volume of the doctrinal assault increased greatly. To a degree not previously noted, pamphleteers, journalists, and clerics now based their critique on their own reading of Scripture.[22]

The core of the theological critique was Protestants' insistence that their beliefs, being based exclusively on the Bible, were more faithful to Christ's teachings. Catholics were accused of taking their teachings not from Scripture, but from Scripture as interpreted by the humans whom the Catholic church invested with authority. The "Bible and the Bible only is the religion of Protestants," while "Catholic tradition is now found scattered through all the writings of the Fathers and the acts and sayings of the Saints and a vast amount of religious literature, to say nothing of what has floated down in oral channels from generation to generation."[23] It was too easy for misinterpretation to creep in as a result of the foibles and failings of ordinary mortals who interpreted the golden words of Scripture. The result of Catholics' reliance on human interpretation was a series of erroneous teachings.

A favourite target of anti-Catholics concerned about the doctrinal deficiencies of Catholicism was the doctrine of transubstantiation. They pointed out that the apostles' words and behaviour did not lend credibility to the notion that the elements used in the eucharist became the real body and blood of the Saviour.[24] Moreover, transubstantiation meant the repeated sacrifice of Christ, even though Protestants held that the Passion was the single and sufficient "sin-offering of the Christian dispensation."[25] In addition to diminishing the significance of Christ's sacrifice, communion that involved transubstantiation led Rome's priests to believe they could fashion god with their own hands. Such a notion, together with the adoration of consecrated hosts, Protestants held to be gross idolatry.[26]

Idolatry was a favourite theme of anti-Catholic writers. Venerating the saints and adoring the Virgin, not to mention the lavish use of imagery in Catholic ritual, encouraged the transference of worship from the deity to human and even material things. At its worst this tendency reduced Catholicism to a "species of paganism disguised in a Christian mask."[27] In the case of the Holy Virgin, Protestants charged that Catholicism had elevated Mary and Joseph into the Trinity along with Jesus. And they objected to the lavish use of statues of the Virgin, and to petitioners' praying to them for intercession. Such practices were nothing less than "abject Mariolatry," a major deviation from scriptural Christianity.[28]

When critics' censorious gaze shifted to Rome itself, it quickly fastened upon the successor to Peter. The alleged defects, both moral and political, of many of the medieval and Renaissance popes constituted a major preoccupation for these enemies of the bishop of Rome. Whether decrying the slaughter of opponents of Catholics, such as Huguenots or Waldensians, or wringing their hands at the peccadilloes of popes who were accused of keeping mistresses in their palaces, these critics charged that Romanism was greatly diminished because of its overemphasis on the papacy, an office that had often been filled with "such monsters as Popes John xxiii [antipope, 1410–15] and Alexander vi."[29] And when the Vatican Council proclaimed the pope infallible when speaking *ex cathedra* on questions of faith and morals, Protestant ire knew no bounds. The very idea of a group of human, and therefore fallible, bishops deciding which of them was infallible was as laughable as it was blasphemous, they claimed.[30] The notion of papal infallibility was the most dangerous of all Rome's many idolatries: infallibility allowed an ordinary "man, as erring as we are, to take the place of God, on earth."[31]

Not only was papal infallibility impious, but the power of the bishop of Rome, as well as certain practices of the church, held the potential for social and political evil. As the French Protestants slaughtered on Saint Bartholomew's Day proved, unrestrained power led to oppression. Celibacy and reliance on such things as penance, purgatory, priestly absolution, and indulgences were almost as dangerous. Prohibition on clerical marriage led to "inevitable consequences, immorality and debauchery."[32] Penance discouraged sinners from confronting their sinfulness and wrestling with it, and indulgences similarly made it all too easy to substitute an outward act for the inner change that was required, according to Scripture, for true forgiveness. The ability of the priest to pronounce absolution simply tempted both penitent and cleric to exaggerate the priest's importance.

Auricular confession, when combined with priestly absolution, was a particular evil. Like absolution, the use of confession encouraged the credulous to transfer their quest for forgiveness from God to the priest. And in the case of female penitents there was a further danger that they would transfer their affections, perhaps physical as well as mental, to the man who heard their most intimate admissions and claimed the power to forgive their transgresssions. The "sanctity of home and family life is made subservient to the tyranny of the confessional," the priest displaced the husband, and the moral health of the family was undermined.[33] The confessional was a "spider's web" in which "your fair wife, your precious daughter" was caught and destroyed, leaving "nothing but a moral skeleton ... after the Pope's black spider has been allowed to suck the very blood of her heart and soul."[34]

As bad as the moral corruption was another danger that flowed from auricular confession. The confessional was the source of Rome's political power as well. It was "what West Point is to the United States, and Woolwich is to Great Britain," a place to train and discipline the pope's soldiers.[35] Bishop Ignace Bourget of Montreal, anti-Catholics charged, used the confessional in his battle against the free thinkers of the Institut canadien. He and his priests "brought to bear the terrors of the confessional to induce them to use the influence of their tears and their fears to compel husbands and brothers to quit their connection with the Institute." By means of the confessional "a terrorism at Montreal which might vie with the Spanish Inquisition" was created.³⁶ Priests transmitted their superiors' commands "by reading and explaining circulars and pastorals at the altar, and by enforcing the instructions they contain through the confessional."³⁷

The confessional was a threat because it was the means by which the church pursued its true, unscriptural objective – earthly power: "Rome claims *power*, power to bless and to anathematize; claims power to define what shall be believed and what shall be rejected; is exclusive against all opinions but her own, and by her decrees, if not by the spirit of her better and more liberal clergy, demands an unhesitating and unswerving subjection of mind and heart and conscience on the part of her followers. But her claims do not end there. She has now proclaimed, by the mouth of her chief officer, that his dictum is infallible; in other words, that his utterances, *be what they may*, are to be received as the utterances of inspired power."³⁸ The reliance on a false basis of authority, church tradition, and the ensuing perversions of doctrine and aggrandizement of human leaders brought Rome inexorably to dictatorship that threatened the political and constitutional foundations of nineteenth-century British America. If that was not bad enough, from that political menace social and economic consequences flowed as well.

Romanism was destructive to the building blocks of a sound society: sturdy individuals and wholesome families. In the hands of a church whose true purpose was the augmentation of its own power, the educational system aimed not at the empowerment and liberation of individuals, but at their enslavement and obedience to the wishes of the church. Catholic leaders desired separate schools to isolate and break down their followers, not, as they claimed, to protect their faith. "The teacher is the great enemy of the priest" because Rome could "only preserve to itself retainers by drilling them out of the reach of the solvent of nineteenth century thought."³⁹ In those schools they "mold every infant mind for five days in the week into a condition of servile dependence on the voice of the priest and worshipful adoration for the person of the bishop."⁴⁰ The Jesuits in particular worked to "clap the padlock on the mind of the young of the government class."⁴¹ Catholic schools aimed to strip a youth "of the brain that nature has given him, and to give him one clipped and pared to the pleasure of the Pope."⁴² The result was the Roman Catholic, a "man who has abdicated the right to think and act for himself in things political and spiritual and whose liberty is in the keeping of an ancient and powerful Italian organization."⁴³

And Romanism destroyed the family by brutalizing and corrupting its heart, the wife and mother. The misogyny of Catholicism was testified to by travellers to Roman countries who complained of seeing "women toiling, like beasts in the field."[44] The institution of priestly celibacy also threatened the woman by denigrating marriage and by depriving priests of the "remedy which God has given to man against his own concupiscence – holy marriage."[45] That was why confession was such a pit for the unwary woman and such a menace to the family. The very safety of the home was placed in jeopardy by Catholicism's deficiencies.

If Rome sacrificed individualism and healthy homes to its pursuit of power, little wonder that Catholic societies were inferior to Protestant societies. Romish exactions, financial and emotional, drained a society of both its wealth and its vitality. The need to support a numerous clergy by tithes and other contributions and the multiplication of holy days on which the faithful were expected to refrain from work also helped to ensure that poverty was the lot of both individual Catholics and Catholic countries. The captains of industry were not Catholics. "Not that they are wasteful, indolent and incapable, but that their energies are paralyzed and their resources gradually absorbed by the Church."[46] The same was true of countries. "Look at Austria, Spain, Portugal, and Italy."[47] "Go to Ireland, and contrast the state of Protestant Ulster as compared with Popish Connaught ... But to come nearer home. Contrast Protestant Ontario and Popish Quebec, and exactly the same state of things is observable."[48] The "intelligence of the one [Quebec] is stagnant and nil, while that of Ontario is aggressive."[49]

The nineteenth-century critique that originated in theological differences evolved ineluctably into a social, economic, and political attack on the place and role of Catholicism in Canada. From the Protestants' favourite foundation, reliance on the bare words of Scripture, the critics traced an elaborate attack on Rome's supposed authority, morality, and social role. The assault culminated in a portrait of the Catholic church and its clergy as pernicious in an individualistic British society such as Canada. Taken to its logical conclusion, it was an indictment that led to the conviction that Catholicism could not be allowed any influence if the morality, liberty, and material well-being of society were to be maintained and promoted.

The nineteenth-century analysis of the evils of Romanism, though widely disseminated in British North America, had its origins chiefly in Britain and the United States. Moreover, so long as Canadian anti-Catholicism was in its predominantly theological phase, it retained this derivative character. The hundreds of books and pamphlets that constituted the anti-Catholic canon had their intellectual, and often their physical origins in British and American teachings. In general,

the intellectual roots – whether of Anglican evangelicals or Presbyterians or Methodists – were from the United Kingdom, but the
people who spread the anti-Catholic message came from both the
United States and Britain.[50] The Loyal Orange Association, obviously,
was an importation from the United Kingdom, and the Protestant
Protective Association that took up its work in Ontario in the 1890s
came from the United States. Canada was a favourite haunt of the
professional anti-Catholic agitator, both British and American, who
flourished in the later Victorian age too. British North America did,
however, repay the debt. Montreal's Hôtel Dieu convent was the
supposed location of the goings-on that were celebrated in the most
infamous of American anti-Catholic tracts, the fictitious *Awful Disclo-
sures of Maria Monk*.[51] And Canada produced one of the continent's
most energetic rabble-rousers, Charles Chiniquy, sometime Catholic
priest, later Presbyterian minister. When it came to anti-Catholic ideas
and the people who propagated them, however, Canada was a net
importer for most of the nineteenth century.

In a parallel fashion, many of the incidents that gave rise to anti-
Catholic agitation were imports, especially before the confederation
of the British North American colonies in 1867. The supposed reve-
lations of Maria Monk to shocked Americans in the 1830s were
followed closely, as were also the anti-Catholic excesses of the Know
Nothing movement in the 1850s and the struggles over Catholic
schooling in New England later in the century. The imitation of
British anti-Catholic causes was even more faithful than emulation of
the American. England's Tractarian controversy and the Anglican
debate over ritualism were faithfully echoed in British North
America. So, too, was the Presbyterian Disruption of the 1840s,
whose importation showed clearly that colonials were dependent for
religious ideas of all kinds on the metropolis. Perhaps most typical
of colonial imitativeness was the 1850 outcry over Papal Aggression,
an incident that had no local relevance whatever. Since English Protestants became upset over Rome's establishment of a complete episcopal organization with English territorial titles, British Americans
followed suit. Copying the uproar in Britain was all the more curious
because British North American Catholicism had enjoyed a full ecclesiastical organization for decades without causing any upset.

Perhaps part of the explanation of the continuing colonialism of
Canadian anti-Catholicism could be found in the entry of the "famine
Irish" in the 1840s. The fact that many of these unfortunate immigrants, especially in the first year of the exodus, were impoverished
and disease-ridden aroused a fear of the newcomers.[52] That trepi-
dation, in combination with traditional suspicions of Catholicism,

hardened into a prejudice against Irish Catholics that, in turn, reinforced the old wariness of Rome and its works. The kinds of charges that were levelled against Irish Catholic immigrants would later find echoes in denunciations of Eastern European immigrants during the western boom or in slurs on native peoples after the Second World War. In all cases, the critics were responding to poverty and its consequences in terms that mistakenly emphasized religion, ethnicity, and race.

Mid nineteenth-century Irish immigrants were held to be a social menace because of their habits, both individual and collective. Their poor physical appearance attracted negative comments, while their poverty provoked more criticism than sympathy. The accompanying social symptoms of violence, alcohol abuse, and family troubles were also loudly deplored. Desperate Irish labourers on the St Lawrence canals who resorted to force to protect their precarious hold on employment were explained in terms of ethnic and religious failings. Urban squalor in such burgeoning centres as Halifax, Saint John, Montreal, and Toronto merely reinforced the stereotype of the Catholic Irishman as someone whose individual failings eventually became a collective burden. As a Toronto politician noted: "They increase taxation for the poor. They render necessary a strong police. They are the keepers of our low tippling houses. They are our chief rioters. They build our Papal churches, and were it not for them our poorhouses, jails, penitentiaries, and Magdalen Asylums would be far less necessary, and frequently empty."[53] What were in fact problems caused by poverty and disease were quickly and mistakenly diagnosed as the consequences of moral failings that could be attributed ultimately to a deficient religious foundation.[54]

These understandable if regrettable anti-Irish feelings profoundly affected British North American public life in the middle of the nineteenth century. Their results were particularly noticeable in the future Ontario. There between 1791 and the 1840s a number of accommodations had been worked out between Catholics and non-Catholics, most notably in the area of education.[55] In the 1850s, however, because of anti-Irish prejudice and rising fear of Ultramontanism within the Catholic church, a full-scale political battle over public support of denominational schooling developed. For some politicians, particularly the voluntarist Protestant George Brown, the appeal of popular anti-Catholicism frequently proved irresistible. In his newspaper, the *Globe*, Brown intermittently pandered to this prejudice for the purpose of consolidating his grip on the Reform party and augmenting its support among the general electorate. In the 1860s the prominence of Irish Catholics in the ranks of the anti-

Confederates helped to keep anti-Irish prejudice alive. By the 1880s, however, the fixation on the alien Irish was weakening. Prejudice against the Irish was being replaced by a disquiet about indigenous Catholics, such as French-speaking Quebecers and the Métis of the Prairie West, who were increasingly seen as obstacles to emerging Canadian nationhood. Moreover, as anti-Catholicism shifted to nationalistic concerns, it became less imitative. Henceforth it was less an echo of theological and social controversies in Britain and the United States, and more a reflection of the ethnic and linguistic divisions that were very much a Canadian problem.

Three factors helped to bring about this transformation and domestication of anti-Catholicism after Confederation. First, the threat of the alien Irish faded as the newcomers adapted to Canada's economic, social, and political systems and as the institutions of Canada, not least of all Roman Catholic ecclesiastical structures in the central provinces, did more to accommodate the immigrants. Second, a renewed menace took centre stage as an upsurge of nationalism and Ultramontanism occurred in Quebec. Finally, Canadian Protestants became increasingly concerned over the acquisition and development of the West.[56]

In Quebec, the upsurge of another wave of Ultramontanism in the 1870s, culminating in the abolition of government control of education and its return to denominational hands in 1875, provoked worried Quebec Protestants to form a Defence League and issue warnings against "Vaticanism" in terms that resembled the fulminations of William Gladstone in Britain. In the 1880s the emergence of Honoré Mercier at the head of a self-described nationalist government provoked still stronger reactions. Mercier's career was a reminder, to some critics at least, that the church was simply "a conspiracy which everywhere employs the particularism of small Catholic races against the modern state."[57] It was mainly because anti-Catholics, particularly those in central Canada, were preoccupied with the anti-national features of Catholicism that Mercier became the provocation for an assault on the Jesuits' Estates Act of 1888 and for rumblings of discontent against French-language instruction in the schools of eastern Ontario.[58] The Estates Act compensated from public funds a variety of Catholic interests that claimed an interest in lands that had been owned by the Jesuits before 1760 and had been taken over by the crown in 1800. Although the measure ostensibly had nothing to do with matters of ethnicity and language, it led to the formation of a so-called Equal Rights Association that soon attacked vestiges of French in Ontario schools. The affair was a striking example of the way in which sectarian animosities were blending into ethnic concerns.

In the West, the Hudson's Bay Company lands had always been a place where Protestants watched warily for the intrusion of Rome. As early as 1718 the HBC's chief officer at York Factory required his men to "swear ... to stand steadfast to the reformed Protestant religion as they [sic] are administered in their kingdoms by law established, and to oppose with all my might all possible pretenders and superstitions ... of the Roman Catholic religion."[59] In 1841 the Reverend John Smithurst reported worriedly from Rupert's Land that "We see the eagle of Rome watching to seize as its prey these precious souls"[60] As these regions were brought into the Canadian confederation, however, and as a mounting stream of settlers poured in from Ontario and from Eastern Europe, Protestant concerns were heightened. To Ontario expansionists, already wary because of Clear Grit influences, the actions of Louis Riel and the Catholic Métis in the Red River Resistance in 1869–70 and the Northwest Rebellion fifteen years later confirmed their suspicions that Rome would oppose the proper – that is, English and Protestant – development of the Northwest. The "apparent complicity of the priests" in the resistance and the alleged connection between the Catholic church and rebellion confirmed the need to prevent the implantation of Romanism on the plains.[61] (Of course, as Goldwin Smith helpfully pointed out, "a celibate priest is well prepared for adventure," even in the form of rebellion!)[62]

The preoccupation with western matters was intensified by Protestant evangelicals' concerns about the Indians in both the Northwest and British Columbia. The Methodist George McDougall worried about the introduction of Catholicism to the southern plains because it was "only less pestiferous and Godless than Paganism itself." Catholic missionaries in the West, he thought, "are anti-British in their national sympathies; and if we may judge the tree by its fruits, anti-Christian in their teachings."[63] After observing a native church service near Lilloet, the Anglican Reverend A.C. Garrett observed the Romish features of the celebration: "Alas! poor creatures they are emphatically walking in darkness. Their native superstitions are bad enough without engrafting upon them a 'Baptised Paganism.'"[64] Church Missionary Society evangelist Samuel Trivett wrote, "I verily believe that the Romish Religion at these places is as bad or worse than the Idoltry [sic] of the Brahmins or superstition of Mohamed."[65] The vulnerability of the indigenous populations to misguided Romanists made Protestant concern about the development of the West all the greater.

This dual concern – about the anti-national tendencies of the Catholic church in the West and the lot of the native populations – helped to focus anti-Catholicism on western issues in the late nineteenth and early twentieth centuries. The fixation took two forms: debates over educational matters and a strong anti-Catholic emphasis to the Protestant missions in the West.

The struggles over the Manitoba and North-West schools questions in the 1890s and over the educational provisions of the bills that created the provinces of Saskatchewan and Alberta in 1905, though ostensibly revolving around constitutional guarantees to religious minorities, in fact turned upon ethnic and nationalistic concerns. The agitators wanted to preserve the West for English-Canadian society by imposing on it a Protestant character. It was more a matter of coercive nationalism than religious bigotry. The point was put most baldly by maverick Conservative MP D'Alton McCarthy, who commented on the Manitoba schools issue: "Let them remain Catholic but not French. That is the object ... to make the people homogeneous."[66] Thus these western controversies stood in sharp contrast to the schools question in the Province of Canada in the 1850s, where the attack had been fuelled by voluntarism and anti-Catholic feeling.

Missions to both the indigenous western population and the immigrant newcomers contained a similar streak of anti-Catholicism. The rapid multiplication of missions and schools throughout the Prairies and British Columbia in the late nineteenth and early twentieth centuries was testimony to anti-Catholicism as well as to Protestants' concern for the souls of the Indians and Métis of those regions. The most effective argument a proponent of a new Protestant missionary project, such as a residential school, could make to the church authorities who controlled the purse strings was that if they did not provide the facility, the Catholics would.[67] The attitudes and motives of those who ministered to European newcomers were parallel to those of the missionaries to native groups. Whether Roman, Greek, or Russian in religious background, these newcomers came with "only a mere caricature of religion" and thereby endangered the Protestant nature of the developing West.[68] In order for them to be "Canadianized," it was imperative for them to "Protestantized."

The emergence of this peculiarly nationalistic brand of anti-Catholicism placed English-speaking Catholics in Canada in an ambiguous position. English-speaking Protestants were no longer their direct antagonists so much as their competitors. Catholics of Irish and Scottish background, especially those in Ontario, also entered the western mission fields, determined to fend off Protestant incursions. At the same time, however, these English-speaking Catholics were becoming more thoroughly integrated into English-Canadian society. As they identified more closely with the predominant culture, they became themselves agents of assimilation among European immigrants. While

they obviously rejected the necessity of "Protestantizing" the newcomers, they readily accepted the necessity of "Anglicizing" them.

Protestants' disappointment at the results of their evangelical
efforts among newcomers and native groups in the West contributed
to a sense of crisis that overtook the non-Catholic churches in the
twentieth century. The census of 1901 that showed that the Protestant
denominations were not growing as quickly as the Catholic communion spurred vigorous efforts for a time,[69] but the "onset of
doubt"[70] about the efficacy of Anglican, Methodist, and Prebyterian
missions was audible in the first decade. The concern about losing
the evangelical race to Catholicism in the West also accounted in at
least some cases for the support of the union of Methodists, Presbyterians, and Congregationalists in 1925. Some of those who advocated the formation of the United Church of Canada did so in order
to equip Protestantism to carry on the battle against Rome.[71]

Such regrouping of the Protestant hosts was but one sign among
many of the waning vitality of those who were opposed to Rome.
That is not to say that the old attitudes about the errancy, social
deviance, and anti-national tendencies of Catholicism passed away
either quickly or completely in the early decades of the twentieth
century. Critics continued to fulminate on traditional grounds. Certainly the dispute over Rome's provocative *Ne Temere* decree issued by
Pope Pius x in an encyclical of Easter 1908 raised in pointed form
what Protestants considered to be Catholicism's presumption to determine social questions unilaterally. Its contention that marriages involving
Catholics had to be performed according to the rite of the Roman
Catholic church was viewed by some as denying the validity of civil
ceremonies. To Protestants this stand was arrogant and unacceptable.
In a fashion reminiscent of the Papal Aggression flurry of 1850, many
Canadian critics protested against the Vatican's posture.[72] And the
Great War raid on the Jesuit novitiate in Guelph, Ontario, by military
authorities in search of Jesuit-inspired shirkers once again drew the
connection that existed in the minds of many Protestants between
religion and national identity, between Catholicism and disloyalty.[73]

In spite of these throwbacks to the traditional nineteenth-century
theological, social, and political campaigns against Catholicism, the
anti-Catholic movement was beginning to wane by the end of the
First World War. In the interwar period, even complaints against such
Quebec Catholic failings as the use of lotteries and failure to observe
the sabbath were fewer in number than in the past, and during the
Great Depression there were instances of cooperation between hard-
pressed Protestant and Catholic groups.[74] Indeed, the overriding problems of depression and world war, along with the anti-Communist

consensus that drew Canadian Protestants and Catholics together against a common, godless foe, helped to damp down even more, from the 1930s to the 1950s, the fires of evangelicals' anti-Catholicism.

Since the middle of the century, moreover, two other forces have continued this process of weakening anti-Catholicism. First, the ecumenical movement, although sometimes more an ideal than a reality, at least discouraged anti-Catholics by removing the veneer of respectability for denunciations of Rome. The second force is secularization.

After 1945, in particular, all forms of religious belief and activity evolved in the midst of the increasing secularization of Canadian society. Although this process affects more than Protestants, it has been reflected among Canadian Protestants in a loss of confidence in the nationalizing mission of their churches, as well as in Protestantism's increased emphasis on sociological rather than theological issues. This emphasis was a response to the challenge of modern thought and to the emergence of an urban and industrial society.[75] The general decline of religion as a formative force in Christians' everyday life has certainly led to a weakening of anti-Catholic fervour.

On its way to becoming an insignificant force, anti-Catholicism went through a number of distinct phases. At first a purely external threat, it became an internal reality in the eighteenth century when British rule replaced French. Thereafter it evolved through successive stages from official to theological and finally to nationalistic forms, becoming in the process more distinctively Canadian in its form and content. During the century after the Treaty of Utrecht (1713), Britain and its new Catholic subjects grappled with accommodating Catholicism and Britain's penal laws. With surprising speed the accommodation was made in favour of the political and civil rights of the Catholic citizenry. As a consequence, British North America did not develop as a series of societies that thought of themselves as strictly Protestant, and the notion of a "Protestant constitution" lacked vitality in British America as well. In the nineteenth century anti-Catholicism shifted its concern from matters of constitutional acceptability to social and political well-being. From a basis in theological differences, anti-Catholics fashioned an analysis of Catholicism as dangerous as well as errant. After Confederation these concerns took more pointed, more exclusive, and more domestic form. Anti-Catholicism became preoccupied with threats to the integrity and growth of the nation, particularly in the West. This nationalistic phase was at its most intense in the generations between 1880 and 1920.

Since the era of the Great War, anti-Catholicism in Canada has experienced a slow decline. A number of considerations account for this mellowing, including the blows of depression and war, the consensus-building tendencies of both the crusade against Communism and the ecumenical movement, and, above all, secularization. In the two centuries between the British Conquest and the Great War, however, anti-Catholicism was a constant and influential force in Canadian life.

NOTES

I should like to thank the Social Sciences and Humanities Research Council of Canada, whose research grant funded most of the research for this article.

1 These "penal laws," as they are generally known, are summarized in J. Garner, "The Enfranchisement of Roman Catholics in the Maritimes," *Canadian Historical Review* (CHR) 34, 3 (1953): 203–4.

2 Treaty of Paris, Article IV, in A. Shortt and A.G. Doughty, eds., *Documents Relating to the Constitutional History of Canada 1759–1791*, 2 vols. (Ottawa: King's Printer 1907), I, 85–6. For the limitations on religious orders see the Capitulation of Montreal (8 Sept. 1760), Article XXVII, ibid., 26.

3 H. Neatby, *Quebec: The Revolutionary Age, 1760–1791* (Toronto: McClelland and Stewart 1966), 109–11

4 R.C. Dalton, *The Jesuits' Estates Question: A Study of the Background for the Agitation of 1889* (Toronto: University of Toronto Press 1968), 12.

5 Shortt and Doughty, eds., *Documents*, I, 403.

6 Neatby, *Quebec*, 138–9.

7 Garner, "Enfranchisement," 205–6.

8 J.S. Moir, *The Church in the British Era: From the British Conquest to Confederation* (Toronto: McGraw-Hill Ryerson 1972), 19, 138; Moir, ed., *Church and State in Canada, 1627–1867: Basic Documents*, Carleton Library (Toronto: McClelland and Stewart 1967), 64–5. See also Garner, "Enfranchisement," 214–16.

9 Moir, *Church in the British Era*, 22, 138; Moir, ed., *Church and State in Canada*, 64–7; Garner, "Enfranchisement," 214–18.

10 Garner, "Enfranchisement," 207–9, 214.

11 Ibid., 212.

12 Ibid., 209–12.

13 Moir, ed., *Church and State in Canada*, 64–5; Garner, "Enfranchisement," 213–14.

14 R.J. Lahey, "Catholicism and Colonial Policy in Newfoundland, 1779–1832," in this volume, n. 1.

15 H. Rollmann, "Religious Enfranchisement and Roman Catholics in Eighteenth-Century Newfoundland," in T. Murphy and C.J. Byrne, eds.,

Religion and Identity: The Experience of Irish and Scottish Catholics in Atlantic Canada (St John's: Jesperson Press 1987), 34–52, esp. 38–9.
16 Governors' instructions, quoted ibid., 36.
17 Rollmann, "Religious Enfranchisement," 39; Lahey, "Catholicism and Colonial Policy," 53; and Raymond J. Lahey, *James Louis O'Donel in New-foundland, 1784–1807: The Establishment of the Roman Catholic Church* (St John's: Newfoundland Historical Society 1984), 13.
18 Lahey, "Catholicism and Colonial Policy," 55–6.
19 Ibid., 63–6.
20 Consider, for example, the heavy emphasis on religious issues in D. Schmeiser, *Civil Liberties in Canada* (Oxford: Oxford University Press 1964), esp. sections III and IV. The Canadian fixation on religion in civil rights matters has not entirely disappeared, even in the late twentieth century when the interests of racial minorities bulk much larger in our thinking. The constitutionality of discriminating in favour of a religious minority – specifically the separate school rights of Roman Catholics in Ontario, the right of separate school boards to discriminate in hiring over "lifestyle issues," and the rights of parents who are members of the Jehovah's Witnesses to interfere with ministrations of medical attendants on their children – are but a few of the more contemporary examples of this continuing preoccupation.
21 E.R. Norman, *Anti-Catholicism in Victorian England* (New York: Barnes & Noble 1968), 15, 19.
22 For a more elaborate description of this phase see J.R. Miller, "Anti-Catholic Thought in Victorian Canada," *CHR* 66, 4 (Dec. 1985): 487–91.
23 W. MacLaren, *The Romish Doctrine of the Rule of Faith Examined* (Ottawa: Henderson & Co. [1872]), 6, 7, 9. See also *The Two Chiniquys: Father Chiniquy vs. Minister Chiniquy* (Montreal: True Witness 1893), 8.
24 J. Jenkins, *A Protestant's Appeal to the Douay Bible and Other Roman Catholic Standards in Support of the Doctrines of the Reformation*, 2nd ed. (Montreal: Wesleyan Book Depot 1853), 330–1.
25 Ibid., 134.
26 D. Hague, *The Protestantism of the Prayer Book*, 3rd ed. (London: Church Association nd [first published 1890]), 187.
27 *Provincial Wesleyan* (Halifax), 31 Jan. 1856; quoted in A.J.B. Johnston, "The 'Protestant Spirit' of Colonial Nova Scotia: An Inquiry into Mid-Nineteenth-Century Anti-Catholicism" (MA thesis, Dalhousie University 1977), 131.
28 W.H. Withrow, *A Canadian in Europe* (Toronto: Rose-Belford 1881), 118. See also Jenkins, *Protestant's Appeal*, 92.
29 MacLaren, *Romish Doctrine*, 12; J.A. Allan, *Orangism, Catholicism, and Sir Francis Hincks* (Toronto: Hart & Rawlinson 1877), 4.

30 *Religious Controversy between Rev. Father Molphy, Roman Catholic Priest, and Rev. Robert Scobie, Presbyterian Minister* (Strathroy, Ont.: Western Dispatch Printing House 1877), 81; *Truth versus Father Damen: A Glance over Eighteen Centuries* (Ottawa: Bell & Woodburn 1872), 5.
31 MacLaren, *Romish Doctrine*, 28–9.
32 Hague, *Protestantism of the Prayer Book*, 4.
33 A. Parent, *The Life of Rev. Amand Parent* (Toronto: William Briggs 1887), 96.
34 C. Chiniquy, *The Priest, the Woman and the Confessional*, 23rd ed. (London: W.T. Gibson nd [first published in French 1875]), 106–7.
35 Ibid., 99.
36 C. Lindsey, *Rome in Canada: The Ultramontane Struggle for Supremacy over the Civil Authority* (Toronto: Lovell Brothers 1877), 116.
37 Ibid., 254.
38 H. Overy, *Rome's Modern Claims* (Saint John: J. & A. McMillan 1874), 7.
39 Toronto *Globe*, 6 March 1863, quoted in M. Cottrell, "Irish Catholic Political Leadership in Toronto, 1855–1882: A Study of Ethnic Politics" (PhD dissertation, University of Saskatchewan 1988), 157; *The Nation*, 1 Oct. 1875, quoted P.F.W. Rutherford, "The New Nationality, 1864–1897: A Study of the National Aims and Ideas of English Canada in the Late Nineteenth Century" (PhD dissertation, University of Toronto 1973), 442.
40 *Montreal Daily Witness*, 7 May 1896.
41 G. Smith, "An Array of Facts," quoted J.J. Roy, *The Jesuit Order, or An Infallible Pope, who 'being dead, speaketh' about the Jesuits* (np: np 1889), 60.
42 Allan, *Orangism, Catholicism, and Sir Francis Hincks*, 5.
43 *Toronto World*, 8 Feb. 1889, quoted L.C. Clark, "A History of the Conservative Administrations, 1891 to 1896" (PhD dissertation, University of Toronto 1968), 11.
44 Withrow, *Canadian in Europe*, 140.
45 Lindsey, *Rome in Canada*, 238; Chiniquy, *The Priest, the Woman*, 37–8.
46 D.H. MacVicar, *Roman Catholicism in Canada* (Montreal: William Drysdale 1889), 9.
47 "Expostulatus" [J. Burland], *Observations: Address in a Series of Letters to the Professors of the Roman Catholic Faith* (Quebec: R. Middleton 1854), 12; M. Richey, *The Spirit of Popery, and the Duty of Protestants in Regard to Public Education* (Halifax: Wesleyan Conference Steam Press 1859), 7, quoted in Johnston, "Protestant Spirit," 54.
48 *Protestant Landmarks: The History of the House of Orange: William and Mary* (Toronto: Maclean and Co. 1876), 23.
49 G. Douglas, *Discourses and Addresses* (Toronto: William Briggs 1894), 303.
50 J.R. Miller, "Bigotry in the North Atlantic Triangle: Irish, British and American Influences on Canadian Anti-Catholicism, 1850–1900," *Studies in Religion/Sciences Religieuses* 16, 3 (1987): 292–3.

51 R.A. Billington, *The Protestant Crusade, 1800–1860: A Study of the Origins of American Nativism*, Quadrangle Paperback (Chicago: Quadrangle Books 1964; first published 1930), 98–102.

52 N. Macdonald, *Canada: Immigration and Colonization 1841–1903* (Toronto: Macmillan 1966), 64–6.

53 George Brown, quoted M.W. Nicolson, "The Irish Vote and the Catholic League: Early Ethnic Politics in Victorian Toronto," unpublished paper, Canadian Historical Association Annual Meeting, University of Guelph 1984, 13.

54 See also W.M. Baker, *Timothy Warren Anglin, 1822–96: Irish Catholic Politician* (Toronto: University of Toronto Press 1977), 18–20; Cottrell, "Irish Catholic Political Leadership," 35–8.

55 J.W. Grant points out, however, that an incident in the 1830s in Upper Canada had caused Irish Catholics to be "regarded in many quarters as socially unacceptable, vaguely subversive, and even threatening to British liberties." *A Profusion of Spires: Religion in Nineteenth-Century Ontario* (Toronto: University of Toronto Press 1988), 82.

56 For more explanation see Miller, "Bigotry," 294–6. The danger of the alien Irish did not completely disappear as concern shifted elsewhere. The prime minister did not want the Canadian Pacific to assist immigration from western Ireland for the Canadian West because these Irish "are bad settlers and thoroughly disloyal. It won't do to have a little Ireland in the North West." Macdonald, quoted in D.N. Sprague, *Canada and the Métis, 1869–1885* (Waterloo, Ont.: Wilfrid Laurier University Press 1988), 151. Macdonald was sensitive to the danger that the Liberal opposition was scare-mongering by attempting "to disseminate the idea that Manitoba is to be a Popish Preserve and this impression will be confirmed unless there is evidence of energetic action in the way of provision for a general immigration." J.A. Macdonald to A.G. Archibald, 1 Nov. 1870, quoted ibid., 93.

57 *Toronto Daily Mail*, 26 June 1889.

58 Miller, "Bigotry," 298–9.

59 Quoted in M. Giraud, *The Métis in the Canadian West*, trans. ed. in 2 vols. (Lincoln and London: University of Nebraska Press 1986), 1:592, n. 18.

60 Quoted in I.M. Spry, "The Métis and Mixed-Bloods of Rupert's Land before 1870," in J. Peterson and J.S.H. Brown, eds., *The New Peoples: Being and Becoming Métis in North America* (Winnipeg: University of Manitoba Press 1985), 114, n. 7.

61 W. McDougall to J.A. Macdonald, 31 Oct. 1869, in D. Owram, *Promise of Eden: The Canadian Expansionist Movement and the Idea of the West 1856–1900* (Toronto: University of Toronto Press 1980), 91.

62 G. Smith, quoted in R. Cook, *The Regenerators: Social Criticism in Late Victorian English Canada* (Toronto: University of Toronto Press 1985), 33.

63 Quoted in J.A. MacGregor, *Father Lacombe* (Edmonton: Hurtig 1975), 210.
64 Archives of the Provincial Synod of British Columbia, RG5, series 5.3, A.C. Garrett, "Sketches of a Missionary Tour to Cariboo," unpublished manuscript, 2 June 1865.
65 S. Trivett to C. Fenn, 24 Oct. 1879, quoted in I.A.L. Getty, "The Failure of the Native Church Policy of the CMS in the North-West," in R. Allen, ed., *Religion and Society in the Prairie West* (Regina: Canadian Plains Research Center 1974), 26.
66 Quoted in Miller, "Bigotry," 298.
67 For example, United Church of Canada Archives, Papers of the Presbyterian Church in Canada, Board of Foreign Missions, Missions to the Indians of Manitoba and the North West, box 1, file 1, R.N. Toms to Mrs Harvie, 12 March 1888; ibid., A. Sutherland Papers, box 6, file 125, Rev. T.C. Buchanan to A. Sutherland, 11 March 1907; General Synod Archives, M 75–1, Bishop J.R. Lucas Papers, undesignated box, J.R. Lucas to Archdeacon J.W. Tims, 16 Dec. 1925.
68 Rev. W.D. Reid, "The Non-Anglo-Saxons in Canada – Their Christianization and Nationalization" (1913), in R.C. Brown and M.E. Prang, eds., *Confederation to 1949*, Canadian Historical Documents (Scarborough: Prentice-Hall 1966), 83. See also J.S. Woodsworth, *Strangers within Our Gates or Coming Canadians* (Toronto: F.C. Stephenson 1909), 281; M.J. Barber, "Nationalism, Nativism and the Social Gospel: The Protestant Church Response to Foreign Immigrants in Western Canada, 1897–1914," in R. Allen, ed., *The Social Gospel in Canada* (Ottawa: National Museum of Man 1975), 210, 212; N.K. Clifford, "His Dominion: A Vision in Crisis," *Studies in Religion/Sciences Religieuses* 2, 4 (1973): esp. 315–19. As has been pointed out implicitly by Michael Owen ("'Building the Kingdom of God on the Prairies': E.H. Oliver and Saskatchewan Education, 1913–1930," *Saskatchewan History* 40, 1 [1987]: 26), the Protestants' concern shifted gradually away from purely religious concerns towards considerations of ethnicity and national identity.
69 P. Dirks, "Finding the 'Canadian' Way: Origins of the Religious Education Council of Canada," *Studies in Religion/Sciences Religieuses* 16, 3 (1987): 305.
70 J.W. Grant, *Moon of Wintertime: Missionaries and the Indians of Canada in Encounter since 1534* (Toronto: University of Toronto Press 1984), title of chap. 9.
71 For example, S.D. Chown, quoted in J.W. Grant, *The Church in the Canadian Era: The First Century of Confederation* (Toronto: McGraw-Hill Ryerson 1972), 134 n. 24.
72 For example, New Brunswick Museum, Archives Section, George T. Baird Papers, *Memorandum [on] Ne Temere Decree* (np, nd), "Issued by the

Committee appointed by the General Synod of the Church of England in Canada."

73 Brian F. Hogan, CSB, "The Guelph Novitiate Raid: Conscription, Censorship and Bigotry during the Great War," Canadian Catholic Historical Association, *Study Sessions*, 1978: 57–80. Wartime seemed to bring out the worst anti-Catholic traditions. See the fulminations of the Rev. T.T. Shields quoted in J.L. Granatstein, *Canada's War: The Politics of the Mackenzie King Government, 1939–1945* (Toronto: Oxford University Press 1975), 390–1.

74 Grant, *Church in the Canadian Era*, 131, 138–9.

75 Clifford, "His Dominion," 321–4; Cook, *The Regenerators*, passim, esp. 6, 229.

3 Catholicism and Colonial Policy in Newfoundland, 1779–1845

RAYMOND J. LAHEY

In the period between Conquest and Confederation, relationships between the Catholic church and the government authorities of British North America underwent a number of subtle, and some not so subtle, transformations. What the spirit of the times emphasised – "freedom" and "toleration" – social and political conditions demanded. The church was too well entrenched to be directly confronted and too important to be ignored. Quebec, of course, with its large French and Catholic population, was a prime case of this process of rapprochement, but throughout the whole of British North America a *modus vivendi* had to be worked out.

Among the English-speaking colonies, Newfoundland affords a vivid example of the same process, perhaps because during much of this period it too had a Catholic majority or near-majority.[1] That in the end it developed its own singular solution to church-state relationships should not obscure the fact that its problems were far from unique – schooling, political rights, church establishment, and changing demographics. In fact, throughout much of the period Newfoundland was something of a microcosm of the contemporary political, social, and religious currents affecting North America.

What might first appear unparalleled about the Newfoundland situation – the unbridled sectarian rivalry that afflicted the island in the decades after 1830 – was in fact also part of a more universal phenomenon, except perhaps in its intensity. One has only to think of Howe's call for Protestant unity in Nova Scotia, the schools controversies in Upper Canada, "nativism" in the United States, and the furore over "Papal Aggression" in England. Indeed, the partisan newspapers of the day graphically reported such controversies to the Newfoundland public, and these reports had their own part in fuelling local conflicts.

Still, while bigotry and intolerance were never far from the surface anywhere, their emergence as dominant factors invariably required a triggering mechanism. In this regard, political factors have not always been given sufficient weight, especially where the absence of electoral contests would make them less obvious. Craig Brown has noted with regard to the later minority schools question in Ontario and the West that "the resolution of these crises was to be found only in politics."[2] In Newfoundland it was clearly the initial failure of the political process to resolve tensions that gave rise to excesses, as, in the end, decades later, it was a political solution that finally laid them to rest. Perhaps, indeed, the only truly distinctive feature of Newfoundland in this period was that, unlike the other colonies, it had no form of self-government and was consequently less well adapted to deal with local problems.

It was in 1832, on the hustings in St John's during the colony's first elections, that the candidate John Kent attempted to rally support by his famous "Irishmen and Catholics" speech, in which he called on them to "connect yourselves together – stand up for your country and creed," and told them he had the support of the bishop and clergy.[3]

But if Kent had injected the religious issue into the Newfoundland electoral scene, he had not created it. Rather, he was reflecting the outcome of a political process to accommodate the Catholic factor that had begun half a century earlier. Kent was the voice of discontent for a growing number of Newfoundland Roman Catholics, by then half the colony's population, who felt anger over the official handling of their grievances. If he appeared radical, he was reflecting a more radical mood among his fellow Catholics than would have been the case even a few years before.

The issues were not generated by the election itself, nor were they the product of traditional hostility between Catholic and Protestant. In fact, several letters to the editor during the 1832 election campaign deplored the sentiments expressed as "incompatible with the well-known Christian cordiality always existing in St. John's" and destructive of that "most perfect unanimity" which usually prevailed among the various social and religious groups in Newfoundland.[4] Even as early as 1804, Governor Erasmus Gower had written that "there is perhaps a greater cordiality subsisting between the Protestant and Romish Communions there than is found in any other situation."[5]

Patrick Morris, the prominent reformer and merchant, said the same thing in 1827, that Newfoundlanders, "though divided into various sects, that bitter sectarian hostility, so frequently seen among people of other countries ... is not observed amongst them. The people of the various religious congregations at Newfoundland have complied with the recommendation of our divine master – *they love one another.*"[6]

Perhaps this was a fair description. However, Governor Thomas Cochrane, writing at the same time, probably put it more accurately and certainly more prophetically when he reported to Lord Bathurst: "a perfect harmony, or should I rather say, tranquillity exists between them [Catholics and Protestants], yet I am persuaded ... that a small spark could excite a flame not easily subdued." He later described this harmony as having been "but a smooth surface covering the seeds of discord, which only required a sufficient exciting cause to shoot into life."[7]

In retrospect, it seems clear that the campaign of 1832 was the "small spark" Cochrane so accurately foresaw. What were the "seeds of discord?" They were not the inevitable product of old-country prejudices. The Irish who had come to Newfoundland were not children of persecution or of famine. They came, young men for the fishery and women for domestic service and for marriage, largely from the farms and the valleys around Waterford and other south-eastern Irish ports. Some Irish no doubt came to Newfoundland as colonizers for Lord Baltimore and Lord Falkland in the 1620s, for both had Irish connections,[8] but it is doubtful that they stayed, and it is not until the 1680s that an Irish presence was notable.[9] Even then, a significant increase in the Irish population of Newfoundland did not occur until the labour shortage created by the opening of the French fishery on the south coast to the British in 1713 by the Treaty of Utrecht. From 1720 to 1750 the combination of labour shortages and periods of depressed agricultural conditions in Ireland acted as stimuli to immigration, so that by 1753 Irish inhabitants were reported as outnumbering the English.[10]

Throughout this time the Irish were tolerated, if inevitably held suspect of loyalty to the French. However, in the mid 1750s three separate events – the murder of the St John's merchant William Keen by Irish Catholics, the appearance on the scene of an Irish Augustinian priest,[11] and the outbreak of war with France – led to a short period of religious persecution under Governor Richard Dorrill. For allowing Mass to be said, Catholics in the Conception Bay area had their houses and stores burned, and for their participation faced fines and even deportation; the priest was hunted by the authorities, although without success.[12] For a few years there was also a fairly strict application, at least in St John's, of the laws against Newfoundland settlement, directed specifically against Irish Catholics.[13] However, this active repression was both an isolated instance and ineffective, for even in the years between 1753 and 1768 the number of Irish Roman Catholic settlers actually increased from 2683 to 6653, a growth of some 248 per cent.[14]

Paraphrasing the article about religion that had appeared in the governor's instructions since 1729, Governor Hugh Palliser noted in 1764 that "a free Exercize of Religion is permitted to all persons except to Roman Catholicks, whose number exceeds the Protestants. It is said they have Priests secreted among them, to the great Disturbance of the Peace and good Government of the Country in the Winter Season."[15] In fact, itinerant Irish priests probably circulated relatively freely in Newfoundland at least from the late 1770s,[16] although removal of the penal laws did not occur until 1779. Events in Newfoundland and elsewhere had made the climate ripe for such a change.[17] The Newfoundland Irish had remained loyal and tranquil during the American Revolution,[18] and the Quebec Act of 1774 had already given *de jure* toleration, and more, to Roman Catholics in Quebec. Even in England and Ireland the worst of the penal laws had been repealed in 1778. When new instructions were framed for Governor Richard Edwards the next year the words "except Papists" were omitted and the article broadened, so that it now read: "It being our intention that all persons inhabiting our islands under your government should have full liberty of conscience and the free exercise of all such modes of religious worship as are not prohibited by law, We do therefore hereby require you to permit all persons within our said islands to have such liberty and to exercise such modes of religious worship as are not prohibited by law provided they be contented with a quiet and peaceable enjoyment of the same not giving offence or scandal to the government."[19] Since the statute laws of Britain did not apply to Newfoundland unless Parliament specifically provided,[20] or unless the governor's commission and instructions gave them application under the royal prerogative, Newfoundland now had no restrictive legal provisions whatsoever against Roman Catholics; moreover, it had no legislature to introduce similar restrictions at the local level. In any event, the priests then in Newfoundland seem to have functioned without constraints.

A few years later the extent of the new toleration became apparent. In 1783 agents for the Roman Catholics of St John's applied to Governor John Campbell for permission to build a chapel and for the approval of regularly appointed resident priests, and the required authorizations were freely given. In fact, so complete was the governor's agreement with these arrangements that in 1784 Rome felt comfortable in establishing Newfoundland as a separate ecclesiastical jurisdiction (the first to be established in North America since Quebec) and officially appointed James Louis O'Donel, the Irish priest chosen by the St John's agents, as its superior or prefect. Here Newfoundland provided a precedent, for a month later Rome took similar action in appointing John Carroll superior of the new mission of the United States.[21] Following the arrival in Newfoundland of Fathers O'Donel and Patrick Phelan, the priest for Harbour Grace, in 1784, Campbell not only issued unequivocal instructions to the magistrates regarding religious toleration but, in the absence of any laws to the contrary, clearly recognized the right of the Catholic priests to perform marriages – something unheard of in England. According to the Anglican rector of St John's, the governor allowed the priests "to act discretionary without any Restrictions whatever."[22]

O'Donel was well chosen for his new position. The former provincial of the Franciscan order in Ireland, he was both politically conservative and personally cautious, urbane (educated in Rome and having taught in Prague), and possessed of a genuine eirenicism towards those of differing religious persuasions. In an era of radical new political ideologies, he remained staunchly loyal to the crown and regarded revolutionary tendencies as an "indelible infamy upon our holy Religion that breaths nothing more than loyalty & obedience to the laws of God & the constituted authorities of every country."[23]

O'Donel had his difficulties. Initially some of the merchants opposed the presence of priests as an encouragement to settlement, and the Anglican clergyman in St John's questioned O'Donel's loyalty.[24] More notable was the physical attack on O'Donel by Prince William Henry (later William iv) in 1786. The prince, a surrogate governor, was venting his outrage over the proselytism and marriage of Anglicans by Father Edmund Burke at Placentia as contrary to law. In any event, O'Donel was not seriously hurt, and the matter died when the prince left the island immediately afterwards.[25] It was significant, however, that even in his correspondence with the prince, Governor John Elliott had defended O'Donel's character.

O'Donel experienced new setbacks between 1788 and 1790, when permission was refused for a chapel in Ferryland and Governor Mark Milbanke even threatened the expulsion of priests from the colony. This situation had been produced by two factors, violence among Irish provincial factions at Ferryland (stirred up, or at least abetted, by the vagrant priest Patrick Power), and the formal complaint to London by an Anglican clergyman that Roman Catholicism had been allowed to become in effect the established religion of

Newfoundland, with Protestantism merely tolerated.[26] For a short time, O'Donel was in a state of uncertainty and anguish, but with the further repeal of the penal laws in England in 1791 and the assurance of full religious freedom given that same year by the first chief justice of Newfoundland, John Reeves, any real threat to the toleration of Roman Catholics ceased. Thereafter their position was secured in both fact and law.[27]

By 1794 the stability of the church was so clearly assured that the Newfoundland Catholics petitioned the Holy See to have the island made a vicariate apostolic, with O'Donel as its first bishop. The initiative for this step came from Archbishop John Thomas Troy of Dublin,[28] O'Donel's Irish mentor, who by this stage had publicly extolled the virtues of the British system[29] and was engaged in negotiations with the crown for the foundation and subsidy of the Maynooth seminary. Rome was certainly unwilling to do anything that would alienate the British government, and asked Monsignor (later Cardinal) Charles Erskine, the pope's representative in London, to test the reaction of the authorities. Erskine spoke to the home secretary, the Duke of Portland, and his predecessor, Lord Grenville, who expressed no objection to the proposal.[30] The good relationship between the civil authorities and the Catholic bishops of Quebec may well have had a bearing on their attitude.[31] The Holy See issued the requisite bulls in January 1796, and O'Donel was consecrated by Bishop Jean-François Hubert in Quebec City on 21 September.[32]

Upon his return to Newfoundland in 1797, O'Donel seems to have experienced more difficulties among his own flock than he did at the hands of government. If a report of General John Skerrett is correct, O'Donel at one stage had such trouble with revolutionary elements that he actually contemplated leaving Newfoundland.[33] It is paradoxical, then, but quite understandable, that the United Irish mutiny in St John's in 1800 actually strengthened immeasurably the position of Roman Catholicism in Newfoundland. By denouncing the revolutionary tendencies of the plotters, whom he felt deluded people into thinking that their cause was religious "while they were openly transgressing the laws of God & their lawful Sovereign,"[34] and by using his influence to calm the civilian population and so confine the outbreak to the garrison, O'Donel ingratiated himself with the administration. Indeed, his handling of the affair cemented an alliance between the government of Newfoundland and the Roman Catholic clergy that was to endure well into the future.[35]

This cooperation worked to mutual advantage. O'Donel's diocesan statutes of 1801, echoing Troy's endorsement of the British Constitution, proclaimed unequivocally the duty of public prayers for King

George III and the Royal Family, and that "priests should use every means to turn aside their flocks from the vortex of modern anarchy; that they should inculcate a willing obedience to the salutary laws of England, and to the commands of the governor and magistrates of this Island."[36] These were not merely pious wishes, but a charter under which the Roman Catholic clergy operated in practice. Their loyalty to government and their work in maintaining law and order among their flock did not go unnoticed. In 1804 Gower could write of O'Donel that "the Government is greatly indebted to his fidelity and piety for the constant preservation of peace and good order among the lower classes of society in this place, as well as throughout the Island."[37] Catholic priests, in turn, were given a degree of deference and public recognition by government that was virtually indistinguishable from that accorded Anglican clergy. In 1805 O'Donel's services were recognized by the award of an annual civil stipend by the British government.[38]

Yet the Roman Catholics were uncompromising in their religious practices, even in the obviously controversial matter of proselytism. Reports repeatedly stressed the activity of the Roman priests in making converts, and this remained a concern of the authorities. Even Gower, who was well-disposed, wrote that "the active zeal which is generally found in the Romish Clergy requires that the utmost diligence should be used, on the part of Government, to support the Established Religion."[39]

Indeed, the success of the Catholic priests produced something of a backlash, for it was unquestionably the strength of Roman Catholicism in Newfoundland that prodded the authorities into increased patronage of the Church of England. Particularly, it led to significant government financial support. From 1804 London agreed to augment the salaries of the Anglican missionaries in Newfoundland by £50 a year.[40] Thereafter, too, successive governors began to use the local Newfoundland revenues from land rents to pay the building or repair costs of Anglican schools and churches and the salaries of Anglican schoolmasters and lay readers.[41] This same fear of Catholic predominance was even reflected in a letter of Governor John Holloway in 1810 that proposed the removal of Chief Justice Thomas Tremlett. The governor cited, among other things, "his not countenancing and supporting by his Presence the Established Church against the Roman Catholic, more particularly as he must have seen the Zeal and Industry of the Priests, to make Converts to that Religion."[42]

At the time, gratified not only to be tolerated but to be held in some respect, with their own bishop in receipt of a stipend, Roman Catholics were hardly in a position to question civil support of the

Anglican church. However, they could not reasonably accede to subsidies deliberately inimical to their own cause; in 1806, for example, Gower wrote of one allowance that it was for "the promulgation of pure Scriptural knowledge, and preventing the encrease of Roman Catholic schools."[43] When in the 1820s, then, Catholics found themselves denied access to the same sources of funding, grants that so obviously favoured the Anglican minority became an increasingly irksome matter.

Before leaving Newfoundland in 1807, O'Donel had placed the choice of a successor entirely in the hands of Archbishop Troy, suggesting only a "man strong in doctrine, patience, suavity and urbanity of manner, lest he should lose the now long standing favour not only of the Governor, but also that of the General, the officers of the garrison and the fleet."[44] Gower had similar concerns, expressing the hope that the new bishop would exhibit "the same spirit of allegiance to His Majesty."[45] Neither was to be disappointed in Patrick Lambert, also a Franciscan, who succeeded O'Donel in 1807.[46] Although never entirely at home in Newfoundland, he was, like his predecessor, a churchman of the old school, and his relationships with the civil authorities continued in the same vein. Government, too, maintained its benevolent attitude towards Catholicism. In 1811, bringing Newfoundland into line with Nova Scotian practice, the Privy Council gave Roman Catholic priests the right to bury the dead, hitherto the official prerogative of the Anglican clergy.[47] More importantly, in 1814, no doubt acknowledging Lambert's loyalty in a time of war with the United States, government went so far as to provide him with a yearly stipend of £75, in virtue of his ecclesiastical position as "Bishop of Chytra and Head of the Catholic Church in this Island."[48] Lord Bathurst, the colonial secretary, was effectively treating the vicar apostolic of Newfoundland like his counterpart in Quebec, where a year earlier Joseph-Octave Plessis had been officially salaried as "Catholic Bishop of Quebec."[49]

Lambert's most serious problem in Newfoundland was the massive Irish immigration that took place between 1811 and 1816, generated by the prosperous Newfoundland economy during the Napoleonic Wars.[50] The Irish who came to Newfoundland were not homogeneous. Although almost all Catholic, they came, probably in near equal numbers, from the rival provinces of Leinster and Munster; they did not even share the same language, since many were still speakers of Irish Gaelic.[51] Foreseeing trouble even in 1813, Governor Richard Keats had proposed that government reinforce Lambert's authority by restricting immigration of priests into Newfoundland to those accredited by the bishop. While the economy was buoyant, things were quiet, but when the fishery collapsed in 1815 and men continued to pour into the country, contending county gangs entered into secret compacts, refusing work at the wages offered and rioting along provincial lines. Lambert and his priests, Leinstermen and few of them Irish-speakers, attempted to quell the troubles, but with little success.[52] They were openly opposed by the suspended priest John Power, a Munsterman from County Tipperary who, if anything, had the larger following, especially among those who spoke Irish.[53] The lawlessness eventually subsided, and immigration was temporarily brought to a virtual halt in 1816 by an act of Parliament regulating passage to Newfoundland.[54] Lambert himself was certainly affected by the faction fighting of 1815, and it undoubtedly precipitated his decision to leave Newfoundland later that year and to transfer the ecclesiastical government to a successor.[55]

Thomas Scallan, the third Franciscan to serve as bishop, and like Lambert from County Wexford, had been curate in St John's since 1812.[56] Hearing of Lambert's intention to leave, Chief Justice Caesar Colclough had written to Lord Bathurst that there was no office in Newfoundland more important "to the Peace and Regularity of the Island at large as that of a Roman Catholic Bishop"; he recommended that the colonial secretary use his influence to secure the appointment of Father Edmund Burke of Halifax.[57] Bathurst seems to have ignored this advice, and in any event Scallan was an intelligent and benevolent man who throughout his episcopate commanded near universal respect.

Immediately he had to deal with the disorders in the colony, especially during the winters of 1816–17 and 1817–18. If anything, they tended to increase the reliance of government on the Catholic priesthood. Scallan did not hesitate to let his priests be enforcers of the law, even to the extent that one commentator lamented: "It is this influence which the priests have over the people which renders their services so valuable in the eyes of the Magistrates, for the priests are our police officers ... and we are taught to believe that we are more indebted to the Catholic priests for our safety and comfort than to any other Class of Men in the Island."[58] At the same time Scallan maintained excellent personal relationships with Governors Sir Charles Hamilton and Sir Thomas Cochrane, as with the Anglican clergy, even to the point of several times attending Anglican church services.[59]

Paradoxically, it was during Scallan's episcopate that serious conflicts developed between Roman Catholic interests and government policy, leading to an alienation that was unresolved at his death. Scallan wrote in 1818: "I am treated with attention by the Governor, visit him frequently, dine with him, and never make an application in vain."[60] Yet, when in 1819 Scallan requested continuation of the stipend paid earlier to O'Donel and Lambert, even the governor's staunch support could not procure it from London. A similar request in 1823, with the same support, produced no different result. It was ironic that even in Upper Canada, where Roman Catholics were a small minority, not only Bishop Alexander Macdonell and but also three Catholic schoolmasters were receiving British government allowances.[61] Scallan did not pursue the matter further, apparently preferring his independence,[62] but Roman Catholics, who were then half the population, could hardly have been happy to see £300 annually paid from public funds to the Anglican archdeacon from 1826 onwards.[63]

Financial discrimination became a further aggravation after the establishment in 1823 of the Newfoundland School Society, a British organization composed largely of merchants and evangelical elements. Nominally Anglican,[64] in Newfoundland the society advertised its schools as nondenominational, one of its brochures explaining: "As the inhabitants of the Colony consist of different denominations of religion, it is the desire of the Society to accommodate its education to the moral wants of those it proposed to benefit, in such a manner, as, without any sacrifice of principle, may, by the blessing of God, most commend it to their acceptance."[65] Newfoundland Roman Catholics had previously supported the St John's Charity School (founded in 1802),[66] open to all and having religious instruction provided by each denomination outside normal school hours. When the Newfoundland School Society opened its doors in 1824, however, Bishop Scallan invoked a Vatican prohibition against schools sponsored by "Bible Societies" to prohibit the attendance of Roman Catholic children at these new schools.[67] He suspected, probably rightly,[68] that despite the protestations of nondenominationalism, they were really aimed at proselytism. As an alternative, and in any case recognizing that the existing schools were inadequate, the Benevolent Irish Society, with the bishop's approval, established a new school in St John's for poorer children, the Orphan Asylum, in 1826.[69] Although in practice this school catered almost entirely to Roman Catholic pupils, it was organized on the lines of the older Charity School – officially nondenominational – but with religious instruction outside regular school hours.[70]

Despite the fact that the Newfoundland School Society schools, the Society for the Propagation of the Gospel schools, and the St John's Charity School all directly or indirectly received government funds, the Orphan Asylum school was unable to obtain similar consideration. The first of its many applications, in 1823, although endorsed by Governor Hamilton, seems to have been passed over in silence. In 1825 another appeal was made directly to Lord Bathurst by Patrick Morris, the Benevolent Irish Society's president, again with the governor's approval. Morris pointed out that £600 had already been raised in Newfoundland and that the BIS was prepared to contribute £100 yearly. What was requested was a government con-tribution towards building costs and a small annual subsidy, both of which had been given to the Newfoundland School Society.[71] These appeals likewise went without result. As late as January 1832 Chief Justice Richard Alexander Tucker, as administrator of the colony, wrote again to the colonial secretary, pointing out that the refusal of aid to the BIS school, which was by far Newfoundland's largest, was seen as discriminatory. He was most anxious, he wrote, "to remove the impression that in the discharge of a duty of such universal obligation as the education of the poor, His Majesty's Government is capable of drawing an unfair line of distinction between Protestants and Roman Catholics." In the circumstances, he asked for an annual contribution of £100, even if the Newfoundland funds were over-drawn. This time Viscount Goderich replied that he would gladly approve such a grant if funds existed, but that the Newfoundland estimates had already gone to Parliament.[72] He suggested that a local legislature could make such a provision when it was established. In fact, the BIS school and the similarly constituted St Patrick's Free School at Harbour Grace (founded by Father Thomas Ewer in 1826) received government aid only after the first local Education Act in 1836.[73]

In Newfoundland, as in all three Maritime provinces and in Upper Canada, one of the most inflammatory religious controversies sur-rounded the right to perform marriages.[74] Prior to 1817 no statute laws applicable to Newfoundland regulated the solemnization of mar-riages, since the British legislation, which normally reserved this function to clergy of the established church, did not apply overseas. Consequently, the celebration of marriage was regulated by local custom, and since there were few clergy of any kind in eighteenth-century Newfoundland, it was common for marriages to be solem-nized by anyone who could read the service, in the presence of two witnesses. With marriages habitually celebrated even by laymen, it was logical that the right of Catholic priests to perform marriages would be unquestioned by the governors, even if this was not British practice, since English canon law clearly recognized Roman orders.[75]

Despite common law, dissenting clergy in Newfoundland were slow to perform marriages. The first local Congregational minister,

John Jones, who died in 1800, did none at all. His successors in St John's were not quite so hesitant, although they apparently performed them infrequently, and only for members of their own congregation. The Methodist clergy seem to have solemnized marriages more freely, although largely in areas where there was no resident Anglican clergyman.[76]

Unclear as to how to handle the issue, Governor Sir John Thomas Duckworth in 1812 sought a formal ruling from the law officers of the crown in England. Their opinion clearly upheld the right of Roman Catholic priests in Newfoundland to solemnize marriages in all circumstances. Marriages performed even by laymen (including dissenting clergy, whose ministerial character was unrecognized in law) could be considered legal when justified by custom or necessity.[77]

There the matter rested until the establishment of a Methodist congregation in St John's in 1815 and the regular performance of marriages in the capital by the Methodist minister George Cubit, notwithstanding that the residence of both Anglican and Catholic clergy did not allow the plea of necessity. James Sabine, the Congregational minister, followed suit. However, they encountered vehement objections from David Rowland, the Anglican rector, angered by what he considered a breach of the privileges of the Church of England. He took no action, however, until Cubit unwittingly performed the marriage, without parental consent and under assumed names, of two underage members of Rowland's own congregation. Upon Rowland's complaint, Governor Francis Pickmore solemnly forbade Cubit and Sabine to perform further marriages under the threat of closing their meeting houses. Pickmore held that the marriage of Protestants by anyone other than an Anglican clergyman – where one was resident – was illegal. This interpretation the two ministers simply refused to accept; indeed, they threatened the governor with legal action if he interfered with them. Unrepentant, they boldly stated their case in the press and continued to officiate openly at weddings.[78]

However, Pickmore was not prepared to let matters rest, and in 1817 he suggested to Lord Bathurst that an act of Parliament might be needed as a remedy. When the law officers again upheld the validity of marriages celebrated by Methodist clergy, Pickmore decided to proceed with legislation.[79] The clear intent was to curtail marriages by dissenting ministers, at least where there were Anglican clergy. Indeed, assurances were given to the Catholics that their rights would not be prejudicially affected.[80]

The 1817 Newfoundland Marriage Act (57 Geo. III, c. 51) was passed without opportunity for public discussion in Newfoundland.[81] Hurriedly drafted, it was a bad law. Its one clear provision was to legalize retroactively all marriages prior to 1 January 1818, no matter how celebrated. Otherwise it said that, except in "circumstances of peculiar and extreme difficulty," the celebration of marriage must henceforth be only by a person in holy orders. This term was thought to be legally specific, referring directly to the Church of England clergy and by extension to Catholic priests and to ministers of the established (Presbyterian) Church of Scotland,[82] groups whose orders were clearly recognized in British civil or canon law.[83]

Methodists and Congregationalists were outraged. They could make at least a *prima facie* case that the phrase "in Holy Orders" was broad enough to include them. However, the legal doubts deterred couples who otherwise might have approached dissenting ministers, especially where there were Anglican or Catholic clergy. Even more infuriating to the dissenters was the advantage the 1817 Act appeared to give to Roman Catholics. It was termed "a most powerful engine of proselytism put into the hands of the Roman Catholic priests ... contrary to the whole spirit of British law,"[84] with a direct tendency "to establish popery and to persecute Protestantism."[85] Less provocatively, William Carson, the great local government advocate, described Pickmore's inept handling of the situation as having "kindled the spark of a Religious Persecution which has diffused itself all over this Island."[86]

A second act in 1824 managed to fuel antagonism even more. This time it was the Methodists, still smarting under the provisions of the 1817 law, who advocated a new act, maintaining, rightly, that the only realistic solution in the Newfoundland situation was legal recognition of marriages solemnized by any minister of religion.[87] Their timing was good, for Sir Francis Forbes, a former chief justice, was then drafting a new judicature act. Accepting that changes were needed, Forbes simply added clauses regarding marriages to his draft.[88] However, he compromised. The 1817 act would be repealed, but it would be provided instead that "where it shall not be convenient to obtain a person in Holy Orders of the United Church of England and Ireland," then it would be lawful for Roman Catholic priests, "or any other Protestant minister of religion," to solemnize a marriage.[89]

When the proposed legislation reached Newfoundland it produced a public outcry from every quarter. Catholics were particularly offended that priests could perform marriages only where it was not "convenient" to obtain an Anglican cleric, since for the first time they were put at a disadvantage. Indeed, taken at face value, the law might render Catholic priests unable to celebrate marriages in heavily Roman Catholic centres like St John's and Harbour Grace, where there were Anglican clergy. If this was unintended, then the bill only served to create confusion. Led by Bishop Scallan, and in massive numbers, Newfoundland Roman Catholics petitioned the British authorities against the proposals, calling them "the most degrading and distressing infliction that could be laid upon them."[90] They had Governor Hamilton's complete support,[91] and in the end their representations carried enough weight that the final version of the act restored the existing provision that anyone "in Holy Orders" could celebrate marriages.[92]

Even Anglicans were upset, for the draft had conceded an explicit legal right to Methodist and other dissenting clergy to solemnize marriages, at least in some circumstances. It also recognized a clergyman of these denominations as a "Protestant minister of religion." These were novelties to British law, and formal protests came from every Anglican missionary in Newfoundland. One of them entreated "that our Venerable Establishment will not be made to bow to the usurpation of Schismatics and Radicals."[93] James Stephen, legal adviser to the Colonial Office, was similarly concerned that a precedent might be created for Britain, although he was prepared to concede that Newfoundland's special situation might justify the concessions.[94] In any event, the Church of England representations were successful. In revision, the offending wording was changed to speak not of a Protestant minister, but "a teacher or preacher of religion," who could assist at marriages only in circumstances of necessity and with a special licence from the governor.[95]

Although the initial intent had been to provide for marriages by Methodist clergymen, their position became progressively worse as the bill went through six draft stages. To them even the first draft was unsatisfactory, since they felt that to provide an alternative only when it was "inconvenient" to have a Church of England officiant was to invite dispute.[96] In the end, they lost even more ground. Their missionaries held an inferior status not only to Church of England clergy, but also to Catholic priests; they were not acknowledged as clerics, and they needed civil licences.[97] Even the conditions of licensing narrowed as the bill was redrafted, at one point being valid only if the woman could not go from her residence to an Anglican church "without *extreme* inconvenience,"[98] and with the marriage certificate to be delivered to an Anglican clergyman. Only the strenuous representations of influential English Methodists procured the removal of the word "extreme."[99]

The Newfoundland Marriage Act (5 Geo. IV, c. 68), by this time a separate bill, passed into law in June 1824. Methodists remained embittered. They could not legally perform marriages where there were Anglican or Roman Catholic priests, and even in other circumstances the act was vague. Its undoubted effect was to discriminate against them. Roman Catholics were angry that the government could have contemplated diminishing a right they had enjoyed for so long; they also objected to the new fee for marriage registration that they were obliged to collect for government. Anglicans in their turn were upset that government had seriously considered recognition of Methodist clergy, a step they felt was calculated to undermine their own church. A hornets' nest had been stirred up, and every denomination had become defensive.[100]

Much more directly harmful to Catholic interests, however, were two controversies that affected their political rights, the first over membership on the Executive Council, the second over Catholic emancipation.

The council was introduced to Newfoundland in 1825 in the governor's commission issued to Sir Thomas Cochrane, a half-measure to appease the agitation for representative government. Appointed, not elected, it had no real legislative power; its primary purpose was the provision of official advice to the governor.[101] So constituted, it could have won general acceptance only with difficulty; in actual fact, the council rapidly became a liability and a cause of dissention. Its problems began at its first session on 8 October 1825. The governor's commission had provided for an interim council to consist of the justices of the Supreme Court and the military commander in Newfoundland. The commander, Lieutenant-Colonel Thomas Burke, was officially sworn in as a member and took the oath of allegiance, but as a Catholic he refused the oath of supremacy and the Test Act declaration against transubstantiation. Governor Cochrane was prepared to waive these requirements, following the lead of Lower Canada, where Bishop Plessis had been a member of the council since 1817. The justices doubted the legality of this procedure, however, and Burke was not seated. Cochrane knew the importance of the issue; he wrote immediately to Lord Bathurst to emphasize that Burke's exclusion could only give serious offence to Newfoundland's Catholic majority.[102]

In fact, Cochrane intended that the council should represent Catholic elements, for when he submitted his list for permanent membership a few months later, it included not only Burke, but also Patrick

Morris, a Catholic merchant, and Bishop Scallan. The bishop Cochrane described as entitled to appointment both by rank and personal
qualifications, but there was also an underlying motive. Cochrane
wrote that Scallan's appointment will ... afford a high gratification to
the whole mass of the Catholic population here, and render them
better satisfied with any measures the Government may wish to
pursue, and which may be supposed to have been adopted with his
concurrence. Cochrane also proposed Burke for administrator of the
colony, with a dormant commission to act in the governor's absence
or incapacity.[103]

Unfortunately the colonial secretary found his hands tied. In fact,
while Cochrane's commission was being drafted, Bathurst himself
had requested that the oaths offensive to Roman Catholics be
omitted, and a commission was prepared without them. However,
when this was referred to the attorney-general, he gave an official
opinion that notwithstanding the precedent of Lower Canada, it was
constitutionally impossible for the king to issue a commission
without these oaths; he had ordered the commission reframed to
include them. In any event, the requirements were now incorporated
in the commission and it would take a new commission to remove
them. Bathurst felt there was no alternative but to decline to submit
the Catholic nominees to the king.[104]

Although Cochrane's nomination of Scallan and Morris was not
public knowledge, Burke's exclusion sparked Catholic resentment.
Public agitation was prevented only by the vigorous efforts of the
bishop himself, who feared it would disrupt the religious harmony
of the colony.[105] Behind the scenes, however, and apparently with
Scallan's support, Morris memorialized the British government in
1828 to ask that the Roman Catholics of Newfoundland not be
deprived of rights that were accorded to them elsewhere in the North
American colonies. The whole question of the exclusion of Catholics
from public office was obviously a sore point, and Morris noted that
in Newfoundland they were not eligible even "to hold the most
unimportant civil situation."[106] Despite Cochrane's strong backing of
this petition, London took no remedial action,[107] possibly owing to
the upheaval then taking place at the Colonial Office.[108] To Newfoundland Catholics the council remained an unpalatable body.

Related to this issue were the changing fortunes in the British
Parliament of a proposed emancipation act. This, it was supposed,
would accord Catholics basic political rights and address such grievances as exclusion from the council. Led by Daniel O'Connell, the
Irish based Catholic Association had fought hard for this act, and
had drawn encouragement from the British general elections of 1826.

Their cause received a setback, however, when the Wellington-Peel ministry assumed power early in 1828, pledged to oppose emancipation. Nevertheless, the government could not withstand the growing agitation in Ireland and was obliged to reverse itself; the necessary legislation (10 Geo. IV, c. 7) finally received royal assent on 13 April 1829.[109] When the news reached Newfoundland, there was general rejoicing among Roman Catholics that the penal restrictions of centuries had been lifted. Bishop Scallan proclaimed 21 May a day of public thanksgiving, and in St John's and elsewhere throughout the island Catholics celebrated the occasion with special masses, parades, and bands.[110] Their joy, however, was short lived, for by December the attorney-general of Newfoundland and the justices of the Supreme Court had rendered concurring legal opinions that held the relief bill inapplicable to Newfoundland. Put simply, they held that since the acts of Parliament repealed by the Catholic Emancipation Act had not applied to Newfoundland, obviously neither did their repeal. However, they held that the Roman Catholics of Newfoundland were still under civil disabilities from Cochrane's commission of 1825, since it had been issued under the royal prerogative and was thus unaffected by statute law.[111]

It was obviously infuriating for the Roman Catholic populace to learn that the acts of Parliament which, in 1825, were held to prevent any commission being framed in their favour did not, in fact, apply, and that the only instrument now excluding them from civil offices was the governor's commission itself. What made matters worse was that elsewhere local legislatures were able to provide their own remedies. In Canada it was not a problem, since Roman Catholics there held full civil rights from the Quebec Act of 1774. Nova Scotia, which had given Catholics the right to vote in 1789, already had passed an act allowing them to hold office as early as 1827; although it had been reserved by London, it could now take effect. Both New Brunswick, where voting rights had existed since 1810, and Prince Edward Island quickly passed the necessary relief acts in 1830.[112] Newfoundland, with a Roman Catholic majority but no legislature, could take no action of its own, and consequently was the only North American colony still to labour under the penal laws.

Catholic feelings were "angry & highly irritated."[113] During December 1829 Roman Catholics held massive protest meetings, which culminated in a petition forwarded to Parliament through Daniel O'Connell and Lord Landsdowne, asking that they be accorded their full rights as British subjects.[114] Both Governor Cochrane and Chief Justice Tucker wrote to ask the Colonial Office to take speedy action to resolve the difficulty.[115] In fact, the draft of a remedial instruction for the governor was prepared as early as March 1830, and Cochrane was given assurances that "immediate steps" would be taken for Roman Catholic relief.[116] When another year of inaction passed, both Bishop Michael Anthony Fleming, who had succeeded Scallan in 1830, and Cochrane, for the second time, urged London to act. Cochrane asked whether his previous letter had been over-looked and stressed that Catholics were "very jealous on the subject and while their disabilities exist a handle is afforded for agitators … to make use of with which to disturb the peace of the community."[117] Perhaps as a sop to public opinion, the government did grant Fleming's request for an annual stipend, the colonial secretary observing to his undersecretary: "To buy a Bishop for £75 is cheap enough."[118]

Things remained unchanged even in early 1832, and Tucker, as administrator in the governor's absence, again tried to impress upon the government the urgency of the situation. He observed that feelings had been calmed only by the assurances given in 1830 that swift action would be taken. "I have every reason to fear," he wrote, "that a much further delay in the gratification of their wishes … would not only lead to the revival of their former angry feelings, but also impart *additional acrimony* to them."[119] Tucker was eventually informed that relief would be given in the new governor's commission, which would institute a House of Assembly for Newfoundland.[120] This was proclaimed on 26 August 1832,[121] so that full civil rights for Roman Catholics and the first general election came together. Strangely, in light of his previous recommendations, Cochrane did not take the one step now available to him to conciliate Catholic opinion – the nomination of a Roman Catholic to the council. (In fact, the first Roman Catholic was appointed only in 1840.)[122] Roman Catholics thus approached the electoral process having just won the struggle for political rights, and without a single one of their number holding any public office.

An elected assembly was a victory also for those in the island, notably William Carson, who had decried the power of the New-foundland oligarchy and had advocated local government. Further, the broad suffrage granted by the proclamation ensured that many voters would have no particular sympathy for mercantile interests.[123] Hence religious, political, and social factors merged to provide a platform during the campaign for anti-establishment views, and it was no doubt this combination that gave special force to the election controversies. Thus Kent could ask Irish Catholics to unite against "the merchants." Despite some heated exchanges, however, the election was not really unruly, even by Cochrane's reckoning.[124] Most outport seats were filled by acclamation, and only in the capital was there any lively campaigning.

Although the campaign marked the beginning of a period of sectarianism in Newfoundland, it was certainly not a clearly defined battle between Protestant and Catholic. In St John's, there were actually five major candidates for the three seats in the House: Kent, who had appropriated the "Irish Catholic" platform; two Anglicans, William Thomas, a merchant, and William Bickford Row, a solicitor; Carson, the "radical" leader and a nominal Presbyterian; and Patrick Kough, another Catholic and a government contractor. Bishop Fleming, put at the centre of the controversy by the *Public Ledger* for his support of Kent,[125] also had endorsed Thomas and Carson; he did not support Kough, the second Catholic contender. As he said himself, "I mentioned the name of an Englishman, Irishman, and Scotsman, a Catholic, Protestant, and Presbyterian."[126]

In fact, the 1832 election was a complex web of many different strands. It pitted the establishment interest as represented by Thomas, Row, and Kough against the more liberal politics of Carson and Kent. Yet even the fact that Kough was a government contractor and Kent the young "radical" does not account for the obvious lack of homogeny in the Irish Catholic vote. An undoubted factor was that Fleming had already fallen out with the more influential St John's Catholics, including Kough, over church matters.[127] It would appear that Kough, from Wexford, got the support of the Catholics from that region,[128] and there could well have been echoes of Irish provincial rivalries in the contest. Kent, Fleming, and those close to them clearly represented the Waterford connection, but Catholics from Leinster (largely Wexford and Kilkenny) were numerically more significant in 1832 than they had been at the turn of the century[129] and may have felt disempowered by the new Catholic leadership that Fleming and Kent represented.

The religious issue worked in other ways as well. On the day the election was proclaimed, Anglican archdeacon Edward Wix denounced Carson, a medical practitioner and a known religious sceptic, for suggesting that cholera was carried by contagion and should not be viewed only as a mysterious visitation of Providence. Wix called Carson's views blasphemous, and the doctor retorted publicly that the archdeacon was promoting religious division with doctrines "more those of Mohammed than of Jesus. He would subject us to a blind fatalism."[130] The debate underscored the fact that the establishment of Anglicanism, the implicit premise on which so much of previous government policy had been predicated, was still very much a concern. It was so live an issue that even the Anglicans, Thomas and Row, openly opposed government financial support for the Church of England.[131]

The results were anticlimactic to the controversies. It was obvious that Kent had found a following, for he led the poll. Thomas and Kough were the other winners, the latter's election clearly a victory for anti-Fleming Catholics and the more "respectable" circles of society. Carson was defeated, finishing fourth. The most decisive result of the election, however, was to shatter whatever racial and religious harmony Newfoundland had hitherto enjoyed. In the press and in politics, denominational ties and church influence henceforth became matters of great importance.

With the clarity of hindsight, it can be seen that the political failure to take Catholic interests into account in the years before 1832 had provided a platform around which many Roman Catholics, especially the working class, were prepared to rally. In their own way such diverse figures as Cochrane, Tucker, Fleming, and Morris had foreseen this eventuality; none of them, however, had succeeded in impressing upon the British government the urgency of the situation.[132] After 1832, new grievances, real and imagined, would be added to the old, and the solidarity of much of the Catholic vote would itself be perceived as a threat by Protestants.

This political failure stemmed largely from two convergent factors. In part it resulted from the tendency of the colonial authorities to act (although without ever espousing it as formal policy) as if the Church of England could be established in a colony where it was a minority.[133] It was also due to the absence of a legislature that would have been more responsive to local grievances: government support of the Newfoundland School Society, the financial subsidies to the Church of England, the marriage question, the exclusion of Roman Catholics from the council, and Catholic emancipation. The other North American colonies had faced similar problems, but the mechanisms in place managed to preclude such a divisive outcome. In the end it was only the home-grown political solution of strict denominational proportionalism that provided Newfoundlanders with the security to regain a degree of that religious harmony that had once been their hallmark.

NOTES

1 The returns for the period are not entirely reliable, but they do give some indication of the relative Protestant and Catholic populations:

Year	Protestants	Catholics	% Catholic
1779	6,473	4,707	43
1786	6,327	5,445	46
1794	8,530	9,207	52
1806	14,310	10,822	43
1815	20,945	19,623	48
1827	28,212	30,928	52
1836	36,089	37,568	51

See Public Record Office (PRO), Colonial Office (CO) 194/34, fols. 88–9 (1779), Admiralty (ADM) 1/472, fol. 225 (1786), War Office (WO) 1/15, fol. 149 (1794), CO 194/46, fol. 78 (1806), ADM 80/151, 269–74 (1815); the figures for 1827 and 1836 are from Gertrude E. Gunn, *The Political History of Newfoundland, 1832–1864* (Toronto: University of Toronto Press 1966), 206.

2 D.G. Creighton, Craig Brown, et al., *Minorities, Schools and Politics* (Toronto: University of Toronto Press 1969), viii–ix.

3 *Public Ledger*, 25 Sept. 1832.

4 Ibid., 21 Sept. 1832.

5 PRO, CO 194/45, fols. 20–38, "Explanatory Observations on Return for 1804."

6 Patrick Morris, *Remarks on the State of Society, Religion, Morals, and Education at Newfoundland; in reply to the Statements made at the Meetings, and in the Reports, of the Newfoundland School Society, and also to a Part of a Speech Delivered by the Bishop of Chester at the Meeting of the Society for the Propagation of the Gospel in Foreign Parts, held at the Freemason's Hall, on the 25th of May last. In a Letter, addressed to the Right Honourable Lord Bexley* (London: A. Hancock 1827), 17.

7 PRO, CO 194/74, fol. 131ff, Cochrane to Lord Bathurst, 1 May 1827; PRO, CO 194/87, fols. 106–11, Cochrane to Lord Stanley, 8 April 1834.

8 See Gillian T. Cell, ed., *Newfoundland Discovered: English Attempts at Colonisation, 1610–1630* (London: Hakluyt Society 1982), 39–54.

9 See, for example, PRO, CO 1/47, no. 52 (i), "Account of Ships … 1681."

10 PRO, CO 194/13, fols. 116–23, Answers to Heads of Enquiry, 1753. See also C. Grant Head, *Eighteenth Century Newfoundland: A Geographer's Perspective*, Carleton Library (Toronto: McClelland and Stewart 1976), 86–94, and Ralph Greenlee Lounsbury, *British Fishery at Newfoundland* (Princeton: Yale University Press 1934), 246–9, 300–4.

11 In 1755 Richard Challoner, vicar-apostolic of London, sent an Irish Augustinian priest to Newfoundland with full faculties; his name is not recorded. See Peter Guilday, *The Life and Times of John Carroll, Archbishop of Baltimore (1735–1815)* (New York: Encyclopedia Press 1922), 144.

12 See, for example, PRO, ADM 80/121, Dorrill to the magistrates at Harbour Grace, 15 Aug. 1755, 10; Provincial Archives of Newfoundland and Labrador (PANL), GN 2/1, Thomas Burnett to Charles Garland, 20 Sept. 1755, and Thomas Burnett to R. Mullen and Charles Garland, 25 Sept. 1755, 256–7, 260.

13 PRO, CO 194/13, fol. 186, Michael Gill to Governor Bonfoy, 22 Nov. 1754; PRO, ADM 80/121, 13, 14, Governor Dorrill's Proclamation, 22 Sept. 1755, and Governor Dorrill to the St John's magistrates.

14 PRO, CO 194/13, fols. 116–23, Answers to Heads of Enquiry, 1753; PRO, CO 194/18, fols. 40–1, Scheme of Fishery, 1768.

15 PRO, CO 194/17, fol. 10, Answers to Heads of Enquiry, 1764.

16 O'Donel to Cardinal Antonelli [18 Dec. 1785], in Cyril J. Byrne, ed., *Gentlemen-Bishops and Faction Fighters: The Letters of Bishops O'Donel, Lambert, Scallan, and Other Irish Missionaries* (St John's: Jesperson Press 1984), 55; United Society for the Propagation of the Gospel (USPG), B6, nos. 215, 218, James Balfour to the secretary of the USPG, 2 and 10 Dec. 1779.

17 This matter is admirably treated by H. Rollmann, "Religious Enfranchisement," in Terrence Murphy and Cyril J. Byrne, eds., *Religion and Identity: The Experience of Irish and Scottish Catholics in Atlantic Canada* (St John's: Jesperson Press 1987), 34–47.

18 PRO, CO 194/33, fols. 5–6, Governor Montague to Lord George Germain, 27 May 1776; PRO, CO 194/35, fols. 133–4, Governor Edwards to Lord George Germain, 6 Dec. 1781.

19 Governor Edwards's Instructions, 27 April 1779, in Rollmann, "Religious Enfranchisement," 36.

20 PRO, CO 194/59, fols. 1–3, Governor Pickford to Lord Bathurst, 7 Jan. 1817; PRO, CO 194/60, fols. 59–62, law officers of the crown to Lord Bathurst, 4 Feb. 1817; PRO, CO 194/78, fols. 259–60, 260–1, Simms, AG, to Captain Bruce, 17 Dec. 1829, and Tucker, CJ, DesBarres and Brenton, JJ, to Governor Cochrane, 21 Dec. 1829.

21 See Raymond J. Lahey, *James Louis O'Donel in Newfoundland, 1784–1807: The Establishment of the Roman Catholic Church* (St John's: Newfoundland Historical Society 1984), 6–9; and Byrne, *Gentlemen-Bishops*, 34–45.

22 USPG, C/CAN/Pre, no. 68, Rev. Walter Price to the secretary, USPG, 25 Oct. 1784.

23 O'Donel to Bishop Plessis, 12 May 1799, in Byrne, *Gentlemen-Bishops*, 162–3; see Lahey, *James Louis O'Donel*, 25, 31–2, and "James Louis O'Donel," *Dictionary of Canadian Biography* (DCB), V: *1801–1820* (Toronto: University of Toronto Press 1983), 631–4.

24 See Lahey, *James Louis O'Donel*, 9–10; and Rollmann, "Religious Enfranchisement," 46.

25 See O'Donel to Bishop Troy, 30 Nov. 1786, in Byrne, *Gentlemen-Bishops*, 58–61; Lahey, *James Louis O'Donel*, 12–13; Lahey, "Edmund Burke," DCB, V: 122–3.

26 See Byrne, *Gentlemen-Bishops*, 69–104; and Lahey, *James Louis O'Donel*, 14–20.

27 See O'Donel to Archbishop Troy, 8 Dec. 1791, in Byrne, *Gentlemen-Bishops*, 115–17.

28 O'Donel to Troy, 28 Nov. [1794], ibid., 125–7; Archives of the Archdiocese of St John's (AASJ), Howley Papers, Sacred Congregation *de Propaganda Fide* (SCPF) transcripts, Edmund Burke et al. to the pope, 20 Nov. 1794, and Troy to Cardinal Antonelli, 10 Jan. 1795. See also Lahey, *James Louis O'Donel*, 23–4.

29 In the second edition of *A Pastoral Instruction on the Duties of Christian Citizens* (1793); see S.J. Connolly, *Priests and People in Pre-Famine Ireland: 1780–1845* (London and New York: Gill and Macmillan and St Martin's Press 1982), 223–4.

30 Howley Papers, SCPF transcripts, Erskine to Cardinal Giacinto Gerdil, 21 July 1795.

31 See, for example, Jean Hamelin and Michel Paquin, "Pierre Denaut," *DCB*, V:246.

32 AASJ, O'Donel Papers, certificate of consecration.

33 PRO, WO, 1/18, fols. 193–7, and CO 194/33, fols. 189–98, Skerrett to the Duke of Kent, 30 April 1800, and Skerrett to Lord Pelham, 22 Sept. 1801.

34 O'Donel to Bishop Plessis, 12 May 1799, and also 14 May 1800, in Byrne, *Gentlemen-Bishops*, 160–3, 171–3.

35 On O'Donel and the United Irish mutiny see Lahey, *James Louis O'Donel*, 25–8.

36 AASJ, O'Donel Papers, diocesan statutes, 2 Aug. 1801.

37 PRO, CO 194/44, fols. 14–15, Gower to Lord Camden, 25 Oct. 1804. Referring to the Catholic church, Gower also spoke of the "attachment of its ministers to the Government"; PRO, CO 194/45, fols. 20–38, Explanatory Observations on the Return, 1804.

38 PRO, CO 195/16, 115–17, Lord Camden to Gower, 20 March 1805.

39 PRO, CO 194/45, fols. 20–38, Explanatory Observations on the Return, 1804.

40 PRO, CO 195/16, 63–4, John Sullivan to Governor Gambier, 1 May 1804.

41 See, for example, Newfoundland Civil Establishment Return, House of Commons, 12 June 1828, which lists expenses from 1823–7; PRO, CO 194/77, fols. 6–8.

42 PRO, CO 194/49, fol. 3, Holloway to the Earl of Liverpool, 26 March 1810. Tremlett and Chief Justice Colclough of Prince Edward Island changed places in 1813; see J.M. Bumsted and K. Matthews, "Thomas Tremlett," *DCB*, VI: *1821–1835* (Toronto: University of Toronto Press 1987), 784–6.

43 PRO, CO 194/45, fols. 5–6, Gower to Lord Castlereagh, 31 Jan. 1806.

44 O'Donel to Pope Pius VII, 15 July 1804, in Byrne, *Gentlemen-Bishops*, 217–19.

45 PRO, CO 194/44, fols. 201–2, Gower to Lord Castlereagh, 28 Nov. 1805.

46 See Lahey, "Patrick Lambert," DCB, V: 473–4.

47 PRO, CO 194/49, fols. 36–46, Governor Duckworth to Lord Liverpool, 25 Nov. 1810; PRO, CO 194/51, fols. 95–8, Privy Council minutes, 24 June 1811.

48 PRO, CO 194/55, fol. 73, Public Accounts, 1814; see PRO CO 195/17, 22–8, Lord Bathurst to Governor Keats. Lambert's "loyalty and patriotism" during the American war was acknowledged by the principal inhabitants in 1815; see Byrne, *Gentlemen-Bishops*, 292. The pension to O'Donel had been to "the Rev. Dr. O'Donnel Romish Clergyman at St. John's in consideration of his important and patriotic services"; PRO, CO 195/16, 125–6, Sir George Shee to Governor Gower, 31 March 1806.

49 See John S. Moir, ed., *Church and State in Canada, 1627–1867: Basic Documents*, Carleton Library (Toronto: McClelland and Stewart 1967), 128–36. Plessis, like his predecessors, had previously received a stipend, but only as "Superintendent of the Romish Church."

50 The official figures show 11,576 immigrants in this period, but are almost certainly low. For example, for 1815 the official figure was 4039, but Governor Keats estimated it at over 6000; see PRO CO 194/56, fols. 105–13, Keats to Lord Bathurst, 10 Nov. 1815.

51 See, for example, the maps in Robert McCrum et al., *The Story of English* (New York: Viking 1986), 170–1.

52 PRO, ADM 80/151, 1–12, 14–15, 16–19, Chief Justice Colclough to Governor Keats, 21 March 1815, Governor Keats to Lord Bathurst, 23 May 1815, Chief Justice Colclough to Henry Goulburn, 22 March 1815; PRO, CO 194/56, fols. 173–5, 45–6, 51–2, Chief Justice Colclough to Governor Keats, 19 March and 6 May 1815, Governor Keats to Lord Bathurst, 12 Aug. 1815. See also Raymond J. Lahey, "John Power," DCB, VI: 613–14.

53 See PRO, CO 194/56, fol. 26, and ADM 80/151, 16–19, Governor Keats to Lord Bathurst, 18 Dec. 1813, and Chief Justice Colclough to Henry Goulburn, 22 March 1815. In reference to Power, a letter of 1812 says that "[Father Philip] Larissy is sent there [Harbour Grace] to speak Irish & quell the mutiny"; the Rev. Thomas Scallan to the Rev. Richard (Francis) Walsh, 22 Dec. 1812, in Hans Rollmann, "Gentlemen-Bishops and Faction Fighters: Additional Letters pertaining to Newfoundland Catholicism from the Franciscan Library in Killiney (Ireland)," *Journal of the Canadian Church Historical Society* 30 (April 1988): 8–10.

54 See PRO, CO 194/57, fols. 132–8, and 194/81, fol. 129, Governor Pickmore to Lord Bathurst, 11 Dec. 1816, and Emigrants to Newfoundland. In 1817, 1818, and 1819, immigration was only 118, 110, and

184, respectively. From 1820 to 1830, however, it returned to a somewhat higher level, averaging over 1000 per year.

55 PRO, CO 194/56, fol. 187, Chief Justice Colclough to Lord Bathurst, 30 March 1815.

56 See Raymond J. Lahey, "Thomas Scallan," DCB, VI: 690–4.

57 PRO, CO 194/56, fol. 187, Chief Justice Colclough to Lord Bathurst, 30 March 1815. Edmund Burke (not the priest of the same name formerly at Placentia) was then vicar-general of the bishop of Quebec and parish priest of Halifax; he became the first vicar-apostolic of Nova Scotia in 1817. See R.A. MacLean, "Edmund Burke," DCB, V: 123–5.

58 Anonymous letter forwarded to Bathurst by Josiah Butterworth [St John's], 4 Nov. 1817, PRO, CO 194/61, fols. 276–7; see also PRO, CO 194/66, fol. 178, Scallan to Sir Charles Hamilton, 22 Oct. 1823. The author of the former letter was likely the Rev. James Sabine, a Congregational clergyman; see James Sabine, *A View of the Moral State of Newfoundland with Particular Reference to the Present State of Religious Toleration in the Island* (Boston 1818), 28–9.

59 See Lahey, "Thomas Scallan," DCB, VI: 691–2.

60 Scallan to Bishop Plessis, 3 Sept. 1818, in Byrne, *Gentlemen-Bishops*, 316–17.

61 PRO, CO 194/62, fols. 143–4, 141, CO 194/66, fols. 178, 166 ff, Scallan to Governor Hamilton, 12 Oct. 1819, Hamilton to Lord Bathurst, 9 Nov. 1819, Scallan to Governor Hamilton, 22 Oct. 1823, Governor Hamilton to Lord Bathurst, 28 Nov. 1823. On Ontario see J.E. Rea, "Alexander McDonnell," DCB, VII: *1836–1850* (Toronto: University of Toronto Press 1988), 546–7, and Franklin Walker, *Catholic Education and Politics in Upper Canada: A Study of the Documentation Relative to the Origin of Catholic Elementary Schools in the Ontario School System*, 3 vols. (Toronto: J.M. Dent 1955), I, 25–8.

62 See Morris, *Remarks*, 19.

63 PRO, CO 194/77, fols. 6–8, Newfoundland Civil Establishment Return, 12 June 1828.

64 Its religious policies were equivocal. Although it maintained the premise that its teachers should always be members of the Church of England, its organizers included dissenters from that church, and in Newfoundland it set up its schools in direct opposition even to Anglican schools operated by the Society for the Propagation of the Gospel. See, for example, *An Account of the State of the Schools in the Island of Newfoundland established or assisted by the Society for the Propagation of the Gospel in Foreign Parts* (London: United Society for the Propagation of the Gospel 1827), 3–11. Governor Hamilton wrote to Sir Robert Wilmot Horton that "the most Strenuous Members of the

[Newfoundland School] Society are Dissenters from the Present Episcopal Establishment," 5 July 1824, PRO, CO 194/67, fol. 125.

65 PRO, CO 194/75, fols. 68–9, *Newfoundland School Society*, (London 1827).

66 See Morris, *Remarks*, 20, 42–3, and PRO, CO 194/83, fol. 12ff, Chief
Justice Tucker to Lord Goderich, 24 Jan. 1832.

67 In this he followed the policy of the Irish episcopate in dealing with
similar schools established there. See Rev. William Herron to Bishop
Plessis, 21 Dec. 1824, in Byrne, *Gentlemen-Bishops*, 338–42; see also a
circular letter from Cardinal Somaglia to Scallan, 5 Aug. 1820, AASJ,
Scallan papers. This letter apparently was translated and sent to all
priests.

68 See, for example, *Proposals for Instituting a Society for the Establishment
and Support of Schools in Newfoundland*, ([?], 1823), and PRO, CO 194/66,
fols. 243, 307–8, Samuel Codner to Lord Bathurst, 14 April 1823.

69 See PRO, CO 194/66, fols. 182–5, Patrick Morris to Governor Hamilton,
12 Oct. 1823, and Michael Anthony Fleming, *Relazione della missione
cattolica in Terranuova nell'America settentrionale* (Rome 1837), 8ff.

70 Fleming, *Relazione*, 8ff.

71 PRO, CO 194/66, fol. 166ff, CO 194/71, fols. 292–3, 290–1, Governor
Hamilton to Lord Bathurst, 28 Nov. 1823, Patrick Morris to Lord Bathurst, 16 Oct. 1823 and 29 March 1825.

72 PRO, CO 194/83, fol. 12ff, Tucker to Lord Goderich, 24 Jan. 1832, 1;
PRO, CO 195/18, 50–1, Lord Goderich to Tucker, 2 May 1832.

73 Nfld. 6 Wm. IV, cap. 13, "An Act for the Encouragement of Education
in this Colony."

74 See Moir, ed., *Church and State*, 58–64, 140–9.

75 PRO, CO 194/53, fols. 79–80, law officers of the crown to the Earl of
Liverpool, 11 May 1812.

76 On Marriages in Newfoundland [1817?], USPG, C/CAN/NFL 2, no. 222;
the author was the Rev. David Rowland; see also Petition of the Protestant Dissenters of Conception Bay to the King [1824?], PRO, CO 194/68,
fol. 476.

77 PRO, CO 194/52, fols. 14–15, and CO 194/53, fols. 79–80, Governor
Duckworth to the Earl of Liverpool, 14 April 1812, and law officers of
the crown to the Earl of Liverpool, 11 May 1812.

78 See USPG, C/CAN/NFL 2, no. 222, On Marriages in Newfoundland
[1817?], PRO, CO 194/59, fols. 1–3, Governor Pickmore to Lord Bathurst, 7 Jan. 1817, and Sabine, *Moral State of Newfoundland*, 12–16.

79 PRO, CO 194/59, fols. 1–3, CO 194/60, fols. 59–62, 63, Governor Pickmore to Lord Bathurst, 7 Jan. 1817, law officers of the crown to Lord
Bathurst, 4 Feb. 1817, Christopher Robinson to Lord Bathurst, 3 March
1817.

80 Sabine, *Moral State of Newfoundland*, 19.

81 Some English Methodists had their say about it, but without effect, except to have its operation postponed for several months.

82 No Presbyterian clergy were then in Newfoundland.

83 PRO, CO 194/68, fol. 112ff, Sir James Stephen to Sir Robert Wilmot Horton, 12 March 1824.

84 PRO, CO 194/69, fols. 500–1, Rev. John Bell to Josiah Butterworth, 3 Feb. 1823.

85 PRO, CO 194/61, fols. 276–7, unsigned extract of a letter from [Rev. James Sabine?] to [Josiah Butterworth?], 4 Nov. 1817. See n. 58.

86 Continued Carson: "where there exists no exclusive privilege or emolument, no invidious distinction, religious animosity will with difficulty be excited, and could not be long supported, but create them and immediately all those passions which demons are said to possess will be engendered in the breasts of the Holy Disputants." PRO, CO 194/60, fols. 130–42, William Carson to Lord Bathurst, 8 Feb. 1817.

87 PRO, CO 194/69, fols. 500–1, 498, Rev. John Bell to Josiah Butterworth, 3 Feb. 1823, and Josiah Butterworth to Sir Robert Wilmot Horton, 5 Feb. 1823.

88 PRO, CO 194/69, fols. 57–8, Sir Francis Forbes, Remarks upon the Objections of His Excellency Sir Charles Hamilton to the Newfoundland Bill and Mr. Butterworth's clauses upon Marriages in Newfoundland, 8 March 1823. Forbes's original sketch of the bill (undated) contained nothing on marriages; see PRO, CO 194/69, fol. 121ff.

89 PRO, CO 194/66, fol. 345ff. An Act for the better Administration of Justice in Newfoundland … House of Commons, 10 July 1823.

90 PRO, CO 194/69, fol. 506, Petition of the Roman Catholics of Newfoundland to the House of Commons [presented 23 March 1824]; see also PRO, CO 194/67, fols. 88–94, 258ff, Memorial of the Roman Catholic Clergy and Laity of St John's, 27 Oct. 1823, and the Petition of the Roman Catholics of Newfoundland to H.M. the King, 10 June 1824.

91 PRO, CO 194/67, fol. 123, Governor Hamilton to Lord Bathurst, 27 Feb. 1824.

92 This revision was first contained in the House of Lords version, An Act for the Better Administration of Justice in Newfoundland, and for making further Provision for the Solemnization of Marriage … 9 April 1824, PRO CO 194/69, fol. 382ff, and was continued in all subsequent drafts.

93 USPG, C/CAN/NFL 3, no. 287, Rev. John Burt to the secretary of the USPG, 12 Jan. 1824.

94 PRO, CO 194/69, fol. 19ff, and CO 194/68, fol. 112ff, Sir James Stephen to Sir Robert Wilmot Horton, 24 April 1823 and 12 March 1824.

95 This wording appeared in the draft as reported from the Committee in the House of Commons, 21 May 1824, An Act to repeal an Act passed

in the 57th Year of his late Majesty King George the Third, intitled ... PRO, CO 194/69, fol. 377ff.

96 PRO, CO 194/68, fol. 229, Josiah Butterworth to Sir Robert Wilmot Horton, 7 May 1824.

97 5 Geo. IV, c. 68.

98 Italics added.

99 PRO, CO 194/68, fols. 232, 234, Josiah Butterworth to Sir Robert Wilmot Horton, 27 and 28 May 1824; see also the draft as reported from the Committee in the House of Commons, 21 May 1824, PRO, CO 194/69, fol. 377ff, An Act to repeal an Act passed in the 57th Year of his late Majesty King George the Third, intitled ... and PRO, CO 194/69, fol. 372ff, the House of Commons bill of the same title, 31 May 1824, which omitted the provisions in question.

100 It is not surprising that one of the first projects of the new House of Assembly in 1833 was a further Marriage Act, which finally gave Methodist clergy the same rights as were enjoyed by the ministers of other denominations. It is significant that the new law had the strong support of Bishop Fleming.

101 See PRO, CO 194/68, fol. 112ff, Sir James Stephen to Sir Robert Wilmot Horton, 12 March 1824.

102 See PRO, CO 194/72, fols. 136–7, and CO 194/70, fols. 153–4, Minutes of Council, 8 Oct. 1825, and Governor Cochrane to Lord Bathurst, 11 Oct. 1825.

103 PRO, CO 194/70, fol. 252ff, Governor Cochrane to Lord Bathurst, 29 Dec. 1825. The council would also have included two Anglican clergy, the archdeacon of Newfoundland, George Coster, whom Cochrane had proposed, and Bishop Inglis of Nova Scotia, who held a royal *mandamus* entitling him to a seat. PRO, CO 195/17, 202–3.

104 PRO, CO 195/17, 225–6, 231–2, Bathurst to Cochrane, 8 Feb. and 10 April 1826. See also PRO, CO 194/73, fols. 142–3, Sir James Stephen to Sir Robert Wilmot Horton, 6 Jan. 1826.

105 PRO, CO 194/76, fols. 221–2, 219–20, Patrick Morris to Governor Cochrane, 2 April 1828, and Governor Cochrane to William Huskisson, 11 April 1828.

106 PRO, CO 194/76, fols. 221–2, Patrick Morris to Governor Cochrane, 2 April 1828.

107 See PRO, CO 194/76, fols. 219–20, Governor Cochrane to William Huskisson, 11 April 1828, and CO 195/17, 321–2, Robert Hay to Governor Cochrane, 17 April 1828. Hay, the undersecretary, simply acknowledged Cochrane's dispatch on Huskisson's behalf, with no comment whatever.

108 Not only had Lord Bathurst, colonial secretary since 1812, been replaced by Lord Goderich and then by Huskisson, but Wilmot

Horton, the undersecretary and the power behind the scenes, had been forced to resign. See Phillip Buckner, "The Colonial Office and British North America, 1801–50," DCB, VIII, xxvii–xxx.

109 See Gearóid Ó Tuathaigh, *Ireland before the Famine 1798–1848*, Gill History of Ireland (Dublin and London: Gill and Macmillan 1972), 70–3.

110 *Newfoundlander*, 14 and 28 May 1829; *Public Ledger*, 22 May and 5 June 1829.

111 PRO, CO 194/78, fols. 259–60, 261ff, James Simms, AG, to Captain Bruce, 17 Dec. 1829, and Tucker, CJ, Des Barres and Brenton, JJ, to Governor Cochrane, 21 Dec. 1829.

112 See Moir, ed., *Church and State*, 64–7, and Edgar Godin, "Etablissement de l'Eglise Catholique au Nouveau-Brunswick," La Société Canadienne d'Histoire de l'Eglise Catholique, *Sessions d'Etude* 48 (1981): 49.

113 PRO, CO 194/80, fols. 405–6, Chief Justice Tucker to Robert Hay, 24 May 1830.

114 *Newfoundlander*, 31 Dec. 1829, and 28 Jan. 1830; PRO, CO 194/80, fol. 376, Petition of the Roman Catholic Inhabitants of St John's to Parliament [1830]; PRO CO 194/80, fols. 280–1, Patrick Morris to Robert Hay, 2 March 1830.

115 PRO, CO 194/78, fols. 257–8, Governor Cochrane to Sir George Murray, 22 Dec. 1829, and CO 194/80, Chief Justice Tucker to Robert Hay, 24 May 1830.

116 PRO, CO 195/17, 390–1, Sir George Murray to Governor Cochrane, 20 March 1830. See CO 194/80, fols. 280–1, Sir James Stephen to Robert Hay, 1 March 1830 (with a note that an instruction had been prepared as Stephen had suggested on 3 March).

117 PRO, CO 194/81, fols. 121–3, Governor Cochrane to Robert Hay, 9 May 1831; see ibid., fol. 283, Bishop Fleming to Lord Goderich [1831?].

118 PRO, CO 194/82, fol. 234, Thomas Spring-Rice to Robert Hay, 27 Dec. 1831.

119 PRO, CO 194/83, fol. 12ff, Chief Justice Tucker to Lord Goderich, 24 Jan. 1832.

120 PRO, CO 195/18, 50–1, Lord Goderich to Chief Justice Tucker, 2 May 1832.

121 PRO, CO 194/83, fol. 217ff, Governor Cochrane to Lord Goderich, 20 Sept. 1832.

122 Gunn, *Political History of Newfoundland*, 203.

123 Ibid., 3–4, 11.

124 PRO, CO 194/85, fol. 30, Governor Cochrane to Lord Goderich, 3 Jan. 1833.

125 *Public Ledger*, 21 Sept. 1832.

126 PRO, CO 194/92, fols. 91–8, Bishop Fleming to Cardinal Capaccini (extracts), 13 June 1835.

127 PRO, CO 194/92, fols. 91–103, Bishop Fleming to Cardinal Capaccini, 13 June 1835; see also Raymond J. Lahey, "Michael Anthony Fleming," *DCB*, VII, 292–3.

128 D.W. Prowse, *A History of Newfoundland from the English, Colonial and Foreign Records* (London: Macmillan 1895), 430.

129 Statistics have been compiled by the present author, using E.R. Seary, *Family Names of the Island of Newfoundland* (St John's: Memorial University of Newfoundland 1977), as a sample. For the Irish whose county of origin is recorded by Seary and who are known to have been in Newfoundland before 1800, 62 per cent came from Munster and 35 per cent from Leinster. For those first recorded in Newfoundland between 1800 and 1815 the figures are respectively 51 per cent and 43 per cent, and for the period from 1816 to 1830, 43 per cent and 52 per cent. More complete figures, but for the whole period from 1790 to 1850, show Munster immigrants at 44 per cent and those from Leinster at 52 per cent; see John J. Mannion, "Irish Migrations to Newfoundland" (unpublished lecture, Newfoundland Historical Society, 23 Oct. 1973), 3.

130 *Public Ledger*, 10 Sept. 1832. Carson had said also: "The very venerable clergyman is a young man, by what prostitution of patronage he could arrive at so high a dignity i [sic] can have no conception." Ibid., 28 Aug. 1832.

131 *Newfoundlander*, 1 Nov. 1832.

132 Morris himself may have had just the opposite effect. See John J. Mannion, "Patrick Morris," *DCB*, VII: 630–1.

133 The first census to subdivide the Protestant population into Church of England members and Dissenters, that of 1836, showed Anglicans as 35 per cent of the total population. Roman Catholics were 51 per cent, and Dissenters, 14 per cent. See Gunn, *Political History of Newfoundland*, 206.

4 Scottish Catholicism in Canada, 1770–1845

J.M. BUMSTED

The history of religion in Canada before Confederation is sufficiently fragmented for central themes to be often lost in a maze of regional, local, and biographical studies. Scattered work is seldom put together, despite its need for synthesis, and the development of Roman Catholicism in early Canada is no exception.[1] Many of the limitations to our understanding of early Canadian Catholic history are themselves common to colonial Canadian society. The Catholic church in early Canada is principally associated with one region (Quebec) and one cultural constellation (French Canadian), to the overall neglect of its own minorities. There were, of course, from the beginning, francophone Catholics outside central Canada and, by the middle of the eighteenth century, Catholics from the British Isles (not all of them anglophone) were moving westward as the course of British emigration and settlement penetrated the heart of the continent.

One of the most stubborn and persistent groups of minority Catholics were those of Scottish origin, particularly from the Highland region of Scotland. These people, chiefly Gaelic-speaking as they departed from their homeland, congregated in three regions of British North America: the Island of St John (or Prince Edward Island after 1798), the Island of Cape Breton and eastern Nova Scotia, and the southeastern district of Upper Canada around Glengarry and Stormont counties. Most Canadians tend to associate the Scots with their "national" Presbyterian church, with all its nineteenth-century schisms and divisions, overlooking the fact that many of the Highlanders retained their Catholic faith and customs – and their Gaelic language – in both Scotland and British North America in the face of considerable difficulties. This study attempts to trace the early history of Scottish Catholicism as both a transatlantic and a British North American phenomenon. To a considerable extent we are dealing not simply with the confessional dimensions of the history of a collectively substantial group of immigrants to British North America, but with their struggles to retain their traditional identity in the New World. The trials and tribulations of early Scottish Catholics are not synonymous with those of early Highland immigrants to British North America, but the story of the latter can hardly be understood without full knowledge of the former. As is often the case, religious and ethnic identities have been inseparable, a point worth emphasizing in the present secular age.

For Scottish Catholics in British North America, the maintenance of faith and identity was attempted against many obstacles, some of which were inherent in the emigration and settlement of early Canada and others peculiar to their situation. All emigrants felt the loss of support from their traditional institutions in their homeland, for example, but for Scottish Catholics emigration was especially difficult. Highland Catholic communities were poor and isolated, their mother church was especially disadvantaged by conditions at home that made it difficult to provide continuing support to those communicants departing Scotland, and the new ecclesiastical authorities understood neither their language nor their customs. Scottish Catholics quickly found themselves neglected by the Scottish Catholic church and caught – both linguistically and culturally – between the dominant francophone Catholicism of the vast majority of the inhabitants of British North America and the rapid growth of anglophone Irish Catholic immigration. The result was twofold and seemingly contradictory: first, their church could not in the short run serve as the protector of their language and identity, which led to some losses to larger assimilative processes; and, second, the church in some areas ultimately was able to assume a central role, less because of its outreach than because of the stubborn insistence by the unassimilated population that it had to provide that function. The survival of Scottish Catholicism owed far less to ecclesiastical authority from above than to the individual and collective efforts of priests and their congregations. The Scottish Catholic community often operated under serious disadvantages in finding a clerical leadership, much less maintaining it.

In the process of seeking to survive in the New World, Scottish Catholicism was forced to assume a new role of political leadership within the framework of the ecclesiastical administration of the church in British North America. Scottish Catholic priests led the way in the dismemberment of the control of the Quebec church over the ecclesiastical affairs of the other colonies through the establishment of new dioceses, which they dominated in a political sense until the early 1840s. A substantial impetus for Scottish leadership in this arena was the perception on the part of its priests that Scottish Catholics in North America had to be served by clergymen who understood both their language and their customs, which in turn required the establishment of appropriate local educational facilities sympathetic to Scottish Catholic traditions. The clerical leadership among the Scottish Catholics was profoundly conservative in all senses of the term. It fully supported the existing British political authorities and system in the colonies in which it was active, even when both authorities and system came under attack from reformist forces in the 1820s and 1830s. Equally important, while it sought internal change within the North American church structure, it did so in order to preserve the traditional ways of its communicants in both religious and secular terms. Not surprisingly, its efforts at conservation were in their own way transforming and dynamic rather than simply conservative. Replicating the old ways in the New World required a leadership of adaptive ingenuity as much as mere traditionalism.

The history of Scottish Catholicism in British North America is complex, yet a few major strands of that history can be identified for analysis. One of those strands is the situation of the mother church in Scotland itself and its relationship with the growing diaspora of its communicants to the northern British colonies. Another is the nature and development of British emigration to and settlement in British North America, particularly on the part of the Scots and the Irish. Related to this theme is a constant current of mutual hostility between Scots and Irish, both layfolk and clergy, which expressed itself in political terms within the church and in the larger society. A third strand is the complicated response of the Quebec church to the growing problems of Catholics in other colonies, and especially to the increasing numbers of Catholics of Scottish origin. Finally, there is the emergence of an articulate and increasingly powerful cadre of clerical leaders of Scottish Catholics in British North America, principally Angus MacEachern in Prince Edward Island, Alexander Macdonell in Upper Canada, and William Fraser in Nova Scotia.

To understand the position of Scottish Catholics in British North America, we must begin with the mother church in Scotland itself. The situation of the Scottish Catholic church changed dramatically between 1770 and 1830, the principal years of emigration of Scottish

Catholics to British North America. The change was a result of a combination of factors: the emigration to America itself, the French Revolution, and the appearance in Scotland of thousands of Irish Catholics after 1790. The status of the Scottish church shifted from one of informal underground toleration to government acceptance. Its communicants altered from a large Gaelic-speaking Highland base to a generally diffused Lowland English-speaking Irish majority. What did not change, however, was an overall atmosphere of poverty on the part of both communicants and the church itself. Both the changes and the lack of them in crucial areas had a significant influence on Scottish Catholics in British North America.[2]

The most striking feature of the Scottish Catholic church over most of the eighteenth century was its survival in the face of substantial anti-Catholicism and persecution. Catholicism had been under public attack since 1560, when the Scottish Parliament had cut ties with Rome and forbade the celebration of Mass. Catholic connections with France and the somewhat unfair association of Catholicism and Jacobitism actually increased penal laws at the opening of the eighteenth century. The failure of the "Forty Five" meant "pacification" of the Highlands for Protestants and Catholics alike. The government shifted after 1745 from a policy of open persecution of Catholicism to a more subtle program of integrating the Highlands into the kingdom, in which the ancient clan chieftains were converted into proper British-style landholders and encouraged to reform their estates.[3]

The new winds of "improvement" set in motion the emigration from the Highlands, partly within the British Isles but also to British North America. British efforts to use Highlanders' martial skills to produce the shock troops of empire – Highland regiments were well represented at the Plains of Abraham – familiarized Highland military officers with North America. The Scottish Catholic bishops themselves estimated that 6000 Highland communicants had served in the British army between 1756 and 1763. After the return of peace, thousands of Highlanders, Protestant and Catholic alike, departed for the New World.[4] Most were driven less by religious than by economic and social factors. Ironically enough, the emigrations were opposed by the reforming lairds, who feared the loss of a labour force. One case of religious persecution against Highland Catholics stands out from the period between the end of the Seven Years' War and the onset of the American Revolution. It involved an attempt by a young laird, Colin MacDonald of Boysdale on South Uist, to force his Catholic tenantry to accept Protestant schooling. The Scottish Catholic church decided to use the landholders' fear of emigration as a weapon against Boysdale. In collaboration with a young tacksman, John MacDonald of Glenaladale, it mounted a scheme to find a religious refuge for persecuted Highland Catholics in British North America, ultimately locating the colony on the remote Island of St John.[5]

Several features of the complex manoeuvring that surrounded the St John's project are important to our story, for they anticipated subsequent themes and developments. In the first place, the Scottish church was impoverished and was able to raise funds (chiefly in London) for the proposed emigration only with great difficulty. Second, the leaders of the church were less concerned with religious refuge per se than with using it as a strategy to end persecution at home; in this respect their policy was successful. Third, ethnicity became involved in several contexts. The emigrants opposed the involvement of an Irish priest who volunteered to accompany them, preferring one of their own people recruited from the thin ranks of Highland missioners. The Scottish bishops recognized that the settlement would be within the jurisdiction of the bishop of Quebec and attempted to gain permission from Rome to allow it to remain subject to the Scottish church. The rejection by Rome of Scottish jurisdiction meant that Highland emigrants to St John's – and to other colonies in British North America – would be totally lost to an embattled national church. Increasingly the church came to view emigration with a jaundiced eye, removing communicants and requiring priests much needed at home to serve them, while producing no commensurate advantages. The demand for Gaelic-speaking priests, which obviously could be best supplied from Scotland, was a constant feature of Highland Catholicism in America for the next half-century.

The Scottish church managed to increase substantially the numbers of Highland priests in the course of the eighteenth century. That success was made possible chiefly by the creation of an autonomous Highland Vicariate in 1731, which was part of a division of Scotland into a mainly Gaelic-speaking Highland district and an English-speaking Lowland district. In the wake of autonomy, the Highland district instituted local seminaries for the preparation of priests, which meant that for most of the eighteenth century intending priests were educated initially in the region before being sent off to Scots colleges in Spain, France, and Rome to complete their education. The eighteenth-century Highland bishops were all related to the clan chieftains. The first three Highland bishops were MacDonalds, and a full 75 per cent of the eighteenth-century Highland priests locally produced were also from MacDonald clans, including three MacEacherns. The Highland priesthood was thus closely integrated into the traditional Highland clan system, and was also bound by complex kinship ties that would be carried over into the New World.

The French Revolution had a significant impact on the Scottish church in a number of ways. Much of the church's revenue was derived from French holdings, and many Scots Catholics were educated in Scottish colleges in France. The anti-clerical hostility to Catholicism during the revolutionary era in France resulted in the confiscation of Scottish Catholic property in 1793, producing a financial crisis for the church. It also frightened Catholics everywhere. The authorities in Britain were equally alarmed by the French Revolution, which threatened to destroy the existing fabric of social and economic relationships. In such a climate, the Scottish church needed revenue at the same time that the British government needed institutional supporters. As a result, the church found itself no longer a clandestine underground operation threatened with imminent persecution, but an organization positively courted by the British authorities. In 1797 the British government and the Scottish church came to a formal understanding, by which the authorities provided subsidies for the Scottish clergy and their educational activities. Scottish Catholicism, particularly in the Highlands, had always been traditional and conservative in its attitudes, the result of the close connections of its leadership with the ancient clan system. By the end of the eighteenth century, it had discovered it could come to terms with the British government; as one scholar has observed, "the Revolutionary and Napoleonic Wars turned the Scottish Roman Catholic clergy into British agents as well as allies of the British Government."[6] For many reasons, Highland priests in British North America had traditional and conservative attitudes, and they shared with their Scottish counterparts an inclination to cooperate with the British authorities and to support opposition to reformist tendencies that might threaten the status quo.

The relationship between Scotland and Ireland, as well as between the Scottish and Irish branches of the Catholic church, was always complex and problematic. Scottish Protestants had been used as colonists by the English authorities as part of their policy of displacing indigenous Irish, particularly in the northern districts of Ulster. In general, no love was lost between Scots and Irish, and there was no positive collaboration between persecuted Irish and Scottish Catholics. The first regiment of Highland Catholics recruited for service within the British Isles, partially organized by Father Alexander Macdonell (later bishop of Upper Canada), was employed in Ireland at the end of the eighteenth century in a brutal suppression of an Irish rebellion. While Macdonell deplored the brutality, he did not question the need for suppression.[7] Scottish priests had a long tradition of suspicion of their Irish counterparts, whom they regarded as unstable and unprincipled. It was true that many footloose Irish priests travelled because of trouble in their homeland. In the Highlands, where many Irish priests had found employment in the days before the creation of a local priesthood, there was much criticism of the Irishmen, often for their inability to speak Gaelic and to understand the traditional clan system. Not all the hostility of the Scots was directed at Irish Catholics. One Scottish priest on Prince Edward Island complained of the Protestant Irishmen active there, calling them "Harpies" operating for "their own greedy oppressive and destructive ends."[8]

From the standpoint of the Scottish church, Irish Catholicism was not merely a matter of the nationality of priests. Irish people began immigrating to the west of Scotland in substantial numbers by the end of the eighteenth century, greatly increasing the number of Catholic communicants that had to be served. As Scottish Catholics moved out of the Highlands to British North America, Irish Catholics moved into the western Lowlands in equal or greater numbers. The Irish leadership in Scotland began demanding their own institutions, but from the standpoint of the Scottish church the Irish represented an additional population that must be served out of limited resources. The attention of Scottish Catholicism was in part deflected from its population emigrating to British North America to its own internal needs by this Irish influx. In any event, the Scottish church, which had earlier seen emigration as a possible solution for persecution, by the end of the eighteenth century no longer feared for its existence. It had its own problems and had little inclination to exert itself to support Catholics who had departed out of its jurisdiction. The correspondence of Scottish Catholic priests in British North America, particularly before 1815, recited a constant litany of their inability to get needed assistance from home. "I received a letter last night from Bishop Cameron of Edinburgh," wrote Angus MacEachern to Quebec in 1805, "but [he] does not promise to send us any clergymen. He even complains of the scarcity of Highland Priests at home with th[em]."[9] According to Captain John MacDonald in 1806, writing to the Highland bishop of Scotland, "we were still a virtual part of the Mission, being Scape Goats sent helpless." Given this lack of encouragement, it was small wonder that Scottish Catholics would be forced to turn to their own resources, especially when they found Quebec equally unable to assist them.

If the situation of Scottish Catholicism in British North America must be understood in light of developments in the church of the mother country, so, too, the patterns of British emigration to the

American colonies, particularly after the American Rebellion, must be considered. In 1763 virtually all Roman Catholics in British North America (with the exception of a few thousand Irish in Newfoundland, an unknown number of Acadians, and a handful in the southern British colonies) were French-speaking residents of Quebec, as the British had come to call New France. By the middle of the nineteenth century there were substantial numbers of non-francophone Catholics in every province of British North America, most of them of Scottish Highland and Irish origin. The Highlanders had come first to most provinces. The first group of Highland emigrations, completed around 1815, were by relatively well-off tenants from the western Highlands and islands, who were driven out of Scotland less by clearance than by vacating of their own volition ahead of it. For the most part they paid their own passage to America, thus requiring a substantial amount of capital. A disproportionate number of these early emigrants were Gaelic-speaking Roman Catholics. These early movements established the colonies of preference for Highland Scots as Prince Edward Island, eastern Nova Scotia and Cape Breton, and southeastern Upper Canada.[11] The second group of emigrations, coming after 1815, was less voluntary and more the result of overt pressure by landlords. While typical emigrants were less prosperous after 1815, they required less capital, because timber vessels were now prepared to carry emigrants to America in preference to ballast and fares ran relatively low.[12]

By 1840 the Highland Catholic emigration had pretty well spent itself but had already been replaced by an Irish Catholic emigration of even greater numbers, which would swell substantially in the next decade because of the potato famine in Ireland. For the most part, particularly before the 1830s, the Irish did not follow the Scots territorially. They went to Newfoundland, to the urban seaports of Nova Scotia and New Brunswick (particularly Halifax and Saint John), to the Miramichi in New Brunswick, and to Sydney in Cape Breton. By the 1830s, however, the numbers of Irish arriving had become so substantial that it was inevitable they should filter into what had previously been Scottish areas, especially on Prince Edward Island and Cape Breton. As the last to arrive among the early British settlers, the Irish were forced to take the least desirable land, usually away from coastal access and substantially less fertile. Most Irish emigrants were no more poverty-stricken than the Highlanders, but in the districts preferred by Highlanders the Irish were later arrivals and ended up with inferior land. What was different between Irish and Highland emigration was that Highlanders tended to travel as extended families, while Irish often arrived alone.

The tiny settlement at Tracadie on the Island of St John was the first enclave of Highland Catholics in what would become Canada. It was also the only Scottish Catholic settlement established before the outbreak of the American Revolution, although substantial numbers of Highland Catholics also emigrated to upstate New York, became Loyalists during the war, and moved northward into adjacent Quebec in the early 1780s. Father James MacDonald, who had accompanied the settlers to the Island of St John in 1772, died in 1785 in isolation. He could not receive the last rites of the church, there being no other priest in the region (of any ethnic background) to administer them.[13] MacDonald's "wretchedness" was used as an excuse by Father Alexander Macdonell of Scothouse when he refused assignment to the island in 1789. Scothouse came from a good family and, after setbacks in the Highlands, accompanied a large emigration of Catholics to Upper Canada in 1786. He had refused to come with these immigrants, who joined those of the Loyalist migrations from New York, until he was properly supported financially. The people of New Johnston (Cornwall) petitioned for him in 1787, "he being the only man that understandes our Country Language." Scothouse finally went in 1792 to Glengarry, where he soon ran into much controversy, fighting with Protestants, with his Quebec superiors over usages (he wanted an amalgamation of Scottish and Quebec customs), and with his parishioners over finances and authoritarian behaviour.[14]

The next Highland Catholic emigration was to the Island of St John (Prince Edward Island) and Pictou County, Nova Scotia, in 1791. It brought Father Angus (or Aeneas) MacEachern to the region. The first Catholic settlements in Antigonish County on the mainland of Nova Scotia were established in the 1780s by disbanded soldiers from Highland regiments, while those in Cape Breton began in 1801, headed by recent arrivals at Pictou who had moved east to find cheaper land and to avoid domination by the powerful Presbyterian majority at Pictou headed by the Reverend John McGregor. Highlanders had also begun trickling into Upper Canada and were joined by Father Alexander Macdonell in 1804, replacing his namesake who had died a year earlier. The Glengarry Fencibles – a regiment largely recruited by Macdonell in the Highlands to fight in Ireland – did not emigrate to Glengarry as a body, although some of them made their way to Upper Canada.

Although the Highlanders, particularly in the Maritimes, often settled in the same regions already peopled by the Acadians, both they and the Acadians tended to remain within their own ethnic enclaves. As Bishop Joseph-Octave Plessis of Quebec observed in Prince Edward Island in 1812: "the Scots always want to live among

Scots, and the Acadians among Acadians. This consideration has often made them blind to everything else … there has not yet been any intermarriage between the two nationalities. Each nationality holds to its own customs and manners, and prefers marriages between its own nationals rather than with strangers at the risk of living in discord."[15] Because of their extreme poverty, many Irish never got beyond the urban seaport in which they landed in British North America. Even when they moved onto the land, because of their late arrival they were forced into the interior regions where the land was often marginal.

Despite their common religion, Acadians, Highlanders, and Irish were divided by language and economic lifestyle.[16] Many of the Acadians, located on the seacoasts, had become a combination of farmer and fisherman. The Highlanders were not much for fishing and tended instead to replicate their familiar agricultural pattern of livestock-raising to the detriment of extensive agriculture. Observers commented on their lack of ambition. "They are apt to be content with a condition but little beyond what they had previously enjoyed," wrote one outsider, "and do not show the same eagerness for further progress that others do."[17] Such traditionalism was particularly the case when the Highlanders were left to themselves, and most chose to be. According to John McGregor: "wherever the Highlanders form distinct settlements, their habits, their system of husbandry, disregard for comfort in their houses, their ancient hospitable customs, and their language, undergo no sensible change. They frequently pass their winter evenings reciting traditional poems in Gaelic, which have been transmitted to them by their forefathers."[18]

The Irish were equally clannish, although their farming practices were quite different from either Highlander or Acadian. Although the language of conversation of the Irish is difficult to determine, few of the Irish priests who came to British North America appear to have had any competence in Gaelic. This limitation probably did not affect their Irish parishioners, most of whom were at least bilingual, but it did matter to the Gaelic-speaking Scots. Irishman Simon Lawlor admitted from Cape Breton in 1826, "I am totally unacquainted with the Gaelic, the prevalent language of the people, and am sorry to state to your Lordship that the benefits which might have resulted from my mission as well as my discourses from the Pulpit are entirely useless, being not at all understood by my congregation." He sought a transfer to Sydney, where "the generality of the people being natives of Ireland," he would be more useful.[19] All ecclesiastical parties agreed that the best situation was one in which ethnic communities had one of their own as priest.

The relationship between Scottish Catholicism on the one hand and the church hierarchy in Quebec and French-Canadian missionaries on the other hand was both complex and ambivalent. There can be no doubt that the Quebec authorities wanted to be supportive of the Highlanders, but they had a number of problems. One was Quebec's own shortage of priests, which made it reluctant to commit itself to clerical assistance and hopeful that the Scottish church would provide. Bishop Plessis in 1809 wrote to Father Edmund Burke in Halifax: "The Scottish missions offer a frightening prospect: Mr. Macdonell alone in Upper Canada, Messrs. MacEachern and Macdonell alone in the missions of the Gulf; and no sign of any successors!!!"[20] Unable to find sufficient numbers of Highland priests, the Quebec authorities attempted to recruit in Ireland young seminarians who spoke Gaelic. Several Irishmen responded, but their linguistic skills did not measure up to their claims. Those few missionaries that Quebec was able to provide were intended in the first instance to serve the Acadians and only secondarily the Highlanders. Most of the French-Canadian priests spoke no Gaelic and their Scottish parishioners neither French nor English. As Father Antoine Gaulin of Antigonish explained his difficulties with Gaelic to his bishop in Quebec: "This language, My Lord, is so very difficult to a foreigner, that, destitute as I am of a dictionary, a grammar, and even a teacher, it would take more than ten years hearing." MacEachern was able to assert to the Propaganda at Rome in 1824, "all the missionaries in Canada are French, and they understand neither English nor Gaelic, nor are they conversant with the customs and institutions of the Scots and the Irish."[21]

If the problem had been merely linguistic, it might well have been more easily resolved. Unfortunately, there was an enormous liturgical gulf between Quebec Catholicism and the practices of the Scottish Catholics. The Quebec bishops understood and appreciated the reasons for the differences, but still had difficulty in remaining completely tolerant about them. Unlike Quebec, where Catholicism and its ritual had always been publicly acceptable – even under the British conquerors – Scottish Catholicism had long been accustomed to an underground status. All external signs of Catholicism not absolutely necessary were suppressed. Scottish priests both travelled and officiated at the sacraments without vestments and proper equipment. "Only a priest brought up in Scotland," wrote Plessis in 1812, "would ever think of celebrating the Sacred Mysteries with the trash" that he was expected to employ on Prince Edward Island.[22] Ritual was decidedly "low church," without singing and ceremony. Plessis on his 1815 tour of the Maritimes commented at Bras d'Or that "the three Scottish priests ... gave authentic proof of their incomparable awkwardness with regard to ecclesiastical customs."[23] Highlanders educated in Quebec developed a different perspective from their Scottish compatriots. Father Alexander MacLeod, who took over Bras d'Or in 1824, confessed his unhappiness with "the indifference of my poor Scots for the honour of the divine cult and the decoration of the holy place."[24] More than mere liturgical differences were often at stake, of course. Fastidious French Canadians could be distressed by Highland customs. Plessis in 1815 refused to sleep in one Highland house at Christmas Island, for fear of "a certain malady (the Itch) which is sometimes contracted in homes of Scottish people of this class."[25]

For their part, the Scottish missionaries responded by insisting that Quebec Catholicism failed to understand their problems. "You have everything regular in Canada," wrote MacEachern to Plessis in 1822. He continued: "The Clergymen, who, as a body, are the most submissive to their superiors, most orderly, and most attentive to their duty under the canopy of heaven, may sleep, if they will, every night in their beds. We must pass many nights in the woods, at the mercy of snow and rain. They have their flocks handy to their daily exhortations, and exposition of the Christian doctrine; and may every Sunday and holyday listen to their homilies on the appropriate parts of the Gospel. The reverse is sorely felt here."[26] The sense of both defensiveness and grievance in these lines is palpable.

Symptomatic of the deep divide between the Quebec authorities and their Scottish missionaries were the differing responses to troubles experienced by Maritime Highland seminarians in Quebec. The Scottish Catholics had subscribed £600, and Plessis in 1812 had agreed to accept six youngsters, two from Prince Edward Island, two from Cape Breton, and two from Nova Scotia. The Scots did not manage to keep sending sufficient funds for these young men, however, and two were actually expelled from their studies for lack of funds. Plessis took over their care, but commented in 1822, "and so their services will not be granted to Nova Scotia, which has abandoned them in this way, but to the diocese which took care of them." MacEachern's view in 1824 was quite different. He noted of the two expelled lads: "They had no friend or money, or the possibility of returning home in the winter, the Ocean frozen and no travelling by land. The Bishop put them in a small seminary of his own. One of them is now in Cape Breton; the other will be down this season. That is all that has ever been done for these outskirts, although Canada abounds in riches."[27] Eventually, both sides came to agree that full administrative separation between Quebec and the "out-skirts" was the best solution.

In the course of his campaign for autonomy, MacEachern was the most outspoken critic of Quebec. To a friend at Rome he expostulated in 1825: "What has Canada ever done for this Island since the Conquest? What provision for the Acadians in spirituals before our people arrived on the Island? And what has been done for us since?"[28] A few years later he added to the same correspondent: "Why, then in the name of almighty God are we kept hanging after *men*, who never cared about us, more than they did, or do about the Hottentots, or the Siberians? The Archbishop and his Coadjutor know nothing about these vast regions."[29] From his perspective, "Canada never raised a student as yet for this Island, altho' they do not want the means, and will not send a Canadian to serve the Acadians."[30]

Scottish (and British) Catholicism in British North America only gradually acquired leadership in the persons of Angus MacEachern, Alexander Macdonell, and William Fraser, the three nonfrancophone bishops after Edmund Burke of Nova Scotia (1818) in British North America. That Scots priests should take the lead in the devolution of the vast Quebec-centred administrative structure of the church is hardly surprising, for they represented the largest body of non-French communicants at the beginning of the nineteenth century. The three men cooperated actively together, with MacEachern serving as the bridge between Upper Canada and Nova Scotia. Macdonell and MacEachern were kinsmen and good friends, often visiting across the distances between their home bases. MacEachern had literally met Fraser at the boat when Fraser first arrived in Cape Breton in 1822, and they remained close collaborators.

All three men were political animals, although their styles were quite different. Macdonell became the classic political priest, an active member and supporter of Upper Canada's "Family Compact" until his death.[31] MacEachern kept his head down and remained out of local politics, although particularly before the enfranchisement of Catholics in Prince Edward Island in 1830 that position was itself political.[32] Fraser cultivated good relations with men of all denominations and persuasions at Antigonish, and his decision to remain there rather than move to Halifax after his surprising appointment as vicar apostolic of Nova Scotia in 1827 reflected a political judgment. Fraser left the Halifax Irish to themselves, an approach that worked until the early 1840s.[33] Perhaps most importantly, all three Scottish leaders shared a perception of the need for administrative autonomy from Quebec, at least partially to have a free hand to create local educational institutions for the training of an adequate clergy.

The division of the enormous Diocese of Quebec had been a subject for discussion since the end of the eighteenth century. As Father Edmund Burke, while in Upper Canada, had observed to the Propaganda at Rome in 1797: "As at present constituted, the diocese of Quebec is most vast in extent, running from the mouth of the St. Lawrence to the Pacific; and no bishop who ever was, or is, or will be, could properly attend to its wants."[34] Bishop Plessis of Quebec himself recognized the problem and wrote about it frequently, although exactly how the diocese should be divided was a matter of some dispute. Two groups of authorities would have to be approached in the matter: the Propaganda at Rome and the British authorities in London. Burke made the first pilgrimage from Nova Scotia to London and Rome in 1815 and, with British approval, the Propaganda erected Nova Scotia into a vicariate apostolic with himself as bishop, providing the bishop of Quebec agreed. Burke was consecrated in 1818. Plessis had already sent Macdonell to London in 1816 to obtain approval of the British government for a proposed division. Macdonell persuaded the British colonial secretary that "Upper Canada, N. Scotia, N. Brunswick and the Islands [Prince Edward Island and Cape Breton Island] ... should be severed from the See of Quebec, that each of the Provinces should be formed into a separate Spiritual Jurisdiction, & the Islands into one by themselves, and that a vicar apostolic, invested with powers to ordain priests, & give confirmation should be appointed to each jurisdiction."[35] Macdonell also persuaded the government that the national sensibilities of the Catholic inhabitants needed to be recognized, since "Irish priests are most fit to manage Irish Catholics and ... Scotch clergymen alone can possess the entire confidence of their Catholic countrymen."[36]

The complex manoeuvring over the creation of new bishoprics – involving the British government, the Propaganda at Rome, the bishop of Quebec, and the various contending factions in the regions – lies beyond the scope of this paper. What is important for our purposes is that the first three bishops worked at cross-purposes, with one of the principal items of disagreement being the elevation of the bishop of Quebec to an archbishop and the resulting status of the remaining bishops. The British government was not in favour of a Quebec archbishopric, and as a result the diocese was, as the bishop of Quebec observed, "only divided into districts for some bishops *in partibus* subject to my authority," with the exception of Nova Scotia. Alexander Macdonell and Angus MacEachern became suffragan bishops under the bishop of Quebec in 1819, the former consecrated in 1820 as bishop of Rhesaena and the latter in 1821 as bishop of Rosen. Only in Nova Scotia was there a vicar apostolic. Macdonell had supervision for Upper Canada, and MacEachern for New Brunswick, Cape Breton, Prince Edward Island, and the Magdalene Islands, but there were no formal dioceses and no real autonomy. Both Macdonell and MacEachern chafed under their situation, particularly because it hampered their ability to organize educational institutions within their own dioceses and therefore to train clergy.

Macdonell made a second visit to London in 1823, again with the approval of Plessis, who still wanted to be metropolitan over a series of suffragan bishops. He succeeded in persuading the British government of the need to erect separate dioceses, and then had to travel to Rome to gain the Propaganda's authorization, assuring the Vatican that the British government now approved the measure. The operation resembled the shuttle diplomacy of the twentieth century. Macdonell's Diocese of Kingston was created first, in 1826, and the Diocese of Charlottetown was not finally sanctioned until 1829. Throughout the decade, MacEachern bombarded friends at Rome with letters about his relations with Quebec, his territory's ability financially to support a diocese, and his desperate need for independence, "as Doctor MacDonell is, the late Doctor Burke was, and Doctor Fraser is."[37] MacEachern's persistence was finally rewarded.

Between Macdonell's consecration to Kingston and MacEachern's to Charlottetown, William Fraser was consecrated as titular bishop of Tanen and vicar apostolic of Nova Scotia, although Nova Scotia was not created a diocese until 1842 amidst considerable turmoil between Scots and Irish factions. As a vicar apostolic, however, Fraser had more autonomy than Macdonell and MacEachern enjoyed when they first became titular bishops, and the pressure for diocesan status came not from Fraser but from the Halifax Irish and the Propaganda. Fraser's appointment as titular bishop had come in 1824 as something of a fluke, Rome acting only after a series of preferred Irish candidates to succeed Bishop Burke (who died in 1820) had refused the position. At one point in his correspondence to Rome, MacEachern commented pointedly about the Scots position in North America: "All the governors in North America, except the Lt. Governor of this Island, are Scotchmen. Three Highland Bishops in B.N. America is a cause of jealousy *somewhere*. It is believed, with reason, we are favourites."[38] Perhaps they were, although MacEachern's tone of exultation came towards the end of the period when Scottish Catholics, particularly in the Maritime region, could remain pre-eminent on the strength of their numbers. Within a few years, the wave of Irish immigration would seriously weaken the relative position of Scottish Catholicism

in Canada. But in 1829, when MacEachern became bishop of Charlottetown, the three leaders of Scottish Catholicism in North America
were at the height of their power, collectively and individually.

One of the greatest needs in British North America was for education. Its absence was particularly acute for minority groups like the
Gaelic-speaking Scottish Catholics, who had difficulty obtaining a
constant flow of appropriately prepared priests. All three of the
Highlander leaders gave considerable priority to education in their
clerical lives, although the ways in which they worked were quite
different.

Father Alexander Macdonell began his efforts in 1815, when he
first projected the scheme of a seminary for Glengarry to train a
local clergy. Unlike his colleagues in the Maritimes, however, Macdonell had fairly grandiose plans for obtaining financial support for
such an institution, hoping to obtain funds from the British government itself. Relying on the known loyalty of Scottish Catholics to the
government, particularly during the recently completed War of 1812,
Macdonell argued that "such an institution would be of all other
means the best calculated to instill on the susceptible minds of youth
the genuine principles of the British constitution," and went on to
maintain that "few men can properly support their authority over
those on whom they depend for their livelihood, and still fewer
however pure their principles, and disinterested their views will feel
so cordially attached to a Government from which they derive no
immediate benefit."[39] Macdonell's arguments were supported by the
acting governor of Upper Canada, and were followed up when Macdonell visited London over the winter of 1816–17 and negotiated with
Lord Bathurst, the colonial secretary of the time. The Glengarry cleric
insisted on the need for Gaelic-speaking teachers for his Catholic
flocks, arguing that "assured by the double barrier of their Language
and Religion they might for a long time stand proof against the
contagious politics of their democratical neighbours."[40]

Bathurst bought this case and allowed Macdonell to recruit three
schoolmasters to be paid by the government out of the colonial civil
list. Getting these men on Upper Canada's civil list was no easy
matter, however. Not until 1822 were their salaries put on the colonial
estimates, and Macdonell recovered the arrears from the British government only in 1824. At this time he argued for government support
for Catholic education everywhere in British North America, not only
for the Scots but for the Irish as well: "Should my Lord Bathurst be
pleased to allow the means of supporting a sufficient number of
Catholic Clergymen & Schoolmasters for Upper Canada & the selection of them be left to me, I would not hesitate for a moment to
become responsible with my life for the general good conduct, &

loyalty of the Irish Roman Catholics, emigrating to Canada, but without I be enabled to maintain the powerful control of Religion over them, it would be impossible for me to become responsible for their conduct, nor could it in justice be expected of me."[41] Always publicly political, Macdonell got support for his seminary by guaranteeing loyalty to the government. Whether he could deliver, especially among the Irish, was a different question.

Matters were not so simple in the Maritimes, partly because there was no Alexander Macdonell to think in such grandiose terms. Not until 1820 did a plan for a seminary for Cape Breton and Prince Edward Island seem possible, but it collapsed with Burke's death in Nova Scotia. The appointment of Fraser as vicar apostolic for Nova Scotia in 1827 seemed to offer an occasion for optimism, and matters finally moved forward when MacEachern received his own diocese and freedom of movement in 1829. By this time Fraser had established a school in Antigonish, which served as a precursor of St Francis Xavier University. MacEachern took a page from Macdonell's book and petitioned the Legislative Assembly on Prince Edward Island for a grant, but he was not successful. He did manage to get twenty-six of his parishioners to promise to contribute £64 each to a school to be located at his own farm at St Andrew's, on the north shore of the island. MacEachern's diocese was poor, and he obtained little support away from the island, but he was ready to move. In 1831 he met an Irish priest named Edward Walsh in Halifax. Like a good many Irish priests who passed through Canada and especially the Maritime region, Walsh had experienced some problems in Ireland and had left under a cloud. He had teaching experience and considerable academic background, however, and the college at St Andrew's was in operation with twenty students by late 1831. It would outlive Angus MacEachern and survive until 1844.[44]

A number of dates could be taken as the high point of Scottish Catholicism in British North America. All the contenders come, however, from the period around 1830. After that time, both the colonial condition and the Catholic church changed fairly rapidly. On the colonial level, the biggest shift came in the increasing challenges to the old political and social order in which Scottish Catholics such as Alexander Macdonell had fit most comfortably as articulate and deliberate defenders of the status quo. On the church level, conflicts with Irish Catholicism that had previously occurred at the priesthood level now took on a more public flavour, as Irish priests found popular support for their positions among their fellow Irish.

There was, of course, some relationship between the pressures for political reform and the increased numbers of Irish. There was also some connection between political reform and an increased use of the press to ventilate religious disagreements within the Catholic church. Father William John O'Grady, who was suspended from the priesthood by Bishop Macdonell and subsequently excommunicated in 1833, established a reform newspaper, the *Canadian Correspondent*, which merged in late 1834 with William Lyon Mackenzie's *Colonial Advocate*. Like Mackenzie, O'Grady was a radical egalitarian who hated privilege and Tories in equal measure. He attacked Macdonell in his newspaper unstintingly.[43] An equally venomous public debate occurred in Nova Scotia in the early 1840s over perceived neglect by Bishop Fraser of what one of his supporters called "the Irish Catholic Schismaticks of the Capital."[44] On Prince Edward Island, Father John McDonald used a privately printed pamphlet to accuse the Irishman who was professor of philosophy at St Andrew's College of being, "as it were, the chaplain of the Escheators [the island's land reformers], during which time the Students of St Andrew's College, committed to his charge, being mostly without a master, were losing their time, going by night to dances and parties of pleasure; and when at home, entertaining their relations and friends at the expense of the College."[45] Both St Andrew's College and Scottish Catholic hegemony on Prince Edward Island may have died in the fallout over escheat.

As one scholar has written of the death of Bishop Macdonell of Upper Canada: "So also would pass from the philosophy of toryism there the values he saw as essential to true liberty – order, stability, deference."[46] The same might well be said for Scottish Catholicism generally in British North America. Ironically enough for a church proscribed in the British Isles for centuries, its Scottish Highland branch was traditionally Britain's staunchest ally by the end of the eighteenth century, seeking to preserve a national order in which a minority culture could survive. It was not reform that broke Scottish Catholic hegemony in British North America but the emergence of the forces that made reform possible. Yet in its heyday, Scottish Catholicism in British North America had helped make Catholicism respectable and acceptable to the governing authorities.

NOTES

1 For an exceptional synthesis see Terrence Murphy, "The Emergence of Maritime Catholicism, 1781–1830," *Acadiensis* 13 (spring 1984): 29–49.
2 Christine Johnson, *Developments in the Roman Catholic Church of Scotland, 1789–1829* (Edinburgh: John Donald 1983).
3 A.J. Youngson, *After the Forty-Five: The Economic Impact on the Scottish Highlands* (Edinburgh: Edinburgh University Press 1973).

4 Ian Graham, *Colonists from Scotland: Emigration to North America 1707–1783* (Ithaca, NY: Cornell University Press 1956); J.M. Bumsted, *The People's Clearance: Highland Emigration to British North America, 1770–1815* (Edinburgh and Winnipeg: Edinburgh University Press and University of Manitoba Press 1982); Bernard Bailyn, *Voyagers to the West: A Passage in the Peopling of America on the Eve of the Revolution* (New York: Alfred Knopf 1986).

5 J.M. Bumsted, "Highland Emigration to the Island of St. John and the Scottish Catholic Church, 1769–1774," *Dalhousie Review* 58 (1978/9): 511–27.

6 Johnson, *Roman Catholic Church of Scotland*, 109.

7 Kathleen M. Toomey, *Alexander Macdonell: The Scottish Years 1762–1804* (Toronto: Canadian Catholic Historical Association 1985), 103–40.

8 J.M. Bumsted, "The Scottish Catholic Church and Prince Edward Island, 1770–1810," in Terrence Murphy and Cyril J. Byrne, eds., *Religion and Identity: The Experience of Irish and Scottish Catholics in Atlantic Canada* (St John's: Jesperson Press 1987), 18–33.

9 Quoted in Angus Anthony Johnston, *A History of the Catholic Church in Eastern Nova Scotia*, 2 vols. (Antigonish: St Francis Xavier University Press 1960, 1971), I, 219.

10 Quoted in Bumsted, "The Scottish Catholic Church," 29.

11 Bumsted, *The People's Clearance*.

12 D. Campbell and R.A. MacLean, *Beyond the Atlantic Roar: A Study of the Nova Scotia Scots* (Toronto: McClelland and Stewart 1974).

13 J.M. Bumsted, "James MacDonald," *Dictionary of Canadian Biography*, IV: *1771–1800* (Toronto: University of Toronto Press 1979), 496–7. Much of the best recent scholarship on early Canadian history is to be found within the pages of the DBC, and early Catholicism in Canada is no exception to this generalization.

14 "Macdonell of Scothouse," DBC, V: *1801–1820* (Toronto: University of Toronto Press 1983), 523–5.

15 Quoted in Johnston, *History*, I, 228–9.

16 Mason Wade, "Relations between the French, Irish and Scottish Clergy in the Maritime Provinces, 1774–1836," Canadian Catholic Historical Association, *Study Sessions* 39 (1972): 9–33.

17 G. Patterson, *A History of the County of Pictou, Nova Scotia* (Montreal: Dawson Bros. 1877), 174.

18 John McGregor, *Historical and Descriptive Sketches of the Maritime Colonies of British America* (New York: Johnson Reprint Company 1968), 184.

19 Quoted in Johnston, *History*, I, 502.

20 Ibid., 219.

21 Ibid., 384–5, 512.

22 Ibid., 231–2.

23 Ibid., 312.

24 Ibid., 478.

25 Ibid., 312.

26 Quoted in Francis W.P. Bolger, "The First Bishop," in Michael F. Hennessey, ed., *The Catholic Church in Prince Edward Island 1720–1979* (Charlottetown: Roman Catholic Episcopal Corporation 1979), 36.

27 Quoted in Johnston, *History*, I, 378.

28 Quoted in Bolger, "The First Bishop," 39.

29 Ibid., 40.

30 Ibid., 43.

31 For Macdonell see J.A. Macdonell, *A Sketch of the Life of the Honourable and Right Reverend Alexander Macdonell* (Alexandria: Office of the Glengarrian 1890); J. Somers, *The Life and Times of the Hon. and Rt. Rev. Alexander Macdonell, D.D., First Bishop of Upper Canada 1762–1840* (Washington: Catholic University of America 1931); J.E. Rea, *Bishop Alexander Macdonell and the Politics of Upper Canada* (Toronto: Ontario Historical Society 1974); Toomey, *Alexander Macdonell*.

32 For MacEachern see E.J. Mullally, "A Sketch of the Life and Times of the Right Reverend Angus Bernard MacEachern, the First Bishop of the Diocese of Charlottetown," Canadian Catholic Historical Association, *Report* 13 (1945–6): 71–106; Bolger, "The First Bishop"; Allan MacDonald, "Angus Bernard MacEachern, 1759–1835: His Ministry in the Maritime Provinces," in Murphy and Byrne, eds., *Religion and Identity*, 53–67; G.E. MacDonald, "The Good Shepherd," *Island Magazine*, no. 16 (fall–winter 1984): 3–8; G.E. MacDonald, "Angus Bernard MacEachern," DCB, IV: *1821–1835* (Toronto: University of Toronto Press 1987), 447-51.

33 For Fraser see A.A. Johnston, "The Right Reverend William Fraser, Second Vicar Apostolic of Nova Scotia, First Bishop of Halifax, and First Bishop of Arichat," Canadian Catholic Historical Association, *Report* 3 (1935–6): 23–30; A.A. Johnston, "A Scottish Bishop in New Scotland: The Right Reverend William Fraser, Second Vicar Apostolic of Nova Scotia, First Bishop of Halifax, and First Bishop of Arichat," *Innes Review* 6 (1955): 107–24; David B. Flemming, "William Fraser," DCB, VIII: *1851–1860* (Toronto: University of Toronto Press 1985), 306–8.

34 Quoted in C. O'Brien, *Memoirs of Rt. Rev. Edmund Burke, Bishop of Zion, First Vicar Apostolic of Nova Scotia* (Ottawa: Thoburn & Co 1894), 34.

35 Quoted in Somers, *Life and Times*, 69.

36 Ibid., 70.

37 Quoted in Bolger, "The First Bishop," 40.

38 Ibid., 38.

39 Quoted in Rea, *Bishop Alexander Macdonell*, 35.

40 Quoted in Somers, *Life and Times*, 54.

41 Ibid., 62.

42 G. Edward MacDonald, *The History of St. Dunstan's University 1855–1956* (Charlottetown: Prince Edward Island Heritage Foundation 1988), 3–42.

43 Curtis Fahey, "William John O'Grady," DCB, VII: *1836–1850* (Toronto: University of Toronto Press 1988), 661–5.
44 Quoted in Flemming, "William Fraser," 307. In general see J.E. Burns, "The Development of Roman Catholic Church Government in Halifax from 1760 to 1853," *Nova Scotia Historical Society Collections* 23 (1936): 89–102; Johnston, *History of the Catholic Church* II, passim.
45 Quoted in MacDonald, *St. Dunstan's*, 35.
46 J.E. Rea, "Alexander McDonell," in DCB, VII, 551.

5 The Policy of Rome towards the English-Speaking Catholics in British North America, 1750–1830

LUCA CODIGNOLA

The nature and composition of the North American Catholic community was profoundly altered in the late eighteenth and early nineteenth centuries by a flood of immigrants from Europe and the British Isles. The Catholic population grew rapidly not only in size but also in diversity. In British North America the French-speaking Catholics of the Province of Quebec and of the former Acadia (from 1784 reshaped into the colonies of Nova Scotia, St John's Island, Cape Breton, and New Brunswick) found themselves surrounded by co-religionists from Ireland, Scotland, and the United States. In the United States the formerly small, unilingual community of English origin was replaced by a disunited church, composed of Irish, Scots, Germans, Belgians, Spanish, and Italians. In both countries the change was traumatic. Major adjustments were required from the newcomers, from the established Catholic communities that received them, and from the ecclesiastical authorities who were in charge of their spiritual care, including the Holy See. Every Catholic in French and British North America was under the ultimate jurisdiction of the Sacred Congregation for the Propagation of the Faith or "de Propaganda Fide" (known as Propaganda), and he or she would communicate with it through the local clergy via the established hierarchies. This agency had been created in 1622 to spread Roman Catholicism among the infidels and to protect the church where Catholics were in direct contact with people of other faiths; from its early days it devised, planned, and implemented the North American policies on behalf of the Holy See.[1] This article will examine when and why

Propaganda recognized the significance of the change that was taking place in the North American community and how it reacted to change by suggesting and implementing new policies.

As soon as Canada became important enough to require a more efficient hierarchical structure, François de Laval was appointed vicar apostolic (1658), later to become full bishop of Quebec (1674). Until John Carroll's appointment as bishop of Baltimore in 1789, the bishop of Quebec was the only bishop in non-Spanish North America. During the French régime and at least until the time of the French Revolution, he was regarded by all, including the cardinals of Propaganda, as the spiritual leader of a community whose growth was matched by the parallel growth of Canada's territory. After the Seven Years' War, when the North American borders were redrawn, the British prelates, theoretically in charge of the English-speaking North Americans, recommended that no innovation be applied to Canada, where there had always been a bishop and a chapter.[2] This was in complete agreement with Rome's attitude. Propaganda never considered altering the jurisdiction and limiting the spiritual authority of the bishop of Quebec. Rather, it suggested an extension by empowering Bishop Jean-Olivier Briand to tour the British continental colonies and provide spiritual help for the local Catholics – although this was never acted upon.[3]

The evaluation of ecclesiastical jurisdiction over British North America was part of a broader North American picture, and it can only be understood by placing it side by side with the course of events in the thirteen American colonies, events that were in some respects similar and in others very different. The American Catholic community did not surface until the mid-eighteenth century, when their numbers, though still small, became noticeable. In 1750 they were but a fraction of the 1,206,000 inhabitants, and only in a limited number of provinces did they exist at all. They were 3000 in Maryland in 1708, and had risen to between 5000 and 7000 fifty years later. Meanwhile, the Catholics of Pennsylvania had grown to 2000. In the rest of the colonies they were virtually nonexistent. On the eve of American Independence, the Catholics of the Thirteen Colonies numbered between 20,000 and 25,000 or about 1 per cent of a population of 2,300,000 – the same percentage they constituted in Britain.[4] In view of these small numbers, Rome's interest in the American Catholics was very limited, and the problem of spiritual jurisdiction over them was not raised until 1745. Responsibility over them had been de facto in the hands of the English Province of the Society of Jesus,[5] although formal jurisdiction, from "time out of mind,"[6] apparently belonged to the vicar apostolic of the London District of England.

According to Benjamin Petre, bishop of Prusa and vicar apostolic, and to his coadjutor, Richard Challoner, bishop of Debra, London enjoyed jurisdiction over all islands and colonies of British America, from Canada to the West Indies.[7]

Propaganda took no action on the matter of the American jurisdiction until 1756, when, for reasons that concerned the West Indies, it became aware of the improper circumstances in which it was exercised. The Sacred Congregation asked Petre "on what ground he enjoyed [his American] faculties."[8] When it became clear that Petre's jurisdiction was not based on any legal document, Propaganda hurried to grant it officially, and later to renew it regularly until 1784, when James Talbot, bishop of Birtha and successor of Petre and Challoner, was relieved of his jurisdiction over the United States, in favour of Carroll.[9] Following independence in the United States, the negotiations between American plenipotentiary Benjamin Franklin and Giuseppe Maria Doria Pamphili, archbishop of Seleucia and nuncio in France, assessed the requests of the American community and allowed Carroll to be appointed superior of the missions in the United Provinces in 1784, later to become bishop (1789) and archbishop (1808) of Baltimore.

This fundamental change in the shape of the American ecclesiastical organization created no major problems. London was relieved of a responsibility that its vicars apostolic had always exercised unwillingly, and the Catholics of the United States received a "local" leader. For its part, Rome regarded it as a major step in the official recognition of the American community, and had no reason to oppose it.[10] As far as the encroaching jurisdictions of Baltimore and Quebec were concerned, political borders well limited either territory, and only the partially unsettled West proved an occasional reason for confusion.[11]

In the mind of the Roman officials, therefore, and indeed of all interested parties in Great Britain, Canada, and the United States, there was no room for debate. The bishop of Quebec was held responsible for French-speaking North Americans, whereas the bishop of Baltimore (or, earlier, the vicar apostolic in the London District) took charge of English-speaking North Americans. This arrangement was straightforward enough until the Seven Years' War, because, until then, political allegiances were in agreement with languages spoken in either community. It was left untouched even after the Treaty of Paris (10 February 1763), when the Catholics of Canada became British subjects. Although it was not openly stated, the assumption certainly was that the Catholics of the United States would continue to be English-speaking and that those of Canada would continue to be French-speaking, even under a British régime.[12] After all, as late as 1800 the society living along the St Lawrence River accounted for about 220,000 of the 350,000 inhabitants of the colonies of British North America, and, of the former, 190,000 were francophones.[13] Nobody, in Rome, London, Baltimore, or Quebec foresaw that immigration would soon change the numbers and the ethnic composition of the Catholic community in both Canada and the United States so drastically.

Between 1800 and 1810 the population of the United States grew from 5.3 million to 7.2 million people. Some 250,000 immigrants are estimated to have arrived in the years from 1790 to 1820, although the Napoleonic Wars made voyages between Europe and the Americas more difficult. Many languages were spoken by the newcomers, and the small Catholic community (60,000 by 1820) was no exception. In 1785 the Capuchin Charles Maurice Whelan suggested that any priest in New York should at least speak Gaelic, English, French, and Dutch, and that some Spanish and Portuguese were also advisable.[14] The formerly unilingual small community of English origin was replaced by a very disunited church, chiefly consisting of people of Irish origin, who coexisted with Scots, Germans, Belgians, Spanish, Portuguese, and Italians, and who were ruled by a predominantly French-speaking hierarchy with its roots in the community of émigré priests of the revolutionary years. By 1815, however, English had won an almost complete victory over its rival languages in the country.[15]

The British North American colonies, meanwhile, underwent similar changes. The resident population of Newfoundland grew from 1653 in 1675 to 10,700 in 1780 and to 25,157 in 1809, by which time it made up 90 per cent of the local population. At the same time, from 90 per cent in 1732, the inhabitants of English origin were reduced to just over 50 per cent in 1770. Except for small minorities of residents of French-Acadian ancestry, or originally from the Channel Islands, Scotland, and the United States, the remainder consisted entirely of people of Irish extraction, mainly from the Waterford and Cork areas. In terms of residential population, their group had experienced an unparalleled growth. From 1732 to 1753 their numbers increased thirteen times. In St John's in 1753 there were 669 Irish to 454 English, and in 1795 two-thirds of the 3000 residents were Irish. Since residents of Irish origin were almost invariably Catholic,[16] their presence posed ethnic as well as religious problems. In 1784–5 St John's had a winter population of about 2000, of whom three-quarters were Catholic.[17]

The case of the Maritime provinces (Nova Scotia, Cape Breton Island, New Brunswick, and the Island of St John, renamed Prince Edward Island in 1798) was even more complicated owing to the existence of language problems. Before the Conquest, the entire population of Acadia consisted of some 2000 to 3000 Micmac and about 12,500 French-speaking Acadians, besides another 2500 in the fortress of Louisbourg. Furthermore, there were 6000 English-speaking newcomers who lived in the British portion of Nova Scotia, mainly in Halifax (founded 1749) and Lunenburg (founded 1753). The pattern changed significantly after 1763, when immigrants mainly from Ireland and Scotland began to pour into the region. The total population of Nova Scotia reached 7800 by 1762. A survey conducted in 1767 in Halifax showed a population of 3022 inhabitants, 667 of whom admitted to be Catholic. Of the latter, only 200 were Acadians, the remainder being Irish newcomers.[18] The 1774 census of Cape Breton Island counted 668 Catholics out of a population of 1013. Of those, 304 were English, 201 Irish, and 502 French.[19] Settlement of Prince Edward Island began only at the end of the 1760s. By 1768 there was a Scottish Highland settlement at Scotchfort. Among the 2300 Acadians still living in the Maritimes, 200 lived in Prince Edward Island (at St Peters, Tracadie, Malpeque, and Rustico). Other homogeneous settlements were at Pictou, Cap-de-Sable, and Baie Sainte-Marie (in Nova Scotia). In sum, in 1800 between 75,000 and 80,000 people lived in Nova Scotia, Cape Breton, New Brunswick, and Prince Edward Island. English- and Gaelic-speaking settlers had rapidly replaced and outstripped the declining French-speaking Acadians and Indians.[20]

Upper Canada, situated west of Quebec (Lower Canada), had at the time of its establishment in 1791 about 10,000 inhabitants, mainly Loyalists or other newly arrived immigrants from the United States, mixed with a few Highland Scots and Germans. They lived in the L'Assomption/Detroit and the Glengarry regions, with pockets of settlement on the north shores of Lake Ontario and Lake Erie, Kingston and Niagara being the principal urban agglomerations.[21]

This radically altered pattern of settlement raised the question of which ecclesiastical authority was responsible for the English- and Gaelic-speaking Catholics who settled in Newfoundland, Nova Scotia, Cape Breton, Prince Edward Island, and Upper Canada. Given the number of the new immigrants, their "new" languages, and their pleas for spiritual assistance, this question had immediate practical implications. Was the bishop of Quebec to send missionaries to the Maritimes, or was this the duty of the vicar apostolic in the London District, or of the Irish bishops? Was any of them able or willing to do something? Since territorial jurisdiction over mission territories was ultimately decided upon in Rome, the opinion of the cardinals of Propaganda was very important.

Although never clearly stated, all parties seemed to take for granted that the jurisdiction of Quebec over Newfoundland had ended with the Treaty of Utrecht (11 April 1713) and that it had been replaced by London. Yet the vicars apostolic were unfamiliar with the island and often wondered whether in fact it still depended on the bishop of Quebec. They knew little, and did even less. Challoner was in fact the only one to mention Newfoundland when he reported in 1756 that an unnamed Irish Augustinian had "recently" gone to the island to assist the fishermen.[22] As in Canada in the seventeenth century before Laval's appointment as vicar apostolic, spiritual authority over the Catholics of Newfoundland probably rested in practice with the bishops of their ports of departure.[23] For actual spiritual assistance, the Catholics of Newfoundland, many of whom were seasonal residents from different European countries, relied on the few priests who accompanied the fishing ships, such as the French missionary Pierre de Neufville in the 1660s or the above-mentioned Augustinian, or on those "strolling priests" of the Irish tradition who ministered without proper faculties and licences.[24] Formally, however, London's jurisdiction over Newfoundland ended only in 1784, when the Irish Recollet James Louis O'Donel was appointed prefect apostolic of Newfoundland.[25]

Spiritual jurisdiction over the Nova Scotia and adjoining territories was also unclear. When the Treaty of Utrecht had consigned the peninsular portion of the province into the hands of the British, the Acadians had continued to regard themselves as spiritually dependent on the bishop of Quebec because they considered themselves on a similar footing with the Acadians who had remained under French rule. Technically, this might not have been the case, at least for those Acadians who had become British subjects. In 1745 Bishop Petre mentioned Nova Scotia as being under his own jurisdiction. In 1756 Propaganda granted him jurisdiction over all British islands and colonies of North America, including Nova Scotia. In fact, as in the case of Newfoundland, the English vicars apostolic never exercised their jurisdiction over Nova Scotia, and knew so little of it that, in 1753, their agent in Rome, Christopher Stonor, wondered aloud whether Nova Scotia, as well as Newfoundland and Hudson Bay, still depended on the bishop of Quebec.[26] The result of this confusion was that the Acadians and the Indians could still regard Qubec as the source of their spiritual guidance, whereas nonfrancophone Catholics were left without leadership and assistance.

Spiritual jurisdiction over the region later to be known as Upper Canada was undoubtedly in the hands of the bishop of Quebec. This arrangement might have changed in 1790, when Edmund Burke, the future vicar apostolic in Nova Scotia, asked John Thomas Troy, the archbishop of Dublin, to obtain on his behalf a mission in the west. In 1794 he was actually sent to Upper Canada as vicar general, on the understanding, however, that he would never be promoted to prefect apostolic. Three years later Burke was still so convinced that a reorganization of the diocese was necessary that he wrote to Cardinal Giacinto Sigismondo Gerdil, prefect of Propaganda, suggesting among other things the erection of a vicariate apostolic in Upper Canada. The plan fell on deaf ears, since the French invasion of Rome had thrown the Holy See into complete disarray.[27] It was only much later that the area was reorganized under Alexander Macdonell, at first vicar-general of the bishop of Quebec with episcopal powers (1818) and later bishop of Kingston (1826).[28]

Both the bishops of Quebec and the cardinals of Propaganda were slow in noticing the change that was taking place in the Maritimes. At first the bishops of Quebec tried to deal with the Maritimes, where most of the nonfrancophones were, as a simple extension of the St Lawrence Valley, as if the Canadian Catholic community had not substantially changed after the Conquest. Whenever they could spare one, they would send a French-speaking vicar-general or missionary to Nova Scotia, Cape Breton, or Prince Edward Island.[29] Although this was hardly an adequate solution, no change in attitude is visible until 1784, when Bishop Louis-Philippe Mariauchau d'Esgly ordered his vicar-general in the Maritimes, Joseph-Mathurin Bourg, to arrange with John Butler, bishop of Cork, the transfer of Irish priests to Nova Scotia. It was, however, Bishop Jean-François Hubert who, in 1787, showed a genuinely new perception of the needs of its Catholic community and began to emphasize the diversity of former Acadia. In a lengthy report that François Sorbier de Villars, his vicar-general in Paris, forwarded to Propaganda, Hubert stated that the Catholics of the Maritimes consisted of families of Acadian, Indian, Scottish, English, and Irish origin. He also mentioned the presence of five hundred Catholic families of various extraction at Baie des Chaleurs, one hundred at Prince Edward Island, and two hundred at Cape Breton. In spite of his own ethnic background, the bishop advocated the sending of more Irish priests to Halifax.[30]

While waiting for the bishops of Quebec to implement their spiritual jurisdiction over them, the Catholics of the Maritimes seized the initiative and began to find their own solutions to their particular needs. In some instances, priests were called to Canada by communities of immigrants who had informed their friends in Ireland or in Scotland. This was the case, for example, of O'Donel (St John's, 1784), of the Irish Capuchin James Jones (Halifax 1784), and of the

Scottish secular priest Angus Bernard MacEachern (Prince Edward Island, 1790). In other instances, priests migrated to North America with their flock and continued to minister to them in the New World. This was the case with the Scottish secular priest James MacDonald, who in 1722 accompanied to Prince Edward Island a group of settlers from South Uist, in the Lower Hebrides, or of Macdonell, who went to Upper Canada with a group of Scottish emigrants in 1804. In most cases, ethnic communities did not mingle and were ministered to by priests of their own extraction. In an urban setting such as Halifax, a sort of dual jurisdiction was approved, by which Jones was in charge of English-speaking missionaries, with responsibility over the English, Irish, and Scots, and Bourg was in charge of French-speaking missionaries, with responsibility over Acadians and Indians.[31]

The cardinals of Propaganda were as slow as the Quebec hierarchy to understand the new developments that were taking place in the Maritimes. From 1658 onwards the bishops of Quebec had always corresponded with Propaganda via Paris. After the Conquest, the three vicars-general of Quebec in Paris, Pierre de La Rue, better known as abbé de L'Isle-Dieu (1734–77), Villars (1777–88), and Martin Hody (1789–93), occasionally assisted by the dean of the Chapter of Quebec, Joseph-Marie de La Corne de Chaptes (1762–79), forwarded to Rome the correspondence dealing with or coming from North America. The appointment of a vicar-general in London, the Irish priest Thomas Hussey (1784–6), did not diminish the importance of Paris, and the cardinals of Propaganda continued to rely on the French capital for their information on North American events.

On account of their close relationship, in the years following the Conquest and prior to the French Revolution, Rome, Paris, and Quebec were in substantial agreement as to the solutions to adopt with reference to Canada. Their common policy hinged on the desire to preserve the free exercise of the Catholic religion for the French-speaking inhabitants. The Quebec clergy, in concert with their representatives in Paris, stressed the necessity for the Canadian Catholics to avoid harsh confrontation, to adjust to the realities of British rule, to assure the new government of their loyalty, and to take advantage of whatever room was legally available to them to recruit new priests. Rome approved this cautious policy, and its major concern in these critical years was never to appear to interfere in the negotiations between the Canadian clergy and the civil authorities in London or to show any sign of arrogance that would annoy the British government. For example, Propaganda took an important but decidedly low-keyed approach to the negotiations that led in 1766 to

Briand's appointment as bishop of Quebec, since it had been warned that the simple suspicion that Rome wanted "to dominate in these lands" would have prevented the new head of the Canadian church from exercising any jurisdiction.[32] Furthermore, when in 1783–4 French priests were brought into Canada surreptitiously, to circumvent the British refusal to admit new priests from France, Propaganda issued a stiff reprimand. A simple order on London's part, it pointed out, would have meant the immediate "loss of the hope to send other [priests]."[33]

Since they viewed Canada and the Maritimes through the eyes of the Quebec hierarchy, the officials of Propaganda were for a long time ill-informed about the new realities of the North American continent and on the needs of its new Catholics. The limitations of the Rome-Paris-Quebec connection were particularly evident in the case of Nova Scotia. When the essential provisions of the Catholic Relief Act (1778) were introduced in the province (1783), Villars, informed by the bishop of Quebec, had been quick to report to Propaganda the new opportunities for Catholic expansion that were taking place in Halifax. According to Villars, many French priests were ready to leave France and move there. Propaganda responded promptly by asking Villars to apply the standard procedure in such cases – to select some missionaries, appoint a prefect among them, forward their names to Rome for the granting of the customary faculties and letters patent, and dispatch the priests to their new missionary stations.[34] Neither Propaganda nor Villars seemed to be aware that the diverse Catholic community of Nova Scotia required sophisticated and varied solutions. This became all the more evident in 1784 when two Irish Recollets, John McManus and Francis McGuire, applied to Pope Pius VI for permission to go to Halifax, where relatives and friends had requested their assistance. The officials of Propaganda did not know what to make of their application. Was not Halifax under the jurisdiction of the bishop of Quebec? Were there any other missionaries there? Would Recollets be appropriate? For that matter, where was Halifax? All these questions were posed to Villars, who responded that the sending of the two Recollets would be a source of confusion. In any event, he explained, the bishop of Quebec's French-speaking vicar-general for the Maritimes, Bourg, had been ordered to move to Halifax from the Baie des Chaleurs and would be arriving there shortly. Propaganda promptly acquiesced to Villars's point of view.[35]

In the meantime, Jones had reached Halifax independently of Quebec and Rome, and in 1786 his first report, gloomy as it was, reached the officials of Propaganda in Rome. Villars, immediately questioned by Propaganda, pretended never to have heard of Jones or of the troubles he described. Villars's proposed solution was, as usual, the sending of more missionaries. But whereas Jones explicitly asked for priests who could speak English, the only language spoken in Halifax, Villars stubbornly suggested French-speaking priests. In Rome, Propaganda could do little but comment that missionaries were certainly scarce, "but this is always a feature of all lands that are so vast and so distant from the centre of Catholicism."[36]

Given the rapid growth of the English-speaking Catholic community, however, Bourg's influence waned, whereas Jones's importance increased. Moreover, it was at about this time, corresponding roughly with Hubert's report of 1787, that Paris was virtually abandoned as Propaganda's major source of information concerning Nova Scotia. The French capital was replaced by Jones and his successor, Burke (1753–1820), who chose to correspond directly with Propaganda or to make use of Irish agents.[37]

The absence of Paris intermediaries made the relationship between Rome and the English- and Gaelic-speaking communities of Prince Edward Island and Newfoundland more straightforward and productive, although correspondence was still limited in volume. The case of the Highland Scots community of Scotchfort, Prince Edward Island, was in fact the earliest instance in which language and ethnic problems were brought directly to the attention of Propaganda. Upon a request coming straight from Scotland in 1771, Pope Clement xiv granted James MacDonald faculties for his Scottish flock. When MacDonald died in 1785, Rome did not find anybody fluent in Scots and Irish Gaelic to replace him, and it was not until 1790 that MacEachern joined the little community.[38]

Newfoundland matters passed via Dublin, not Paris. Villars and his colleagues were never informed of, let alone interested in, what happened on the island, and they did not influence at all Propaganda's dealings or opinions with reference to the Newfoundland Catholic community. When in 1783 and 1784 freedom of religion was extended to the island, the Irish inhabitants, like their compatriots in Nova Scotia, resorted to their links with the Irish church and, with Rome's approval, they secured O'Donel's appointment as prefect apostolic (1784), later to become vicar apostolic.[39]

From Rome's point of view, it was in the mid 1780s that the various pieces of the North American puzzle began to fit together and the hazy picture of its Catholic community started to make sense. The Diocese of Quebec continued to be the centre of it all, its loyalty to the British during the War of American Independence having made its position even stronger than before. Yet it was becoming increasingly evident to Propaganda that North American Catholics were no longer limited to the old Canada of New France. This decade was marked by the extension of religious liberty to Nova Scotia (1783) and Newfoundland (1783, 1784) Catholics. The year 1784 also saw Carroll's and O'Donel's appointments in the United States and Newfoundland, as well as the naming of Hussey as vicar-general of the bishop of Quebec in London. Three years later, Jones was appointed superior of the missions for Nova Scotia, with Hubert's report emphasizing the diversity of former Acadia. The hopes and expectations of the end of the 1780s, however, were severely threatened and partly dispelled by the coming of the French Revolution.

The French Revolution and the ensuing political and military events threatened the very existence of the Catholic church in France and in the Papal States. Correspondence between Rome and North America was disrupted, official documents delayed, and travel made hazardous. In Paris the Séminaire des Missions-Etrangères and the Séminaire de Saint-Sulpice were closed in 1790, while the Séminaire du Saint-Esprit suffered the same fate in 1792. As for the Papal States, the French invaded them in 1797 and occupied Rome in 1798, and from 1797 to 1800 Propaganda operated out of Padua and Venice. In 1798 the eighty-one-year-old Pius VI was exiled, destined to die in France in 1799. Pius VII was elected in 1800, but the annexation of Rome to the empire, proclaimed in 1809, caused the pope's exile, from which he was not to return for good until 1815. The Holy See was simply overwhelmed by the magnitude of events that no government in Europe had been able to anticipate. The events of the turn of the century significantly disrupted the missionary network that Propaganda had been organizing via Paris for decades, and effectively ended the role of the French capital as the organizational and moral centre of the network linking the Catholics of North America with the Holy See.

At the same time, these events also accelerated the process of separation of the nonfrancophone Catholic communities from Paris and Quebec that had already started in the late 1770s and early 1780s. In fact, in the 1790s and 1800s Rome's officials were increasingly concerned with their own survival and paid less attention to North American affairs, leaving the Catholics of Quebec, the Atlantic provinces, and the United States to their own resources and initiatives. Later, in the mid 1810s, when relations between Rome and North America were regularly resumed, their nature was deeply changed. The Paris connection was almost nonexistent (it continued to apply regularly only to Saint-Pierre and Miquelon), having been replaced by many direct relations between the Holy See and the various North American communities. Quebec matters went via London, whereas Newfoundland, Nova Scotia, and Prince Edward Island preferred Ireland and Scotland. The correspondence between the United States and Rome occasionally continued to be forwarded via London and Paris, but Leghorn, in Italy, increasingly became the port of entry and departure.[40]

The fragmentation of the North American community, both in Canada and in the United States, and the bitter rivalries and often enmities that prevented large portions of the clergy from trusting either the bishop of Quebec or the archbishop of Baltimore, strengthened the direct links of the various communities with the Holy See. Whereas before the 1780s direct communication with Propaganda was an exception, in that the unilingual and uninational clergies relied on the bishops who represented them, after the 1780s the bishop's voice was only one, albeit the most authoritative, of the many voices that reached the Holy See.[41] In the case of British North America, the relations between the bishops of Quebec and the spiritual leaders of the Irish and Scottish communities were in fact based on mistrust and suspicion rather than cooperation and mutual understanding. To varying degrees, Burke, MacEachern, and Macdonell fought against Bishop Joseph-Octave Plessis, accusing him not only of neglect towards the English-speaking Catholics of his diocese but also of resisting their efforts aimed at the establishment of independent bishoprics throughout Canada. When in 1790 and 1797 Burke tried to convince the cardinals of Propaganda that a reorganization of the diocese was necessary, he did it in a way that was revealing of his profound distrust of Hubert, whom he had not even cared to inform of his projects. When he became vicar-general for Nova Scotia, Burke's attitude towards Quebec did not change. In the summer of 1815, feigning medical reasons, he travelled to Ireland, England, and eventually to Rome to campaign for the erection of Nova Scotia into an independent vicariate apostolic. Again, Burke acted without informing his bishop, from whom he expected fierce opposition.

MacEachern was not as convinced as Burke that the only way to deal with Plessis was to fight him or to circumvent him; yet his experience in Prince Edward Island and in the adjacent territories had proved that little, if anything, could be expected from Quebec. The diocese was so vast that it required not one distant francophone bishop but a good number of vicars apostolic who would be familiar with the languages, customs, institutions, and national features of the people they led. By 1824 both MacEachern and Macdonell had lost all hope in Quebec, and the Macdonell decided to follow Burke's example and personally take his case before the cardinals of Propaganda in Rome. Like the late vicar apostolic of Nova Scotia in 1815, Macdonell did not inform the bishop of Quebec of his initiatives.

No matter what Burke, MacEachern, and Macdonell imagined, they were actually in substantial agreement with the bishops of Quebec, and with Plessis in particular. The latter were certainly not opposed to these initiatives, and actually supported them when they could. They were conscious that their jurisdiction was immense and were relieved to see their own burden eased. Hubert had always been in favour of a subdivision of his diocese. Moreover, Burke, MacEachern, and Macdonell had always been Plessis's candidates, as he had repeatedly written to the Holy See. Plessis's successor, Bernard-Claude Panet, shared the late bishop's views on this matter.[42] The fact remained that the relations between the bishops of Quebec and the spiritual leaders of the Irish and Scottish communities proved to be strained, being based on mistrust and suspicion rather than cooperation and mutual understanding.[43]

Since it was in Rome that final decisions concerning episcopal appointments or ecclesiastical censures were made, in order to be heard, or at least to ensure that their viewpoint was not misrepresented, each community hired local ecclesiastics to foster and protect their interests with the Roman bureaucracy. Some individuals, often residing in the foreign colleges, became regular correspondents, lobbyists, agents, or unofficial representatives of North American interest groups. At the Venerable English College, Rector Robert Gradwell was for a long time Plessis's agent in Rome. At the Scots College, Rectors Paul Macpherson and Angus MacDonald represented Macdonell and MacEachern. At the Irish College of St Isidore, the brothers James and Michael MacCormick, both superiors at different times, had a special relationship with the Franciscan Recollets of Ireland and, consequently, with the vicars apostolic of Newfoundland. As for the religious orders, the Jesuit John Thorpe was the agent of the English Jesuits and for a long time represented his former confrère, Carroll. Abbé L. de Sambucy was the French Sulpicians' representative, and as such he also became in the 1820s the voice of the Montreal Seminary against Plessis and the future bishop of Montreal, Jean-Jacques Lartigue. These same remote communities often sent their own representatives to the Holy See, and, whenever they felt it necessary, the bishops went to Rome in person. To mention but a few visitors, Burke and Louis-Guillaume-Valentin Dubourg, the future bishop of New Orleans, travelled to Rome in 1815–16, Plessis in 1819–20, Montreal lawyer Michael O'Sullivan in 1824–5,[44]

Macdonell in 1825, the Sulpician superior of the Montreal Seminary, Jean-Henry-Auguste Roux, in 1826–7, and the Quebec priests Pierre-Antoine Tabeau and Thomas Maguire in 1829–30.[45]

A visit to the centre of the Roman Catholic world could become a frustrating experience for those Catholics – bishops, simple priests, laymen – who personally went to Rome to present the case of their communities before the Holy See. They all had come from far away and felt that some important decisions had to be made immediately. They all were kept in waiting for days, weeks, and months. Bishop Plessis was particularly resentful of the way he had been treated by the Holy See. He was confident that his church enjoyed a special right, given its "parfait dévouement au S. Siège Apostolique," and that he was entitled to "puiser la source féconde dont les eaux se répandent sur toutes les parties de l'Univers Catholique." When in Rome (c. 10 November 1819–10 February 1820), he took up residence in via Poli, a few yards from the palace of Propaganda, to whose archives he was specially admitted on 11 December 1819. About a month later he compiled a memorandum comprising very simple questions, which, he maintained, required little work on the part of the cardinals. He apologized for being so pressing, but he was "un pauvre évêque qui vient du bout du monde." "Puisqu'il se trouve au centre de la lumière," he explained, "il doit tâcher d'en saisir autant de rayons qu'il en pourra emporter." He soon became uneasy about the slowness of the Roman bureaucracy. Nobody seemed to know in which office his case was being assessed. He was then obliged to leave Rome before his requests had been fully answered and, six months later in London, he bitterly complained to the prefect of Propaganda, Francesco Cardinal Fontana, that the latter had failed to deliver what he had promised to do.[46]

Since the fragmentation of the North American Catholics was so well mirrored in Rome by the representatives of the various communities, the cardinals of Propaganda could not refrain from noticing that the viewpoints of Quebec and Baltimore needed to be assessed against a more complex gamut of available options. Dissenting voices, or simply different opinions, made Rome's decisions more difficult, but they also gave more power to the Holy See. As far as this was practically possible, all opinions were weighed, all voices heard. In the end Burke was appointed vicar apostolic of Nova Scotia and Macdonell bishop of Kingston, but no decision was made before Plessis had been heard on the matter. Although Ambrose Maréchal, archbishop of Baltimore, had violently accused the Irish communities of Norfolk, Virginia, and Charleston, South Carolina, of being schismatic, Propaganda was careful enough to allow some Irish representatives to go to Rome and actually to meet some cardinals. Amidst such dissenting opinions, Rome's attitude was that, often, no decision was preferable to a wrong decision.[47]

Thus the cardinals of Propaganda became entrusted with decisions that theoretically had always been within their jurisdiction but for which they had until then mainly relied on the opinions of the bishops of Quebec and Baltimore. This sense of increased power, together with the growing importance of the United States and Canada in the Western world, produced another major change in the relationship between Rome and North America. Contrary to what had happened in the eighteenth century, in the nineteenth century Rome began not only to react to requests and queries coming from Canada and the United States, but also to envisage an autonomous policy against which those requests and queries were assessed. The cardinals of Propaganda re-emerged from the dark years of the turn of the century with some ideas for an orderly development of Catholicism in North America. Before a special committee (*congregazione particolare*) of 4 March 1808, Cardinal Bartolomeo Pacca, an influential member of Propaganda soon to be appointed pro-secretary of state, reviewed the state of religion in the United States and recommended the erection of a number of new bishoprics and the promotion of the Baltimore see to archbishopric. According to the Dominican Richard Luke Concanen, who was the agent of the Irish clergy in Rome, the new bishoprics would rely solely on the contributions of their flock, a customary arrangement for the four archbishops and twenty-two bishops of Ireland and for the vicars apostolic in England, Scotland, and Newfoundland. In the end, four bishops were appointed and the new dioceses of Boston (Maréchal), New York (Concanen), Philadelphia (Michael Francis Egan), and Bardstown (Benedict-Joseph Flaget) were erected. The promotion of Bishop Carroll to archbishop of Baltimore was also approved.[48] In 1820 this policy was confirmed by the erection of new bishoprics in Charleston (John England) and Richmond (Patrick Kelly).[49]

A few years later the Diocese of Quebec underwent a major reorganization that closely resembled the 1808 subdivision of the Diocese of Baltimore. The general congregation (*congregazione generale*) of Propaganda of 23 November 1818 approved the recommendation of Antonio Cardinal Dugnani, a senior member of the congregation, and appointed Macdonell and MacEachern vicars-general with episcopal powers respectively for Upper Canada and the region comprising Prince Edward Island, Iles de la Madeleine, and New Brunswick. By the same token, they promoted Plessis archbishop of Quebec. One year later, at the general congregation of 24 January 1820, Cardinal

Lorenzo Litta, a future prefect of Propaganda, recommended that Cape Breton be attached to MacEachern's jurisdiction. At the same time, Lartigue and Joseph-Norbert Provencher joined ranks with Macdonell and MacEachern and were entrusted respectively with the district of Montreal and with the Northwest, including Hudson Bay.[50] The American appointees were full bishops and the Canadian appointees only vicars-general with episcopal power (technically they were suffragan bishops, auxiliary to the bishop of Quebec, on whom they still depended). Yet the Canadians would have all been put on the same footing with the Americans had Plessis not advised against it. In Plessis's view, Burke's experiment in Nova Scotia as an independent vicar apostolic had resulted in a net loss, because the Irish prelate had lost all his Quebec priests without being able to recruit new missionaries on his own. Conversely, the new appointees' capacity as suffragan or auxiliary bishops granted them a sufficient degree of independence, without making it impossible for them to retain or receive priests from Quebec. Furthermore, Plessis feared that the British government might try to enforce its alleged right to make the final selection of the candidate for the bishopric.[51] By and large, then, the cardinals of Propaganda acted differently vis-à-vis Canada and the United States only because they were asked to do so.

Propaganda's decisions regarding the United States and Canada were also alike in that they both involved the appointment of archbishops. Plessis had sought a promotion to archbishop in 1817 on the grounds that a much younger church such as the American had been granted the privilege some years previously and that such a move would preserve unity to a territorial jurisdiction soon to be subdivided. When the appointment actually came in 1819, its timing took him by surprise and caused him serious problems for many years. Neither Plessis nor Propaganda had foreseen the British government's opposition to the creation of an archbishopric.[52]

Two appointments do not fit into the orderly pattern described above, namely, Dubourg's as bishop of New Orleans (1815) and Burke's as vicar apostolic of Nova Scotia (1817). They were, indeed, exceptions to the rule. The Diocese of New Orleans was not comparable to any other in the United States on account of its Spanish and French heritage and of the strong opposition that part of the local clergy waged against Dubourg.[53] As for Nova Scotia, Burke's appointment was a direct consequence of the candidate's own intense lobbying. Burke was not, however, appointed full bishop, but vicar apostolic, like O'Donel in Newfoundland.[54] This was what Burke himself had requested, but it is also a possible indication of the mixed feelings of the cardinals of Propaganda, who later implicitly conceded that, in separating Nova Scotia from Quebec, they had made a mistake.[55] Incidentally, both Dubourg (August 1815–January 1816) and Burke (December 1815–April 1816) had personally travelled to Rome to advance their own cause.

Although it was not explicitly mentioned at the time, Propaganda's master plan for an orderly development of North America was certainly there. Some years later, in 1823, Cardinal Francesco Saverio Castiglioni, later to become Pope Pius VIII, recalled it before a plenary session of Propaganda in a way that seems to express a general agreement on a matter of common knowledge among the cardinals. According to Castiglioni, the appointments of MacEachern, Macdonell, Lartigue, Provencher, and even Burke were part of a general plan to have North America united under two archbishoprics and a number of bishoprics. In fact, he pointed out, after Burke's death (1820), that the general congregation of 21 May 1821 had deferred the appointment of his successor, Dennis Lyons, in order not to hamper any decision concerning the reunion of Nova Scotia and New Brunswick. In Castiglioni's scheme, if the two provinces were united, then Newfoundland could also be reattached to the archbishopric of Quebec, "and thus implement that noble idea of completing the Christian world on that side [of the world] with the Archbishop of Quebec and his suffragan bishops."[56]

The outcome of this plan is of little consequence. We now know that Nova Scotia and New Brunswick were never reunited, that Newfoundland was not reunited with Quebec, and that the British government did not recognize Quebec as an archbishopric until 1844. At the same time, by 1829 English-speaking bishops reigned in all the regions of British North America where Irish and Scottish Catholics outnumbered their French-speaking counterparts. (The latest additions were Macdonell, appointed bishop of Kingston in 1826, and MacEachern, appointed bishop of Charlottetown in 1829. Meanwhile, Thomas Scallan had succeeded as vicar apostolic of Newfoundland in 1816, and Fraser had been elected vicar apostolic of Nova Scotia in 1826.) The point, however, is that such a scheme existed, was entirely devised in Rome, and that in its apparent symmetry it took little account of the complex nature of the North American church. The scheme was formulated perhaps as early as the mid 1810s, certainly by the early 1820s, and it was the background against which the cardinals of Propaganda made their decisions vis-à-vis the requests coming from North America. It was also a plan of which the North American Catholic leaders seemed to have no knowledge at all. Their frustrations when visiting Rome were certainly caused by poor public relations on the part of the Holy See and to the inefficiency that is inherent in every bureaucracy. Yet one wonders whether they or their agents were not also faced by a deliberate slowness in the decision-making process that might have interfered with Propaganda's grand scheme. If so, an impatient North American clergy mistook for inefficiency and callousness what was at times deliberate deferral.

The years from the early 1760s through the late 1820s changed significantly the relationship between the Holy See and the Catholics of North America, and, consequently, Rome's policy towards what are now Canada and the United States. Unity and uniformity were replaced by fragmentation and diversity. The Holy See, which until then had relied almost solely on the bishops of Quebec and Baltimore (most often via Paris), was now confronted with direct relations with various North American communities with leaders in such diverse places as Quebec, Halifax, Newfoundland, New York, Baltimore, Norfolk, Charleston, and New Orleans. These communities were mainly characterized by ethnic allegiances and origins, rather than by the sharing of the same territory or by the borders of the same ecclesiastical jurisdiction. Although at first confused by these new developments, the cardinals of Propaganda (who were fully responsible for the Holy See's North American policies) did not oppose in principle this fragmentation and largely accepted the idea that the various communities of North America had different needs, mainly of an ethnic origin, and needed to be treated separately. In the end, this fragmentation made Propaganda's decisions more difficult, but it also gave Rome more power and allowed the Holy See in the nineteenth century to re-emerge forcefully as the centre of Ultramontanism.

NOTES

1 Propaganda was officially founded by Pope Gregory xv on 22 June 1622, with the bull *Inscrutabili divinae providentiae*. Canada and the United States were withdrawn from the jurisdiction of Propaganda by Pope Pius x on 29 June 1908, with the bull *Sapienti consilio*. The standard reference work on Propaganda is Niccolo' Del Re, *La curia romana: Lineamenti storico-giuridici* (Rome: Edizioni di Storia e Letteratura 1970), 185–203. On Propaganda and North America see Luca Codignola, *Guide to the Documents Relating to French and British North America in the Archives of the Sacred Congregation "de Propaganda Fide" in Rome 1622–1799* (Ottawa: National Archives of Canada 1991); Codignola, *Guide to the*

118   Luca Codignola

Documents of Interest for the History of Canada in the Archives of the Sacred Congregation "de Propaganda Fide" in Rome, 1800–20 (Ottawa: National Archives of Canada 1991), especially 1–8.

2 Westminster Diocesan Archives (WDA), B, vol. 46, no. 64, Challoner to Stonor [London], 20 May 1763 ("I suppose the diocese of Quebec is out of the question, because it has its own Chapter, and capitular vicars"). Partially printed in Edwin Hubert Burton, *The Life and Times of Bishop Challoner (1691–1781)*, 2 vols. (New York: Longmans, Green 1909), II, 132, and in Laval Laurent, *Québec et l'Eglise aux Etats-Unis sous Mgr Briand et Mgr Plessis* (Montréal: Librairie St-François 1945), 7.

3 Luca Codignola, "The Rome-Paris-Québec Connection in an Age of Revolutions, 1760–1820," in Pierre Boulle and Richard A. Lebrun, éds., *Le Canada et la Révolution française: Actes du 6e colloque du CIEC. 29, 30, 31 octobre 1987* (Montréal: Centre interuniversitaire d'Etudes euro-péennes/Interuniversity Centre for European Studies 1989), 120. See also Laurent, *Québec*, 14–17.

4 For figures on American population see Robert V. Wells, *The Population of the British Colonies in America before 1776: A Survey of Census Data* (Princeton: Princeton University Press 1975), 46–7, 49, 61, 147, 284; John J. McCusker and Russell R. Menard, *The Economy of British America, 1607–1789* (Chapel Hill: University of North Carolina Press 1985), 54, 136, 203. For contemporary estimates of American Catholics see WDA, B, vol. 45, no. 135, Fisher [*vere* Challoner] to [Stonor], [London], 14 Sept. 1756; copy in Archives of the Sacred Congregation "de Propaganda Fide," Rome (APF, SOCG), vol. 767, fols. 273rv–6rv, as Stonor to Propaganda, [Rome, Dec. 1756]; partially printed in Burton, *Life of Challoner*, II, 125–7; WDA, A, vol. 41, no. 133, Challoner to [Castelli], [London], 10 Sept. 1773; copies in Southwark Curia Diocesan Archives, London (SDCA), ms 37, 525–30; and in APF, Fondo Vienna, vol. 37, fols. 305rv–6rv; printed in J.H. Whyte, "The Vicars Apostolics' Returns of 1773," *Recusant History* 9, 4 (Jan. 1968): 208. See also Charles H. Metger, *Catholics and the American Revolution: A Study in Religious Climate* (Chicago: Loyola University Press 1962), 138–53; James J. Hennesey, *American Catholics: A History of the Roman Catholic Community in the United States* (New York: Oxford University Press 1981), 42, 55. Catholics in England and Wales were 80,000 in 1770, with an overall population of 6.5 million in 1750 and of 9.4 million in 1780. See John Bossy, *The English Catholic Community 1570–1850* (London: Darton, Longman & Todd 1975), 185; Ian R. Christie, *Wars and Revolutions: Britain 1760–1815* (London: Edward Arnold 1982), 3, 158–9.

5 The vicar apostolic and his associates mentioned the Jesuit question in APF, SOCG, vol. 729, fols. 47rv–8rv, Petre and Challoner to Propaganda (PF), [London], 3 Sept. 1745; APF, Congressi, America Antille (C, AA), vol. 1,

fols. 529rv–3orv, [Stonor] to [PF], [Rome, Feb. 1753]; WDA, B, vol. 45, no. 135, Fisher [*vere* Challoner] to [Stonor], [London], 14 Sept. 1756; APF, SOCG, vol. 767, fols. 273rv–6rv, Stonor to PF, [Rome, Dec. 1756]; WDA, B, vol. 46, no. 73, Challoner to Stonor, [London], 15 March 1764; copy in SDCA, ms 37, 70–1; WDA, B, vol. 46, no. 77, Challoner to Stonor, [London], 28 Aug. 1764. See also Peter Keenan Guilday, *The Life and Times of John Carroll, Archbishop of Baltimore (1735–1815)* (New York: Encyclopedia Press 1922), 142–6; Francis O. Edwards, *The Jesuits in England: From 1580 to the Present Day* (Tunbridge Wells: Burn & Oates 1985), 123–5, 130.

6 WDA, B, vol. 45, no. 135, Fisher [*vere* Challoner] to [Stonor], [London], 14 Sept. 1756.

7 APF, SOCG, vol. 729, fols. 47rv–8rv, Petre and Challoner to PF, [London], 3 Sept. 1745; APF, C, AA, vol. 1, fols. 529rv–3orv, [Stonor] to [PF], [Rome, Feb. 1753]; APF, SOCG, vol. 767, fols. 273rv–6rv, Stonor to PF, [Rome, Dec. 1756]; WDA, B, vol. 45, no. 135, Fisher [*vere* Challoner] to [Stonor], [London], 14 Sept. 1756; WDA, B, vol. 46, no. 58, Fisher [*vere* Challoner] to Stonor, [London], 11 June 1762.

8 APF, Acta, vol. 126, fols. 352v–8r, Rome, General Congregation (GC) of 6 Dec. 1756. See also Thomas Aloysius Hughes, *History of the Society of Jesus in North America Colonial and Federal: Text and Documents*, 4 vols. (London: Longmans, Green 1917), II, 578.

9 APF, Acta, vol. 126, fols. 352v–8r, Rome, GC of 6 Dec. 1756 and papal audience of 17 Jan. 1757; APF, Lettere, vol. 190, fols. 21v–2r, [PF] to Petre, Rome, 29 Jan. 1757; APF, Lettere, vol. 244, fols. 524rv–5r, [PF] to Talbot, [Rome], 19 June 1784.

10 Codignola, "Rome-Paris-Quebec Connection," 120–1. For a discussion of the question of the American jurisdiction see Burton, *Life of Challoner*, II, 123–48; Hughes, *History*, II, 580–3; Guilday, *Life of Carroll*, 134–50; Laurent, *Québec*, 5–7; John Tracy Ellis, ed., *Documents of American Catholic History*, 4 vols. (Wilmington: Michael Glazier 1987), I, 124–5.

11 See, for example, APF, SOCG, vol. 876, fols. 386rv–7rv, Carroll to [Antonelli], [Baltimore], 13 March 1786; printed in Thomas Hanley O'Brien, ed., *The John Carroll Papers*, 3 vols. (Notre Dame: University of Notre Dame Press 1976), I, 216–17; and APF, SOCG, vol. 876, fols. 385rv, 388rv, Carroll to [Antonelli], [Baltimore], 12 Jan. 1787; printed in Hanley, ed., *Carroll Papers*, I, 236–8. See also Hennesey, *American Catholics*, 73.

12 After the Conquest, however, there were in Quebec anglophone Catholics and non-Catholic francophones. See Honorius Provost, *Les premiers anglo-canadiens à Québec: Essai de recensement 1759–1775* (Québec: Institut Québécois de Recherche sur la Culture 1984); David Thiery Ruddel, *Québec City 1765–1832: The Evolution of a Colonial Town* (Ottawa: Canadian Museum of Civilization 1987), 39–40; John Hare, Marc Lafrance, and David Ruddel, *Histoire de la ville de Québec 1608–1871* (Montréal: Les

Editions du Boréal Express 1987), 113, 145–9; Marianna O'Gallagher, "The Irish in Québec," in Robert O'Driscoll and Lorna Reynolds, eds., *The Untold Story: The Irish in Canada* (Toronto: Celtic Arts of Canada 1988), 253–7.

13 Serge Courville, "A Mari Usque Ad Mare: La grande saga canadienne," *Revue d'histoire de l'Amérique française* 12, 3 (hiver 1989): 437. See also "Canada in 1800," in Cole Harris and Geoffrey J. Matthews, eds., *Historical Atlas of Canada*, i: *From the Beginning to 1800* (Toronto: University of Toronto Press 1988), 171–3. For a general discussion of immigration and the Catholic community see Terrence Murphy and Cyril J. Byrne, eds., *Religion and Identity: The Experience of Irish and Scottish Catholics in Atlantic Canada* (St John's: Jesperson Press 1987).

14 APF, C, AC, vol. 2, fols. 442rv–3rv, Whelan to [Doria Pamphili], [New York], 28 Jan. 1785. See also Hennesey, *American Catholics*, 75.

15 On emigration at the turn of the century see Marcus Lee Hansen, *The Atlantic Migration 1607–1860: A History of the Continuing Settlement of the United States* (New York: Harper & Row 1961 [1st ed. 1940]), 65–72; Marshall Smelser, *The Democratic Republic 1801–1815* (New York: Harper & Row 1968), 21. On emigration and the Catholic community see Thomas Timothy McAvoy, *A History of the Catholic Church in the United States* (Notre Dame: University of Notre Dame Press 1969), 75–91; Hennesey, *American Catholics*, 102; Jay P. Dolan, *The American Catholic Experience: A History from Colonial Times to the Present* (Garden City, NY: Doubleday 1985), 101–31; James Stuart Olson, *Catholic Immigrants in America* (Chicago: Nelson-Hall 1987), 9, 20, 31–7. See also Codignola, "Conflict or Consensus? Catholics in Canada and in the United States, 1780–1820," Canadian Catholic Historical Association, *Historical Studies* (1988): 43–59.

16 This has been questioned by W. Gordon Handcock, who suggests a larger English immigration or a larger non-Catholic Irish immigration, although somewhat later. See W. Gordon Handcock, "English Migration to Newfoundland," in John J. Mannion, ed., *The Peopling of Newfoundland: Essays in Historical Geography* (St John's: Memorial University of Newfoundland 1977), 32–3. See also W. Gordon Handcock, *"Soe longe as there comes noe women": Origins of English Settlement in Newfoundland* (St John's: Breakwater Books 1989), 23–142.

17 On population estimates see Raymond J. Lahey, "Church Affairs during the French Settlement at Placentia (1662–1714)," unpublished paper presented at the Placentia Area Historical Society, 1 Dec. 1972, 17–18; John J. Mannion, *Irish Settlement in Eastern Canada: A Study of Cultural Transfer and Adaptation* (Toronto: University of Toronto Press 1974), 19; Wells, *Population*, 46–7; Grant Head, *Eighteenth Century Newfoundland: A Geographer's Perspective* (Toronto: McClelland and Stewart 1976), 82–92, 98, 232; Mannion, ed., *Peopling*, 6–7, 12–13; Handcock, "English

Migration to Newfoundland," ibid., 20–1, 27–40; Patrick O'Flaherty, *The Rock Observed: Studies in the Literature of Newfoundland* (Toronto: University of Toronto Press 1979), 18; Glanville James Davies, "England and Newfoundland: Policy and Trade 1660–1783" (PhD dissertation, University of Southampton 1980), 329–30, 340–1, 344; McCusker and Menard, *Economy*, 111–12; George Casey, "Irish Culture in Newfoundland," in Cyril Byrne and Margaret Harry, eds., *Talamh An Eisc: Canadian and Irish Essays* (Halifax: Nimbus Publishing 1986), 208–9, 212; Mannion, "Patrick Morris and Newfoundland Irish Immigration," ibid., 183; Kildare Dobbs, "Newfoundland and the Maritimes: An Overview," in O'Driscoll and Reynolds, eds., *Untold Story*, 177–85. For the latest and the best summary of data see John J. Mannion, W. Gordon Handcock, and Alan Macpherson, "The Newfoundland Fishery, 18th Century," in Harris and Matthews, eds., *Historical Atlas*, plate 25; Mannion, "St John's," ibid., plate 27.

18 On population estimates see Angus Anthony Johnston, *A History of the Catholic Church in Eastern Nova Scotia: 1611–1827* (Antigonish, NS: St Francis Xavier University Press 1960), 103–4; William Stewart McNutt, *The Atlantic Provinces: The Emergence of a Colonial Society 1712–1857* (Toronto: McClelland and Stewart 1965), 94, 117–19; Andrew Hill Clark, *Acadia: The Geography of Early Nova Scotia to 1760* (Madison: University of Wisconsin Press 1986), 58, 211–12, 276, 335, 340, 351; Wells, *Population*, 60–2, 260, 284; Leslie Francis Stokes Upton, *Micmacs and Colonists: Indian-White Relations in the Maritimes 1713–1867* (Vancouver: University of British Columbia Press 1979), 32–3; Terrence M. Punch, "The Irish Catholic, Halifax's First Minority Group," *Nova Scotia Historical Quarterly* 10, 1 (March 1980): 28–9; Punch, "'Gentle as the Snow on a Rooftop': The Irish in Nova Scotia to 1830," in O'Driscoll and Reynolds, eds., *Untold Story*, 215–29; Muriel Kent Roy, "Peuplement et croissance démographique en Acadie," in Jean Daigle, ed., *Les Acadiens des Maritimes: Etudes thematiques* (Moncton: Centre d'Etudes Acadiennes 1980), 166; Terrence Murphy, "James Jones and the Establishment of the Roman Catholic Church Government in the Maritime Provinces," Canadian Catholic Historical Association, *Study Sessions*, 48 (1981): 29; Murphy, "The Emergence of Maritime Catholicism 1781–1830," *Acadiensis* 13 (spring 1984): 31- 2; McCusker and Menard, *Economy*, 111–12. On the Loyalists, a good summary is John G. Reid, *Six Crucial Decades: Times of Change in the History of the Maritimes* (Halifax: Nimbus 1987), 59–90. For the latest and the best summary of data see Graeme Wynn and Debra McNabb, "Pre-Loyalist Nova Scotia," in Harris and Matthews, eds., *Historical Atlas*, I, plate 31.

19 Public Record Office, London (PRO), Colonial Office (CO) 217, vol. 5, fols. 22rv–6rv, F. Legge to W. Legge, Earl of Dartmouth, Halifax, 12 Nov. 1774.

20 On population estimates see Clark, *Three Centuries and the Island: A Historical Geography of Settlement and Agriculture in Prince Edward Island, Canada* (Toronto: University of Toronto Press 1959), 55; J.M. Bumsted, "James Macdonald" in *Dictionary of Canadian Biography*, VI, : *1771–1800* (Toronto: University of Toronto Press 1979), 497; Muriel Kent Roy, "Peuplement," 144, 160, 170–6; Michel Roy, *L'Acadie des origines à nos jours: Essai de synthèse historique* (Montréal: Editions Québec/Amérique 1981), 330–5; Brendan O'Grady, "A 'New Ireland' List: The Irish Presence," in O'Driscoll and Reynolds, eds., *Untold Story*, 203–7.

21 Gerald Marquis Craig, *Upper Canada: The Formative Years 1784–1841* (Toronto: McClelland and Stewart 1963), 1–19, 124–44; Cole Harris and David Wood, "Eastern Canada in 1800," in Harris and Matthews, eds., *Historical Atlas*, I, plate 68; Robert Choquette, *L'Eglise Catholique dans l'Ontario français du dix-neuvième siècle* (Ottawa: Editions de l'Université d'Ottawa 1984), 30–1.

22 WDA, B, vol. 45, no. 135, Fisher [*vere* Challoner] to [Stonor], [London], 14 Sept. 1756. See also Raymond J. Lahey, *James Louis O'Donel in Newfoundland, 1784–1807: The Establishment of the Roman Catholic Church* (St John's: Newfoundland Historical Society 1984), 1.

23 This was the legal ground of the claims of the archbishop of Rouen, François de Harlay de Champvallon, against Laval's appointment. See Lucien Campeau, *L'Evêché de Québec (1674): Aux origines du premier diocèse érigé en Amérique française* (Québec: La Société Historique de Québec 1974).

24 WDA, A, vol. 42, no. 44, Keating, Gaul and Commins to [Talbot], Waterford, 14 Jan. 1784; APF, SOCG, vol. 867, fols. 32rv–3rv, Keating, Gaul, Commins and Maddock to Talbot, [Waterford], 14 Jan. 1784; Archives of the Archdiocese of Dublin, Dublin (AAD), Troy, I, no. 109, O'Donel to Troy, St John's, 24 Dec. 1789. See also Howley, *Newfoundland*, 180–1; Codignola, *Guide*, 5–6; Cyril J. Byrne, *Gentlemen-Bishops and Faction Fighters: The letters of Bishops O'Donel, Lambert, Scallan and Other Irish Missionaries* (St John's: Jesperson Press 1984), 99; Lahey, *O'Donel*, 13.

25 Archives de l'Archidiocèse de Québec, Quebec (AAQ), Eglise du Canada, I, 122, Conseil de la Marine, Paris, 15 May 1717; APF, SOCG, vol. 729, fols. 47rv–8rv, Petre and Challoner to PF, [London], 3 Sept. 1745; APF, C, AA, vol. 1, fols. 529rv–30rv, [Stonor] to [PF], [Rome, Feb. 1753]; APF, C, AA, vol. 2, fols. 36rv–7rv, Challoner to Castelli, London, 2 Aug. 1763; APF, C, America Centrale (AC), vol. 1, fols. 290rv–1rv, [Challoner] to Clement XIII, London, 2 Aug. 1763; APF, SOCG, vol. 867, 31rv, 38rv, PF's internal memorandum [Rome 1784]; APF, Lettere, vol. 244, fols. 480rv–1r, [PF] to Talbot, Rome, 5 June 1784; APF, Lettere, vol. 248, fols. 370rv–1r, [PF] to Talbot, [Rome], 1 July 1786. See also Howley, *Ecclesiastical History of Newfoundland*, 160; Daniel Woodley Prowse, *A History of Newfoundland from the English, Colonial, and Foreign Records*

(London: Macmillan 1895), 276–83; Lahey, "Church Affairs," 17–18;
Mary Mulcahy, "The Catholic Church in Newfoundland: The Pre-Eman-
cipation Years," Canadian Catholic Historical Association, *Historical
Studies* (1985): 5–6.

26 APF, SOCG, vol. 729, fols. 47rv–8rv, Petre and Challoner to PF, [London],
3 Sept. 1745; APF, C, AA, vol. 1, fols. 529rv–30rv, [Stonor] to [PF],
[Rome, Feb. 1753]; APF, SOCG, vol. 767, fols. 273rv–6rv, Stonor to PF,
[Rome, Dec. 1756]; APF, Acta, vol. 126, fols. 352v-8r, Rome, GC of 6 Dec.
1756 and papal audience of 23 Jan. 1757; APF, Lettere, vol. 190, fols.
21v-2r, [PF] to Petre, Rome, 29 Jan. 1757; APF, C, AC, vol. 1, fols. 290rv–
1rv, [Challoner] to Clement XIII, London, 2 Aug. 1763; APF, C, AA, vol.
2, fols. 36rv–7rv, Challoner to Castelli, London, 2 Aug. 1763.

27 George Paré, *The Catholic Church in Detroit, 1701–1888* (Detroit: Gabriel
Richard Press 1951); Michael Power, *A History of the Roman Catholic
Church in the Niagara Peninsula 1615–1816* (St Catharines: Roman Cath-
olic Diocese of St Catharines 1983), 155–73; Codignola, "Rome-Paris-
Quebec Connection," 121–4; Codignola, "Conflict or Consensus?" 49–
50.

28 Lucien Lemieux, *L'établissement de la première province ecclésiastique au
Canada 1783–1844* (Montréal: Fides 1968), 93–8, 228–48; Choquette,
Eglise dans l'Ontario, 27–46.

29 Codignola, "Rome-Paris-Quebec Connection," 118–19; Codignola, "Conflict or Consensus?" 46.

30 AAQ, 20 A, II, 10, [Mariauchau d'Esgly] to Bourg, Quebec, 23 Oct. 1785;
copy in AAQ, 22 A, V, 187; APF, C, AS, vol. 1, fols. 466–7, [Hubert] to
[Villars], [Quebec, after 15 Oct.] 1787; copy in AAQ, 312 CN, I, 12; and
in AAQ, 22 A, V, 270. Historian Léon Thériault criticizes Hubert for his
pro-Irish stance (Thériault, "L'Acadianisation de l'Eglise catholique en
Acadie, 1763–1953," in Daigle, ed., *Acadiens*, 301). See also Murphy,
"Jones," 27–9; Murphy, "Emergence," 72–3; Codignola, "Rome-Paris-
Québec Connection," 119.

31 Codignola, "Rome-Paris-Québec Connection," 119; Codignola, "Conflict
or Consensus?" 47–8.

32 Archivio Segreto Vaticano (ASV), Missioni, vol. 53, fols. not numbered,
Pamphili Colonna to Castelli, Paris, 14 March 1764. See also Codignola,
"Rome-Paris-Quebec Connection," 115–18.

33 APF, Lettere, vol. 244, fols. 559rv–60r, [PF] to Villars, Rome, 4 July 1784.
See also Codignola, "Rome-Paris-Quebec Connection," 117–18; Codignola, "The Failure of an International Scheme: The Old Province of
Quebec and the Savoy Priests, 1779–1784," *Revue d'histoire de l'Amérique
française* 43, 4 (print. 1990): 559–68.

34 APF, C, AS, vol. 1, fols. 364rv–5rv, Villars to [PF], 22 Dec. 1782; APF,
C, AA, vol. 2, fols. 419rv, 422rv, Villars to [PF], 22 March 1783; APF,
Lettere, vol. 242, fols. 327rv–8rv, [PF] to Villars, 16 April 1783. See also

Bernard Ward, *The Dawn of the Catholic Revival in England 1781–1803*, 2 vols. (London: Longmans, Green 1909), I, 1–17; Johnston, *History*, 102–3; Lemieux, *Etablissement*, 14; John Garner, *The Franchise and Politics in British North America 1755–1867* (Toronto: University of Toronto Press 1969), 144; Murphy, "Emergence," 70; Hans Rollmann, "Richard Edwards, John Campbell, and the Proclamation of Religious Liberty in Eighteenth-Century Newfoundland," *Newfoundland Quarterly* 80, 2 (1984): 5–7.

35 APF, C, AC, vol. 2, fols. 423rv–4rv, McManus and McGuire to Pius VI, [1784]; APF, Lettere, vol. 244, fols. 981v-2r, [PF] to Villars, Rome, 23 Dec. 1784; APF, C, America Settentrionale (AS), vol. 1, fols. 423rv–4rv, Villars to [PF], Paris, 17 Jan. 1785; APF, Lettere, vol. 246, fols. 82v-3rv, [PF] to Villars, [Rome], 19 Feb. 1785.

36 APF, Lettere, vol. 248, fols. 515rv–16r, [PF] to Villars, [Rome], 19 Aug. 1786. See also APF, C, AS, vol. 1, fol. 449rv, [Villars] to [Antonelli], [Paris], 12 Dec. 1785; APF, C, AS, vol. 1, fols. 452rv–3rv, Callanan to J. McCormick, Cork, [1786]; APF, Lettere, vol. 248, fols. 355rv–6rv, [PF] to Villars, [Rome], 24 June 1786; APF, C, AS, vol. 1, fols. 454rv–5rv, Villars to [PF], Paris, 17 July 1786.

37 Codignola, "Rome-Paris-Quebec Connection," 119.

38 Ibid., 118–19.

39 Raymond J. Lahey, "Religion and Politics in Newfoundland: The Antecedents of the General Election of 1832," unpublished paper presented to the Newfoundland Historical Society, 15 March 1979, 4; Byrne, ed., *Gentlemen-Bishops*, 10, 88; Codignola, *Guide*, 1–2; Lahey, *O'Donel*, 5–10, 15–17; Hans Rollmann, "John Jones, James O'Donel and the Question of Religious Tolerance in Eighteenth-Century Newfoundland: A Correspondence," *Newfoundland Quarterly* 80, 1 (1984): 24; Rollmann, "Edwards," 5–10; Mulcahy, "Newfoundland," 6, 14; Rollman, "Religious Enfranchisement and Roman Catholics in Eighteenth-Century Newfoundland," in Murphy and Byrne, eds., *Religion and Identity: The Experience of Irish and Scottish Catholics in Atlantic Canada* (St John's: Jesperson Press 1987), 34–52; Codignola, "Rome-Paris-Quebec Connection," 119–20.

40 Codignola, "Rome-Paris-Quebec Connection," 121–5.

41 Codignola, "Conflict or Consensus?"

42 APF, SOCG, vol. 944, fols. 109rv–10rv, Panet to Della Somaglia, Quebec, 17 July 1816; copy in AAQ, 210 A, XII, 524; AAQ, 210 A, XII, 546, Panet to MacEachern, Quebec, 23 Aug. 1826.

43 Codignola, "Conflict or Consensus?," 47.

44 O'Sullivan was Bishop O'Donel's nephew, was educated by the Sulpicians, and ended up an opponent of Plessis. See AAQ, 30 CN, I, 17, O'Donel to Plessis, St John's, 10 June 1801; AAQ, 210 A, XII, 124, Plessis to Poynter, Quebec, 20 Oct. 1824.

45 On the official agents in Rome of the bishops of Quebec see Ivanhoë Caron, "Les évêques de Québec, leurs Procureurs et leurs vicaires généraux, à Rome, à Paris et à Londres (1734–1834)," *Mémoires de la Société Royale du Canada*, 3ème sér., 29 (mai 1935): sec. I, 153–78.

46 APF, C, AS, vol. 2, fols. 269rv–70rv, Plessis to Litta, Quebec, 23 Nov. 1816; copy in AAQ, 210 A, IX, 67; APF, C, AC, vol. 3, fols. 564rv–5rv, Plessis to Litta, 26 April 1817; APF, C, AS, vol. 2, fols. 303rv–4rv, Plessis to [Fontana], Rome, 12 Dec. 1819; APF, C, AS, vol. 2, fols. 305rv–6rv, Plessis to Fontana, Rome, 4 Jan. 1820; APF, C, AS, vol. 2, fols. 307rv–8rv, Plessis to Fontana, [Rome], 30 Jan. [1820]; C, AS, vol. 2, fols. 324rv–5rv, Plessis to Fontana, London, 5 June 1820.

47 Codignola, "Conflict or Consensus?" 44–5, 51–7; Codignola, *Guide*, 17–18.

48 APF, Acta, vol. 177, fols. 309rv–44rv, CP of 4 March 1808.

49 Hennesey, *American Catholics*, 100.

50 APF, Acta, vol. 181, fols. 203rv–8rv, 211rv, 222rv, GC of 23 Nov. 1818; APF, Acta, vol. 183, fols. 4rv–11[a]rv, GC of 24 Jan. 1820. See also Lemieux, *Etablissement*, 87–137; Hennesey, *American Catholics*, 89–100; Codignola, "Rome-Paris-Quebec Connection," 7–8; Codignola, "Conflict or Consensus?" 44–5.

51 APF, SOCG, vol. 919, fols. 148rv–51rv, Plessis to Litta, Quebec, 6 Dec. 1817; copy in AAQ, 210 A, IX, 284. See also Codignola, "Conflict or Consensus?," 52.

52 APF, SOCG, vol. 919, fols. 148rv–51rv, Plessis to Litta, Québec, 6 Dec. 1817; copy in AAQ, 210 A, IX, 284.

53 APF, Acta, vol. 177, fols. 276rv–87rv, PF's internal memorandum, [Rome, July/Aug. 1815]; APF, Acta, vol. 178, fols. 289rv–95rv, 296rv–304rv, Doria Pamphili to PF, [Rome, Dec. 1815]. See also Annabelle M. Melville, *Louis William DuBourg, Bishop of Louisiana and the Floridas, Bishop of Montauban, and Archbishop of Besançon 1766–1833* (Chicago: Loyola University Press 1986), 328–48.

54 APF, Acta, vol. 179, fols. 34rv–42rv, GC of 1 April 1816; AAQ, 12 A, H, fol. 133 [Litta] to Plessis, [Rome], 16 April 1816; copy in APF, Lettere, vol. 297, fols. 67v–70r; APF, Acta, vol. 180, fols. 2rv–18rv, 20rv–48rv, GC of 19 May 1817.

55 APF, Acta, vol. 186, fols. 76rv–82rv, [Castiglioni] to [PF], [Rome, Feb. 1823].

56 Ibid.

6 Trusteeism in Atlantic Canada: The Struggle for Leadership among the Irish Catholics of Halifax, St John's, and Saint John, 1780–1850

TERRENCE MURPHY

The formative period for the English-speaking Catholic communities of Atlantic Canada was 1780 to 1850. Before that time, a certain number of Irish Catholics had settled in Newfoundland and Nova Scotia, but it was only after 1780 that the total number in any one location reached the level at which viable Catholic congregations could take shape. Increased immigration from Ireland and Scotland, together with the arrival of Catholic Loyalists and disbanded soldiers after the American revolutionary war, ensured that by the turn of the century each of the Atlantic colonies had a significant and rapidly expanding Catholic population.[1] This rapid growth, however, put an intense strain on the meagre resources of the Roman Catholic church in the region. Nova Scotia, New Brunswick, and Prince Edward Island were still under the jurisdiction of the bishop of Quebec, while Newfoundland, like the former American colonies, had been placed under the vicar apostolic of the London District. Neither bishop could effectively supervise or provide for such distant territories. Few stable missions were established, and vast areas went for long periods without the regular services of a priest.[2]

In these circumstances, the task of founding Roman Catholic institutions fell largely to laymen. Lay initiative was especially important in the major towns, such as Halifax, St John's, and Saint John. The growing Catholic populations of these centres were almost exclusively Irish, but while ethnically homogeneous they were socially differentiated, comprising most occupations from merchant to unskilled labourer. Leadership was assumed by the more prosperous members of the community – merchants, professionals, shopkeepers, and independent artisans – who became the founders and principal benefactors of the new urban churches. The efforts of these men had a definite political dimension, since at the beginning of the period Catholics in each of the Atlantic colonies were subject to one form or another of legal restraint. Before they could establish Catholic parishes they had to obtain the permission of the government. Once freedom of worship was secured, however, lay leaders purchased land, erected chapels, and recruited priests. In the process they became the legal proprietors of church property, since the laws of incorporation, designed to favour the established Church of England, offered no practical alternative to vesting temporalities by civil title in the hands of local trustees.

What began as a matter of necessity, however, was soon transformed into a question of principle, as lay trustees began to see themselves as the "patrons" of their congregations, with all that that implied in terms of proprietorial rights. In two of the major centres in the region – Halifax and Saint John – long and bitter conflicts developed when trustees tried to assert their authority over the temporal and even spiritual affairs of the local church. In the third case – that of St John's – the role of lay trustees was initially more restricted and therefore less controversial, but lay committees did exist at certain crucial times, and a major political controversy erupted between the bishop and a portion of the laity which reflected many of the issues underlying trustee conflicts elsewhere. Episcopal authority eventually triumphed throughout the region, especially as the spread of Ultramontanism fostered more authoritarian and centralizing concepts of church government, but this occurred only after a long period of turmoil.

The role of lay committees in the emerging Catholic communities of Atlantic Canada closely resembles the much more famous activities of American Catholic lay trustees. Lay involvement in ecclesiastical matters and attempts by lay trustees to control congregational affairs were so widespread in the United States during the late eighteenth and early nineteenth centuries that trusteeism is usually considered a basic characteristic of American Catholicism during this period. Recently, American Catholic historians have reinterpreted trusteeism by rejecting the clericalist view that it was an unconscionable revolt against legitimate ecclesiastical authority in favour of the idea that it was a natural consequence of the legal and cultural circumstances of Catholicism in the United States. This change has occurred, however, without upsetting the fundamental assumption that trusteeism was a distinctly American phenomenon. If anything, this assumption has been strengthened. Patrick Carey,[3] who provides by far the most up-to-date and sophisticated interpretation of trusteeism, argues that the movement must be seen primarily as a constructive attempt to adapt European Catholic institutions to the republican environment of the United States by "democratizing" church government. Carey recognizes that comparable examples of Catholic congregationalism can be found elsewhere in the English-speaking world (in English cities such as London and Lancaster, for example, where large numbers of Irish immigrants settled),[4] but he treats them as analogues to the American experience, reserving trusteeism properly speaking for the United States.

The evidence from Atlantic Canada, however, suggests that we are dealing with essentially the same phenomenon and that it flourished in an anti-republican as much as a republican environment. The lay committees of management that emerged in Atlantic Canada were identical in form and function to American boards of trustees. The first to take shape (Halifax) was in existence and engaged in conflict with the clergy as early as the first trustee controversy in the United States (New York). Moreover, the trustees of Atlantic Canada closely resembled their American counterparts in their social background and in their values and attitudes. Drawn from the small but rising Catholic bourgeoisie and from the independent artisan class, they were eager to be accepted in "respectable" society. This encouraged among them a desire to improve the image of Catholicism in the eyes of their Protestant neighbours and a generally accommodating attitude towards the predominant culture. They were deferential in politics and conciliatory in matters of religion. They attended Protestant worship occasionally and gladly accepted Protestant contributions to their church building funds. The very formation of lay committees, inasmuch as it was a conscious imitation of Protestant church polity, reflected their desire to conform to prevailing norms. Like their American counterparts, the lay committees seem also to have emulated Protestant worship by stressing the importance of preaching. They were sincere Catholics but minimized those aspects of Catholic practice, including eucharistic piety, that might be construed as superstitious. Judging by the complaints of the clergy, they attended the sacraments only infrequently. Besides the desire for social acceptance, they may have been influenced in some measure by the "enlightened" spirit of the times, with its stress on tolerance and rationality in religion.

The majority of trustees on both sides of the border, however, were more concerned with building up Catholic institutions than with theological concerns or the devotional life of the church. They were preoccupied with the ownership of property and with maintaining a privileged status within their congregations. Conflict with the clergy occurred not only when priests and bishops tried to limit their proprietorial rights but also when they tried to inhibit their social ambitions by forcing them to cut their ties with Protestants. Class distinctions meanwhile divided them from the majority of their fellow parishioners. Ethnic rivalries also exacerbated trustee controversies, but in Atlantic Canada these tensions developed between congregations of one nationality (Irish) and clergy of another (Canadian or Scottish) rather than within congregations of mixed ethnic background, as sometimes happened in the United States.

The first major centre in Atlantic Canada where laymen assumed leadership of the Catholic community was Halifax. A lay committee was formed there in 1781 for the purpose of achieving relief from the penal statutes imposed a generation earlier by the Nova Scotia legislature. By 1783 Catholic spokesmen had secured the first Nova Scotia relief act, allowing clergy to exercise their functions without risk of punishment and also permitting Catholics to acquire land by deed and inheritance.[5] The same committee purchased land,[6] built a chapel, and recruited as their priest an Irish Capuchin named James Jones.[7] This was done without prior approval from Bishop d'Esgly of Quebec, but d'Esgly not only sanctioned the arrangement after the fact but also named Jones superior of the mission for Nova Scotia.[8] The title "superior of the mission" was used imprecisely, for Jones's appointment did not involve erecting Nova Scotia as a separate ecclesiastical jurisdiction. His powers were really those of a vicar-general.[9] Nevertheless, the intervention of the lay committee had decisively altered the situation of Catholics in the region. Jones was the first English-speaking missionary to serve in Nova Scotia, and the position entrusted to him by the bishop of Quebec recognized the changing nature of the Catholic population of the Maritimes.

The original lay delegates in Halifax were militant in asserting their rights over the clergy. Styling themselves church wardens, they insisted on control of church property and on a decisive voice in the appointment of additional priests. They offered no clear justification of their claims apart from the notion that as the founders and principal benefactors of the parish they deserved a say in its management. From Jones's arrival in 1785 until 1792 they engaged him in a series of bitter disputes, interfering with his use of the presbytery, challenging his decisions concerning burials in the churchyard, and resisting his attempt to appoint an assistant pastor without their consent.[10] At the height of controversy they also formed an alliance with William Phelan, a priest stationed at Arichat whom Jones was attempting to discipline for irregular conduct. Matters came to a head in 1792, when, armed with evidence supplied by Phelan, they threatened to take Jones to court over his management of money entrusted to him by the bishop of Quebec.[11] The total failure of this court case seems to have been followed by a period of relative peace, but when Jones was preparing to leave Halifax in 1800 the wardens threatened him with arrest,[12] again on the grounds that he was attempting to misappropriate church funds.[13] Subsequent events proved that Jones was innocent of wrongdoing,[14] but the fact that the accusation was made at all shows how much mistrust existed.

Furthermore, tensions had developed among the Halifax laity, both between the prosperous pewholders and the less affluent majority and between older members of the congregation and relative newcomers. These conflicts rose to the surface in the wake of Jones's departure. For his replacement he had appointed an Irish Dominican, Edmund Burke, on whom the wardens were able to impose their demands for the control of temporalities.[15] As part of their plan to manage church finances, however, they were also determined to change the way in which money was raised from the congregation. Hitherto financial support had come almost entirely from the minority of parishioners included among the founding fathers and pewholders. The wardens wished to redistribute the burden by forcing the rapidly increasing rank and file to participate in a system of compulsory subscriptions. To enforce compliance they denied the rights of parishioners, including burial in the churchyard, to noncontributors.[16] At the same time, they wanted to retain the practice of allowing only pewholders to elect the wardens.[17] These measures sparked an open revolt against their authority from the less affluent parishioners. Leaders for the popular party were found among merchants and artisans who seem to have been excluded from the cliquish committee of management because they had arrived in the city after the parish was established.[18] With the support of at least two hundred parishioners, they proposed a program of reform that would restore a strictly voluntary system of support, give all members of the congregation a vote in elections, and dedicate a much larger share of parish revenues to the relief of the poor.[19]

After an attempt to reach a compromise between the wardens and their opponents had failed, the wardens referred the dispute to Bishop Pierre Denaut of Quebec.[20] This appeal opened the way for the assertion of episcopal authority over the Halifax congregation. Denaut rebuked both lay factions, not just for causing dissension but especially for assuming powers that properly belonged to him.[21] He replaced Edmund Burke as pastor and vicar-general by a man with the same name, an Irish secular priest with several years experience in Quebec and in the Upper Canadian missions. Acting on the bishop's instructions, the newly appointed Burke arranged the election of new wardens by a procedure even more restrictive than the original one.[22] The new committee met only in his presence and all its decisions had to receive his written approval. Whenever there was a risk that one of their measures encroached on episcopal prerogatives, it was passed with a suspending clause making it subject to the bishop's approval.[23]

Denaut made a pastoral visitation to Halifax in 1803, during which he was able personally to suppress the few traces of lay independence still in evidence.[24] For the time being, clerical authority had achieved a major victory. Burke established himself as a widely respected figure in the Halifax community and remained firmly in control of the congregation for the rest of his term of office. In 1817 he was himself raised to the episcopate and named first vicar apostolic of Nova Scotia.[25] The appointment of a local bishop enjoying widespread popular support neutralized for the time being the forces of Catholic congregationalism.

The 1820s, however, saw a fresh outbreak of controversy in Halifax. The immediate crisis was caused by Bishop Burke's failure to arrange a suitable successor for himself. His death in 1820 was followed by an interregnum of six years during which Nova Scotia was without a bishop and the rapidly expanding Halifax congregation was in the care of Burke's nephew, John Carroll, a newly ordained and very inexperienced priest. Carroll's ineffective leadership allowed the initiative to pass once again to the middle-class laity, who asserted their independence in the face of faltering clerical authority. One witness declared that "Halifax was in an uproar during his tenure."[26]

A new bishop, William Fraser, was finally consecrated in 1827, but his appointment only made matters worse. Instead of moving to Halifax, Fraser maintained his residence among his Scottish countrymen in eastern Nova Scotia. Ethnic resentment now began to play a part alongside strictly ecclesiastical differences, although much more was involved than tensions between Irish and Scots. Fraser placed Halifax in the care of an Irish vicar-general, John Loughnan, who proved very unpopular with the Catholic middle class, especially when he tried to prohibit mixed marriages.[27] Two members of the prominent Tobin family, leading merchants in Halifax, were actually married in the Anglican church.[28] At the same time, middle-class leaders were accused of currying favour with Protestants by minimizing distinctively Catholic practices. Evidently, some of them promoted the use of English in the liturgy and advocated the idea that hymn-singing and preaching, rather than the eucharistic sacrifice, were the heart of Catholic worship.[29]

Convinced that Fraser was ultimately indifferent to their needs, the Halifax laity persuaded him to apply to Archbishop Murray of Dublin for two additional Irish priests.[30] Murray sent them Richard Baptist O'Brien and Joseph Dease. In some respects, the arrival of Dease and O'Brien marks a new departure for Catholicism in Halifax. Both men proved highly satisfactory to the laity and cooperated with them in promoting the further growth of Catholic institutions. They helped, for example, to plan a second parish for the city (intending that Dease would become pastor) and collaborated with lay governors in founding St Mary's College (O'Brien was appointed first principal). Yet they also acted as an important link between Halifax and the Catholic revival then gathering momentum in Ireland. In particular, they introduced to the city branches of the new voluntary societies that were helping to transform Irish Catholicism. By sponsoring religious education and by promoting popular devotions, these organizations served to increase conformity among the laity to official standards of observance. At the same time, they offered an alternative sphere for lay involvement, one that was ultimately more subject than trustee boards to clerical supervision. When O'Brien and Dease arrived in Halifax in 1839, there were no Catholic confraternities in the city; by the time O'Brien left in 1845 (Dease departed earlier), at least six had been established. Not all can be traced directly to their efforts, but their names often appear alongside those of their lay supporters in lists of officers or in the proceedings of the various societies.[31]

Meanwhile, other important changes were taking place among the lay leaders of the Halifax congregation. By 1840 most of the original trustees and their immediate successors had died or left the city, and they were being replaced by a new generation of merchants and professionals, such as Michael Tobin, Jr, and Laurence O'Connor Doyle. Like the newer clergy, these lay spokesmen were profoundly influenced by the course of events in Ireland. The successful campaign for Catholic emancipation, besides opening up political life to Catholics, increased their self-respect. A new confidence developed in their capacity for collective self-improvement, which was reinforced by other popular movements such as Father Theobald Mathew's temperance crusade. In pragmatic terms, Daniel O'Connell, the Irish "Liberator," had shown how much was to be gained by organizing and mobilizing the Catholic rank and file. Inspired by his ideals and methods, the younger lay activists in Halifax abandoned the purely elitist attitudes and anti-clericalism of their predecessors in favour of a position as co-leaders with the clergy of a progressive and united Catholic population, whose relative influence in the community was increasing with rapid growth. Most of them were also ardent nationalists, and in 1843 they established at Halifax a branch of O'Connel's Repeal Association.

The final emancipation of Nova Scotia Catholics, which immediately followed the British Emancipation Act, allowed them to participate on an equal footing in local politics. Doyle was elected to the Nova Scotia Assembly in 1832, only the second Catholic to achieve this status. The political power and the unity of Catholics was growing steadily. During the election of 1843, when the Reformers (supposedly the allies of the Catholics) failed to include Doyle or any other Catholic among their candidates for the Halifax city riding, Tobin and other well-known lay spokesmen organized a boycott of the election by Catholic voters which resulted in the defeat of a Reformer by a Tory candidate. Awareness of their new-found strength made Catholic leaders less reliant on the support of sympathetic Protestants and therefore less accommodating to Protestant standards.

Despite the harmony between O'Brien and Dease and the rising generation of lay spokesmen, the two priests were sharply at odds with Bishop Fraser and John Loughnan, who resented their very presence in the diocese.[32] A confrontation occurred over the plans for a second parish in Halifax, which Loughnan saw as a threat to his position. The laity were determined to have Dease as pastor of the new church and wrote to Fraser requesting his appointment. Fraser described their petition as the work of a "few purse-proud Pedlars and Butchers" and rejected it on the grounds that the appointment of clergy was exclusively an episcopal prerogative.[33] Dease afterwards requested and received permission to leave the diocese. A thousand members of the congregation petitioned to have him reinstated.[34] Fraser replied that their petition had been "committed to the flames."[35] Dease's departure, however, was followed by vigorous lobbying at Dublin and Rome,[36] with the result that the Vicariate of Nova Scotia was converted into a diocese and an Irishman, William Walsh, appointed as coadjutor to Fraser. Fraser, who learned about the change through the newspapers, deeply resented the way in which Walsh's appointment had been made, and in this he was supported by a majority of his clergy.[37] Efforts to establish a satisfactory working relationship between the two bishops failed, so that after an interval of two years Rome had to intervene again, this time dividing Nova Scotia into two dioceses, one under Fraser in the east and the other under Walsh at Halifax.

The erection of a separate diocese of Halifax with an Irish bishop at its head was a clear victory for the lay activists. Ironically, however, it marked the end of the system that had given them effective control over parish affairs. Walsh attracted tremendous support among the inarticulate majority of Catholics and quickly emerged as the living focus of a united Catholic community. The lay leaders whose agitation had led to his appointment, and who therefore regarded him as the champion of their cause, offered no resistance when he began to assert his authority. At a meeting held shortly after his arrival, he easily persuaded them to surrender into his hands the management of church property.[38] He also took effective control of St Mary's College by replacing the lay board of regents with seven clergymen.[39] O'Brien was replaced as principal by Father Frechette, a Canadian priest;[40] O'Brien evidently found this arrangement unacceptable, and left the diocese.[41] Walsh consolidated these steps in 1849 by establishing an episcopal corporation whereby he and his successors were recognized as a body corporate for the purpose of acquiring and holding real estate.[42] This method of regulating the ownership of church property, first used at Baltimore in 1833 and subsequently adopted by other American and also some British North American dioceses (Quebec and Saint John, for example), provided the first effective alternative to congregational boards of trustees. Walsh was challenged in the courts, but only by one member of the congregation, who acted largely from personal motives.[43] Given the failure of other laymen to support him, his efforts ended in inevitable defeat. After 1849 socially prominent laymen continued to exercise considerable influence among Halifax Catholics. Their sphere of activity, however, shifted more and more to politics, where they were relatively autonomous, and to Catholic voluntary societies, where they operated within the framework of a solidly episcopal polity.

Another centre in Atlantic Canada where a lay committee assumed leadership of the Catholic community was St John's. In 1783 four Irish merchants operating out of Newfoundland appealed to the governor of the colony for permission to build a Roman Catholic chapel and to invite a priest to come to the island.[44] Having obtained a favourable response, they invited James Louis O'Donel, a prominent Irish Franciscan, to serve as their pastor.[45] O'Donel was willing to do so but was required first to apply to Bishop Talbot, vicar apostolic of the London District, for authorization. O'Donel impressed upon Talbot the need to have not only priestly faculties but also the powers of vicar-general in order effectively to serve Newfoundland.[46] Talbot listened sympathetically to O'Donel's arguments and in fact referred the matter to Rome with a recommendation that the Newfoundland mission be established as a separate ecclesiastical territory. On 30 May 1784 the Holy See named O'Donel prefect apostolic (or superior of the mission) for Newfoundland.[47] This arrangement preceded by one month the appointment of John Carroll to the same position for the United States[48] and was very likely part of a broader plan on Rome's part to put the North American church on a more independent footing.

Laymen continued to play a role in ecclesiastical affairs after O'Donel's appointment. The names of five Catholic businessmen, for example, appear with O'Donel's on the lease for the chapel site in St John's.[49] Unlike Halifax, however, lay leadership and lay proprietorship of church property did not immediately give rise to controversy. It is not even clear whether a lay committee of management was formed at this stage. Routine administration of parish finances seems to have been left in O'Donel's hands, although he took for granted the need to keep the laity informed about his decisions.[50] This spirit of cooperation, moreover, was based on an underlying unity of purpose between O'Donel and the merchants who recruited him. In seeking a resident priest, they had hoped he would regularize the affairs of the church in Newfoundland, not least of all by banishing the wandering, irregular clerics who had previously infiltrated the colony, scandalizing and embarrassing Catholics.[51] They therefore had a strong incentive to support his authority, and their support was soon rewarded as he chased these clerical vagabonds off the island. At the same time, the Catholic merchants wanted a priest who would share their policy of peaceful accommodation with Protestants and the government. O'Donel fit this requirement perfectly. He was a product of the Catholic Enlightenment, tolerant, conciliatory, and deeply respectful of legitimate civil authority. He was quick to inculcate in his flock respect for law and order, and on this basis constructed a durable alliance with the Protestant authorities. In 1794 eighteen Catholic laymen, obviously well satisfied with his leadership, joined the Newfoundland clergy in successfully petitioning Rome for his promotion to the episcopate.[52] He was the first Roman Catholic bishop appointed to British North America apart from the bishop of Quebec. His episcopal rank increased even further his stature in the Newfoundland community, and the aspiring Catholic bourgeoisie were able to participate indirectly in this added prestige.

The same pattern of harmonious relations between Catholics and Protestants and between the clergy and the Catholic middle class persisted into the terms of O'Donel's two immediate successors, Patrick Lambert and Thomas Scallan. Lambert and Scallan carried on O'Donel's eirenic and accommodating policies and continued to accept lay involvement as a normal part of congregational life. Lay leadership meanwhile found a variety of outlets, in philanthropic endeavours and politics as well as parochial affairs, with the same individuals taking the lead in all three areas. In the sphere of philanthropy, the key institution in the opening decades of the nineteenth century was the Benevolent Irish Society, founded in the last year of O'Donel's episcopate. Dedicated to poor relief and to educational ventures, the BIS was officially nondenominational in character, but its membership was overwhelmingly Catholic, and Catholic spokesmen assumed an increasingly prominent role on the society's executive with the passage of time.[53] In the political arena, laymen cooperated with the clergy in pressing the government to provide funds for the schooling of Catholic children, to remove restrictions on the performance of marriages by Roman Catholic priests, to admit Catholics to the newly formed Executive Council of Newfoundland, and to extend to Newfoundland the provisions of the Catholic Emancipation Act. Strongly worded petitions were submitted to the government on all these issues, and in the case of the Emancipation Act lay leaders also presided at large Catholic rallies.[54] In parochial administration, a lay committee was formed under Scallan's administration, or possibly even earlier. Little is known of the activities of the committee, except that it coooperated well with the bishop. In 1824 the members passed a resolution assuring Scallan of their total support and pledging themselves always "to abide by his friendly and pastoral advice."[55] This statement may be interpreted as evidence of an exceptionally compliant attitude on the part of the committee, but, especially in light of other information we have concerning Scallan's policies, it might also be taken as an indication that he seldom resisted them.

The entire situation in Newfoundland began to change in 1823, with the arrival of Michael Anthony Fleming. Fleming served six years as curate to Bishop Scallan in St John's before becoming his coadjutor in 1829 and his successor as vicar apostolic in 1830.[56] He was a young man even when he succeeded to the bishopric, and like the newer clergy in Halifax he reflected the new expansive mood of Irish Catholicism. In Fleming's case, this took a particularly uncompromising form, more confident but also more sectarian and more authoritarian in spirit. Almost from the outset, he quarrelled with the leaders of the Catholic laity. For example, while Fleming was still Scallan's curate, he collected a large sum for the purpose of enlarging and improving the chapel. He wanted to retain control of these funds, but the parish committee insisted this was their prerogative. The committee appealed to Scallan, who forced Fleming to turn over the money to them. According to Fleming, they then squandered it by making useless alterations to the church.[57]

While the control of temporalities was an important issue for Fleming, the underlying cause of his quarrels with lay leaders was their relationship with Protestants. On this issue there was a growing division among the laity themselves, precipitated partly by Fleming's policies but due also to a growing polarization in Newfoundland society. As Philip McCann has observed, the social cleavage in Newfoundland was along religious, ethnic, and economic lines,[58] with Irish Catholics forming a vastly disproportionate share of the labouring class. Fleming identified closely with the poor. He was incensed, however, by the behaviour of a small, influential circle of Catholic merchants who, in his view, would do anything to ingratiate themselves with the Protestant elite. In his bitter attacks on this group, he referred to them variously as "pretended liberals," "indifferent Catholics," or "Orange Catholics." He took special exception to their habit of participating in Protestant worship. After going to Mass on Sunday morning, he reported, they routinely attended a Protestant service at night. They rejected and even ridiculed distinctively Catholic beliefs and practices, including the Real Presence and the use of holy water.[59] In his reports to Rome, Fleming placed much of the blame for fostering and condoning this behaviour on Bishop Scallan. Scallan, he said, often appeared at important Protestant funerals or at Protestant services to mark official events in full ecclesiastical dress, thus "countenancing the worship of heretics."[60]

Another conflict between Fleming and the laity occurred over the Orphan Asylum School. This charitable institution was founded three years after Fleming's arrival in St John's by the Benevolent Irish Society. A number of prominent Catholic laymen, including some of the so-called "liberals" (Timothy Hogan and McLean Little, for instance), were appointed to the school's board of directors.[61] Since the BIS was officially nondenominational in character, a formal policy had been adopted of excluding from the curriculum religious books or catechisms that might arouse sectarian feelings.[62] All of the teachers and most of the students, however, were Roman Catholic, and Fleming was outraged that these Catholic pupils should be denied religious instruction. He tried personally to teach catechism in the school, but was "pre-emptorily forbidden" to do so by a majority on the board of directors. Forced to instruct the students outside of school in the evenings, he nevertheless succeeded in preparing several hundred of them for First Communion. Some of the lay spokesmen, however, appealed to Scallan to prevent Fleming from holding a public procession for fear such a display would offend

Protestants. Scallan as usual acquiesced in their wishes, and Fleming was limited to a private ceremony. Still, he regarded the eventual outcome of this incident as a major victory. Having shown how much could be accomplished by regular instruction of disadvantaged children, he promptly convoked a meeting of the principal financial sponsors of the Orphan Asylum School, who apparently overruled the policy of the board by giving Fleming a free hand to teach religion.[63]

Fleming's ability to impose his will on his Catholic opponents was greatly strengthened when he succeeded Scallan as bishop in 1830. New sources of conflict also developed, however, as political tensions were added to the ecclesiastical differences that already existed. In 1832 Newfoundland was granted its first representative assembly. During the ensuing general election Fleming threw his support behind three candidates for the St John's riding, two of whom (William Carson, a Unitarian, and John Kent, a Catholic) were sharp critics of the ruling oligarchy. Against the reform candidates, the Catholic "liberals" supported one of their own circle, Patrick Kough, who represented mercantile interests.[64] The results of the election were inconclusive in the sense that both Kent and Kough were elected, while Carson went down to defeat. Fleming was attacked for interfering in politics, however, by his Catholic critics as well as by Henry Winton, Protestant editor of the *Public Ledger*.[65] Furthermore, in a by-election of the following year, Fleming again endorsed Carson over one of the Catholic "liberals," Timothy Hogan. When Hogan accused Fleming of exercising undue influence and withdrew from the contest on this account, most of the Catholic population boycotted his business until he issued a public apology.[66] A Catholic crowd also demonstrated against Winton for his continued attacks on the bishop, gathering outside his house on Christmas night. The garrison had to be called out to suppress the demonstration, and a number of particpants were bayonetted.[67]

After 1833 the anti-Fleming forces among Catholics became more isolated from their co-religionists. Fleming enjoyed the support of the vast majority of priests (many of whom he had recruited directly from Ireland) and also of the great bulk of the laity. Father John Thomas Troy, Fleming's high-handed vicar-general, took the lead in denouncing the dissidents and in stirring up feeling against them. At one stage (whether at Troy's instigation is unclear) a placard appeared in the chapel identifying seven merchants as subscribers to the *Public Ledger*, by now the symbol of opposition to Fleming, and calling for a boycott of their businesses.[68] This measure was so effective that five of the denounced individuals publicly apologized and severed their connections with the newspaper.[69] Virtually the only support lay dissidents enjoyed within the Catholic community came from Father Timothy Browne, a long-time missionary in Newfoundland who was engaged in a dispute of his own with Fleming.[70] Fleming's lay opponents shared their grievances with one another and endorsed one another's complaints to the ecclesiastical authorities in Rome.[71] In 1841, when Browne travelled to Rome to submit and defend his case in person, his trip was paid for largely by donations from the anti-Fleming Catholics and from sympathetic Protestants.[72]

The more isolated Fleming's opponents became from their fellow Catholics, the more closely they identified themselves with the government. In 1835, for example, McLean Little, one of the principal members of the group, submitted a formal protest to the governor of Newfoundland, asking him in effect to protect him against Fleming and Troy.[73] He and other like-minded Catholics, he said, had been mercilessly persecuted for refusing to accept clerical direction in politics, with the result that their rights both as Catholics and British subjects had been denied. Government officials in turn used such evidence of clerical tyranny as part of a campaign of their own against Fleming. Depicting him as a threat to the stability and good order of the colony, they attempted first to have him censured by Rome and then to have him removed from office.[74] The breaking-point in their relations came in 1840, when Fleming again intervened in an election.[75] This led indirectly to the setting up of a Select Committee of the House of Commons to investigate the situation in Newfoundland. In effect, the committee was an inquiry into Fleming's activities, relying heavily on hostile testimony from Catholic dissidents. The report of the committee was a major blow to the cause of political reform in Newfoundland, as it resulted in the restriction of the franchise and the introduction of an amalgamated house of nominated and elected members.[76]

Proceedings against Fleming at Rome, however, were entirely unsuccessful. Although Pope Gregory xvi personally insisted on the removal of Troy,[77] Fleming was not only continued in office but in 1847 his vicariate was raised to a regular diocese. By that date, independent lay opinion in St John's had completely given way to episcopal leadership. Fleming enjoyed enormous support among the Catholic populace, manifested not least in their contributions (both physical and financial) to the building of his cathedral.[78] This close identification with the people was the key to his success. Even the Catholic bourgeoisie, however, had never been unanimous against him, for Fleming's political allies, such as John Kent, came from essentially the same social background as his Catholic opponents.

Like the new lay leadership in Halifax, they were prepared to cooperate rather than compete with the clergy. In sum, Fleming was the first clear example in Atlantic Canada of an Ultramontane bishop, uncompromising in religion but progressive in politics, whose popular clericalism signalled a new alliance between prelates, priests, middle-class reformers, and the Catholic rank and file. This united Catholic body was more self-reliant and confident of its strength but also more susceptible to authoritarian forms of church government.

Saint John was a third example of a centre in Atlantic Canada where laymen assumed a position of leadership in the emerging Catholic community. The first evidence of a lay committee there dates from 1793, when four Catholic spokesmen sought and obtained permission from Governor Guy Carleton to bring a priest to the city.[79] These efforts faltered, however, and no serious steps were taken towards organizing a congregation until the arrival in 1814 of an Irish Dominican named Charles Ffrench. Having arrived in British North America the year before, Ffrench had been stationed by Bishop Plessis of Quebec at Bartabog on the Miramichi River. On his own initiative, he visited Saint John and launched a project to build a church. His efforts to raise money for this purpose took him to both St John's and Halifax, where his "charity sermons" were rewarded with donations totalling several hundred pounds.[80] Since the Saint John congregation was still very small, the sums he collected seemed excessive, and this, combined with his absence from his appointed mission, earned him a reprimand from Plessis.[81] The lay representatives of the Saint John Catholics were delighted by his success, however, and in 1815 they applied to have him appointed as their resident priest.[82] Plessis replied that he was unable to comply with their request, since Ffrench had indicated his intention of leaving his diocese for the United States.[83] On 28 May 1816 he appointed another Irish priest, Paul McQuade, whom he had recruited from Albany, New York.[84]

Like Halifax, Saint John had church wardens who, as the legal proprietors of church property,[85] insisted from the outset on a decisive voice in the administration of the parish. Plessis's refusal to appoint Ffrench, which stemmed from the genuine belief that he wished to leave for the United States, was interpreted by the trustees as insensitivity to their wishes.[86] This misunderstanding sparked a controversy that racked the Saint John congregation for the next decade. The trustees resisted not only McQuade[87] but any clergyman whom they regarded as a rival to Ffrench. When McQuade resigned owing to lack of financial support[88] and was replaced with a Canadian missionary, J.-E. Morissette, ethnic tensions exacerbated the conflict.

Two parties emerged among the laity, one supporting Morissette, the other determined not to have a French-speaking pastor.[89] Morissette bombarded Plessis with complaints[90] and pleaded for a transfer.[91] The wardens renewed their efforts to obtain the appointment of Ffrench, who had temporarily withdrawn to the United States. But Ffrench had already become involved in another, widely reported trustee conflict in New York.[92] Meanwhile, evidence came to light that he had been guilty of sexual impropriety during his tenure at Bartabog.[93] In the face of mounting evidence of irregular conduct on his part, Plessis stiffened in his refusal to appoint him.[94]

Initially Plessis attempted to resolve the difficulties by replacing Morissette with yet another Irish priest, Michael Carroll. Like Ffrench, however, Carroll was found guilty of irregularities – in his case the problem was drunkenness.[95] This led Plessis to reinstate Morissette,[96] which only heightened tensions in the congregation. Both Morissette's supporters and opponents were by this time represented on the committee of wardens, but his opponents enjoyed far greater popular support.[97] Increasingly, they took on the character of an "Irish party," agitating for a clergyman of their own nationality.

For the time being Carroll remained their nominee, evidence of misconduct notwithstanding, but there is reason to believe that he owed his popularity largely to an alliance he had formed with Ffrench. Ffrench had made his way back to the city by this time, and Plessis suspected he was the real instigator of opposition to Morissette.[98] When Carroll died suddenly in 1824, Ffrench attended him at his deathbed.[99] Shortly afterward the congregation met and "elected" Ffrench as pastor.[100]

The attempt to elect their own pastor was a high point in the lay agitation at Saint John. Nevertheless, Plessis refused to take any cognizance of such proceedings and issued a stiff reminder that it was the bishop's prerogative to appoint clergy.[101] Ffrench defied Plessis by officiating at Saint John without authorization,[102] and a rumour circulated briefly that he intended to apply to Rome to have New Brunswick removed from Plessis's jurisdiction.[103] This scheme, if it ever existed, came to nothing. By steadfastly refusing to grant Ffrench even temporary faculties, Plessis eventually convinced many of his supporters that their cause was hopeless. In May 1825 the wardens reversed their policy and informed Ffrench that in view of Plessis's refusal to give him licence to exercise his priestly functions they would no longer permit him to perform divine service in the chapel.[104] Plessis appointed a new pastor, Patrick McMahon, and dispatched a trusted Maritime missionary, William Dollard, to prepare Saint John for his arrival.[105] Dollard's intervention, followed by

McMahon's arrival as a duly authorized priest, destroyed the last traces of support for Ffrench. After a brief attempt to operate a school in Saint John,[106] he left the city for the last time to take up a position in the United States.[107]

Even though Ffrench's departure removed a major source of conflict, disturbances continued to divide the congregation. Controversy shifted to the method of choosing trustees. On the instructions of the new bishop of Quebec,[108] Bernard-Claude Panet, McMahon had appointed five wardens for life.[109] This caused widespread disaffection and led to demands for the election of wardens "in the sacred name of liberty."[110] Meanwhile, John Carroll, the young priest who had succeeded Edmund Burke at Halifax, arrived in Saint John in 1827 to replace McMahon. With his support,[111] spokesmen for the congregation persuaded Panet to permit the introduction of the Halifax electoral system whereby twenty-five pewholders were chosen as electors to select six wardens.[112] This limited concession to democracy, although achieved against the wishes of the existing trustees, seemed to alleviate tensions briefly.

In 1829, however, a major change in church government occurred in the region with the appointment of Angus Bernard MacEachern as bishop of Charlottetown with jurisdiction over Prince Edward Island, Cape Breton, and New Brunswick. In 1832 MacEachern visited Saint John and found that Carroll's relationship with the new wardens had soured to the point that he refused to have anything more to do with lay committees.[113] The congregation was in such an uproar over financial matters that MacEachern had to spend the entire winter in Saint John in an effort to restore order. He appointed new wardens and issued instructions governing their relationship to the clergyman and their handling of church revenues.[114] Carroll responded to this initiative with a stream of invective, questioning MacEachern's authority over New Brunswick and declaring he would never be governed by a Scottish bishop.[115] He was supported in his resistance to MacEachern by a portion of his flock, largely on the strength of appeals to national sentiment. MacEachern quoted him as saying: "Irishmen look to yourselves, and appoint your own Officers, and do not allow yourselves to be put down by a miserable Scotchman."[116] Nevertheless, with backing from Bishop Panet, MacEachern eventually drove Carroll from the city and replaced him with William Dollard. MacEachern also implemented new regulations that confirmed the role of church wardens in parish administration but placed them firmly under the control of the priest.[117]

This direct exercise of episcopal authority inaugurated a decade of relative peace in Saint John. Genuine stability was achieved, however, only after one more round of controversy had taken place. The central figure in the early stages of this final conflict was James Dunphy, who succeeded William Dollard in 1832 as parish priest. Dunphy was an "uncompromising advocate of clerical supremacy," and he tried in various ways to undermine the role traditionally assigned to lay wardens.[118] A crisis occurred in 1841 over plans to build an additional parish in the city when Dunphy insisted that the property be registered in the bishop's name rather than held in trust by a committee of parishioners.[119] The Catholic merchants who were leading the fundraising drive dissolved their own committee in protest and published an account of the proceedings that was highly critical of Dunphy.[120] This development met with immediate protests from members of the congregation, including some members of the building committee.[121] Matters were further complicated when Dunphy quarrelled publicly with his assistant priest, William Moran, who enjoyed the support of a portion of the congregation.[122] The situation in Saint John was so volatile that it is not always easy to determine which laymen belonged to which faction. Prominent figures, such as the merchant Thomas Watters, who had previously supported episcopal authority against the renegade Charles Ffrench, now found themselves part of an antiepiscopal minority as they resisted MacEachern's appointee, Dunphy. The change seems to have been due to Dunphy's direct attack on lay ownership of church property, not the immediate issue in earlier conflicts in Saint John. The majority of the congregation, however, once supporters of the charismatic (if disreputable) Ffrench, were now just as squarely behind Dunphy, the new symbol and embodiment of their group identity.

Clerical authority was strengthened even further in 1842 when New Brunswick was removed from the unmanageable Diocese of Charlottetown and placed under the supervision of Dollard as first bishop of Fredericton. Nevertheless, the disaffected Catholic minority in Saint John continued to agitate against Dunphy. Following a public meeting in November 1843, twenty-three parishioners petitioned Dollard for Dunphy's removal from office.[123] Dollard chose instead to transfer his own residence to Saint John in an effort to restore order. Upon his arrival he was presented with another petition, signed by twenty dissidents, not only repeating the request for Dunphy's removal but also demanding guarantees for the election of church wardens and the control of parish finances by the pewholders.[124] At this stage, Dollard decided to settle the question of church temporalities once and for all by the formation of an episcopal corporation. His decision preceded the same development in Halifax by five years. The incorporation bill encountered stiff opposition from Catholic merchants in Saint John and from some members of government.[125] In 1844 it was turned back by the Legislative Council.[126] In 1845 it was obstructed in the House of Assembly.[127] Finally, in 1846, it was passed into law.[128] In the midst of the controversy, 112 Saint John laymen petitioned against the measure. The bishop's supporters, however, responded with a petition of their own bearing 1400 signatures.[129] After 1846 all church property was vested in the Roman Catholic bishop and his successors, and the legal basis for the claims of lay wardens was destroyed.

By the middle of the nineteenth century, therefore, full episcopal authority was established among Catholics in St John's, Halifax, and Saint John, the three most important centres of population in Atlantic Canada. The precise course of events that led to this result varied according to the situation, but common elements can be discerned in all three locations. The fact that local controversies were part of a broader pattern gives them their significance. Not only did events in the major towns of Atlantic Canada resemble one another, but they were also similar to contemporary developments in the United States. Lay spokesmen in British North America were just as actively involved in ecclesiastical affairs as their American counterparts, and their involvement took essentially the same form. They also were drawn from the same class of aspiring merchants, professionals, and independent artisans, and their social ambitions made them just as strongly inclined to conform to the standards of the dominant culture. Although some American trustees (but by no means all)[130] undoubtedly appealed to republican principles to justify their actions, thus lending their approach a peculiar American colouring, this does not mean that trusteeism as such was exclusively American or republican. Demands for a measure of ecclesiastical democracy have a broader context than adaptation to American values. Lay trustees in British North America lived in the midst of, and sometimes participated in, campaigns for constitutional reform. They did not consciously link this political struggle to controversies over ecclesiastical government; their notion of democracy, like that of American trustees, clearly reflected the ideas of the times. Democracy for both groups meant the acquisition of power by the middle class through representative institutions based on the rights of property.

Trusteeism, or Catholic congregationalism, was characteristic of a certain phase in the development of Roman Catholic communities in the English-speaking world. It occurred when large numbers of Catholic immigrants poured into cities where the institutional framework of the church was inadequate to receive them, where clergy were in relatively short supply, where episcopal government was weak, and where the principal means of financial support was the contributions of the emerging Catholic bourgeoisie. It was a product of time and circumstance as much as place, reflecting conditions in the Catholic diaspora, not only in the United States. Its importance lies largely in the insight it gives us into the experience of the first few generations of Catholic immigrants as they laid the foundations of ecclesiastical life. For all the rancour and controversy associated with their activities, lay trustees succeeded in providing basic parochial insitutions for themselves and for their less prosperous co-religionists. The decline of trusteeism, however, signalled the beginning of a new era. Approximately in the middle of the nineteenth century, a process of institutional expansion and elaboration began that saw the rapid creation of a wide array of Catholic social agencies, educational institutions, devotional societies, and philanthropic organizations. Unlike the formative period, this phase of development depended principally on the initiative of bishops and priests. Leadership in the Catholic community had passed to the clergy, whose authority was stronger than ever. Middle-class laity could still play a role, but only to the extent that they accepted clerical supervision.

NOTES

1 The Catholic population of Newfoundland, which can be estimated at 3500 in 1775, had risen to approximately 5500 in 1786 and 8500 in 1795. See Alison Earle, "From the Governors' Returns: Showing the Distribution of Roman Catholics and Protestants in the Various Communities," Religion in Newfoundland Archive (RNLA), Memorial University of Newfoundland, 13–000–00. (I am grateful to my colleague Hans Rollmann for furnishing me with this unpublished paper and other materials from RNLA.) In 1816 the total Catholic population of mainland Nova Scotia was 8500 and that of Cape Breton, 7000. See Edmund Burke to the Sacred Congregation for the Propagation of the Faith, 12 Feb. 1816, Scritture Riferite nei Congressi, II, fol. 261, Archivio della Sacra Congregazione de Propaganda Fide (APF). The first statistics available for New Brunswick and Prince Edward Island date from 1829, when the Catholic population of the former was said to be 21,500 and of the latter, 12,500. See APF, fols. 248–61, Acta of the Sacred Congregation for the Propagation of the Faith, 1829.

2 Terrence Murphy, "The Emergence of Maritime Catholicism: 1781–1830," Acadiensis 13, 2 (spring 1984): 31–3.

3 Patrick W. Carey, People, Priests, and Prelates: Ecclesiastical Democracy and the Tensions of Trusteeism (Notre Dame: University of Notre Dame Press

1987). The preface to this book provides a good overview of the historiography of trusteeism, and an extensive bibliography is also included.

4 Ibid., 35ff. For a fuller discussion of Catholic congregationalism in England see John Bossy, *The English Catholic Community, 1570–1850* (London: Darton, Longman and Todd 1975), 337ff.

5 Public Archives of Nova Scotia (PANS), RG1, vol. 222, nos. 91–3, John Mullowney et al. to Governor Hughes, 5 July 1781, John Cody et al. to Hammond, undated, and John Cody et al. to Governor Hammond, 2 July 1782. For the first relief act see *Statutes of Nova Scotia*, 23 Geo. III, c. 9.

6 Archives of the Archdiocese of Quebec (AAQ), Nouvelle Ecosse (NE), II, 29. Indenture between John Mullowney et al. and William Meaney, 16 Oct. 1782.

7 AAQ, NE, II, 2, John Mullowney et al. to James Jones, 24 May 1785.

8 AAQ, Registre D, fol. 95, D'Esgly to Jones, 20 Oct. 1787.

9 See Terrence Murphy, "James Jones and the Establishment of Roman Catholic Church Government in the Maritime Provinces," Canadian Catholic Historical Association, *Study Sessions* 48 (1981): 26–42.

10 AAQ, NE, I, 37, Jones to Bishop Hubert, 24 March 1792.

11 Ibid.

12 AAQ, Angleterre, I, 20, Jones to [John Stealing], 9 May 1801.

13 AAQ, NE, II, 55, Bartholomew Sullivan et al. to Bishop Denaut, undated.

14 AAQ, Evêques de Québec, III, 73, J.O. Plessis to Denaut, 4 Sept. 1800.

15 AAQ, NE, III, 57, Edmund Burke, OP to [Plessis], 15 May 1801.

16 AAQ, NE, II, 19, extracts from the proceedings of a meeting of parishioners, 17 Aug. 1800.

17 AAQ, NE, II, 37, E. Phelan et al. to Denaut, 25 Aug. 1801.

18 On the exclusion of relative newcomers see ibid. For the leaders of the popular party see AAQ, NE, II, 26, John Sands et al. to Burke, 7 March 1801.

19 *Resolves of the Delegates Appointed by the Congregation of the Roman Catholic Church in Halifax To Make Amendments in the Bye-Laws and Regulations of the Temporal Affairs of the Said Church* (Halifax: Gay and Merlin [1801]), copy in AAQ, NE, II, 34.

20 AAQ, NE, II, 37, John Stealing et al. to Denaut, 25 April 1801.

21 AAQ, Registre F, fol. 69, Denaut to the Catholics of Halifax, 8 Sept. 1801.

22 Archives of the Archdiocese of Halifax (AAH), Wardens' Minute Book, fols. 23–4.

23 Ibid.

24 AAQ, NE, II, 57, Denaut to the [wardens and] electors, 28 June 1803.

25 R.A. McLean, "Edmund Burke" *Dictionary of Canadian Bibliography: 1801–1820* (Toronto: University of Toronto Press 1983), (DCB), V, 123–5.
26 Angus Bernard MacEachern, as quoted in A.A. Johnston, *A History of the Catholic Church in Eastern Nova Scotia*, 2 vols. (Antigonish: St Francis Xavier University 1960, 1971), II, 78.
27 Terrence M. Punch, "The Irish in Halifax, 1863–1871: A Study in Ethnic Assimilation" (MA thesis, Dalhousie University 1976), 126.
28 Ibid.
29 *Letters of Hibernicus* (Pictou, NS: The Observer 1842), 105–7.
30 Michael Tobin, Sr, et al. to Fraser, 12 July 1838, copy in AAH, Wardens' Minute Book, entry for 17 July 1838, and Fraser to Archbishop Murray, 20 July 1838, copy in *Letters of Hibernicus*, 115.
31 See, for example, Archives of the Archdiocese of Halifax (AAH), Fraser Papers, I, 47, minutes and accounts of the St Mary's Catechistical Society, and the report of a meeting of the Association for the Propagation of the Faith, *Register*, 21 Jan. 1845, 19.
32 See undated notes in the hand of Bishop Walsh, AAH, Walsh Papers, IV, unnumbered document.
33 AAQ, NE, VII, 126, Fraser to Archbishop Signay, 13 Sept. 1842.
34 AAH, Fraser Papers, 9, Michael Tobin, Jr, to Fraser, 18 Nov. 1841.
35 AAH, Fraser Papers, 4, Fraser to Michael Tobin, Jr, 20 Nov. 1841.
36 Johnston, *History*, II, 182–4.
37 AAQ, NE, VII, 126, Fraser to Signay, 13 Sept. 1842, and AAH, Walsh Papers, I, 3, Clergy to Walsh, 28 May 1842.
38 AAH, fols. 114–15, Wardens' Minute Book.
39 AAQ, NE, II, 121, Father Frechette to Signay, 8 Nov. 1842.
40 Ibid.
41 AAH, Walsh Papers, III, 235–6, O'Brien to Walsh, 31 Aug. [1842] and "Sunday."
42 An Act to Incorporate the Roman Catholic Bishop in Halifax, 31 March 1849, *Private and Local Acts of Nova Scotia* (Halifax: Richard Nugent 1851), 80–2.
43 AAH, Walsh Papers, I, "Carten Excommunication."
44 Raymond J. Lahey, *James Louis O'Donel in Newfoundland, 1784–1807: The Establishment of the Roman Catholic Church* (St John's: Newfoundland Historical Society 1984), 6.
45 Archives of the Archdiocese of Westminster (AAW), O'Donel to Talbot, 14 Jan. 1784, printed in Cyril J. Byrne, ed., *Gentlemen-Bishops and Faction Fighters: The Letters of Bishops O'Donel, Lambert, Scallan, and Other Irish Missionaries* (St John's: Jesperson Press 1984), 37–8.
46 Ibid.
47 Lahey, *O'Donel*, 8.
48 Ibid., 9.

49 Indenture between John Rogers and James O'Donel, Andrew Mulleny, Garret Quigley, William Burke, Edward Cannon, and Luke Maddock, transcript in RNLA, 10–003–07.

50 See Archives of the Archdiocese of Dublin, Troy Papers, I, 109, O'Donel to Troy, 24 Dec. 1789, printed in Byrne, ed., *Gentlemen-Bishops*, 98–101, where O'Donel speaks of his having delivered an account of the chapel debt and annual expenses to the congregation. See also Public Archives of Newfoundland and Labrador, GN2/I/A16, 500–1, O'Donel to Gambier, 13 Oct. 1802, printed in Byrne, ed., *Gentlemen-Bishops*, 197.

51 AAW, James Keating et al. to Talbot, 14 Jan. 1784, printed in Byrne, ed., *Gentlemen-Bishops*, 37–8.

52 Brother Edmund Burke et al. to Pius VI, 20 Nov. 1794, printed in M.F. Howley, *Ecclesiastical History of Newfoundland* (Boston: Doyle and Whittle 1888), 196–9.

53 *Centenary Volume, Benevolent Irish Society, St. John's, Newfoundland* [St John's, 1906].

54 See, for example, the petitions contained in Public Record Office (PRO), Colonial Office (CO) 194/66, fols. 182–3; 194/67, fols. 88–94 and 258–60; 194/69, fol. 507; 194/71, fols. 290–3; 194/76, fols. 221–2; 194/80, fols. 280–1 and 376. See also *The Newfoundlander*, 31 Dec. 1829 and 28 Jan. 1830.

55 Scallan to Walsh, 29 Oct. 1824, printed in Hans Rollmann, "Gentlemen-Bishops and Faction Fighters: Additional Letters Pertaining to Newfoundland Catholicism from the Franciscan Library at Killiney (Ireland)," *Journal of the Canadian Church Historical Society* 30, 1 (1988): 3–19.

56 Raymond J. Lahey, "Michael Anthony Fleming," DCB, VII: *1836–1850* (Toronto: University of Toronto Press 1988), 292–300.

57 Fleming to Capaccini, 13 June 1835, enclosed in PRO, CO 194/92, 91–8. I am grateful to Bishop Raymond Lahey for supplying me with this and other important documents relating to Fleming's career.

58 Phillip McCann, "Bishop Fleming and the Politicization of the Irish Roman Catholics in Newfoundland, 1830–1850," in Terrence Murphy and Cyril J. Byrne, eds., *Religion and Identity: The Experience of Irish and Scottish Catholics in Atlantic Canada* (St John's: Jesperson Press 1987), 82.

59 PRO, CO 194/92, 91–8, Michael Anthony Fleming, *Relazione della missione cattolica in Terranuova nell'America settentrionale* (Rome 1837), 15, and Fleming to Capaccini, 13 June 1835.

60 Ibid.

61 Noel A. Veitch, "The Contribution of the Benevolent Irish Society to Education in Newfoundland from 1827 to 1875" (MEd thesis, St Francis Xavier University 1965), 38.

62 Ibid., 50–1.
63 Fleming recounts the entire course of events concerning the Orphan Asylum School in his *Relazione*, 8–9, and in Fleming to Capaccini, 13 June 1835, PRO, CO 194/92, 91–8.
64 McCann, "Bishop Fleming," 85.
65 Ibid., 87, and Lahey, "Fleming," 293.
66 Lahey, "Fleming," 293.
67 Ibid., 294.
68 PRO, CO, 194/90, fols. 167–77, Little to Prescott, 9 March 1835.
69 Ibid.
70 Raymond J. Lahey, "Timothy Browne" DCB, VIII: *1851–1860* (Toronto: University of Toronto Press 1985), 106–8.
71 See Archives of the Sacred Congregation *de Propaganda Fide* (APF), S.C. Am. Setten. 5 (1842–8), fols. 375r–7v, Simms to Acton, 1 June 1843; and Browne to Acton, 31 July 1843, APF, S.C. Am. Setten. 5 (1842–8), fols. 388r–9r.
72 Fleming to DeLuca, 2 April 1842, APF, S.C. Am. Setten. 5 (1842–8), fol. 77.
73 PRO, CO 194/90, fols. 167–7, Little to Prescott, 9 March 1835.
74 Lahey, "Fleming," 294–7.
75 Ibid., 296, and McCann, "Bishop Fleming," 92.
76 McCann, "Bishop Fleming," 93.
77 Lahey, "Fleming," 296.
78 Ibid., 297.
79 Thomas Sealey et al. to Governor Thomas Carleton, undated, and Jonathan Odell to Charles Brannen, 6 May 1793, printed in D.G. Bell, ed., *Newlight Baptist Journals of James Manning and James Innis* (Hantsport: Lancelot Press 1984), 250–1.
80 AAQ, NE, IV, 95, Burke to Plessis, 30 Aug. 1814; Royal Gazette, St John's, Nfld, 17 Nov. 1814; AAQ, Nouveau Brunswick (NB), VI, 143, Ffrench to Plessis, 30 May 1815; AAQ, Terre Neuve (TN), I, 47, Ewer to Plessis, [?] Dec. 1815, printed in Byrne, ed., *Gentlemen-Bishops*, 293–4.
81 AAQ, Registre des lettres, VIII, 352–3, Plessis to Ffrench, 26 Aug., 1815; AAQ, NB, VI, 144, Ffrench to Plessis, 20 Oct. 1815.
82 AAQ, NB, II, 1, John Toole et al. to Plessis, [?] Nov. 1815.
83 AAQ, Registre H, fol. 116, Plessis to Catholic inhabitants of Saint John, 26 Feb. 1816.
84 AAQ, Registre H, fol. 118, Plessis to McQuade, 28 March 1816.
85 AAQ, NB, VI, 143, Ffrench to Plessis, 30 May 1815; and AAQ, NB, II, 9, McQuade to Plessis.
86 AAQ, NB, VI, 4, John Toole to Plessis, 25 April 1816.
87 AAQ, NB, II, 10–10a, Bernard Kiernan et al. to Plessis, [Feb. 1817] and 25 March 1818.

88 AAQ, NB, II, 21, McQuade to Plessis, 7 May 1818.

89 See, for example, Thomas Watters et al. to Plessis, [16 July 1824], and Daniel O'Sullivan et al. to Plessis, 10 Oct. 1824, NB, II, 50 and 53. The former petition was in favour of Morissette, the latter opposed to him.

90 AAQ, II, 28–30, Morissette to Plessis, 23 July and 27 Aug. 1821, [Sept. 1821].

91 AAQ, NB, II, 35, Morissette to Plessis, 2 April 1822.

92 AAQ, Registre des lettres, X, 74–6, Plessis to Connolly, 6 Sept. 1820, and Plessis to Fontana, 7 Sept. 1820.

93 AAQ, Registre des lettres, IX, 189, Plessis to Ffrench, 26 March 1817; AAQ, NB, VI, 149, Morissette to Plessis.

94 AAQ, Registre des lettres, X, 362, Plessis to Connolly, 23 Feb. 1822, and Plessis to Morissette, 24 Feb. 1822.

95 AAQ, Registre des lettres, XII, 80–1, Plessis to Michael Caroll, 20 Sept. 1824.

96 AAQ, Registre des lettres, XII, 81, Plessis to James Gallagher et al., 20 Sept. 1824.

97 A petition opposing Morissette's reappointment and denouncing the "few calculating and self-interested individuals" who had supported it bore twenty-two columns of signatures. See AAQ, NB, II, 53, Daniel O'Sullivan et al. to Plessis, 10 Oct. 1824.

98 AAQ, Registre des lettres, XII, 128, Plessis to Morissette, 29 Oct. 1824.

99 AAQ, NB, II, 59, Ffrench to Plessis, 2 Dec. 1824.

100 AAQ, NB, II, 60, Peter McNamara et al., 15 Dec. 1824.

101 AAQ, NB, II, 60a, Plessis to Catholic inhabitants of Saint John, undated.

102 AAQ, NB, VI, 162, Dollard to Plessis, 5 Feb. 1825; and AAQ, NB, III, 105, Gagnon to Plessis, 23 Feb. 1825.

103 AAQ, NB, II, 70, James Gallagher et al. to Plessis, 30 March 1825.

104 AAQ, NB, II, 73, Peter McNamara et al. to Ffrench, [c. 5 May 1825].

105 AAQ, NB, II, 74, Dollard to Plessis, 9 June 1825.

106 AAQ, NB, II, 77, McMahon to Plessis, 4 Oct. 1825.

107 AAQ, NB, II, 87–8, McMahon to Plessis, 31 Oct. 1826 or 4, 12 Dec. 1826.

108 AAQ, Registre des lettres, XIV, 34–5, Panet to William Watters et al., 6 April 1829.

109 AAQ, NB, II, 95, William Watters et al. to Panet, 17 Feb. 1829.

110 Ibid.

111 AAQ, NB, II, 96, John Caroll to Panet, 18 Feb. 1829.

112 AAQ, Registre des lettres, XIV, 34–5, Panet to William Watters et al., 6 April 1829.

113 AAQ, NB, II, 104, MacEachern to Panet, 29 May 1823.

114 AAQ, Ile du Prince Edouard (IPE), I, 125, MacEachern to Catholic inhabitants of Saint John, 21 April 1832.

115 AAQ, NB, II, 104, MacEachern to Panet, 29 May 1832.

116 Ibid.

117 AAQ, IPE, I, 126, MacEachern to church wardens, 20 June 1832.

118 On the conflict between Dunphy and the Saint John wardens see T.W. Acheson, *Saint John: The Making of a Colonial Urban Community* (Toronto: University of Toronto Press 1985), 101–5.

119 *New Brunswick Courier*, 26 June 1841.

120 Ibid., 3 July 1841.

121 Ibid., 26 June and 24 July 1841.

122 Ibid., 24 Sept. 1842, 4 and 11 Nov. 1843, and 10 and 24 Feb. 1844.

123 Archives of the Diocese of Saint John (ADSJ), Dollard Papers, 520, parishioners to Dollard, 28 Nov. 1843.

124 ADSJ, Dollard Papers, 535, parishioners to Dollard, 7 Oct. 1844.

125 *New Brunswick Courier*, 10 and 17 Jan., 7, 14, and 28 Feb., 7 March, and 10 April 1846.

126 Ibid., 6 April 1844.

127 Ibid., 5 April 1845.

128 *New Brunswick Statutes*, 9 Vic., c. 72.

129 Acheson, *Saint John*, 103.

130 Carey, *People, Priests, and Prelates*, 154.

7 The Growth of Roman Catholic Institutions in the Archdiocese of Toronto, 1841–90

MURRAY NICOLSON

When examining the growth of Roman Catholic institutions in English-speaking British North America, certain patterns emerge that are common to all regions and that also resemble developments in the United States. Institutional growth began in the late eighteenth and early nineteenth centuries with the introduction of stable missions consisting of established parishes with resident priests. About the middle of the nineteenth century, however, that primitive organization expanded in response to a rapidly growing population. The first step was the erection of local dioceses, with bishops in the principal towns governing a network of urban and rural parishes. These dioceses were in turn organized into ecclesiastical provinces as archbishops were named in centres such as Baltimore, Quebec, and Halifax. The introduction of this metropolitan system, nearly as old as the church itself, opened the way for the recruitment of religious orders, the introduction of Catholic schools and colleges, and the provision of Catholic social services through hospitals and orphanages. Lay organizations also played a key role, as is evident from the activities of philanthropic associations such as the St Vincent de Paul Society and temperance leagues.

Certainly the church in Upper Canada did not function as a metropolitan institution in the first half of the nineteenth century. When the pioneer clergyman Alexander Macdonell arrived in 1804, it was a neglected mission, an appendage of the Diocese of Quebec, with only three churches and two priests in the entire colony. The Catholic population did not exceed a few thousand in number and was concentrated in two areas – the Scots in Glengarry in the east and the French in Sandwich in the west. Although Macdonell was made vicar-general to the bishop of Quebec in 1807, he was often the only priest in Upper Canada. His consecration in 1819 as bishop of Resina *in partibus infidelium* was a limited measure, for it did not make him head of a separate ecclesiastical jurisdiction but simply vicar epis-copal (or vicar-general with episcopal powers) to the bishop of Quebec. He gained little more than the power to confirm and ordain, and increased stature in the eyes of the government.[1]

Although the colonial government had divided the old Province of Quebec into the two political and national entities of Upper and Lower Canada in 1791, no division of the Diocese of Quebec had taken place. Out of fear of multiplying the hierarchy, requests for ecclesiastical division, even within Quebec proper, had been denied. This impeded the development of the metropolitan system because there was no opportunity for the creation of an ecclesiastical prov-ince.[2] But Irish immigration in the 1820s increased the Catholic pop-ulation in the central area of Upper Canada, creating an Irish fact at the time that York (later Toronto) was emerging as the metropolis of the province.[3] In response to the rise in Catholic population, the colonial government acquiesced and in 1826 allowed the creation of an independent diocese covering the whole of Upper Canada with Macdonell as bishop. Macdonell, however, chose Kingston as his see in the mistaken belief that the Rideau Canal would make it the most important town in the colony. This left him geographically isolated from the true centre of his diocese in York and the Home District, while he was also ecclesiastically isolated from the bishop of Quebec. Macdonell's mode of operation was better suited to the conditions of a mission church than to emerging metropolitan structures.

For his successor, Macdonell wanted a titled Englishman rather than a Scot or an Irishman. No doubt he believed that an English cleric of high social standing would be more readily accepted to the colonial administration and the Family Compact elite. He had hoped to make Dr Thomas Weld his coadjutor, but this plan was foiled when Weld was made a cardinal. Meanwhile, Macdonell's preoccu-pation with the selection of such a candidate cost him the services of several qualified men, including Joseph Quiblier, a Sulpician from Quebec, John Larkin of the Seminary of Montreal, and John Mur-doch, suggested by the Sacred Congregation for the Propagation of the Faith. Finally in 1833, Jean-Jacques Lartigue, the future bishop of Montreal, was able to gain the position of coadjutor for Rémi Gaulin, a French-Canadian priest. Gaulin was a veteran of the Maritime missions who was chosen chiefly because he spoke French, English, and Gaelic. Through his appointment, however, Quebec hoped to re-establish ecclesiastical hegemony in Upper Canada.[4]

When Macdonell died on 14 January 1840, Gaulin became bishop of the Diocese of Kingston, but he could not cope with the administrative responsibilities the position entailed. Gaulin suggested a division of his diocese and asked that the bilingual Michael Power, vicar-general of Bishop Ignace Bourget of Montreal, be made coadjutor to assist him in the Diocese of Kingston. In 1841 Bourget and Power were in Rome and, at Gaulin's request, discussed the division of the diocese with Propaganda. Pope Gregory XVI agreed and sent Bourget and Power to London to obtain the assent of the British government.[5] Power had written to Lord Stanley that Kingston was too large a diocese to deal with the present Catholic population. In attempting to gain British approbation for the proposed division, Power had the wisdom to explain that it would strengthen clerical authority over a sometimes unruly population: "A Catholic bishop in case of emergency will provide more authority over those committed to his care than an ordinary clergyman, his presence and his advice may also prove highly serviceable to Her Majesty's Government in quelling that spirit of insubordination and fierce democratic spirit which unhappily exists in a formidable degree in many parts of the frontier line."[6] Despite their reservations about the multiplication of Roman Catholic bishops, colonial officials welcomed the prospect of additional supervision in an area which in 1837 had been a centre of political upheaval. Bourget and Power were encouraged to proceed with the plan for division.

On 16 December 1841 the pope issued a bull dividing from the Diocese of Kingston all that part of Upper Canada lying west of the district of Newcastle. On the same day Michael Power, born in Halifax in 1804 and ordained in Montreal in 1827, was named the first bishop of the new diocese. Power was granted permission to choose the city and title of his see and, in 1842, was consecrated bishop of Toronto.[7]

The formation of this new diocese, however, did not complete the implementation of traditional church government. The absence of an ecclesiastical province restricted communication among the various dioceses under the supervision of the bishop of Quebec. Power and the other bishops of Upper and Lower Canada petitioned the pope to create an ecclesiastical province. By 1844 the four dioceses – Quebec, Montreal, Kingston, and Toronto – were united into a single ecclesiastical province under the name and title of the Metropolitan Province of Quebec, wherein the Diocese of Quebec became the archdiocese under the jurisdiction of Archbishop Joseph Signay. In a pastoral letter, Signay advised his laity of this achievement: "Let us pray that this complete Ecclesiastical organization may tend to the more rapid progress of the Catholic faith, bind together more firmly all the members of the Church, afford to Her now well established hierarchy, the means of labouring together in more perfect unity of design, and by the united efforts of her first Pastors, of infusing new vigour and fresh energy to the most remote and most infant portions of the Catholic Church in this province."[8] The creation of the ecclesiastical province of Quebec meant that British North American Catholics achieved full hierarchical government six years earlier than their counterparts in England. Nicholas Wiseman, who would be named archbishop of Westminster in 1850, recognized the significance of this step and heartily congratulated the Canadian bishops: "You, on your side, have experienced the blessing of a properly constituted ecclesiastical government, sufficiently to understand our eagerness to obtain the same privilege."[9]

There were immediate, positive results from the formation of the ecclesiastical province. This arrangement strengthened communication links, established lines of authority with delegated responsibility, and provided the opportunity for the interchange of ideas. Archbishop Joseph Signay ruled between Bishop Patrick Phelan of Kingston, who had replaced Gaulin, and Bishop Power over the division of the pension granted to the whole of Upper Canada by the civil government. In this way, official matters regarding church policy did not become public knowledge and provoke unfavourable secular reaction.[10] More pertinently, this expanded organization afforded Power, and his successor Armand de Charbonnel, confidential contact with Bishop Ignace Bourget, one of the architects of Canadian Catholic Ultramontanism.

Power's attempts to organize and modernize the church in the Diocese of Toronto were limited by a short tenure of five years. His efforts reveal a growing interest in establishing institutions, increasing and regulating the clergy, centralizing power in a cathedral city, stimulating the laity towards a more ordered devotionalism, and furthering education. Power brought the Jesuits to Toronto, but they directed their efforts to the mission field among the Indians. He invited the Christian Brothers and the Sisters of Loretto to come to the city to establish schools, although neither arrived until after his death. And, in the hope of expanding the knowledge and concern of the laity for the problems of the worldwide church, he introduced the Association of the Propagation of the Faith into the diocese.[11]

When Power arrived in Toronto there was a single church, St Paul's. Land was secured to build a cathedral and a bishop's palace. It was an age of cathedral building in North America, and Power was stimulated by similar projects undertaken in Kingston, Philadelphia, Chicago, Mobile, and Louisville. For this cathedral, Power asked for a contribution of at least five shillings from each worker, which amounted to a day's pay for a skilled worker such as a printer. As well, he invited the investment of funds on loan to build the cathedral.[12]

The building of St Michael's Cathedral created accounting problems and the need for monetary and fiscal control. Surviving subscription lists show that the church was partly dependent upon a transient, labouring population. The majority of addresses were unknown; some subscribers were denoted as having become Protestants. Nonetheless, among those who contributed, there was a spirit of voluntarism and cooperation. The people donated what money they could afford and paid half-yearly, quarterly, or monthly; some provided labour, usually a half-day's work; and others provided materials such as stone and brick or services like carting. The old Compact families, Catholic and Protestant, including the Anglican Bishop John Strachan, received donations at their homes, as did the few members of the rising Catholic middle class. Upper Canada College, the House of Parliament, banks and business firms accepted contributions on behalf of the cathedral debt. This venture showed the need for fiscal organization for the diocese.[13]

In 1842, soon after he took possession of his see, Power called the clergy of the diocese to a retreat and synod in St Paul's Church. Sixteen priests attended a five-day retreat under the guidance of a Jesuit. At that time the diocese was consecrated to the Sacred Heart of Jesus to encourage a more spiritual life among priests and people. Power drew up statutes for the government of the diocese that were adopted by the clergy, and announced that a seminary college was necessary to educate Canadian priests for the diocese.[14]

Qualified priests were essential as a link in the emerging metropolitan system of the Diocese of Toronto. Power, in writing to Bishop William Kinsella of Ireland in 1844, outlined some essential elements in forming a modern church: "I have but twenty clergymen throughout the whole country ... I have neither colleges, nor schools, nor men ... I pray to God most earnestly that the Irish College for Foreign Missions may prosper and fully answer all our expectations ... I am determined to have a whole district without any spiritual assistance rather than to confide the poor people into hands of improper or suspended men."[15] In fact, however, the building of the cathedral and the bishop's palace, the external symbols of the metropolitan institution, took priority in both time and money, and the needed seminary was neglected.

Power realized that his priests' synod and retreat were not enough to bring about significant change in the existing personnel. On 31 December 1846 he issued a pastoral letter to his secular clergy in which he announced reforms and regulations to effect more direct episcopal control. He stipulated that only he, his vicars-general, or archdeacons could authorize priests to say Mass or perform sacerdotal functions in his diocese. Priests from his diocese would require his permission to perform similar functions in other dioceses. This regulation was needed to curtail the activities of wandering American clerics as well as transiency among his own clergy. Moreover, to curb a developing financial independence and an allegiance to civil or military authority over that of his own, Power denied clerics the right to receive salaries without his knowledge of all arrangements. Any infractions of these regulations met with excommunication. Priests who organized or showed defiance of the bishop's authority to transfer or remove a cleric would be suspended immediately, and those who falsely asserted authority or attested title from beyond the diocese were suspended.[16] The purpose of the regulations was to bring an end to the clerical insubordination that thwarted the growth of metropolitan structures.

In addition, Power was successful in 1845 in obtaining a bill incorporating the Catholic church that ended the requirement for priests, groups of laymen or the bishop to hold church property. This act placed church land beyond the manipulation of clergy, which often had jeopardized the church's title or prohibited sale, although it did not grant the church permission to mortgage capital assets.[17]

Bishop Power divided the diocese into six rural deaneries under the supervision of senior clergy: St Michael's for the Home and Simcoe districts; St Mary's for the Gore, Niagara, and Talbot districts; St Ignatius for the Western District; St Gregory's for the London and Brock districts; St Ambrose for the Wellington and Huron districts; and St Francis Xavier's for the missions on the borders of Lake Huron and Lake Superior. The deans were authorized to hold meetings of the clergy through which local problems were solved and discipline effected. At this particular time, the vast diocese was largely Irish but contained minority groups of French, Scottish, German, and native Catholics. In these areas the rural dean was also vicar forane, which extended his authority to act more independently of the bishop.[18]

Power's accomplishments, though real enough, were limited by the circumstances of his episcopate. He had become bishop in an era of social and political change in Upper Canada, and the movement towards democratic representation left him uncertain of his power base. From his correspondence, one senses a prelate who was capable of exercising authority but who was inhibited by the fear that involvement in public disputes might compromise his office. In the field of education in particular, he failed to take the episcopal initiative necessary in a hierarchial system. Apparently believing that the impulse for Catholic education should come instead from the grass roots, he acquiesced, as chairman of the Board of Education for Upper Canada, in an emerging secular educational system. Had his term of office been prolonged, it is doubtful whether the separate school system would have developed beyond this appendage to the public system.[19]

In 1847, however, Toronto was faced with an influx of famine Irish. These destitute and nominally Catholic people were in need of immediate material and spiritual assistance, but the diocese was unprepared for the crisis. City authorities set up fever sheds to contain the infectious diseases the immigrants carried. Fear of contagion made them an alien group from the moment of their arrival. Power, a few priests, and one Catholic layman ministered to their needs; as a result, Power became ill and died.[20]

Power's death left Toronto without a bishop, and the interregnum lasted three years. The immigrant Irish who arrived at this time were an unskilled, uneducated group and by 1851 they formed one-quarter of the city's population. Their social needs were beyond the resources of the church and the city. They crowded into the tenements and single dwellings in Cabbagetown and on the waterfront, or lived in the shanty towns in the Don Basin or in barns on the periphery of the city, subsisting on what they could grow, beg, or steal. In addition, they retained past forms of social adjustment, or defence mechanisms, which had been common in Ireland, including violence as a weapon against prejudice, drunkenness as an escape from a harsh environment, distrust of civil authority, and reliance on their own forms of justice, all of which, when applied in the new urban milieu, resulted in crime, penal servitude, and family instability. Lack of employment opportunities accounted for transiency, prostitution, and abandoned wives and children. Because of a high adult mortality rate, orphans were numerous. Having lost contact with their church in Ireland, the immigrants nevertheless carried with them older belief patterns seen particularly in the practice of the wake, which made them appear a superstitious group.

Detachment from the church allowed the Irish to avail themselves of whatever aid was forthcoming in the Protestant city. Acceptance of many forms of material assistance required a denial of Catholicism, and the church feared the loss of its laity, particularly to Protestantism. This seepage created a dilemma for the Diocese of Toronto and even threatened the existence of the developing local church, for these Irish, in absolute numbers, were the Catholics of Toronto.[21]

In the midst of this situation, Armand-François-Marie de Charbonnel, DD, arrived in Toronto. This French Sulpician, who had been a professor of dogma and history in Lyons, was offered but refused the Legion of Honour and a seat in the National Assembly of France. He came to Canada first as a missionary working with the Irish in Montreal from 1840 to 1847. While assisting the famine immigrants, he became critically ill with typhus and was recalled to France to convalesce.[22] The Canadian hierarchy, aware of Charbonnel's qualifications, asked Propaganda to appoint him to the vacant see of Toronto. Charbonnel was a reluctant candidate but complied with the will of Pope Pius IX, who bestowed the episcopal dignity on 26 May 1850.

Charbonnel was faced with a major task because Power had only begun to develop mature ecclesiastical institutions. From his arrival in Toronto, change was inevitable. He knew he had to salvage the remnants of the ill-adjusted, socially deprived Irish laity by providing for their religious, social, and educational needs. His past experience with the Irish in Montreal had made him aware of their positive traits – voluntarism, love of associations, and close kinship patterns. First, though, he had to build an integral diocesan structure from which would evolve the social institutions and educational facilities that could help the Irish improve their lot.

Charbonnel was able to import into the Diocese of Toronto necessary personnel, money, ideas, and methods through the well-established external communications network of the church. Trained in Europe, he was aware of the social work instituted by St Vincent de Paul, the devotional and moral renewal of Alphonsus de Liguori, and the effectiveness of the new religious orders that combined cloistered life with service to the poor. He saw in them possible models for building the internal diocesan framework and providing solutions for the pressing problems of the Irish Catholics.[23]

As a suffragan, Charbonnel attended the Quebec Provincial Council to consult with his metropolitan and, perhaps more particularly, with Bishop Ignace Bourget of Montreal, a genius in central church organization. He also visited Baltimore several times to confer with Bishop M.J. Spalding, and attended the Plenary Council of the Catholic Church in America held there in 1852. His friendship with Spalding, Archbishop John Hughes of New York, and Bishop Colin McKinnon of Nova Scotia, and with prelates in Ireland and Italy, gave him insight into the problems of management and the recruitment of priests.[24]

Charbonnel soon realized that the extension of ecclesiastical control depended on the adaptation of the classical form of church government over smaller units. By decentralizing, local urban nuclei could more effectively administer their own hinterland. In 1854 he wrote to Father Elzear Taschereau of Quebec (later the first Canadian cardinal) with the proposal that the existing Diocese of Toronto be divided into three separate areas: Toronto with six counties and 40,000 Catholics; Hamilton with eight counties and 22,000 Catholics; and London with nine counties and 10,000 Catholics. He believed that there were sufficient resources for three bishops. All three needed twenty additional priests, churches, and presbyteries, and forty schools. He warned that, as in the United States, "wandering or vagabond priests are increasing like a disease," and that, similarly, "mixed schools are the burial place of children."[25] In addition, Charbonnel advised the cardinal prefect of Propaganda that the Catholic population was growing rapidly in all three major areas of this diocese and that two of these sections were far removed from his see and difficult to administer. He complained about the lack of priests and said he planned to go to Europe to obtain them.[26]

At the Second Council of Quebec in October 1855, Charbonnel again made an appeal for dividing his diocese. He stated:

Also Protestantism reigns supreme in the Diocese of Toronto, powerful, rich and zealous, it has at its beck and call landed property, business and labour and numerous clergy, well endowed, teaching in schools in every branch and degree, churches and magnificent schools in abundance, elections and all the seats in Parliament, almost all public employment, houses of charity, the press and secret societies. The Bishop of Toronto is insulted in the streets of this city and in several counties there have been different attempts on the life of the missionaries. However, the presence of the Bishop, his visits, and his incipient institutions have produced a certain betterment which will be much better with two new Sees and the action of their bishops.[27]

Charbonnel was ultimately successful in his pleas and in 1856 the Diocese of Toronto was divided into the three areas he had suggested. He recognized that, with two additional bishops, the number of clergymen, schools, churches, and religious institutions must increase.[28] With the reduction in size of the diocese, Charbonnel was able to expend maximum effort and tighten control in his own city and its vicinity. Furthermore, it was his foresight that predetermined the creation, during the episcopate of his successor, of an ecclesiastical province in Upper Canada. Although Charbonnel was not a true metropolitan, throughout his career as Bishop of Toronto he spoke for the Catholics in all dioceses of Upper Canada.[29]

Charbonnel also launched a comprehensive program of reform affecting both clergy and laity. In 1852 he made a tour of the diocese, during which he assessed the current state of his flock and devised measures to overcome abuses. In September 1852 he convoked a seven-day clerical retreat, ending with a two-day synod. As preparation, he issued a circular emphasizing certain points of parish practice. Priests were reminded of the importance of founding Catholic schools and advised they were trustees and superintendents of these institutions *de jure divino*. There was also a clear warning against the danger of mixed marriages, the proliferation of heretical books, and the use of Protestant prayers in mixed schools. The overriding concern was the risk of seepage from the church and the need to establish independent Catholic institutions.

Charbonnel was also determined to improve clerical discipline and to make priests more accountable to their ecclesiastical superiors. Any priest unable to attend the 1852 synod was to notify the bishop in writing.[30] Those who did attend were to bring with them the vestments for divine office, the decrees of the Council of Quebec, the statutes of the Diocese of Toronto, and parish registers of baptisms and marriages. Charbonnel subsequently insisted that no priest should be absent from his parish without notifying him of the reason. He also demanded that his clergy wear the soutane (or at least the abbreviated soutanelle), even though this meant an added expense and the risk of insults or injury in the streets. By his own example, he set a standard of frugal, even austere living that he expected his clergy to imitate.[31]

To improve communications and to facilitate reforms within the diocese, Charbonnel revived and expanded the system of deaneries. Deans were ordered to bring to the diocesan synod detailed reports on their districts, including recommendations for improvement. Meanwhile, the deaneries were established as preliminary tribunals where local cases could be heard. If such cases required the decision of a higher court, they were referred to the bishop's tribunal composed of the bishop and the officers of the diocesan curia.[32]

With diocesan structures thus improved, Charbonnel was able to build up institutions adequate to the pressing needs of the rapidly growing and socially deprived laity. In doing so, he turned to Europe and especially France for both methods and personnel. Like contemporary bishops elsewhere in British North America, he strengthened the ties of the local church with its parent institution in Europe, importing both religious orders and charitable foundations that had already proven successful abroad. The proliferation of these new orders and philanthropic associations was part of a general tendency towards ecclesiastical centralization that characterized the Roman church in the mid nineteenth century.[33]

Four sisters of Loretto had come to Toronto from Ireland at the time of Power's death and, with great personal difficulty, they began to teach in the elementary schools. Their efforts were complemented by a few Christian Brothers who arrived from France in 1851, taking over the teaching of elementary and senior boys.[34] In the same year, the French-based Sisters of St Joseph, a versatile order of women, established themselves at the Nelson Street orphanage, where they shared deplorable conditions with the children.[35] They soon became involved with all aspects of social work and with education. Charbonnel selected the Basilian Fathers from France to train Canadian priests, and in 1852 they assumed control of the amalgamated St Michael's College, originally set up by the Christian Brothers.[36]

During Bishop John Joseph Lynch's tenure (1860–88), the Sisters of Charity of St Vincent de Paul from the United States took on the more specialized task of training disadvantaged girls and women. They, however, were dismissed from the diocese following a conflict with Lynch, and their work was taken over by the Sisters of the Good Shepherd,[37] who faced tremendous hardship. It was under Archbishop William Walsh that the order's work with women in trouble with the law gained the recognition and support it deserved. Additionally, Lynch called from Quebec the Sisters of the Precious Blood, a cloistered order, who supported themselves by making communion bread and altar linens. The German Redemptorist Fathers arrived from the United States at Lynch's request in 1879 to administer St Patrick's Church and to assist with the restructuring of Catholic family life by conducting missions and retreats.[38]

By 1889, when Walsh took over the jurisdiction of the diocese, substantial growth had occurred among the religious orders in the city. There were 293 sisters, of whom 144 belonged to St Joseph's order, 17 Basilians, 20 Christian Brothers, and 7 Redemptorists.[39] Bound by rules of conduct and vows of poverty, chastity, and obedience, the religious orders were efficient, effective candidates for works of service.[40] They sought and attained public charity to finance social programs, and they gained some independence through tutoring private pupils and teaching in separate schools, all of which helped pay for the expansion of institutions.

The laity, too, began organizing for charitable work. The principal organization was the St Vincent de Paul Society, which began in 1850 in Toronto with one conference and seven members. Its primary purpose was to provide aid to the poor and sick, and, to avoid secularization, it was strictly regulated and bound by obedience to rules laid down by the Central Council in Paris. It soon branched out to cover various facets of care, financing itself through collections from members, poor boxes, and public donations and later sponsoring picnics, bazaars, and concerts for additional funds. Initially, most members were from the upper and middle classes, but it evolved into a working-class organization, directed by successful men. By 1889 there were ten conferences in the city, with more than 245 active members, and five conferences outside the city.[41]

Complementing the St Vincent de Paul Society was a group of women's organizations composed mainly of the wives and relatives of society members. These parish-oriented associations began in the 1850s to raise money through bazaars for such charitable endeavours as providing food and clothing for school children. Under the auspices of the St Vincent de Paul Society, the Catholic Ladies Aid Society was founded to attend to cases that could not be reached by men. One of its branches, the Catholic Ladies Hospital Visiting Society, expanded its role to visit the reformatory and the jail, preparing and delivering knitted clothing, special baskets, and books to female prisoners. Members worked to restore released prisoners to family life and to find jobs for them.[42]

Together these religious orders and lay fraternities sponsored an expanding and increasingly complex program of social action. Over a period of half a century, they established programs and institutions that touched on nearly every aspect of a Catholic immigrants' life and that emerged as a mirror image or parallel network to Protestant social institutions. By the end of the nineteenth century, an orphanage, training schools, house of providence, savings bank, childrens' protection society, shelter for destitute or delinquent women, boys' reformatory, hostels for men and women, senior citizens' home, and hospital had been established in the Diocese of Toronto, as well as wide-ranging programs of outdoor relief and home visits to those in need of nursing services. Although each of these programs and the organizations that sponsored them were discrete units, they functioned ultimately as a corporate entity, complementing rather than competing with one another, under the ultimate authority of the bishop.[43]

Some idea of the scope and magnitude of these social programs may be gained by examining the activities of the St Vincent de Paul Society. Members of the society collected furniture, bedding, household utensils, and clothing throughout the city and also purchased wood or coal to be distributed to the poor. Food staples such as bread and cereal grains were supplied according to family need. These basics were later supplemented with vegetables, meat, milk, and tea. In 1889 alone, the society assisted 1045 persons. Some 31 tons of coal and 131 cords of wood were delivered, and 9884 pounds of bread was distributed. Society members also visited the sick, teaching them methods to improve personal hygiene and control disease, and also supplying medicines and procuring the services of doctors, dentists, and practical nurses. They intervened with the authorities to have acutely ill people admitted to hospital and to extend the stay of those who required extra care. They offered financial support to families whose bread-winners were incapacitated because of illness or accident. Finally, they comforted the dying and assumed the cost of pauper burials, providing shrouds, coffins, and grave plots and also paying stipends so that masses could be said for the dead. The society followed up with financial aid to widows and assistance in placing orphans.[44]

Within the broad spectrum of social action, an area of special concern was education. Education was seen both as a means of self-improvement for immigrants and as a way of preserving their faith. Whereas Power had more or less acquiesced in the development of a secular school system, Charbonnel insisted absolutely on the need for Catholics to have their own educational institutions. From the outset, he was embroiled in conflict with Egerton Ryerson, the Methodist architect of Ontario's public school system. Both Ryerson and Toronto city officials saw the public schools as a means of assimilating Irish immigrants to the standards of the English-speaking and Protestant charter group. This was precisely the result that Charbonnel feared. In order to promote separate schools, he used every method available, including the influence of bishops and politicians from Canada East and coercive pastorals to compel the faithful to comply with his approach. Typical of this coercion was the Lenten Pastoral of 1857, which declared that absolution could be withheld from priests, parents, electors, and legislators who supported mixed schools to the prejudice of separate schools.[45]

A series of school acts, from the Common School Act of 1841 to the Scott Act of 1863, slowly legalized the existence of separate schools, and the British North America Act of 1867 guaranteed Catholics the educational rights they had at Confederation. Even then, Catholics had to struggle for an equitable portion of the school grant, and the operation and expansion of separate schools posed a major financial problem for both the hierarchy and the laity.[46]

Teaching and the administration of the Catholic schools was entrusted to the religious orders. Early interaction with the poor in their homes had gained them the confidence of the laity. At the same time, the assistance of various Catholic philanthropic associations was required to make school attendance possible for a number of needy children. Members of the St Vincent de Paul Society assumed the role of truant officers, kept attendance records, and followed up on absenteeism. By 1889 the religious orders operated twenty-seven schools in the city, with a student body of 4602. The Sisters of St Joseph operated nine parochial girls' schools, six parochial boys' schools, one convent school, the girls section of De La Salle Institute, and two schools in the orphanages. The Sisters of Loretto ran one parochial girls' school and two convent schools. The Christian Brothers had four parochial boys' schools and the boys' section of the De La Salle Institute, which included a commercial program. Finally, the Basilian Fathers operated St Michael's College, founded in 1852 largely to train local candidates for holy orders.[47]

Economic hardship nevertheless prevented some Catholic youth from pursuing their education under the religious orders. To accommodate these students as well as to serve some adults, the St Vincent de Paul Society initiated a program of night classes. English was taught to the small Italian minority to ease their adjustment into the city. Society members also cooperated with the clergy in an effort to stimulate church and separate school attendance among Toronto's French-Canadian population. Under the impetus of Charbonnel and the Catholic Institute (founded in 1851), libraries, reading rooms, debating clubs, and religious sodalities were organized. These served to keep young people occupied and to channel interest towards approved, censored literature of religious, devotional, and nostalgic Irish content.[48]

Closely linked to many of these philanthropic and educational enterprises were attempts by the clergy and lay activists to reform certain forms of behaviour among Catholic immigrants. Home visits were used to teach disease control and to demonstrate methods to improve personal hygiene and for the correct disposal of human waste. Lack of training and the impression that immigrants were careless, lazy workers left them with few employment opportunities in the city. To dispel this generalization, charitable organizations attempted to secure labouring jobs, domestic positions, and apprenticeships for immigrant workers. They supplied tools for capable workmen entering the emerging construction trade, and guaranteed businesses to promote a middle sector. They provided small wares for women to sell from their homes. To help immigrants escape poverty and their dependence on charitable assistance, the charities encouraged thrifty habits and promoted the Toronto Savings Bank as a depository for security in old age, times of unemployment, illness and death, and for the education of children. They also urged children to save by using penny banks set up in the schools.[49]

Drunkenness and violence associated with Irish wakes were subdued by the exemplary attendance of St Vincent de Paul members, who set a more religious tone. To avert the paganism surrounding extravagant funeral trappings, a purgatorial society was formed to promote more simple burial customs. Church-oriented temperance groups spurred the formation of sodalities and the League of the Cross, which demanded a vow of abstinence. Moreover, benevolent societies, like the Irish Catholic Benevolent Union and the Catholic Mutual Benefit Association, promoted abstinence while offering insurance and disability benefits. In this way, they became important stabilizing factors and self-help agencies among the laity.[50]

Finally, Catholic social action included the distribution of devotional literature and religious aids, which were handed out with material help to Catholics. This promotion of a devotional and moral renewal was assisted by the proliferation of Catholic bookstores in the city. In addition, the church beautified its buildings and service so that the working class might be imbued with a sense of peace and pride, a momentary relief from the stresses of the real world. To perpetuate this religious renewal, the church developed a productive method for achieving moral and social control. The retreat or mission, introduced to the laity by Charbonnel, was perfected in the late 1870s by the Redemptorist Fathers, founded by Alphonsus de Liguori. Each parish was involved in an intense program of devotional and moral renewal and, during the mission or retreat, the laity was separated into groups of men, women, and children for specific teaching. As skilled orators, the Redemptorists delivered sermons condemning intemperance, immorality, violence, sloth, and deviance in family roles or family life. They gave the laity guidelines for self-examination, which was followed by confession, penance, and communion, and a promise to change. Few Catholics could evade the experience because to miss a retreat was to incur community censure.[51]

Ecclesiastical metropolitanism was essential to control an ever-growing and spatially dispersed laity. Following a standard structure of classical church government, the diocese was held together by an interlocking communications system that formed part of the universal church's internal network. Inherent in the system was a double thrust: promoting and protecting the religious faith and spiritual welfare of its adherents, and upholding human dignity through charitable endeavours that would satisfy basic needs. Rules governing the various segments fostered a unified approach and denied innovation that could lead to secularism. The application of proven concepts and models allowed for a progression from simple mechanisms to the creation of vital, complex religious and social institutions that assisted Catholics to live in this world while preparing for the next.

The Catholic institutions that developed in Toronto between 1850 and 1900 provided the means for a minority group to escape the pressures of assimilation into the charter English-Protestant society. In opposition to the Protestant majority, the successive bishops in Toronto fought to acquire a separate system of education and other social institutions and agencies so as to retain and protect the religious rights of their flock. The laity, however, was composed predominantly of an Irish, urban-dwelling peasantry, a small portion of the New World Irish diaspora that strove to maintain its distinctive ethnic identity. As a result, the Catholic institutions that evolved in the metropolitan centre and spread throughout most of the English-speaking areas of the province were a religious response to urban conformity, eventually to become a significant part of Ontario's culture.

In concentrating on the Archdiocese of Toronto, it becomes evident that its institutional growth was not a unique phenomenon. It exemplifies what occurred within all regions of English-speaking North America where a similar form of church government was adopted to create the classical structure of ecclesiastical metropolitanism. Quite clearly, by promoting, developing, and supporting a self-contained system of institutions which paralleled those of the dominant Protestant culture, Catholics enhanced their religious life and preserved their identity in a pluralistic society.

NOTES

1 W.J. Macdonell, *Reminiscences of the Late Hon. and Right Rev. Alexander Macdonell, First Catholic Bishop of Upper Canada* (Toronto: Williamson 1888), 23.
2 Ibid., 21–4.
3 Archives of the Roman Catholic Archdiocese of Toronto (ARCAT), Macdonell Papers, A Report on the Missions in the Diocese of Kingston, 22 June 1835.
4 L.J. Flynn, *Built on a Rock: The Story of the Roman Catholic Church in Kingston 1826–1976* (Kingston: Brown and Martin 1976), 21.

5 H.F. McIntosh, "The Life and Times of the Right Rev. Michael Power, D.D., First Bishop of Toronto," in J.R. Teefy, ed., *Jubilee Volume: The Archdiocese of Toronto and Archbishop Walsh* (Toronto: G.T. Dixon 1892), 109–40.

6 ARCAT, Power Papers, Power to Lord Stanley, 27 Sept. 1841.

7 *The Cross* (Halifax), 23 Oct. 1847; McIntosh, "Power," 109–40.

8 Power Papers, pastoral letter, 8 May 1842; Gregory XVI, Sovereign Pontiff, 12 July 1842; Pastoral Address on the Occasion of the Erection of the Four Dioceses of Canada in an Ecclesiastical Province, Having Quebec for the Metropolitan See, 29 Dec. 1844.

9 Power Papers, Nicholas Cardinal Wiseman to the Right Reverend the Bishops of Canada, undated true copy.

10 Ibid., Power to Bishop Phelan, 5 March 1844.

11 McIntosh, "Power," 109–40.

12 Power Papers, pastoral address, Inviting the Catholics of the Diocese of Toronto to Contribute towards the Building of the Cathedral Church of St. Michael's in the City, 29 Dec. 1846; Edward Kelly, *The Story of St. Paul's Parish* (Toronto 1922), 105–9.

13 ARCAT, Sundry Books and Records, names and residences of defaulters of donations to the Cathedral building 1848–9. The persons undermentioned have contributed information as to residence 1848–9; St Michael's Cathedral Fund, Feb. 1843–Aug. 1845.

14 Kelly, *St. Paul's Parish*, 84–95; McIntosh, "Power," 109–40.

15 Power Papers, Power to Bishop Kinsella, 8 July 1844.

16 Ibid., pastoral letter, 31 Dec. 1846.

17 Ibid., An Act to Incorporate the Roman Catholic Bishops of Toronto and Kingston in Canada, in *Each Diocese* 82, 29 March 1845.

18 Ibid., pastoral letter, 31 Dec. 1846.

19 Although Power believed in the need for Catholic education, his detachment from the problem is evident from the paucity of correspondence on the subject. See ibid., Power to S. Sanderl, 28 June 1844; Power to T. Roothaan, 12 Nov. 1842; Power to Monseigneur Reisache, 8 May 1847.

20 Kelly, *St. Paul's Parish*, 96–104.

21 The condition of the famine Irish in Toronto is well recorded in ARCAT, Record Books, Minute Books and Annual Reports of the St Vincent de Paul Society. As well, see the Annals, Institutional Records and Letters in the Archives of the Sisters of St Joseph, Toronto, Ontario. Proselytism and Souperism is documented in D. Bowen, *The Protestant Crusade in Ireland 1800–70* (Montreal and Kingston: McGill-Queen's University Press 1978), and ARCAT, Charbonnel Papers, passim.

22 J.R. Teefy, "The Life and Times of the Right Rev. Armand Francis Marie Comte de Charbonnel, Second Bishop of Toronto," in Teefy, ed., *Jubilee Volume*, 143–60.

23 M.W. Nicolson, "The Irish Catholics and Social Work in Toronto 1850–1900," *Studies in History and Politics* 1 (1980): 29–54.
24 Teefy, "De Charbonnel," 143–60.
25 ARCAT, Charbonnel Papers, Charbonnel to Father Taschereau, 26 June 1854.
26 Ibid., Charbonnel to the Prefect of the Congregation of Propaganda, 25 May 1855.
27 Ibid., Charbonnel to all the Bishops during the Second Council of Quebec, 20 Oct. 1855.
28 Ibid., Circular of His Lordship the Bishop of Toronto to his Clergy on the Subdivision of the Diocese, 1856.
29 For Charbonnel's influence, direction, and leadership of the church see the *Mirror* and the *Canadian Freeman*, 1850–60.
30 Charbonnel Papers, circular to the clergy, 18 July 1852.
31 Ibid., J. Kennedy to Charbonnel, 25 June 1853. ARCAT, Lynch Papers, note in Lynch's handwriting, 29 April 1879; Lynch to J. McBride, 15 July 1881.
32 Power Papers, pastoral letter, 31 Dec. 1846; Charbonnel Papers, J. Kennedy to Charbonnel, 25 June 1853.
33 Nicolson, "The Irish Catholics and Social Work," 29–54.
34 Christian Brothers Archives (CBA), Annals of the Brothers of the Christian Schools, 1851–3.
35 Archives of the Sisters of St Joseph (ASSJ), Community Annals of the Sisters of St Joseph, 1851–3.
36 James Hanrahan, *The Basilian Fathers (1822–1972): A Documentary Study of One Hundred and Fifty Years of the History of the Congregation of St. Basil* (Toronto 1973), passim.
37 Archives of the Sisters of the Good Shepherd (ASGS), Annals of the Sisters of the Good Shepherd, 1875–6.
38 *Mission Book of the Redemptorist Fathers: A Manual of Instructions and Prayers Adopted To Preserve the Fruits of the Mission* (New York 1897), 315–425.
39 *Hoffman's Catholic Directory and Clergy List* (Milwaukee 1889), 556–60.
40 SSJA, *Constitutions and Rules of the Congregation of St. Joseph in the Archdiocese of Toronto* (Toronto 1881).
41 *Manual of the Society of St. Vincent of Paul* (London: Bailly, Divry and Co 1851).
42 ARCAT, St Vincent de Paul Society Papers (SVDP), *Report of the St. Vincent de Paul Society, Toronto* (Toronto 1886, 1887, 1888, 1889), 39–46, 43–50, 48–50, 39–42.
43 Murray W. Nicolson, "The Catholic Church and the Irish in Victorian Toronto" (PhD dissertation, University of Guelph 1981), 211–50.
44 SVCP, minutes, 16 Dec. 1855, 19 Dec. 1871, 12 March 1854, 20 Jan. 1856; *Report of the Society of St. Vincent de Paul* (Toronto 1883, 1886), 23, 24.

45 Murray W. Nicolson, "Irish Catholic Education in Victorian Toronto: An Ethnic Response to Urban Conformity," *Social History* 17, 34 (Nov. 1984): 287–306.
46 Nicolson, "The Catholic Church and the Irish," 364–435.
47 Nicolson, "Irish Catholic Education," 287–306.
48 Nicolson, "The Catholic Church and the Irish," 211–50.
49 Ibid., 211–50.
50 Ibid.
51 *Irish Canadian*, 7 Dec. 1872; *Canadian Freeman*, 9 April 1863; *Toronto Mirror*, 29 May 1851; *The Mission Book of the Redemptorist Fathers*, 315–425.

8 "Improvident Emigrants": John Joseph Lynch and Irish Immigration to British North America, 1860–88

GERALD STORTZ

"Canada is a nation of immigrants" is a cliché that, in the age of government-sponsored multiculturalism, has come to dominate political speeches in the last two decades. It is a phrase, however, that would have been equally appropriate in describing Canada in the second half of the nineteenth century. The difference was that, in the nineteenth century, the overwhelming majority of immigrants were from the British Isles, among them a large member of Irish Catholics. This migration had a profound effect upon the development of all institutions, and in Ontario none was reshaped more than the Roman Catholic church.

The Catholic church in Ontario had initially been simply an offshoot of its Quebec parent, beginning as a missionary effort dating back to the era of the Canadian martyrs, then evolving into attempts to provide services for small pockets of French-Canadian Catholics in Sandwich (now Windsor) in Essex County.[1] In 1804 this small group was joined by Scottish Catholic immigrants led to Glengarry County by Father (later Bishop) Alexander Macdonell. Although Macdonell enjoyed unexpected success in achieving status for the Catholic church, largely through his friendship with Anglican Rector (later Bishop) John Strachan of York (Toronto), it was not until the 1840s that Catholics became a numerically significant minority in Upper Canada, which in 1867 became the Province of Ontario.[2] The internal result was an overwhelmingly "Irish" church, now predominantly English-speaking, often antagonistic to French Canada in terms of orientation, hierarchical structure, and ritual. Similarly, Irish-

Canadian Catholicism encountered an Ultra-Protestant backlash, which included such extreme measures as attempts at outright conversion. Within the Catholic church, there were those such as Bishop Thomas Louis Connolly, bishop of Saint John (1852–9) and archbishop of Halifax (1859–76), who felt that emigration to Canada, whatever problems the emigrants might face, was preferable to the poverty of Ireland.[3] Connolly was, however, in a minority among not only the Canadian but the North American hierarchy.

The views of Archbishop John Joseph Lynch of Toronto, who had a dualistic attitude towards Irish Catholic immigrants, were more typical among Catholic churchmen. Lynch's initial task was to do everything possible, through the expansion of an extensive charitable network, to ease the problems he saw plaguing his charges, such as poverty, cyclical unemployment, and drunkenness.[4] The second task, more important in his eyes, was to discourage immigration to Ontario cities, which, unlike the countryside, were seen to be part of the problem. To this end, Lynch steadfastly opposed Irish immigration schemes. There was an exception in the early 1880s when he was involved with a "star-crossed" scheme with the federal government for an agricultural colony, as part of the National Policy, in rural Manitoba. The purposes of this article are to explore the genesis of Lynch's ideas, the extent of his anti-immigration efforts, and the ill-fated attempt at establishing the religiously based settlement in Manitoba.

The arrival in Toronto in 1859 of the Ulsterman John Lynch, after postings in Texas, Missouri, and New York, to succeed Comte Armand de Charbonnel coincided with the end of large-scale famine migration to Canada.[5] Lynch, who was consecrated as third bishop of Toronto in 1860, soon realized he was living in "the Belfast of Canada." If he had had any doubts, they would quickly have been dispelled by the sectarian violence surrounding the Prince of Wales's 1860 visit to Canada or by the "ritualized" violence surrounding such religiously based feasts as St Patrick's Day, Corpus Christi, the "Glorious" Twelfth, and Guy Fawkes Day.[6] Endemic prejudice against Irish Catholics in Toronto added to the fervour of his belief that the problems of the North American urban environment did not extend to those willing to go to rural areas. As the *Catholic Weekly Review*, Lynch's official newspaper, argued late in his career, "It would be difficult to find a more practical and wholesome lesson than is often shown them [urban Catholics] than by their fellow Catholics in districts less favoured with opportunities to enjoy the frequent and full services of the church."[7] This point of view seems to be validated by recent studies that suggest that Catholics settling in rural areas also avoided the economic pitfalls of their urban counterparts and were, on the whole, successful agriculturists.[8]

Whatever doubts Lynch may have had about speaking out on this issue were dispelled by 1864. In that year he published a pamphlet, *The Evils of Improvident Emigration*, in which he vividly described the plight of impoverished Irish Catholics who poured into North American cities. Although marked confidential and ostensibly for the eyes only of the Irish hierarchy, the letter appeared first in the Irish, then in the North American press. Lynch argued that although his action led to mild censure from the Vatican, it was necessary because four million Irish "have disappeared from that land and alas for their descendants ... the Irish are banished by proud and unjust laws and a secret conspiracy by the Irish landlords. The loss of souls alone affected me." He contrasted Irish immigrants with "the Germans, French and even the Norwegians [who] came provided with the means of establishing themselves either as farmers or mechanics; but the large majority of Irish come absolutely penniless; and hence they cannot reach the interior of the country and are obliged to look for the cheapest lodgings in the cities and everyone knows that such places are the haunts of vice ... They and their children are lost to morality, to society, to religion and finally to God." This was why, claimed Lynch, "the hospitals, the poorhouses and jails ... have more than their proportion of inmates of Irish or their descendants." In Toronto, he concluded, "the criminal calendar is made up almost exclusively of those ... having been driven in the country in an impoverished condition and consequently forced to take up their abode in the haunts of vice." The solution was to aid "our persecuted and impoverished brethren in the well grounded hope that England in her wisdom will see the necessity of doing justice to Ireland."[9] Lynch was supported in his position by a number of Canadian and American bishops, including Peter Richard Kenrick, archbishop of St Louis. Kenrick wrote to Lynch that a statement such as his was badly needed to correct "the misapprehension entertained by people in Ireland on the subject of emigration. Your statement was rather defective than exaggerated for the whole truth could not be told."

In a letter to Alessandro Cardinal Barnabo, prefect of Propaganda, Lynch defended his actions, in that he had marked the letter confidential, but reiterated that it was immigration of the Irish to urban areas, not immigration per se, to which he was opposed: "without possessing land they have not bettered their position by coming to this country." He indicated that he would give wholehearted support to an *agricultural* scheme.[10] It was a stance Lynch maintained even at the risk of appearing hardhearted, as in 1872 when he vetoed a proposal to bring Irish slum children to Toronto.[11] Ironically, when Lynch did get a chance to establish his dream of an agricultural colony, it remained an unfulfilled dream. Yet the failure of "New Ireland," as the colony was to be called, had less to do with Lynch or the concept than with external factors.

Early in his career in Toronto, Lynch had developed an alliance with the Liberal-Conservative party of John A. Macdonald and George-Etienne Cartier. It was a quid pro quo relationship, with Lynch providing what was considered to be the block Catholic vote representing nearly 20 per cent of the population. With Confederation in 1867 and the formation of Macdonald government, this alliance was continued. In the first federal election, for example, Lynch issued letters indicating his preference for Macdonald's party. By the early 1870s, however, Conservative strategists began to doubt the archbishop's ability to deliver the vote. In several instances in which he intervened, the Conservative candidate lost. In addition, a group known as the Catholic League was formed by John O'Donohoe, a layman and Liberal politician. Although ostensibly neutral, the party ties were obvious. The Conservatives therefore decided to sever the ties with the archbishop. Although wooed by Alexander Mackenzie's Liberals, Lynch never did form an alliance with them. In an era in which Canada languished in depression, it was a wise move.

Certainly it seemed more than coincidence that Lynch's newspaper began in 1876 to speak of the need for "a National Policy" for Canada at precisely the same time that John A. Macdonald was crisscrossing the country touting an economic program of the same name.[12] The scheme that led to an 1878 election victory for the Conservatives had three aspects: a protective tariff, the construction of a transcontinental railway, and development of the West through immigration.[13] One idea with regard to immigration was to establish colonies on the basis of religion and nationality. "New Ireland," for example, was to be located in Manitoba. Since this was exactly what Lynch had argued since 1864, the government decided to ask him to participate in the project – but only after it had sought the approval of Henry Edward Cardinal Manning in Britain.[14] Manning was agreeable, but suggested the scheme would not be viable unless the approval of the Canadian hierarchy was obtained. Otherwise the scheme would be seen simply as a means for Irish landlords to rid themselves of troublesome tenants. Lynch proved the stumbling block, however, arguing that the Irish hierarchy who opposed emigration would never agree. As Lord Lorne, the governor general, described the situation: "I very nearly got the Canadian hierarchy to put their names on an invitation to the Irish people to come here. All were willing to sign except an old Fenian archbishop of Toronto who kicked wildly at the last moment and as he was the senior, the others said they must wait for him."[15]

In the meantime, Lynch had visited Ireland and England, where he met the Duke and Duchess of Marlborough and saw the miseries of Ireland firsthand. He had also been invited to the Court of St James to express his views on the fate of Ireland, the first Roman Catholic bishop in more than two hundred years to be given such a reception.[16] In his absence from Toronto and after his return, other Irish leaders expressed their support for the establishment of "New Ireland" in Manitoba. The *Irish Canadian* newspaper, for example, encouraged such an idea to include young priests from Ontario. Manitoba was described as "the North-Western Canaan of Milk and Honey."[17] By the end of 1880 John Costigan, a prominent representative of Canada's Irish Catholics, had indicated his approval of the colonization scheme. He complained that appeals to the politicians in Ottawa "have been met in an unworthy spirit" and indicated that he felt he would be able to raise fifty thousand dollars.[18] The preliminary work on behalf of the colony, however, had been taking place even as Costigan's complaints were being made public. Canadian officials had informed British authorities of the terms they would request for the scheme. Immigration was to be voluntary, and low interest loans would be provided. The immigrant would receive a free grant of 160 acres, for which he would pay a £2 registration fee. The settler would also have the option to buy the 160 acres of land adjoining his grant.[19] At the end of December 1880 Canadian officials formalized this proposal and sought British approval.[20]

Up to the early part of 1880, Lynch continued to oppose the scheme. During the course of the year, he changed his mind, possibly for a variety of reasons. He was undoubtedly aware of the success that a similar project, headed by John Ireland, coadjutor bishop of St Paul, was enjoying in Minnesota.[21] He must also have been aware that Icelanders had been settled by the Canadian government in the same area suggested for New Ireland.[22] Another reason for the change of heart may have been the involvement of Archbishop Alexandre-Antonin Taché of Saint-Boniface. Taché had spent a great deal of largely unrewarded effort attempting to establish colonies of French-Canadian Catholics in the North-West.[23] By 1880 he had lost patience with his fellow French-Canadian bishops and had come to the conclusion that Irish and Scottish Catholics in the West were preferable to no Catholics at all.[24] The combination of rural settlement and the offer by the government of a trip to Ireland for Lynch probably also played a significant role in Lynch's change of mind. He wrote to Vatican officials, outlining the plan and asking permission to make the trip to his homeland to persuade the Irish hierarchy to encourage emigration to New Ireland.[25] In the meantime, while Taché selected a probable site for the colony, Lynch, through the auspices of trusted laymen, began to promote the scheme in Toronto.[26] Macdonald personally continued to encourage Lynch's involvement. The prime minister warned that it would be difficult to persuade the Irish hierarchy of the acceptability of the scheme because they feared a loss of faith among emigrants. Macdonald, however, wanted Lynch to encourage priests to take part in the scheme. Priests, he said, could be enticed by the prospect of "Congregations of well-to-do farmers instead of a flock of starving and dissatisfied Irishmen."[27] Lynch argued, in turn, that assisted emigration might render the scheme generally more acceptable: "If the government was prepared to support and help them according to their needs and necessities then you can bid for the prize ... but you are a great politician and I am a great churchman and you know we cannot always agree on every question."[28]

Lynch personally travelled to Manitoba to inspect the proposed site. On his return to Toronto, the archbishop described the site "as in many respects unsurpassed in the world."[29] The project was delayed only by the failure of Rome to approve the project. In the meantime, Lynch, Taché, and Macdonald agreed that the colony need not be exclusively Irish, but that it would be settled by religion – in clusters of Catholics with priests.[30] Taché also was instrumental in choosing the specific township sites for those he and Lynch had inspected. Any subsequent settlement would be dependent on the success of the initial colony. It was left up to Lynch to decide during his trip to Ireland when the colonists would arrive and how many there would be in each phase.[31]

The year 1882 marked the high point for the scheme. The Macdonald government was still in the throes of making arrangements, but Ontario's Irish population had indicated their enthusiastic response for the colony.[32] Lynch had also finally received permission from the Vatican to go to Ireland.[33] Arrangements were made for him to meet Taché in Toronto to make preparations for the journey. Early in February Lynch departed for Ireland with the expectation that there would be general opposition to the scheme on the part of the Irish hierarchy. He warned Macdonald, "many [of the hierarchy] fear that they [the emigrants] only exchange climates and country but not masters and landlords."[34] The reaction of the Irish was, however, far more favourable than Lynch had anticipated. Not only was the hierarchy willing to accept the scheme, but the government administration in Ireland was also enthusiastic. The British government encouraged the scheme by offering low-interest loans. In Lynch's own estimation, he had "succeeded beyond my expectations."[35]

Lynch left Ireland for England full of enthusiasm. His arrival was heralded by English Catholic notables. One prominent Catholic advised Lynch that his visit in England in 1879 had been a triumph that could be repeated in 1882.[36] Another, the Duke of Norfolk, issued an invitation to Lynch to stay at his home, and was accepted.[37] Lynch also assumed he would be meeting with the British prime minister, William Ewart Gladstone, since Alexander T. Galt, the Canadian high commissioner to Britain, had made the arrangements.[38] Gladstone's 1881 Land Act included an emigration clause, and Lynch reasoned that colonization societies such as the one he was proposing were required for the clause to work.[39] The archbishop's enthusiasm was soon dashed, however, by a message indicating that Gladstone was too busy to see him and that there was little chance of his government's accepting Lynch's plan.[40] Galt attempted to soften the blow by suggesting that Lynch would be able to see Gladstone at a later date. He also warned, however, "the delay is evidence of a want of appreciation of the Irish situation."[41] Although Lynch remained in London through part of the summer, Gladstone consistently refused to meet with him, and the expected approval of the British government for the emigration scheme was not forthcoming.[42]

The refusal was the product of events in Ireland and in Canada. The Phoenix Park murders has just taken place in Ireland. Two English noblemen, Lord Spencer and Lord Cavendish, who had only the night before taken the oath of office, were stabbed to death by Irish nationalists.[43] The result was an anti-Irish backlash in Britain. Almost simultaneously, the Canadian Parliament passed a resolution calling for Home Rule for Ireland.[44] Credit for passing the resolution was given to the Irish Catholics of both Houses of the Canadian Parliament.[45] Lord Kimberley advised Lorne that British officials were not pleased. He warned, "they are not in a temper to be trifled with by anglers for Irish votes at elections for colonial legislatures."[46] Kimberley might also have added that the British were not disposed to grant favours to an Irish Catholic archbishop with well-known sympathy for Home Rule for Ireland. There was no longer any hope of British participation in the colonization scheme.

The British refusal to participate did not mark the end of the scheme. The Canadian government continued actively to portray Canada to the Irish as a land of opportunity.[47] A prospectus outlining the boundaries of the colony was also prepared. To replace the British money, the Canadian government offered £100,000 to finance the colony.[48] Galt, in particular, was enthusiastic about the possibilities for success. He wrote to Lynch: "I trust with your valued aid I shall be asked to do some good to these poor people and change their lot for a happier one; [count on] my using every prosecution to attain honest industrious people such as you may confidently recommend to your local clergy."[49]

As the year ended, Lynch was still enthusiastic about the immigration plan, as the Macdonald government also seemed to be. The scheme was seen as a success, and others aware of the archbishop's involvement sought his help for colonization projects of their own.[50] Lynch's enthusiasm for the New Ireland scheme was undoubtedly heightened by news of new economic difficulty facing Irish tenants. The failure of both the oat and potato crops led to extreme famine conditions.[51] There was continued British opposition from such sources as Lorne, who argued: "Under the scheme we would have a piece of Ireland whose social organization would be sown with the seeds of family quarrels with 'sores' of old standing, with smouldering enmities, hatred of British government, of the protestant religion, of our system of education, frequently of our government and owing allegiance only to dictation of leaders of their own nationality and creed and to the priesthood."[52]

The Conservative government continued to support the scheme into 1883. As late as August of that year, Lynch was still being encouraged by the prime minister in his support of the colony. Macdonald advised Lynch that he felt fifty families would be a good basis on which to found the colony. The males in these families would be able to earn $2.50 per day, helping to build the Canadian Pacific Railway, while the wives and children could grow potatoes on the homestead.[53] In Toronto the plan was hailed by the Tory newspaper, the *World*. It argued that the Irish were acceptable because they were unskilled, and therefore were not taking jobs away from Canadian mechanics.[54]

By the end of 1883 the New Ireland scheme was, as far as Lynch was concerned, a dead issue. Like the British, the Canadian Conservatives withdrew their support for political reasons. Lynch and the federal Conservatives had become embroiled in a dispute over the archbishop's direction of the Catholic vote to the Liberal party of Oliver Mowat in provincial elections.[55] The direction of colonization projects for the North-West was turned over to Lynch's colleague, Bishop John Walsh of London, Ontario, a friend and sometime supporter of Ontario Conservative leader William R. Meredith. By the time Walsh assumed the role, many colonization projects in the North-West had foundered. Presumably because enthusiasm for such plans was dampened, New Ireland did not become a reality under Walsh's direction.[56]

Lynch's response was to retreat to his 1864 position. In an 1883 letter to the bishops and clergy of Ireland, Lynch explained that North American conditions had obliged him to speak out in 1864. He also claimed that once Pope Pius ix had been sent a copy of the letter, the pontiff had written thanking him for his efforts. Lynch claimed the situation had not improved. He cited evidence that many Catholics had become "staunch Protestants." He enumerated the "causes of the loss of souls in America ... 1st the scarcity of priests; 2nd, the fact that the great majority of Irish emigrants arriving in America, till very lately were so poor that they were unable to push their way into the country and there follow their old occupation of tilling the land." Lynch then described the "overcrowded tenement houses in the poorest and most unhealthy parts of the city." Fresh air was available in the streets, where children fell into bad company and ended up either in jail, shipped to the West, or, if fortunate, in Catholic-run orphanages and asylums.

Distance from church, inability to afford "good clothes," and impassable roads for much of the year were also cited as threats to Catholicism, especially if a Protestant church was closer. Common schools, in which Catholicism was often ridiculed by both teachers and fellow students, were also a consistent problem. Mixed marriages rendered Catholics "far from church and the influence of its teachings."

All of these calamities, claimed Lynch, were the product of the unpreparedness of the emigrants. The children, in particular, were vulnerable because once their families achieved some measure of comfort, they became bitter at their parents. Also, "the children quickly surpass in general knowledge, their parents and if their religion do not come to their aid, they are attempted to neglect or be ashamed of them."

"Drink is another cause of loss and of great misery and untimely deaths," continued the archbishop. "The Celtic blood is so strong and hot that very little spirits, in too many cases, will set it in a blaze." Drunkenness, in turn, led to crime and imprisonment. Finally, "the Irish came isolated, without organization, not knowing what part of the country to settle in." In particular, Lynch lamented the fate "of the young women and girls who, in great numbers, came unprotected," some of whom were "allured by the wily agents of iniquity and who are lost: but we hope not eternally." He regretted also "young men and boys ... scattered through the country, on railroads, canals, steamboats, farms and workshops." Married men often came with the idea that they "would acquire means to bring them out. Alas! some of them fail miserably."

Lynch concluded, "what could not be effected in Ireland by religious persecution, loss of land and homes, social disabilities and starvation, has been accomplished here in too many instances by the enemy of good and all his agents." He urged instead that the Irish remain in Ireland, claiming, "patriotism is a God-given virtue, and the people of a country are bound to and do give up their lives to preserve their altars and their homes."[57]

Because there was no alleged attempts at secrecy, there was, in this instance, no reaction from the Vatican, although some Irish officials were critical and the archbishop was pilloried by the Toronto Conservative and Protestant newspapers. This was especially the case after it was revealed that he had vetoed a plan to bring Irish workhouse girls to the city because they tended to immorality. The *Sentinel*, the paper of the Orange Order, said this proved that priests, not landlords, were at the root of the Irish problem because of their inability to instil morality in their flock.[58] The populist *World* put the problem in a larger context, arguing that "the present condition of Ireland is due simply to the Romish priests who really would keep the people in ignorance and poverty rather than control them. Hence, the opposition of the Irish patriot Archbishop Lynch who publicly opposes the plan of the British government for assisting the unfortunate priest ridden Romanists to emigrate."[59] Such criticisms did nothing to change Lynch's opposition to further Irish immigration, which he maintained staunchly until his death in 1888.

From a twentieth-century perspective, some of Lynch's views on the Catholic immigrants seem almost ludicrous or at best tragi-comic. Certainly, as even he himself admitted, the portrayal of the typical Irish Catholic urbanite seemed to confirm the stereotype of a drunken, unemployed criminal element more often associated with nativist groups, such as the Orange Order, than with a Roman Catholic archbishop. Lynch's extremely negative view of the typical Irish Catholic immigrant may have reflected a class bias on his part. That the archbishop was not of peasant stock is indicated by his parents' ability, after initial education at the "hedge schools," to arrange for their son to be taught by a graduate of Dublin's Trinity College. Even regional considerations may have come into play, for the immigrants of whom Lynch was so critical were predominantly from the south, while he was from the relatively prosperous northeast of Ireland. Such factors, however, must not blind us to the element of truth in what Lynch had to say about the Irish Catholic population of Toronto. Catholic immigrants were indeed exposed to physical and spiritual hazards, including the risk they would lose their faith. In the city's hospitals and prisons, they were bombarded by the proselytizing efforts of Protestant zealots distributing evangelical tracts, often making relief from poverty contingent upon renunciation of Catholicism.[60] Nor should we ignore the depth of Lynch's concern for his flock and of his commitment to philanthropic undertakings. His episcopal motto – "Evangelizare Pauperibus Misit me [He has sent me to bring the good news to the poor], Luke 4:18" – was reflected in his efforts to expand the charitable network that had been established by Charbonnel as a response to the new problems brought about by the twin processes of industrialization and urbanization. When he observed the havoc that had been wrought, it made sense not to multiply the problem by having more Irish Catholics emigrate to the cities. It made similar sense to encourage migration to pastoral areas where these problems did not exist. Within a few years of Lynch's death in 1888, the whole nature of immigration changed. Irish Catholics were but a minor trickle in the Wilfrid Laurier/Clifford Sifton era. The Catholics who arrived were predominantly from Europe. Suddenly the paramount problem for the church was not the Irish, who by century's end had begun to assimilate into the larger society, but how to provide services for Poles, Italians, Slovaks, and others.

NOTES

1 For an overview see John S. Moir, *Church and State in Canada West 1841–1867* (Toronto: University of Toronto Press 1967).
2 For details of Macdonell's career see J.E. Rea, *Bishop Alexander Macdonell and the Politics of Upper Canada* (Toronto: Ontario Historical Society 1974).
3 See Robert Choquette, "English-French Relations in the Canadian Catholic Community," and J.R. Miller, "Anti-Catholicism in Canada: From the British Conquest to the Great War," in this volume. For details of Connolly's episcopal career see Fay Trombley, *James Louis Connolly (1815–1876): The Man and His Place in Secular and Ecclessiastical History* (Saint John: The author 1983).
4 For details of charitable efforts see Gerald J. Stortz, "The Charitable Endeavours of John Joseph Lynch, c.m.," *Vincentian Heritage* 5, 2 (1984): 85–106.
5 See Gerald J. Stortz, "John Joseph Lynch, Archbishop of Toronto: A Biographical Study of Religious, Political and Social Commitment" (PhD dissertation, University of Guelph 1980).

6 The terms "Belfast of Canada" and "ritualized" violence are used in G.S. Kealey, "The Orange Order in Toronto: Religious Riot and the Workingclass," in P. Warrian and G.S. Kealey, eds., *Essays in Canadian Working-class History* (Toronto: McClelland and Stewart 1976).

7 *Catholic Weekly Review*, 14 March 1891.

8 This view, which has gained considerable support among scholars, first appeared in D. Akenson, "Ontario: Whatever Happened to the Irish?" in D. Akenson, ed., *Canadian Papers in Rural History*, vol. 3 (Gananoque: Langdale Press 1982), 204–56.

9 The full text of the pamphlet can be found in Gerald J. Stortz, ed., "Archbishop Lynch's *The Evils of Wholesale and Improvident Emigration from Ireland*," in *Eire-Ireland* 18, 2 (1983): 6–16.

10 Archives of the Sacred Congregation de Propaganda Fide (APF), Scritture Riferite nei Congressi, America Settentrionale, vol. 8 (1862–4), fol. 869; Lynch to prefect of Propaganda, 28 Sept. 1864; Archives of the Roman Catholic Archdiocese of Toronto (ARCAT), Archbishop Kenrick to Lynch, 15 Oct. 1864; APF, Lynch to Cardinal Barnabo, 29 Sept. 1864.

11 Archives of the Archdiocese of Quebec, Archbishop Taschereau Papers, Lynch to Vicar-General C.F. Cazeau, 11 Feb. 1873.

12 *Toronto Tribune and Catholic Vindicator*, 13 Oct. 1876.

13 The simplest summary of the National Policy is J.H. Dales, "Protection, Immigration and Canadian Nationalism," in Peter Russell, ed., *Nationalism in Canada* (Toronto: McGraw-Hill 1966), 164–7.

14 For an earlier treatment of many of these themes see Gerald J. Stortz, "Archbishop Lynch and New Ireland: An Unfulfilled Dream for Canada's Northwest," *Catholic Historical Review* 68, 4 (Oct. 1982): 612–24.

15 W.S. MacNutt, *Days of Lorne* (Fredericton: Brunswick Press 1945), 168.

16 H.C. McKeown, *The Life and Labors of the Most Rev. John Joseph Lynch* (Toronto 1886), 116–17.

17 *Irish Canadian*, 18 Feb. 1880.

18 Ibid., 15 Dec. 1880.

19 National Archives of Canada (NA), Lord Kimberley Papers, J.H. Pope to the Duke of Newcastle, 30 Oct. 1880.

20 Ibid., J.D. Cole to Newcastle, 26 Dec. 1880.

21 C. Wittke, *The Irish in America* (New York: Russell and Russell 1956), 72–3.

22 N. Macdonald, *Canadian Immigration and Colonization 1841–1903* (Aberdeen 1966), 208–13.

23 A.I. Silver, "French Canada and the Prairie Frontier," *Canadian Historical Review* (CHR) 50, 1 (1969): 13.

24 R. Painchaud, "French Canadian Historiography and Franco-Catholic Settlement in Western Canada 1870–1975," CHR 59, 4 (1978): 458.

25 ARCAT, Lynch Papers, Lynch to prefect of Propaganda, nd [1882].

26 NA, Sir John A. Macdonald Papers, Lynch to Macdonald, 5 Jan. 1881.
27 Lynch Papers, Macdonald to Lynch, 7 May 1881.
28 Macdonald Papers, Lynch to Macdonald, 11 May 1881.
29 *Globe*, 31 Oct. 1881.
30 Archives of the Archdiocese of Saint-Boniface (AASB), Archbishop Taché Papers, Macdonald to Lynch, 9 Dec. 1881.
31 Ibid., Taché to Lynch, 23 Dec. 1881.
32 Lynch Papers, J. McMahon to Lynch, 13 Jan. 1882.
33 Archives of the Archdiocese of Kingston, Archbishop James Vincent Cleary Papers, Lynch to Cleary, 2 Feb. 1882.
34 Macdonald Papers, Lynch to Macdonald, 20 Feb. 1882.
35 Taché Papers, Lynch to Taché, 19 April 1882.
36 Lynch Papers, unidentified to Lynch, 15 May 1882.
37 Ibid., Duke of Norfolk to Lynch, 30 April 1882; Lynch to Norfolk, 13 May 1882.
38 Ibid., Sir Alexander Galt to Lynch, nd [1882].
39 Ibid., Galt to Lynch, 1 April 1882.
40 Ibid., Lord Kimberley to Galt, 28 April 1882.
41 Ibid., Galt to Lynch, nd [1882].
42 Ibid., J.S. Cohner to Galt, 8 July 1882.
43 Emmet Larkin, *The Roman Catholic Church and the Creation of the Modern Irish State 1878–1886* (Philadelphia: American Philosophical Society 1975), 183.
44 S.W. Horall, "Canada and the Irish Question: A Study of the Canadian Response to Irish Home Rule, 1882–1893" (MA thesis, Carleton University 1966), 18.
45 Macdonald Papers, Macdonald to Lorne, 2 May 1882.
46 Lord Kimberley Papers, Kimberley to Lorne, 2 May 1882.
47 See, for example, C.A. Pringle, *Manitoba and the Northwest* (Ottawa 1882), a typical pamphlet touting the benefits of emigration to Canada.
48 Lynch Papers, Galt to Lynch, 18 Oct. 1882.
49 Ibid., Galt to Lynch, 27 Oct. 1882.
50 See, for example, ibid., M. Bedford to Lynch, 1 Dec. 1882.
51 Ibid., Bishop Bartholemew Woodlock to Lynch, 3 Jan. 1883.
52 J.E. Collins, *Canada under the Administration of Lord Lorne* (Toronto 1884), 165–6.
53 Macdonald Papers, Macdonald to Lynch, 3 Aug. 1883.
54 *Toronto World*, 26 June 1883.
55 For an explanation of the dispute from the archbishop's point of view see Archives of Ontario, Pamphlet Collection, no. 19, *An Important Protest: The Mail's Vilification of Archbishop Lynch Denounced: The Manifesto of Senators Smith and O'Donohoe Criticized: Facts for Catholic People to Consider* (Toronto 1882).

56 Peter Dembski, "William Ralph Meredith: Leader of the Conservative Opposition in Ontario 1878–1894" (PhD dissertation, University of Guelph 1977), 100–1.
57 The full text of the letter is in McKeown, *Lynch*, 249–60.
58 *Sentinel and Orange and Protestant Advocate*, 1 Nov. 1883.
59 *World*, 3 Nov. 1882.
60 See, for example, Metro Toronto Central Reference Library, Baldwin Room, Minutebook of the Irish Protestant Benevolent Society.

9 The Parish and the Hearth: Women's Confraternities and the Devotional Revolution among the Irish Catholics of Toronto, 1850–85

BRIAN CLARKE

Any attempt to understand the religious life of Catholic immigrants to Canada must begin with a knowledge of the religious situation in their country of origin at the time of their departure. The religious background of Irish Catholic immigrants, such as those who poured into Toronto in the wake of the Great Famine, has been expanded by historians like Emmet Larkin who have examined the impact of the Ultramontane revival on the religious practice of the laity. These historians have pointed out that the Ultramontanes were dedicated to effecting a far-reaching program of religious renewal. In addition to regularizing the laity's observance of canonical duties, such as attendance at Sunday Mass, the Ultramontanes also sought to extend the range of lay piety. Devotions newly authorized by the papacy, paraliturgical rituals such as the rosary and the benediction of the Blessed Sacrament, were to become part of the everyday piety of the laity.

Historians of Irish Catholic immigrants, both in Britain and the United States, have observed that women were far more likely than men to attend church and to embrace the wide range of piety advocated by Ultramontane reformers.[1] Nevertheless, women's devotional organizations, or confraternities as contemporaries called them, have not as yet been examined in any depth. This lacuna is all the more puzzling since it is often assumed that women's predominance in these organizations is directly related to their high level of devotional practice. One of the reasons why these confraternities have been overlooked is that historians have generally disregarded the role of the laity in the parish. All too often when the laity and their parochial organizations are examined, they are viewed as extensions of the clergy. Consequently, lay activism, especially that of women, is largely ignored.

Since the Catholics of Ireland are today a church-going people with one of the highest rates of attendance in the world, it is often assumed that they have always been so. In his pioneering article, "The Devotional Revolution in Ireland," Larkin maintained that before the Great Famine of 1845–9 Irish Catholics were not noted for their religious observance, at least when measured by the usual official indices of church attendance.[2] Rather, he argued, the Catholics only became a church-going people in what he characterized as a devotional revolution during the quarter-century following the famine. Larkin's essay has provoked much discussion and debate among historians of Ireland. Some scholars, most notably S.J. Connolly, have argued that the revolution in lay religious observance was almost exclusively a post-famine phenomenon.[3] Others, especially Patrick Corish and K.T. Hoppen, have maintained that there was a marked continuity in the growth of religious practice among the Irish before and after the famine.[4] Before the famine, church attendance had reached about 40 per cent, which means that by any measure a considerable proportion of the population were practising Catholics. As Larkin has subsequently pointed out, while the devotional revolution had made greater headway before the famine than he had originally allowed, its diffusion was still largely limited to the prosperous social classes and, in general, to the English-language regions of the country.[5] A devotional nucleus did exist in pre-famine Ireland, but even in areas such as the southeast, where the devotional revolution had made progress, religious observance had not yet reached anything like the universal level it was to gain in the three decades after the famine. Nor did devotional practice match the intensity and quality that marked that of post-famine Ireland. Even though the devotional revolution began before the famine, it was consolidated in the following generation, when an extraordinarily high level of religious observance became all but universal.[6]

The debates of Irish historians over the timing and scope of the devotional revolution in Ireland have an important bearing in determining the religious background of those Irish Catholics who came to Toronto. The Catholic population of Toronto was largely composed of immigrants who arrived in Canada during or shortly after the Great Famine of 1845–9. In 1841 there were some 2400 Irish Catholics in the city; by 1851 the Irish Catholic population had jumped to 7940 people, a more than three-fold increase over one decade.[7] What exposure would these immigrants have had to the beliefs and practices of the Catholic church in their home counties before departing for North America? Religious practice in pre-famine Ireland was differentiated along both class and regional lines. Substantial farmers and their families were the most likely to attend church and, as a class, were the backbone of the devotional revolution. While substantial farmers did not emigrate to North America in large numbers in this period, agricultural labourers were the mainstay of Irish Catholic emigration to Canada.[8] Official Catholicism had made few inroads among this population, who tended to stay away from church on Sundays as at any other time.[9] Other Irish Catholic immigrants to Toronto, albeit a minority, came from modest backgrounds either in small-scale farming or in the trades.[10] The exposure of these immigrants to the official teachings and rituals of the Roman Catholic church would vary according to where they grew up in Ireland.

Information on the regional origin of Irish Catholic immigrants is exceedingly rare. Fortunately, parochial marriage records make it possible to paint a regional profile of young adult immigrants married in Toronto between 1850 and 1859.[11] The vast majority of these immigrants, nearly one-half of the total, were from Munster. Those from Leinster came in a distant second, comprising a little over one-quarter of the sample. Immigrants from Connaught and Ulster together made up the remaining quarter. Of all these immigrants, only a handful came from cities, where in almost all regions church attendance was generally high, somewhere in the range between 60 and 70 per cent.[12]

In rural Ireland the Catholic church was weakest in Ulster and, above all, in Connaught. In these two provinces, the population far outstripped the institutional resources and personnel of the church, and, as a consequence, the majority of people did not attend church regularly. The situation was a good deal better in Munster, but even here the people's contact with the church was mixed. In County Clare, the leading county of origin for immigrants from the province, the church was an exceptionally vibrant institution. Nevertheless, in many parts of Munster, including areas in Counties Limerick, Tipperary, and Cork, which ranked consecutively after Clare in the number of immigrants recorded in the parochial marriage registers of Toronto, the church's parochial network was greatly overextended. Only in Leinster, with the exception of the Diocese of Meath, was the church a vibrant religious institution capable of reaching the laity in the region, and as a result church attendance was uniformly high in the province. Given their class backgrounds and their regional origins, many of those who emigrated to Toronto could hardly have had extensive exposure to the official beliefs and practices of the Catholic church before leaving for North America.[13]

During the 1850s the majority of Irish Catholic immigrants in Toronto stayed away from church on Sundays and continued to ignore the canonical injunctions of the church, much as they had done in Ireland. When Armand de Charbonnel assumed his duties as the second Roman Catholic bishop of Toronto in 1850, only two churches served the entire Catholic population. Although these churches were reasonably well filled on Sundays, only two-fifths of those Catholics who were required to attend church could have actually done so, a rate that compares favourably to the national pattern found in Britain at the time.[14] While the ecclesiastical authorities could have reasonably taken solace in the Roman Catholic turnout on Sundays, they saw things differently.

As dedicated reformers, Bishop Charbonnel and his clergy judged lay religious practice from a standard far more exacting than that of their predecessors. The clergy could only view the laity's religious behaviour with shock and horror. "I have everywhere met a great deal of ignorance," Charbonnel sadly admitted.[15] Besides ignoring the religious obligations of canonical Catholicism, too many Irish Catholic immigrants, Charbonnel believed, were totally ignorant of the essentials of their faith, such as how to say the Hail Mary, to hear Mass, and to make their confession.[16] In response to this situation, the clergy not only sought to elevate the standard of religious practice, but they also endeavoured to extend the range of Catholic piety. The laity were to discharge their canonical obligations of attendance at Sunday Mass as well as the fulfilment of Easter duties and, in addition to this canonical minimum, to perform a wide variety of devotions. Instructed in the ideals of Ultramontanism, the clergy of Toronto in effect redefined what it was to be a practising Catholic.

The clergy were also deeply disturbed by the social behaviour of the Irish Catholic immigrants. Drunkenness and idleness, Charbonnel complained, were far too common among the Irish, and he was certain that the dissolute pastimes of the Irish were responsible for their indifferent religious observance. The moral reform of the laity, he concluded, was essential to effect their spiritual renewal. The Roman Catholic clergy, like their evangelical counterparts, set out to reform popular recreation: dancing, drinking, parties, and other amusements were denounced as "immediate occasions of sin alike to those who indulge in them and to willing spectacles [sic]."[17] What was at stake was nothing less than a way of life. The traditional work rhythm of the Irish, with its intense activity followed often by equally intense festivities and drinking, was incompatible with the demands of canonical Catholicism, which stressed the necessity of a well-regulated life. Self-discipline, punctuality, and the tenets of Catholicism were mutually reinforcing. The rationalization of social life and the promotion of the regular discharge of religious duties went together.

With only two churches, both located in the east end of city, and with little in the way of social institutions, the Catholic church at the time of Charbonnel's arrival in 1850 was in a poor position to influence either the religious or the social behaviour of the laity. One obvious response to the situation was to make the church more accessible to the laity. Over the next eight years Charbonnel built three more churches to give Roman Catholicism an institutional presence throughout the city. It was one thing to provide adequate accommodation for the Catholic population, quite another to attract people who were not in the habit of going to church to attend Mass.

Parish missions, the Catholic version of the revival meeting, were one method by which the church sought to awaken the lukewarm. During services held morning and evening over several days, mission preachers would impress upon the laity how perilous their spiritual state was on account of sin, a condition that could only be redeemed by a conversion sealed by the sacraments of the church. The high point of the parish mission was the call to the confessional, followed by the reception of communion.[18] By stressing the immediate necessity of conversion, the mission fostered an experiential and personal form of piety. Yet the sporadic and episodic character of these services meant that the church had to turn to other means to sustain the laity's commitment to the church. In order to realize the church's twin mission of moral and spiritual renewal, the parish had to become the social and religious centre of the Irish Catholic community. The most effective means to achieve that end were parochial voluntary organizations that offered the laity a religiously informed alternative to the pastimes available outside of the church. Through its network of parish-based voluntary associations, which occupied the laity's leisure time, the church sought to influence both the social and religious behaviour of the laity.

Parochial organizations were of many types – social service, recreational, and devotional – but confraternities were the linchpin in the clergy's campaign for spiritual renewal. Charbonnel began founding parochial confraternities in the early 1850s. By the early 1860s two of the largest confraternities, the Sodality of the Blessed Virgin Mary and the Children of Mary, were well established in the city's parishes. The Apostleship of Prayer or League of the Sacred Heart was introduced to the city by Charbonnel's successor, Bishop

John Joseph Lynch, during the mid 1860s and, by the following decade, its parochial branches had become a fixture. The one significant latecomer, the Archconfraternity of the Holy Family, was not generally organized in the parishes until the early 1880s.[19] These devotional associations for adults, with the significant exception of the St Vincent de Paul Society, which Charbonnel introduced to the diocese in 1850, were supported almost exclusively by women, even though most confraternities were open to men.

Most of the devotions promoted by the confraternities – the devotions to Mary, to the Blessed Sacrament or eucharist, to the Sacred Heart of Jesus and the way of the cross – were not new. Nevertheless, Catholic piety underwent a dramatic change both in style and content during the nineteenth century. The papacy's adoption of particular devotions by granting papal authorization and indulgences served to standardize these devotions according to Roman norms and usage.[20] Moreover, the papacy's energetic promotion of these devotions resulted in Catholic piety being recast into a complex of devotions that were articulated to one another, so much so that this form of Catholicism can be aptly termed devotional Catholicism. Catholic piety became characterized by the repeated performance of ritualistic actions that were to inspire the devotion of the faithful, as for example in the rosary.

All Catholic devotions sought to induce the faithful to forge a personal and familiar bond with Jesus, Mary, or one or another saint.[21] By entering into a relationship with these supernatural beings through the various devotions of the church, the believer could participate in the communion of the saints and share in the salvific economy of prayer and merit mediated by the Roman Catholic church. Through Mary, the Mother of God, the manual for the Archconfraternity of the Holy Family assured the faithful, "we have the most certain means of obtaining [the] inestimable gift of divine love, since she has been appointed by her Son, the Treasurer and Dispenser of all graces, and is therefore our most compassionate intercessor and advocate with God."[22] Devotions provided a highly ritualized entry into this redemptive universe. It is through these devotions that the religious world of Irish Catholic women is revealed.

Among the devotions promoted by the confraternities, it is perhaps the resurgence of Marian piety that most clearly illuminates the development of devotional piety among Irish Catholic women in Toronto. All the parish religious societies – the Association of the Children of Mary, the Sodality of the Blessed Virgin Mary, the Archconfraternity of the Holy Family, the Apostleship of Prayer also known as the League of the Sacred Heart – promoted devotions to

Mary, especially the saying of the rosary. The rosary was a series of prayers, usually counted on a string of beads, in which the faithful recited fifteen decades of the Hail Mary, with each decade preceded by an Our Father and followed by a Glory Be to the Father. Associated with each decade was a meditation on the life of Mary and Jesus that linked Mary's purity and maternal solicitude with the salvific work of Jesus.

The rosary could be easily performed both in the church and in the home. Consequently, the rosary became an intensely private devotion. During the celebration of the Mass, the attention of many women was usually directed towards saying the rosary.[23] Few could understand Latin, and Catholic prayer books, because of Pius ix's prohibition of translations of the liturgy, usually provided only "Mass devotions and meditations" rather than liturgical texts.[24] Individually as well as collectively, these devotions imparted the distinctive doctrines of the Roman Catholic church. The rosary, like other Catholic devotions, was the prism through which the laity interpreted the Mass. Far from isolating its devotees, the rosary inevitably led to communal affirmation through the reception of the sacraments.

The purpose of the rosary, Charbonnel explained, "is to unite ourselves, in the course of our daily actions and sufferings [sic] to the Blessed Virgin Mary, to Her thoughts, Her Judgments, Her feelings, Her conversations, so that we may live and die as she did for God alone."[25] Mary's devotion to Jesus provided lay women with a model of true piety and maternal solicitude. As the Mother of God and a divine mediator, Mary was the spiritual mother of the faithful. Her graces and spiritual favours, purchased through her sacrifice and suffering, led her devotees to Christ crucified.[26] In the meditations the laity were encouraged to engage in while reciting the rosary, the sufferings of Mary were associated with Christ's sacrifice and his loving offer of salvation given up in the Mass. The Passion was thus central to the rosary, as it was to all other devotions. Marian devotionalism bridged the seemingly infinite gulf between the sacred and profane and made the sacraments much more accessible to the laity. By establishing such an intimate relationship with Mary, a relationship rooted in Christ's passion, the rosary inspired Irish Catholic women to receive the sacraments and so unite themselves with Christ. Without the sanctifying grace conveyed by the sacraments, Archbishop Lynch warned, "we can make no progress towards eternal life."[27] When informed by the sacraments, "the most indifferent works become eminently meritorious and of truly apostolic efficacy."[28]

The rosary fostered a personal quest for holiness that centred on the sacraments of the parish church. As a result, all women's confraternities advocated the frequent – monthly – reception of the sacraments.[29] As this piety was a form of sacramental nurture, it was firmly rooted in the collective affirmation of the Roman Catholic faith, the sacrifice of the Mass. By stressing the sacramental foundation of Catholic piety, the confraternities made an essential contribution to the establishment of parochial piety. Not only did they encourage the performance of private devotions at Mass and the regular reception of the sacraments, as the mark of a practising Catholic, but they also provided an important impetus for the public celebration of parochial devotions, such as the benediction of the Blessed Sacrament. In the interval between the reception of the sacraments, the performance of these devotions served to reinforce the sacramental relationship between the faithful and the divine forged in the sacrifice of the Mass offered up in the parish church. At the same time that the devotion to Mary led lay women to the altar, it was designed to suffuse day-to-day life with the sacraments.[30] The rosary, like all devotions, fostered a distinctive way of life for Irish Catholic women.

Both in style and in content, Marian devotions were a microcosm of the piety favoured by the Ultramontanes. All devotions – the way of the cross, the forty-hours devotion, the devotions to the Sacred Heart of Jesus – had the same ultimate aim and followed the same general pattern as the rosary. As schools of piety, confraternities played a leading role in popularizing these devotions. Besides promoting the saying of the rosary, women's confraternities encouraged daily prayers, usually the reciting of the Our Father and Hail Mary, as well as the use of other devotional aids: the crucifix with or without the miniature *Via Crucis*, the *Agnus Dei*, scapulars, medals, and prayer cards. One confraternity, that of the Holy Family, went so far as to advocate lotteries of such devotional aids as a means of encouraging their use. These portable aids fostered the practice of private home devotions among Irish Catholic women.[31] The day of a confraternity member was punctuated by short devotions such as the litany of the Blessed Virgin Mary, short exclamatory prayers ("My dear Jesus, I love you"), and, if possible, a visit to the Blessed Sacrament or a statue of the Blessed Virgin in the parish church.[32] As with the rosary, the purpose of these devotions and devotional aids was to integrate the grace communicated by the sacraments into the daily lives of members of the parish societies.

Although some devotions could be performed almost anywhere, their emphasis on the sacraments meant that they were church-centred forms of piety. Yet, as the proponents of the confraternities understood, such piety was best imparted and sustained in intimate groups rather than in the general anonymity of the larger congregation. Through their regular weekly meetings and collective devotions, confraternities created a social setting in which women could practise Catholic piety and appropriate its way of life. Most confraternities had a special room for their meetings where the members could engage in various religious exercises and in the business of formal meetings. These rooms were also used by the smaller devotional circles into which most confraternities were divided, where they could meet without the usual comings and goings of the parish church. In the privacy of these smaller meetings, each member was encouraged to participate and contribute to the group's activities. Not only did the repeated performance of the devotions cement the members' commitment to the Catholic church, but these exercises enabled members to get to know each other better and to form new friendships.[33] By providing mutual support, parochial devotional organizations sustained their members in the practice of piety and enabled them to integrate these devotions into their daily lives.[34]

The purpose of the confraternities was to popularize the devotions of the church. Yet how many Catholic women in fact joined these parish organizations? Unfortunately, complete and detailed reports on parish confraternities are extremely rare; only one full parish report, from St Mary's parish in 1881, has survived in Toronto. In this parish of 5000, there were 1620 confraternity members or almost a third of the total Catholic population. This figure apparently includes 570 school children, which if deducted from the total membership leaves 1050 or roughly a quarter of the remaining parish population.[35] This large enrolment was not at all unusual. At about the same time, the Apostleship of Prayer in St Paul's parish alone had some eight hundred members. While a substantial segment of the parish population joined confraternities, the available figures from St Mary's do not indicate where the true strength of these organizations lay. In the city-wide Saint Joseph's Society, for example, men accounted for only a tenth of the membership, three-fifths of whom were married to women who had previously joined the society.[36] Membership in some of the parish confraternities for adults were limited to women only, but even those that were open to men, such as the Archconfraternity of the Holy Family or the Apostleship of Prayer, failed to attract significant male support.[37] In St Paul's parish, the leadership of the two main confraternities, the Apostleship of Prayer and the Archconfraternity of the Holy Family, was wholly composed of women, a good indication that their adult membership was almost entirely female.[38] Contemporary newspaper accounts confirm that women in other parishes made up the vast majority of the confraternities' adult membership.[39] The sex-specific membership of the confraternities is significant in establishing their impact on Irish Catholic women in general. How great an influence the parish confraternities had can be seen when the enrolment statistics from St Mary's are examined more closely. If it is assumed that women made up about half of the parish's adult population and nine-tenths of the confraternities' membership in the parish, then some 42 per cent of all women in that parish belonged to one or another of the parish confraternities.[40]

Even these figures probably discount the full impact of the parish confraternities on the female population. The Saint Joseph's Society, for example, had an average membership of 158, yet over ten years some 336 people, the vast majority of them women, at one time or another belonged to the society.[41] This membership turnover indicates that static membership figures underestimate women's involvement in the parish confraternities. St Mary's may not have been a typical parish, but it is clear that confraternities enjoyed extensive support among Irish Catholic women. By contrast, very few men joined confraternities. Although it is likely that more men took up devotions than their membership in confraternities would suggest, there was a marked difference between men's and women's religious behaviour. Not only did women attend church more regularly than men, but they were also far more involved in its devotional life. The correspondence between the world view of the devotions and the social role of women, particularly in the family, provides the answer.

The general expectation, certainly one encouraged by the church, was that women would marry, unless they were destined for a religious life. While the evidence is admittedly scanty, it would appear that the vast majority of Irish Catholic women eventually did marry.[42] After marriage, most Irish Catholic women worked in the home rather than outside.[43] Industrialization resulted in the growing separation between the home and men's place of work, a development that led many women to regard their homes as their distinct sphere. At the same time, industrialization sharpened the distinction between the paid work done by men in the workplace and the unpaid work women performed in the home.[44] Even though the work women did in the home was essential to their families' survival, they were economically dependent on their husbands, whose wages were the household's main source of income. Such dependence undercut the ability of women to exercise authority in the home, a situation that inevitably led to many a domestic quarrel.

Catholicism, however, developed a cult of domesticity that through its devotional observances sacralized the home as well as women in their capacity as the preservers and defenders of the home's sanctity. This process is especially apparent in the devotions to Mary, for the Virgin Mary represented feminine attributes raised to a supernatural level. Her divine qualities of maternal solicitude and service to others were precisely those that women were expected to fulfil, albeit on a more mundane level. Further, these qualities were not mere attributes, but virtues. If the Virgin Mary represented the sum total of feminine qualities, she also embodied virtue *tout court*. Nor was this combination of femininity with virtue in the person of Mary coincidental, for the two were seen as synonymous. In this sense, the Virgin Mary personified the idealization of womanhood, and a particular type of womanhood at that: woman as the repository and embodiment of self-sacrificing virtue, purity, and motherhood.[45] At the same time that Catholic piety validated the domestic role of women, it legitimized their authority in the home.

Devotional Catholicism also drew a sharp contrast between the home and the world: the home was a moral haven in a materialistic and immoral world.[46] According to this cult of domesticity, when at leisure the man's place was in the home, shielded from the dangers of the world, especially those of the tavern, by the comforting and virtuous influence of his wife. Women were to protect the sanctity of the home, and it was their responsibility to encourage the religious observance of their husbands.[47] In this way, confraternities bestowed upon women a moral power and influence over those on whom they were dependent.

If the devotions of the church encouraged women to exercise initiative in the privacy of the home, what role did the members of confraternities play in the parish church? It is not clear who the activists in the confraternities were and what went on in the confraternity meetings. Catholic newspapers generally took little notice of parish confraternities and their leaders, except when they were raising funds for the church. Even then, newspapers tended to emphasize the contributions of the wives of well-known Irish Catholic laymen. The others were referred to by their last name only, if they were noticed at all. This usual anonymity of confraternity activists shows that confraternities, like women's work in general, were undervalued in the male power structures of the church and of the Irish Catholic community. Yet confraternities required a large number of leaders, activists who were willing to commit their time and talent to the confraternity week in and week out. Most confraternities, such as the Apostleship of Prayer or the Archconfraternity of the Holy

Family, were divided into prayer circles with no more than twenty-five members, each with its own leader. A large parish confraternity would depend upon some forty circle leaders to conduct its monthly or biweekly meetings.[48]

The composite structure of the confraternities had important consequences for lay leadership among Irish Catholic women. Most confraternities had both plenary sessions as well as assemblies of the individual circles. The plenary meetings were usually of a set format and often required the presence of the parish priests to offer instruction, initiate new members, or perform the benediction of the Blessed Sacrament. In contrast to the plenary sessions presided over by the clergy, there were so many separate meetings of the confraternity circles that an overworked clergy must have left the circle leaders to their own devices. Parish confraternities thereby provided a limited outlet for lay leadership. Circle prefects would lead their members through a set round of devotions, but they were also expected to offer a short instruction and demonstrate ingenuity in making the meetings both lively and entertaining. Each circle leader was responsible for the general administration and well-being of her circle: she was to collect fees, console sick members, reassure the faint hearted, and recruit new members.[49]

As members of confraternities, women also exercised leadership in the parish at large. The women's confraternities were the most successful parish fund-raisers. While men, usually members of the St Vincent de Paul Society, sat on the committee of management to supervise financial arrangements, it was the women who prepared the food, decorated the hall, made articles to be sold or auctioned off, and above all persuaded the public to contribute their mite.[50] The fund-raising of the confraternities was essential not only for the continuing operation of the church's social institutions and parishes, but also for the construction of new buildings. By 1872 Catholic church buildings and social institutions were valued at more than half a million dollars, far outstripping any other denomination in Toronto, an impressive achievement for a largely lower-working-class denomination.[51] In addition to fund-raising, a few women's confraternities were directly involved in charity work through their auxiliaries, popularly known as sewing societies, whose members visited the sick and provided warm clothing for the poor in winter.[52] When fund-raising, staging of parish socials and entertainments, conducting of confraternity meetings, organization of volunteers for various parish projects, holding of various sewing and baking bees, and operation of the benevolent societies are added up, it becomes clear that parish confraternities offered Irish Catholic women an opportunity to demonstrate their administrative ingenuity as well to exercise leadership.[53]

Nonetheless, the field for lay leadership open to women, even to middle-class women, was restricted. The parish priests' authority was "always supreme" in the confraternities, and lay leaders were to concern themselves solely with "material administration."[54] In contrast to parochial organizations for men, where elections for the executive prevailed, the parish clergy usually appointed lay leaders from among the prominent ladies of the parish. The confraternities' leadership reflected the social hierarchy of the parish.[55] The manner in which the clergy directed these societies and appointed their leadership was unmistakably paternalistic. Women were frequently relegated to a position of service and subordination. The founding of the Society of Our Lady of Perpetual Help, a women's benevolent society in St Michael's parish, illustrates how women dealt with this paternalism. The wives of some of the wealthiest laymen in the parish respectfully requested Archbishop Lynch to call a meeting so that the society, which now had numerous members, could be "properly organized." They further asked that the archbishop "speak in favorable terms of it in the Cathedral."[56] The society was already organized, but its leaders recognized that a proper show of deference was necessary to obtain the necessary ecclesiastical sanction. These women obviously knew what they wanted and how to get it, but this petition also demonstrates that they usually depended on the good will of others to achieve their goals. Power remained firmly in the hands of the clergy.

Yet for many women the religious and social life of the parish confraternity was attractive. For one thing, the Roman Catholic church provided one of the few forms of respectable recreation available to Irish Catholic women outside the home. Then, too, in the confraternities, women could find much needed moral support and receive assurance they were living up to the new and demanding role of the angel in the home. Perhaps of greater significance was the opportunity confraternities offered to their members to associate with other women and engage in corporate action with them. Many of the social relations that circumscribed women's social life were either prescribed by traditional ties, as in the case of kin, or by an accident of geography, as in the case of neighbours. In the parish confraternity women could form close friendships and collaborate with other women of their own choosing who shared their interests and ideals.

The influence of the confraternities extended far beyond their largely female membership. Confraternities played a critical role in the development in the public performance of devotions in the parish church, such as vespers, the benediction of the Blessed Sacrament, and the forty-hours devotion.[57] When these parish-centred devotions were first introduced, the confraternity members were their most fervent practitioners. The observance of these rituals by the members of the confraternities galvanized the parish and acted as a leaven, encouraging others to participate in these devotions of the church. Confraternities also played an important role in changing the ethos of the parish and the tone of Catholic worship. In rural, pre-famine Ireland, Catholic services were frequently punctuated by the continual traffic of the congregation as they entered or left the church, the yelping of dogs, and the loud conversations of parishioners. After Toronto's devotional revolution, contemporary observers frequently commented on the reverential behaviour of the laity when in church: while the priest said Mass, save for the occasional protest of an infant in arms, only the whispers of the faithful telling their beads and the rustling of the congregation as they knelt and rose could be heard.[58]

Confraternities reinforced the parish as the locus of piety, but confraternity members also exercised their influence in a much more informal and personal way. Many sons and daughters, not to mention husbands, were introduced to the devotions and teachings of the church by women belonging to the confraternities. As a result, few families could escape contact with Catholic values and rituals. The appeals of these women in the privacy of their homes are now unfortunately beyond the reach of the historian, but they were effective. Reliable figures on church attendance are hard to obtain, but an enumeration of Sunday services by the *Globe* in 1882 reveals that slightly over 70 per cent of all Catholics of canonical age attended Sunday Mass. Women were still more likely to attend church, but this figure indicates that many men, perhaps a bare majority, now assisted at Mass. Yet if men increasingly discharged their canonical obligations, they still lagged behind in taking up devotions. The predominance of women in the parish confraternities underlines the uneven diffusion of devotional Catholicism in Toronto. By the late 1880s the Roman Catholic church finally managed after many failed attempts to establish parish societies for men on a secure footing, but these organizations emphasized recreational pursuits rather than devotional observances. Only after the turn of the century did confraternities gain a large following among Catholic men.[59]

According to the clergy, as Jay Dolan has remarked, the laity were to pray, obey, and, of course, pay the bills.[60] In practice, the laity, women in particular, did much more than that. Women's confraternities were a major agency for popularizing devotional piety. As a result of their efforts, the practice of devotions became common among Irish Catholic women. Confraternities offered Irish Catholic women an associational life in the parish that wedded female sociability to devotional Catholicism and its world view. This form of piety imparted to its practitioners a social as well as a religious identity that were mutually reinforcing. Confraternities offered women the opportunity to create a religious and social world. Within the male-dominated power structures of the Roman Catholic church they could not make that world in any way that they chose to, but they successfully claimed a social vocation both in the home and in the parish as their own.

NOTES

1 Lynn Hollen Lees, *Exiles of Erin: Irish Migrants in Victorian London* (Ithaca, New York: Cornell University Press 1979), 184–5; and Ann Taves, *The Household of Faith: Roman Catholic Devotions in Mid-Nineteenth-Century America* (Notre Dame: University of Notre Dame Press 1986), 18 and 87.

2 Emmet Larkin, "The Devotional Revolution in Ireland, 1850–75," *American Historical Review* 77 (June 1972): 625–52; reprinted in Emmet Larkin, *The Historical Dimensions of Irish Catholicism* (Washington: Catholic University of America Press 1984).

3 S.J. Connolly, *Priests and People in Pre-Famine Ireland: 1780–1845* (London and New York: Gill and MacMillan and St Martin's Press 1982).

4 Patrick J. Corish, *The Irish Catholic Experience: A Historical Survey* (New York: Michael Glazier 1985), 232; K.T. Hoppen, *Elections, Politics and Society in Ireland* (Oxford: The Clarendon Press 1984), 197–224; Desmond J. Keenan, *The Catholic Church in Nineteenth-Century Ireland: A Sociological Survey* (London: Gill and Macmillan 1983), 242–5.

5 Larkin, *Historical Dimensions of Irish Catholicism*, 8.

6 Ibid., 5–9.

7 *Journals of the Legislative Assembly of Canada*, 1842, appendix M, and *Census of Canada*, 1851–52, I, 30–1 and 66–7.

8 Cecil J. Houston and William J. Smyth, *Irish Emigration and Irish Settlement: Patterns, Links, and Letters* (Toronto: University of Toronto Press 1990), 57–63; S.H. Cousens, "Emigration and Demographic Change in Ireland, 1851–1861," *Economic History Review*, series 2, 14 (1961): 275–7.

9 Connolly, *Priests and People*, 277–8; Archives of the Roman Catholic Archdiocese of Toronto (ARCAT), Lynch Papers, "The Evils of Wholesale and Improvident Emigration From Ireland."

10 S.H. Cousens, "The Regional Pattern of Emigration during the Great Famine," Institute of British Geographers, *Transactions and Papers* 28 (1960): 128–33; ARCAT, J.M. Jamot, "Census of City Wards," c. early 1860s.

11 ARCAT, St Paul's Parish, Marriage Register, 1850–9; St Michael's Cathedral, Marriage Register, 1852–9; St Mary's Parish, Marriage Register, 1857–9.

12 David Miller, "Irish Catholicism and the Great Famine," *Journal of Social History* 9 (1975): 87.

13 Corish, *Irish Catholic Experience*, 174, 176, 181–2, 184, and 208–9; Miller, "Irish Catholicism and the Great Famine," 85–8; Connolly, *Priests and People*, 91–2 and 94–5.

14 ARCAT, Charbonnel Papers, Bishop Armand Charbonnel to Cardinal Giacomo Fransoni, 26 May 1851; W.S.F. Pickering, "The 1851 Religious Census – A Useless Experiment?" *British Journal of Sociology* 18 (1967): 382–407.

15 Charbonnel Papers, Bishop Charbonnel to M. de Merode, 12 July 1852 (my translation).

16 Ibid., Bishop Charbonnel to Cardinal Fransoni, 30 May 1852, and Bishop Charbonnel to John Wardy, 1 Dec. 1854.

17 Ibid., pastoral 1856, pastoral 1858, and "Regulations for the Retreat preceding St. Patrick's Feast," 1859.

18 Jay P. Dolan, *Catholic Revivalism: The American Experience: 1830–1900* (Notre Dame: University of Notre Dame Press 1978), 77–8, 83–4, 95–6, and 112.

19 *Mirror*, 15 Sept. 1854; Charbonnel Papers, Saint Paul's Parish Report, c. 1859; Lynch Papers, St Michael's Cathedral Report, c. 1861, and J.C. Pouxel to Bishop John Joseph Lynch, 23 Nov. 1863; *Canadian Freeman*, 1 June 1865; *Irish Canadian*, 31 May 1883.

20 Taves, *Household of Faith*, 27 and 94–6.

21 Ibid., 48–51, 81, and 83–8.

22 *Manual of the Archconfraternity of the Holy Family* (np, nd), 2.

23 Charbonnel Papers, Rev. M. O'Shea to Bishop Charbonnel, 15 Jan. 1858, and Rev. F. Rooney to Bishop Charbonnel, 1858; Edward Kelly, *The Story of St. Paul's Parish* (Toronto: Private 1922), 252.

24 See *Rules of the Society of St. Vincent of Paul* (Toronto 1861), 53–123.

25 Charbonnel Papers, pastoral, 2 Feb. 1855.

26 *Catholic Weekly Review*, 12 May 1887; *Exercise of the Via Crucis* (Rome: Sacred Congregation de Propaganda Fide 1834), 30–1.

27 *Irish Canadian*, 1 March 1876; *Third Glorious Mystery, Fourth Glorious Mystery, Fifth Sorrowful Mystery*, and *Fifth Joyful Mystery* (Montreal: D. and J. Sadlier, nd).

28 *Apostleship of Prayer – Ticket of Admission*.

29 Ibid.; ARCAT, St Michael's Cathedral, Book of Announcements, Third Sunday after Lent, 1882, and Second Sunday after Easter, 1884.

30 H. Ramière, *The Apostleship of Prayer: Explanation and Practical Instruction* (Baltimore: John Murphy 1864), 6; *Bulletin of the Society of St. Vincent of Paul (Bulletin)*, Sept. 1872, 218, and June 1879, 173.

31 Lynch Papers, Archbishop Lynch to Rev. T. Wardy, 9 Dec. 1862, pastoral, Aug. 1869, and J.M. Jamot, "Confraternity of the Scapulary of Mt. Carmel"; *Bulletin*, Sept. 1872, 298; *Manual of the Archconfraternity of the Holy Family*, 106–12.

32 *Manual of the Archconfraternity of the Holy Family*, 9–10 and 127–9.

33 *Apostleship of Prayer – Ticket of Admission*; Ramière, *Apostleship of Prayer: Explanation*, 6; *Bulletin*, April 1872, 126; *Work of the Holy Agony of Our Lord Jesus Christ* (np 1863); Kelly, *Saint Paul's Parish*, 254–63; Mary Hoskins, *History of St. Basil's Parish, St. Joseph Street* (Toronto: Catholic Register and Canadian Extension 1912), 63–6, 81–2, and 92.

34 *Apostleship of Prayer – Ticket of Admission*; Ramière, *Apostleship of Prayer: Explanation*, 6; *Bulletin*, April 1872, 126; *Work of the Holy Agony of Our Lord Jesus Christ*.

35 Lynch Papers, St Mary's Parish Report, 15 Aug. 1881.

36 ARCAT, "Register of the Saint Joseph's 'Bona Mors' Society," 1863–73.

37 ARCAT, St Michael's Cathedral, Book of Announcements, Twenty-Fifth Sunday after Pentecost, 1882, and Second Sunday after Pentecost, 1883.

38 Kelly, *Saint Paul's Parish*, 251–64.

39 *Globe*, 20 June 1881 and 1 June 1883; *Catholic Weekly Review*, 14 June 1890; *Irish Canadian*, 5 June 1872 and 17 May 1888.

40 These calculations are based on the sex ratio found in *Census of Canada, 1880–81*, I, 73.

41 ARCAT, "Register of the Saint Joseph's 'Bona Mors' Society," 1863–73.

42 *Canadian Freeman*, 23 March 1871; *Irish Canadian*, 22 Jan. 1879; "Register of the Saint Joseph's 'Bona Mors' Society," 1863–73.

43 Jamot, "Census of City Wards," c. early 1860s; Hazier Diner, *Erin's Daughters in America: Irish Immigrant Women in the Nineteenth Century* (Baltimore: Johns Hopkins University Press 1983), 51–2.

44 Joan W. Scott and Louise A. Tilly, "Women's Work and Family in Nineteenth-Century Europe," *Comparative Studies in Society and History* 17 (1975): 52–3; Nancy F. Cott, *"Bonds of Womanhood": Women's Sphere in New England, 1780–1835* (New Haven: Yale University Press 1977), 61–2 and 69; Alison Prentice, Paula Bourne, Gail Cuthbert Brandt, Beth Light, Wendy Mitchinson, and Naomi Black, *Canadian Women: A History* (Toronto: Harcourt, Brace, Jovanovich 1988), 121–2.

45 Charbonnel Papers, pastoral 1854; Ramière, *Apostleship of Prayer: Explanation*, 5.

46 *Irish Canadian*, 20 March 1870.

47 John Francis Maguire, *The Irish in America* (New York: Sadlier 1873), 123.

48 *Archconfraternity of the Holy Family; Apostleship of Prayer – Ticket of Admission;* Kelly, *St. Paul's Parish*, 263.

49 *Bulletin*, April 1882, 126; Lynch Papers, St Mary's Parish Report, 15 Aug. 1881; *Catholic Weekly Review*, 14 June 1890.

50 *Irish Canadian*, 7 July 1869, 13 Dec. 1870, 10 Sept. 1873, and 18 Nov. 1886; *Canadian Freeman*, 29 Dec. 1864, 6 June 1867, 4 June 1868, and 17 Feb. 1870; ARCAT, St Paul's Parish, Book of Announcements, First Sunday in September, 1872, Sixteenth Sunday after Pentecost, 1875, Second Sunday after Advent, 1875, and Fourth Sunday after Easter, 1876; St Michael's Cathedral, Book of Announcements, Twelfth Sunday after Pentecost, 1881, Third Sunday after Easter, 1882, and Fifth Sunday after Easter, 1882; *Globe*, 28 Oct. 1880.

51 *Globe*, 16 May 1872.

52 *Irish Canadian*, 7 Nov. 1877, 20 Nov. 1878, and 19 Nov. 1879; *Catholic Weekly Review*, 19 Nov. 1887, 21 April 1888, and 28 March, 4 and 25 April 1891; Lynch Papers, Helen Crawford et al. to Archbishop Lynch, 8 Dec. 1874.

53 *Manual of the Archconfraternity of the Holy Family*, 11–17; *Bulletin*, May 1873, 152; Lynch Papers, St Mary's Report, 15 Aug. 1881; St Paul's Parish, Book of Announcements, Second Sunday after Easter 1871, 2 July 1871, Palm Sunday 1873, Twenty-second Sunday after Pentecost 1873, Fourteenth Sunday after Pentecost 1874, Second Sunday after Advent 1875, Sexagesima Sunday 1876, Sixth Sunday after Pentecost 1876, Twentieth Sunday after Pentecost 1876; St Michael's Cathedral, Book of Announcements, Seventeenth Sunday after Pentecost 1881, Twentieth Sunday after Pentecost 1881, and Septuagesima Sunday 1882.

54 *Archconfraternity of the Holy Family; Bulletin*, April 1872, 125, and June 1879, 173.

55 *Archconfraternity of the Holy Family; Canadian Freeman*, 28 Nov. 1861, 23 Jan. 1862, 1 Jan. 1863, and 1 June 1865; *Irish Canadian*, 16 June 1869, 16 Feb. 1870, 19 July 1871, 4 Feb. 1874, 20 Nov. 1878, 4 Oct. 1883, 29 July 1886, and 6 Sept. 1888; *Globe*, 8 Oct. 1874, 28 Oct. 1880, and 18 Nov. 1884; *Catholic Weekly Review*, 19 Nov. 1887, 1 Feb. 1890, and 18 April 1891; Hoskins, *St. Basil's Parish*, 96–8; Lynch Papers, Archbishop Lynch to Miss Banks and the Children of Mary, nd, and Helen Crawford et al. to Archbishop Lynch, 8 Dec. 1874.

56 Lynch Papers, Helen M. Crawford et al. to Archbishop Lynch, 8 Dec. 1874.

57 *Canadian Freeman*, 22 June 1865 and 22 June 1871; *Irish Canadian*, 21 Sept. 1875; *Globe*, 7 Feb. 1882.

58 John Ross Robertson, *Landmarks of Toronto*, 6 vols. (Toronto: Toronto Telegram 1914), 4, 324–5.
59 *Globe*, 7 Feb. 1882. My calculations have been based on *Census of Canada, 1880–81*, I, 174–5, and II, 100–1, and have been adjusted to reflect population growth over one year. Almost 27 per cent of the city population was under the age of twelve, the usual age among Catholics for first communion and confirmation. I have used this figure to calculate the rate of attendance of Irish Catholics.
60 Jay P. Dolan, *The Immigrant Church: New York's Irish and German Catholics, 1815–1865* (Baltimore: Johns Hopkins University Press 1973), 165.

10 Toronto's English-Speaking Catholics, Immigration, and the Making of a Canadian Catholic Identity, 1900–30

MARK McGOWAN

In the introduction to his seminal work on imperialism in Canada, Carl Berger comments that "there have been many varieties of Canadian nationalism, and, while they have been inspired by the same nation, the manner in which the character and issues have been interpreted vary enormously."[1] The Manichean struggle between French-Canadian nationalism, as exemplified in the writing of Henri Bourassa, and the imperialist-nationalism of many English Canadians has long dominated historical analysis of late Victorian and Edwardian Canada. English-speaking Catholic thought, however, has not received a great deal of attention, nor have scholars identified these Anglo-Celts as willing participants in the imperialist versus nationalist struggle. This is an unfortunate lacuna in Canadian historiography, since English-speaking Catholics in central Canada adopted a tenuous middle position between the nationalism of their French-Canadian co-religionists and the anglophilia of their Anglo-Protestant neighbours. Although English-speaking Catholics remained steadfast in their fidelity to the church, they adapted themselves to Anglo-Canadian socio-economic mores and envisaged an independent Canada in an empire of interdependent equals. By 1930 English-speaking Catholics had cultivated a unique vision of Canada – a nation they believed destined to be English in speech but Catholic in faith.

The coming of thousands of Catholic immigrants to Canada between 1900 and 1930 helped clarify this vision in the minds of English-speaking Catholics, and, in effect, entrenched them more firmly in their self-identification as English Canadians. Led in large measure by the hierarchy and laity of the Archdiocese of Toronto, central Canada's English-speaking Catholics were as zealous as Canada's Protestants in their attempts to evangelize and assimilate the new Canadians. Inspired by Pope Pius x's motto *Instaurare Omnia in Christo* [to restore all things in Christ], Canadian English-speaking Catholics directed their missionary efforts at Southern and Eastern European Catholics, who ventured to Canada without priests and sufficient funds, to help them rebuild their formal religious life in the new world.[2] The principal fear of the anglophone hierarchy and laity was the aggressive Protestant home-missionary activity both in Toronto and the West that threatened to lure Catholic immigrants away from "the true Faith." English-speaking Catholics considered the loss of their immigrant co-religionists to be an embarrassment for the church and a major setback in terms of the church's overall numerical power across Canada.

For English-speaking Catholics in Ontario, this arrival of a Catholic polyphony from Europe was the greatest test of their resolve since the famine migration and "no-popery" outcry of the 1840s and 1850s. On the one hand, the Catholic church prepared itself to battle the Presbyterian and Methodist home missionaries, who were anxious to liberate "the foreigners" from the clutches of Rome. On the other hand, the establishment of new "ethnic" or "national" parishes for poor immigrants taxed the resources of the English-speaking Catholic hosts and threatened the Irish and Scottish attempts to solidify their control over Catholic dioceses and institutions outside Quebec. The pressures from proselytizers outside the church and the onerous task of protecting the integrity of various Catholic rites and practices, without compromising the essentials of Anglo-Celtic devotion, forced English-speaking Catholics to come to terms with their own position as Catholic citizens of Canada.

The problems posed by the "immigrant question" forced English-speaking Catholics to define themselves and to remind new Canadians of their duties as citizens. Reassured by Archbishop John Bourne's plea at the 1910 Eucharistic Congress for the spread of Catholicism through the medium of the English language,[3] and frightened by the Protestant missionaries' anglicization programs, English-speaking Catholics actively sought the "healthy assimilation" of Catholic immigrants, while they themselves embraced more fully Canadian life and values. By the second decade of this century, leaders of the Catholic home-mission movement in Toronto eagerly extolled the manifest destiny of the English language, Canadian institutions, and British law. They also exuded a new confidence in their self-ordained mission as Canadian Catholic nation builders. One leader of the Catholic Church Extension Society, a Catholic fund-raising society for preserving the faith of immigrants and native peoples, boldly asserted that "religious duties and patriotic endeavours" would not work at cross purposes.[4] It was this society, more than any other, that articulated Catholic immigration policy and epitomized the central Canadian control of the Catholic home-mission effort, especially on the Prairies. In the long term, the CCES's double-edged sword of Catholicization and anglicization of immigrants contributed to the fractured relations between French- and English-speaking Catholics.

This article addresses two fundamental issues regarding the "immigration question" and the maturation of English-speaking Catholic identity. First, since Toronto was the nerve centre, focus of leadership, and dissemination point for English-speaking home-mission efforts, the article will examine briefly the ideological and social transformation of Toronto's Catholic community. Much of the Catholic ethos evident in the home-mission efforts was rooted in a new confidence among Toronto's Catholics themselves. Socio-economic mobility, the indigenization of the clergy, and the Canadianization of separate schools and Catholic associations all contributed to the maturing of the English-speaking Catholic Canadian identity. Much of this confidence was transferred to the Extension Society, which in turn spread the vision, while gathering together like-minded Catholics from across Canada. Second, this article will discuss how the new Canadians, especially those in the West, provided the first major test of English-speaking Catholic identity as it had been developed prior to 1914. In the cultural contact that ensued, "foreigners" were offered the Catholic faith and the English language as the prerequisites to solid citizenship. While these home-mission projects met with only moderate success, a more fundamental transformation was taking place in the Canadian church, partly as a result of the "immigrant question." By 1930 English-speaking Catholics had pushed themselves into the Canadian mainstream, while their co-religionists in Quebec drifted further away from the locus of English-Canadian life.

The English-speaking Catholics whom immigrants encountered in the first two decades of this century were very different from the Scots and Irish who had entered Canada in the early and mid nineteenth century. Prior to the 1890s, Toronto's largely working-class Irish Catholic population created an ethno-religious subculture in the city, complete with independent social, pedagogical, and recreational services. Regarded as a religious and social threat to the Protestant ascendancy in Toronto, Irish Catholics were described by hostile

commentators as "vicious," "ignorant," and as "brutish in their superstitions as Hindoos."[5] Such stereotypes died hard in the print media,
as did the reputation of local "Irish nationalists" for their frequent
condemnations of British rule in Ireland. These religious, social, and
political cleavages between the host community and the Irish Catholics caused the latter initially to create a closed, exclusive, and defensive subculture as a means of survival in Toronto.[6]

By the turn of the century, however, Toronto's English-speaking
Catholics had entered the twentieth century with considerable confidence, both in their faith and in their status as citizens of Canada.
Their integration into the society of "Orange Toronto" was noticeable
at several levels – economic, social, and intellectual. Prior to the First
World War, the English-speaking Catholic success at entering the
white-collar workforce, owning property, and intermarriage with
non-Catholic men and women gave the city's Catholic community
some assurance that religion was not necessarily a barrier to good
Canadian citizenship. In fact, many clergy and lay leaders thought
that the ideals and loyalty inbred in Roman Catholicism made Catholics the best material from which citizens could be moulded.[7] "We
are all Canadians," they boasted, "and as Canadians, loving our
country and honouring her laws, do we desire to be judged."[8]

The Catholics of Edwardian Toronto were remarkably mobile in
terms of their employment, place of residence, and standard of living.
No Catholic ghettos survived in the city as they had in Boston,
Chicago, or New York. By the time of the Great War Catholics could
be found in all areas of the city, especially in the new and more
affluent suburbs in Toronto's northern, western, and eastern frontiers.
In such suburban parishes as St Helen's, Holy Rosary, St Monica's, St
Peter's, and Holy Name, English-speaking Catholics had joined the
ranks of white-collar workers in greater numbers and had participated in Toronto's home ownership boom of the Laurier years. In
1910 more than half of the assessed Catholic household heads in
some suburban parishes owned their own home – a rate that
exceeded the city-wide levels at that time. Although the level of
Catholic poverty and unskilled labour was more prevalent in the inner
city, Catholics across Toronto were found to be employed in clerical,
business, and professional occupations at the greatest level since the
inception of the diocese.[9] English-speaking Catholics had quite
simply outgrown former ethnic and class stereotypes. Women
embarked on careers in the clerical sector, and men found employment even in such Protestant bastions as the fire and police departments. In short, the English-speaking Catholics were at a stage where
they could measure themselves against the rest of the community

and feel satisfied that "the day ... when a Catholic would be rejected on account of his religion is rapidly passing, even in Toronto, and our young men and women are given places of trust wherever honesty and capability are recognized."[10]

Canadian
born priests

While English-speaking Catholics had begun to integrate into the socio-economic fabric of Ontario's capital city, the church itself had also rooted itself in the Canadian landscape. By 1920 Catholic priests and bishops of the archdiocese were largely Canadian born and Canadian educated. These indigenized clergy preached not only the gospel of Christ but the gospel of Canada as well, advocating patriotism, loyalty to the crown, social mobility, ecumenism, and pride in freedoms afforded by Canadian citizenship.[11] Similarly, Canadian clergy often sanctioned local liturgical customs – marital, musical, ceremonial – even if these practices deviated from the strict application of Canon Law.[12] The laity, too, developed a more Canadian attitude to their piety, devotions, and moral life. The Irish nationalist ethos, once the driving force behind large St Patrick's Day parades, faded into memory as Catholic parades assumed a distinctive devotional character, through the agencies of the Holy Name Society and the patriotic Knights of Columbus. Similarly, pilgrimages were made to Canadian Catholic shrines, especially the local shrine to the Canadian martyrs at Midland. At the family level, devotional life was greatly influenced by existence in a Protestant world, and, by 1920, at least one in three marriages blessed by the church were interfaith.[13] The frequency of denominationally mixed marriages, and the laity's opposition to any episcopal restrictions on such unions, underscored the level to which new generations of Catholics in the city were willing to integrate with the community around them. Moreover, the fact that several priests permitted mixed marriages as a lesser evil than the "apostasy" of Catholic youth attests to the fact there was little the clergy could do about the laity's desire to cultivate relationships with non-Catholic neighbours.[14]

The Canadianization of Toronto's Catholics was underscored by the curriculum and social activities in Toronto's separate schools. At the turn of the century, the city's Catholic schools were experiencing growth in terms of enrolment, certification of teaching personnel, modifications to school structures, and construction of new schools in the burgeoning suburbs. Within these schools Catholic children were exposed to a strict Tridentine Catholic catechism and a formal introduction to the principles of loyalty to the crown and good citizenship. Readers, history texts, and geography books placed a great emphasis on Canada, the history of the British Empire, and the duty of a child to the nation. Even in the Canadian Catholic Series, a series of readers specially prepared for separate schools in 1899, there were explicit references to "this great northern heritage," a strong "northern race," and rule by a "northern Queen."[15] Fragments of students' own poetry and prose were frequently patriotic in tone, and the themes and songs of student concerts, Empire Day celebrations, and the establishment of school-based cadets bore convincing testimony that the patriotic lessons learned at school made an easy transition from the classroom to the schoolyard and the outside world.[16] It comes as no surprise that, shortly after the Great War, Archbishop Neil McNeil could comment: "No one can claim ... that the graduates of Separate Schools in Ontario lacked either patriotism in enlisting or courage in battle."[17]

Toronto's male and female Catholic associations and mutual benefit societies also reflected the maturation of Canadian English-speaking Catholics. Nineteenth-century Irish Catholic nationalist associations disintegrated, as new North American societies took their place and advocated a message that was both piously Catholic and proudly Canadian.[18] Within such societies as the Knights of Columbus, Catholic Mutual Benefit Association, Holy Name Society, and the Catholic Women's League, Catholics were able to enjoy recreation, conduct charitable work, grow in the understanding of their faith, and garner self-confidence to the extent they could proclaim themselves as "brave soldiers – holding aloft our banner of patriotism to our beloved country and of invioble [sic] fidelity to our glorious faith."[19] In addition to being ideological crucibles for Catholic Canadianism, these associations also reflected the rise of a Catholic middle class and the consolidation of white-collar control over lay activities in the Toronto. In 1909 over 80 per cent of the charter members of the Knights of Columbus in Toronto were engaged in white-collar work, and most of these men were from the Catholic growth areas in the suburban parishes and churches on the fringe of the inner city.[20] Prior to 1920, white-collar Catholics became the driving force in Catholic associations and were the primary builders of a new Catholic self-confidence, resting in the assurance that their Catholic morality and faith constituted "the universal principle" upon which good citizenship was based.[21]

The maturation of a Canadian identity among Toronto's English-speaking Catholics was clearly articulated by the Catholic weekly press. The editorials and news reports of the *Catholic Register*, *Catholic Weekly Review*, and the London-based *Catholic Record* demonstrated a shift away from concern with Irish issues and their impact on Irish-Canadian expatriates. Instead, journalists redirected their primary concern to Canadian politics, society, and geography. Gone were the maudlin expositions of the suffering "kinfolk" in Ireland, and with them the emotional anti-British diatribes, so typical of Toronto's *Irish Canadian* in the nineteenth century.[22] Instead, the press turned its attention to Canada, a land editors recognized as the prime focus of Catholic loyalty:

Canada is a colony now growing to be a fine young lady ... She is no longer an infant and the time has passed when every inhabitant in this land must refer to some old-country centre as his birthplace. The majority of the people of this grand country were born right here; in very many cases their parents are natives of this land too. While no one can find fault in a Canadian feeling proud of his English, Irish, Scotch, or French blood, nevertheless we have gotten beyond that stage where we feel that this is an adopted home only. The majority of our people are proud to acknowledge Canada as their native land ... Canada is rapidly becoming the land of Canadians; of Canadians who know no other love than that toward their glorious country. It is as it should be. A country is but a conglomeration of nations that can never attain its full growth until the several races have been assimilated and merged into one great union ... When we have attained that growth in this country; when the inhabitants of this land know no other, then we shall have come to the stage where Canada will stand ready to declare herself to the world.[23]

Such heartfelt pride in Canadian citizenship was not unusual for Catholic periodicals in the period.[24] Catholic papers also cultivated a new love and respect for the British monarchy, especially the aged Queen Victoria, and her "tolerant" heir Edward VII. In the process, editors recognized that the crown was above political parties and petty nationalisms and, as such, Catholic disagreement over policies emanating from Westminster was in no way a slur against the crown.[25]

The greater Catholic identification with Canada also prompted a re-evaluation of Canada's role in the empire. Caught between the pull of the American republic to the south and the vociferous British imperialists at home, English-speaking Catholics found themselves in an awkward position. From 1890 through to the First World War, the Catholic press in Toronto rejected annexation to the United States, fearing the lower moral standards and general American intolerance to the Catholic church, while at the same time criticizing Joseph Chamberlain's empire-building and the jingoism of the "colonial-bred jackass."[26] Resisting formal alignment with either the continentalist or the imperialist positions, English- speaking Catholic spokespersons formulated a unique policy that stood midway between Canadian independence and imperial federation. The *Catholic Register*, while sustaining Canadian endeavours in the South African War, clearly rejected Chamberlain's vision of a centralized empire in favour of Canadian autonomy within the context of the empire.[27] At the *Catholic Record*, editor James Foley was equally as pointed: "'A nation within the Empire' is Imperialism enough for most of us who don't relish the tendency to eliminate the first term of the motto."[28] Catholics neither rejected the empire nor entirely embraced the nationalist-imperialist rhetoric; they simply sought an independent Canada within an imperial partnership of equals.

This maturation of a Canadian identity among English-speaking Catholics was consecrated in blood on the fields of Flanders. In 1914 Toronto's Catholics, joined by thousands of their Celtic Catholic co-religionists from Cape Breton to Burnaby, answered the call to defend their "country and to share in the burdens of Empire."[29] Toronto offered more than 3200 English-speaking Catholic volunteers prior to 1917, as well as strong support for war-bond drives, national registration, the patriotic fund, and conscription.[30] Archbishop McNeil encouraged recruiting, ladies auxiliaries formed sock committees to provide clothes and confections to the troops, and at least one church was turned into a barracks.[31] The war gave Catholics the opportunity to advertise the loyalty to king and country they had cultivated for nearly three decades. While many men went overseas for adventure, escape from unemployment, or as a result of peer pressure, Catholic volunteers came from all walks of life, many had militia experience, and many possessed trades and skills needed in Toronto at the time of their enlistment. Catholics simply recognized this fight as their fight too.[32]

By the end of the Great War, English-speaking Catholics in Toronto, as in other centres, had pushed their way into the mainstream of Canadian life. They recognized that their primary loyalty was to Canada and no other land. They were suspicious of the United States and firm in their demand for more equality among the constituent dominions of the empire. They aspired to better jobs, acquired new skills and improved literacy, and looked favourably on the myth of the "self-made man." English was usually their only language, and it was this linguistic identification that bound them more and more to the non-Catholic Canadians around them. With this identity in mind, they embarked on a bitter struggle to hold French-Canadian nationalism at the Ottawa River, while nurturing and moulding Catholic immigrants in their new "Canadian" Catholic image.

Much of what English-speaking Catholics knew about Eastern and Southern European Catholics was learned through their initial contacts with these immigrants in the cities of eastern Canada. In

Toronto the new Canadians were an exotic oddity to the Irish and Scots, whose only previous contact with a non-English-speaking Catholic minority had been the French Canadians of Sacré Coeur parish or the Syrians of the Maronite rite, who practised their ancient ritual at St Vincent's chapel.[33] The Catholic press offered mixed reviews of the newcomers, at one time offering stories and platitudes regarding the liturgies of the Maronite and Greek Catholics, and in other instances warning Canadians of undesirable immigrants. Irish and Scottish contact with immigrant Catholics, though infrequent, was generally characterized by the hosts' curiosity or by complete indifference. Mischievous altar boys sneaked around church vestry doors to catch glimpses of the strange practices of the foreigners who used "Irish" churches for Eastern rite masses, while some English-speaking pastors were less than hospitable to their new parishioners.[34] Until the installation of Archbishop Fergus McEvay, in 1908, English-speaking Catholics in Toronto did little for European Catholic immigrants.

The rising tide of immigration to Ontario, particularly by Italians, Poles, and Ukrainians, the majority of whom were Catholic, blasted English-speaking Catholics from their apathy. The sheer numbers of the newcomers in comparison with waning Irish immigration threatened to disrupt the Celtic control of the church in Toronto and other cities. In 1891 less than 5 per cent of Toronto's Catholics had been born outside the British Empire or the United States. By the turn of the century foreign-born Catholics had increased to approximately 7 per cent of the denomination's strength in Toronto. Within ten years, this figure nearly doubled to 14 per cent and, by 1921, 20 per cent of Catholics in the city were of continental European birth.[35] The increasing numbers of non-English-speaking immigrants could no longer be treated by Catholics of Irish or Scottish extraction as an exotic passing fancy.[36]

The Catholic immigrant presence was felt most acutely at the parish level, especially in the inner city and the west end. These districts were close to the workshops, garment factories, and manual occupations that were the mainstay of immigrant employment. In 1890 St Mary's parish, at the corner of Bathurst and MacDonell Square, was over 90 per cent English-speaking in composition. Over the next thirty years, the Irish and Scots dropped to little more than 64 per cent, as Poles, Ukrainians, and Italians flooded into the neighbourhoods to the north and south of Queen Street, west of Spadina Avenue.[37] In St Patrick's and St Mary's parishes, baptismal registers confirm the increase in the number of Italian, Polish, and other European children entering the church.[38]

The distinctive immigrant neighbourhoods of Toronto's southern and western districts were by no means safe havens for preserving the religious traditions of Catholic newcomers. English-speaking Catholics considered Methodist missionaries of Italian origin to be the biggest Protestant threat to the Catholicity of Toronto's new Canadians. A Methodist mission house was established in the heart of each Little Italy in Toronto, with the expressed intent of converting the Italians, whom they considered "not sincere or earnest Roman Catholics."[39] Italian men were believed to be the most promising converts, since their participation in Sunday Mass and associated parish activities was perceived as minimal. Responding to the enthusiastic claims of the *Christian Guardian* regarding the conversion of Toronto's Italians, the *Catholic Register* complained that Methodist successes were due, in large part, to the slow response of English-speaking Catholics to the needs of their immigrant co-religionists.[40] After the congress of the "Protestant Laymen's Missionary Movement," the *Register* warned Catholics: "We have unfortunately in the past been too prone to consider all charitable obligation as beginning and ending with the parish. The really great Catholic mission work of the Church Universal was either ignored altogether, or at best poorly considered. Now we know that we are all obligated, in the love of the Master ... to see to it, whether we be laymen or cleric, that there be no portion of our country wherein the blessing of religion is not brought within the reach of all and we are able to procure it."[41] This fear that Catholics were being outflanked in their own back yard by more zealous Protestants was repeated by both the hierarchy and influential laypersons, in order to muster Catholic support for immigrant aid.[42]

Part of the answer to this urgent need of the Toronto church was furnished by Archbishops McEvay's and McNeil's initiatives to establish ethnic or "national" parishes. In 1908 McEvay founded the first major national parish in the city, Our Lady of Mount Carmel Church for Toronto's Italian Catholics. By 1920 Toronto's Italians had two other parishes in addition to Mount Carmel, the Poles had two, and the Syrians and Ukrainians each had one.[43] McEvay's successor, Neil McNeil, was so anxious to get immigrant groups quickly established in parishes, that he ignored canonical procedures requiring him to seek permission from Rome for the creation of special national parishes. After his death in 1934, his successor, James McGuigan, applied to the Vatican for recognition of these parishes after the fact.[44] McNeil's omission testifies both to his dislike of ecclesiastical red tape and to his burning desire to provide immigrants with familiar places of Catholic worship.

The church's immigrant aid program was in effect a double-edged sword, with Catholicization sharing the stage with Canadianization. While congratulating themselves for the tolerant pluralism in the local church, English-speaking Catholics were aware that immigrants from all countries would have to conform to "Canadian civilization." According to the *Catholic Register*:

We have under the aegis of the British flag, peace and prosperity, liberty to the individual both in the political and the religious rights of man, and why should we not rejoice in the enjoyment of these blessings, whatever may be our religious convictions – whatever may be the religious nationality of our forefathers – English, Irish or Scotch, French, German, Polish, Doukhobor or Galician? Yes, even the strange-mannered Doukhobor from the wilds of Russia is not to be placed beyond the embrace of fraternal charity, though we must insist as a young and rising nation that such foreigners as make of Canada their home conform themselves to the reasonable demands of Canadian civilization, law, and order.[45]

The *Register* considered that the surest way of making the foreigners into good Canadians was to make them good Catholics. The paper once again saw Catholics, by their spiritual commitment, as the best kind of citizens.[46]

Making good citizens out of Toronto's Catholic immigrants, however, required more than just a church building and the request that Irish and Scots be tolerant and refrain from using the word "dago."[47] English-language education was considered a prerequisite for the adaptation of Catholic immigrants to Canadian society. Noting that immigrants were eager to learn English, especially for job-related reasons, Toronto's English-speaking Catholics set up night schools and adult education classes for Catholic immigrants. In 1910–11 members of the Catholic Church Extension Society's Women's Auxiliary conducted English classes for foreigners in their own homes. Ukrainian pastor Charles Yermy reported to the *Register*: "There was another need which confronted us; viz., the inability of our Ruthenian people to talk the English language. This was a great drawback and when the matter was brought to the notice of the Women's Auxiliary of the Canadian Church Extension Society, the convener of the teaching committee ... generously gave up her home two evenings a week during the winter months for foreigner's classes. The young ladies of the Auxiliary gave their services as teachers and were at their posts punctually, every teaching night, in spite of rain or storm."[48] Although they had criticized Protestants for enacting similar policies of "anglicization," Toronto's Catholics actively engaged in a program to acculturate the foreigner both linguistically and behaviourally.

Catholic voluntary associations in the city were also enthusiastic in their effort to integrate new Catholic Canadians. In addition to its principal aims of instilling the values of prayer and clean speech, the Holy Name Society attempted to preserve the faith among Catholic immigrants.[49] The middle-class Catholics who controlled most of the Holy Name executive positions feared that if the influence of the Catholic church was not extended to new Catholic immigrants from Southern and Eastern Europe, these newcomers would fall prey to Protestant proselytizers and socialists, thus causing irreparable damage to the growth of Catholicism in Toronto. The executive balanced this concern for the foreigners' soul with an effort to teach Catholic immigrants the principles of Canadian citizenship and the "conditions, customs, and tongue" of Anglo-Canadians.[50] As a means to this end, Anglo-Celts coordinated the establishment of ethnic branches of the Holy Name Society. As early as 1913 the Italians of Our Lady of Mount Carmel parish formed a branch of 150 members and sent five delegates to the union's annual meeting. By 1918 forty-nine Italians in St Clement's parish and forty men in St Agnes parish claimed membership in separate branches. Italian executive members tended to reflect the occupational stratification of their community, many being fruiterers, pedlars, labourers, or skilled workers.[51] Branches consisting of working-class immigrants were also established in the Ukrainian, Lithuanian, and Maltese Catholic communities, and a tiny but "model" branch of the society was active among Syrian Melchite rite Catholics in Assumption parish.[52]

The strength of the newly established branches among Catholic immigrants was questionable. Most immigrant branches folded after only a few years' operation. Catholic sojourners, for example, left Toronto for home or for seasonal employment in northern Ontario, draining these fledgling associations of their members. Some immigrants preferred to establish voluntary associations with origins in their home villages and more akin to their cultural ambience. Others saw the Holy Name Society for the assimilative vehicle it was.[53] By the end of the First World War only 6 per cent of all Holy Name Society members in Toronto were from ethnic parishes.[54] By 1924 Vice President James O'Hagan reported little success in forming permanent branches among the new Canadians.[55]

Perhaps the most dramatic evidence of English-speaking Catholic concern that the newcomer adapt to Canadian customs and language was the push to enrol Catholic immigrants in separate schools. It was believed that a Catholic education would, first and foremost, preserve the faith of the immigrant child, and second, prepare the child for duties as a Canadian citizen. McNeil viewed the separate schools of Ontario as strong agents of the "assimilating power" of the Catholic religion on the many foreign nationalities that constituted the church in Toronto. Although not promising that the first generation could be assimilated, McNeil was confident that voluntary assimilation could be achieved by the immigrant child's exposure to Canadian art, literature, and religion, under the guidance of teachers and in the company of English-speaking Catholic children.[56]

From 1905 to 1920 the initiation of Catholic immigrants to Toronto's separate schools brought mixed results. As early as 1907, 50 per cent of the boys and 60 per cent of the girls in the first form junior class at St Patrick's School were Italian. The inspector of separate schools reported that language difficulties prohibited these students from doing well, and, as a result, few foreign children reached the fourth form, equivalent to today's seventh and eighth grades.[57] By 1919, however, immigrants were beginning to accommodate themselves to English Catholic separate schools. At St Patrick's School three of five honour students in the senior class were Italian, while at St Clare's the ratio was two in five.[58]

Attracting priests to these new parishes was another major difficulty. Bishops often enlisted the services of an ethnic priest to recruit clergy from his particular culture. One such agent, Italian Pietro Pisani, however, usually enlisted the support of priests with questionable reputations, who were more than eager to leave Italy. Sexual indiscretions, shady business dealings, and the fact that many priests from northern Italy irritated the largely southern Italian and rural *paesani* of Toronto made the recruiting effort a nightmare.[59] These priests had been trained primarily for the missions in Italy's African colonies, and their approach to the southerners of Toronto reflected their northern bias as well as missionary techniques intended to civilize and Catholicize un-Christian Africans. English-speaking bishops soon found themselves scrambling for replacements.

Such problems were repeated in the local Polish Catholic community. In 1907 the first missionaries to the Poles complained that their parishioners were susceptible to Protestant missionaries and to rogues posing as Catholic priests. Father J.P. Schweitzer of Berlin reported to Archbishop Denis O'Connor that "a bogus priest" had charged one dollar per head for hearing confessions and had smoked cigarettes liberally while in the confessional.[60] By 1911, however, the Poles had a priest and a permanent house of worship dedicated to St Stanislaus Kostka.[61] Priests and parishioners quarrelled constantly over issues of lay control of the parish, or allowed partisan politics to divide the parish between Poles born in Russia, Austria, and Germany. After one priest had been assaulted with accusations of being a "Judas, cannibal and wild beast," McNeil issued an uncharacteristically stern warning to the Polish laity to obey their priest: "the parish Priest may serve to everybody, if he wishes to, but he must do it only for those, who are his parishioners and go according to the parish constitutions. The church law says: 'THE PASTOR IS A PASTOR FOR HIS PARISHIONERS; THE PARISHIONER IS THIS, WHO FULFILLS THE DUTY OF THE PARISHIONER.'"[62] The incident prompted the defection of a group of parishioners who, in 1922, established a Polish National Catholic church nearby.[63]

Toronto's Ukrainian or Ruthenian Catholics[64] also had problems with clergy. The fifteen hundred Ukrainian Catholics in the city had emigrated from the provinces of Galicia and Bukovynya in the Austro-Hungarian Empire. Roughly 80 per cent of them were Eastern rite Catholics in union with Rome, who were permitted to celebrate the Mass in the Byzantine Greek rite but were subject to Canon Law and Roman Catholic dogma.[65] Byzantine rite priests were permitted to marry, but owing to protests from the Latin rite hierarchy in the United States, the Vatican, in 1894, prohibited further emigration of married priests to North America. In Canada, Latin rite priests complained of the existence of married clergy in the country, fearing that the presence of this group might disrupt the status quo among celibate Latin rite clergy.[66] Ukrainian celibates were few in number, and efforts to recruit this small minority to Canada ended in vain. As one observer commented, the celibate Basilian monks who enlisted earned little respect from the Ukrainian people, because they were usually drawn from among the lowest ranks of Ukrainian society.[67] The English-speaking Catholic hierarchy found it nearly impossible to entice Eastern rite priests to serve the thousands of Ukrainians in agricultural colonies on the Canadian Prairies and in central Canadian urban ghettos. Toronto's English-speaking Catholics relied heavily on Byzantine rite celibates from long-established parishes in the United States.[68]

By 1920 the English-speaking Catholic attempt to Catholicize and Canadianize the newcomer in Toronto was neither a failure nor a complete success. The first pillar of English Catholic policy towards Catholic immigrants – preserving the faith – was relatively successful. There had been some defections to Methodism, Anglicanism, Presbyterianism, and Russian Orthodoxy, but most Italians, Poles, Ukrainians, and others remained in the Catholic fold. Each ethnic group, however, taught the Irish and Scots valuable lessons regarding cultural persistence, lay control of church property, and respect for the non-Latin rites within the church. Faced by problems of immigrant nonconformity to North American church practices and customs, English-speaking Catholics occasionally resorted to heavy-handedness, or used European priests to advance episcopal interests within the respective ethnic communities. Their reliance on misinformation about ethnic communities and on the services of unpopular immigrant clergy frequently created tension within ethnic communities, which sometimes led to schism and abandonment of the church. Yet by 1920 there were at least nine ethnic congregations in the city, housed in seven national churches, all of which had been built since 1908. The relative inactivity of the O'Connor years had been transformed into policies of action and concern under McNeil and McEvay.

The second pillar of the program – the gentle assimilation of the immigrant into Canadian life – was far less successful. While the separate schools demonstrated some progress in Canadianizing immigrant children, the national parishes proved to be shelters in which the ethnic groups clung to their traditions, customs, and family networks of the old world.[69] When faced by the efforts of Irish and Scots to consolidate their control over all ecclesiastical institutions in Toronto, the ethnic parishes were more likely to reinforce their cultural distinctiveness than to conform to the demands of their English-speaking co-religionists.[70] Ironically, the only real success in the acculturation process was made among English-speaking Catholics themselves, who, when dealing with new Catholic Canadians, became more intensely aware of their own identification with Canada, its institutions, opportunities, and freedoms. Cultural encounter among Catholics was as much concerned with the identity of the Catholic host as with the "peculiarity" of the Catholic foreigner.

Attempts to Catholicize and Canadianize Catholic newcomers in Toronto provided the impulse for a nationwide movement that was equally assimilative in its design. West of Ontario lay the vast Canadian Prairies, which became the principal destination for Eastern European Catholic settlers after 1900. Without the manpower or resources to sustain the huge influx of Catholics, a cloud of doubt hung over the viability of Catholicism in the West, except in the small cities and mission centres where French Canadians had already established formal ecclesiastical structures. The familiar problems of Protestant proselytism, lack of Catholic clergy, paucity of national churches, and scarcity of Catholic schools were magnified in the Prairies on account of the large numbers of Catholic newcomers there and the vastness of the territory they inhabited. Under the leadership of Archbishop McEvay, the *Catholic Register*, and prominent laypersons, Toronto became the nerve centre of a nationwide movement by English-speaking Catholics to save the frontier for the church and to incorporate the newcomers into Canadian society.

The principal vehicle for the English-speaking Catholic home-mission movement was the Catholic Church Extension Society. Although the first extension society was founded in the United States in 1905, its founder, Monsignor Francis Clement Kelley, and first episcopal patron, Archbishop James Quigley of Chicago, were both Canadian born. This Canadian connection facilitated a dialogue between American and Canadian clergy regarding home missions and, by June 1908, Father Kelley, Archbishop McEvay, Apostolic Delegate Donatus Sbaretti, Father Alfred E. Burke (Kelley's former pastor in Prince Edward Island), Father Alfred Sinnott, and Chief Justice Charles Fitzpatrick founded a completely independent Canadian Extension Society in Toronto. Burke was appointed president of the society and McEvay was made chancellor, a job that would fall upon each of his successors to the see of Toronto. The remaining governors of the CCES reflected both the Toronto-based support for the society and the home-missionary impulse among Catholics of wealth and power across Canada. Early governors included Toronto brewer and philanthropist Eugene O'Keefe, Toronto publisher George P. Magann, the Rosedale-based chief engineer of the Lachine Canal, Michael J. Haney, Ottawa contractor Michael P. Davis, Berlin entrepreneur George Lang, Alberta Supreme Court Justice Nicholas Beck, and CPR president Sir Thomas Shaughnessy.[71] The board also had token representation from Quebec in the persons of Archbishop L.N. Bégin, Bishop Joseph Archambault, and politician Alexandre Taschereau.

According to the society's initial charter and the subsequent pontifical constitution awarded it by Pope Pius X in 1910, the CCES was to be a fund-raising organization whose main task was to build churches and furnish the spiritual and religious needs of Catholics "in the country districts and among immigrants."[72] Board members, working from society headquarters in Toronto, would coordinate a dominion-wide fundraising campaign, sponsor the building and furnishing of churches on the Prairies, recruit and fund the education of missionary clergy, establish Catholic schools in immigrant districts, and propagate the faith through Catholic literature and newspapers. The chief recipients of aid were Ukrainian, Hungarian, and Polish Catholics on the Prairies, although money was also provided for first nations and frontier missions in other parts of Canada and Newfoundland.

The underlying mission of the society, however, was far more subtle, and less trumpeted by members. Catholicization was in essence only one edge of the double-edged sword of Catholic home-missionary activity. Central Canadian Catholics, who by 1908 heavily identified themselves with Anglo-Canadian values, promoted Prairie home-mission programs and schools that frequently exposed immigrants to Canadian customs, laws, and the English language.[73] In 1910 McEvay informed dissatisfied French-Canadian governors that while the CCES deemed it important to recruit clergy who spoke the languages of various immigrant groups, the society had been unable to find sufficient numbers of European clergy for the Prairies. In light of this "failure," McEvay added that the society recruited "those who speak the English language which is that of the majority in the West and which is the language the foreigners must learn of necessity if they are successfully to procure a livelihood."[74] The society's hidden agenda of anglicization was sustained on several occasions by Burke and his ally on the board, Charles Fitzpatrick, both of whom were noted for their imperialist-nationalism. Burke included the society in his vision of Canada, a land which "the Catholic Church alone can make it what God seems to have intended … the home of a great race destined to achieve the highest ideals of religion and civicism."[75] In the *Catholic Register*, purchased by the society in 1908 as its official organ,[76] Burke proudly asserted that: "Propinquity to the United States, the preponderance of Britain in the world, the commercial character of this age and of the age to come will make for a common vehicle of intercourse and that will not be French but English. We may like it or not, but we cannot and would be foolish to shut our eyes to what is coming and fail to prepare for it … The way of our statesmen and Churchmen is bestrewn with difficulty, but it must be kept clear for the advance of British civilization and effective religion."[77] The leaders of the CCES maintained that their "religious duties and patriotic endeavours" would not work at cross purposes,[78] and all the while they promoted English-speaking Catholicism as a force in the English-Canadian mainstream.

The Catholic Church Extension Society was neither exclusively Torontonian nor elitist in its membership or support structure. The home-mission impulse that emanated from Toronto soon spread to other English-speaking dioceses in Ontario and the Maritimes. Donors, members, and episcopal support were evident in the sees of Alexandria, Sault Ste Marie, Hamilton, Peterborough, Antigonish, Charlottetown, and Halifax.[79] Similarly, at the parish level women's auxiliary councils were founded in Toronto, Montreal, Edmonton, and Calgary. By 1920 there were fourteen parish auxiliaries in Toronto alone, boasting a total membership of 600. Each of these councils distributed Catholic literature, sent toys to immigrant children, raised money for the construction of chapels, made vestments for priests of the Latin and Byzantine rites, purchased altar plate for "national" parishes in the West, and established inner-city hostels and night schools for Catholic immigrant women.[80] Above all, the extension auxiliary provided the needed grass-roots organization that helped to sustain the CCES at the parish level.

At all levels the Catholic Church Extension Society became the messenger of a "crisis" in Canadian Catholicism. For Alfred Burke, his allies, and successors, the crisis in the fledgling Prairie immigrant churches had several dimensions: the immigrants lacked clergy and churches, they were falling away from the faith, and aggressive Protestant missionaries were scooping up these lost souls. As tribune of the home missions, Burke made several pleas to Catholics on behalf of the Ukrainian and Hungarian Catholics in the West and also took his message to the assembled bishops at Canada's First Plenary Council (1909) and the First American Catholic Missionary Congress in Chicago (1908). His impassioned address won him the attention of American Catholics, allies among missionaries in the Canadian West, as well as a pledge of $5000 per diocese per year for the immigrant missions from the Canadian bishops.[81]

The rise of the Protestant Laymen's Missionary Movement and the success of Presbyterians among Ukrainian Catholics in the three Prairie provinces sparked a major investigation by agents of the CCES. In 1909 Burke sent two Toronto priests, J.T. Roche and H.J. Canning, to Manitoba to investigate rumours that the Presbyterian Home Mission Board was assimilating Ukrainian Catholics into an Independent Greek Church. After a tour of the immigrant districts in the province, both priests reported that the allegations were correct and that Presbyterians had concocted a hybrid service combining Protestant doctrine and adaptations of the Byzantine rite.[82] CCES leaders were particularly shocked because the Ukrainians, numbering some 150,000, were the largest of the new Catholic immigrants groups, and one that seemed to have great potential for producing "good" citizens.[83]

The English-speaking Catholic reaction to this "crisis" was two-fold. First, they attempted to help the Ukrainians on the Prairies recreate their traditional ecclesiastical structures, preserve their liturgies, and educate their children. Under the auspices of the CCES, they poured thousands of dollars into the Ukrainian church over the next twenty years. Special diocesan collections were taken for the Ukrainian church in 1912; financial support was extended to the new Ukrainian metropolitan of Canada, Nicetas Budka, for his passage and that of his secretary; moneys were allotted to help found a

Ukrainian Catholic newspaper, the *Kanadyskyi Rusyn*; CCES funds established new Ukrainian chapels and schools; clergy were recruited from the Austro-Hungarian Empire; and Canadian-born Ukrainian candidates to the priesthood were admitted to a special program at St Augustine's Seminary in Toronto. From 1919 to 1927 alone, the CCES supplied $264,947.78 in cash to Bishop Budka.[84] The metropolitan himself admitted: "The substantial support from The Most Reverend Bishops and Catholic Societies is indispensably necessary in order to keep the Ruthenian people in the faith of our fathers."[85]

The second approach to the Ukrainian crisis consisted of swinging the entire weight of the Extension Society's Toronto-based propaganda machine behind the Prairie missions. Through the pages of the *Catholic Register*, Burke relentlessly attacked any and all Protestant groups that threatened the Ukrainians and other Catholic immigrants. Presbyterians, in Burke's eyes, were little more than "wolves in sheep's clothing," who tricked Ukrainians out of their faith by means of "bogus priests" and bribes of alcohol.[86] Similarly, when the small Hungarian Catholic colonies in Saskatchewan were locked in controversy with local Hungarian Calvinists and the Austro-Hungarian consul to Canada, the *Register* and its editors dashed into the fray to defend Catholic interests. The *Register* frequently printed letters from Jules Pirot, a Belgian-born missionary to the Hungarians in Kaposvar and Esterhazy, and eventually printed a pamphlet defending him against charges that he was trying to "frenchify" his flock.[87] Burke's wild bombast on behalf of the Hungarians and Ukrainians made excellent press and appeared to lure English-speaking readers to the *Register* in record numbers. From 1909 to 1911 the circulation of the *Register* soared from a modest 3000 paid subscribers to 17,000.[88] In addition, donations to the CCES increased to over $16,000 per year.

English-speaking Catholic involvement in Prairie home missions, however, was beset by cultural mine fields, old and new. English-speaking Catholic relations with Catholic communities that were non-English-speaking and, in the case of the Ukrainians and some Hungarians, non-Latin rite were often tense and frustrating for all parties concerned. The problems experienced at the local level in Toronto and Hamilton were frequently replayed in the West. Church buildings erected by the CCES frequently fell into the hands of dissident factions within the Ukrainian community who converted to Orthodoxy. In addition to the loss of property, English- and French-speaking Catholics still found it difficult to recruit sufficient clergy for the "new Canadians," especially priests of Eastern European origin. Hungarians in Saskatchewan relied on Hungarian-speaking

Germans and Belgians,[89] while Ukrainians were served by a corps of celibate Ukrainian Basilian monks and by Belgian and French-Canadian priests who had been transferred to the Eastern rite. Vatican prohibitions on married clergy in North America, the Canadian clergy's protest against working with existing married clergy,[90] and the paucity of celibate Ukrainian priess, made the CCES job of securing more clergy for Ukrainians acute, until the Eastern rite program was established at St Augustine's.[91] Five years after his installation, Bishop Budka had a net gain of only two priests. By the close of the Great War, twenty-nine priests, most of whom were non-Ukrainian, served nineteen parishes and 139 missions.[92] Given this high incidence of non-native-speaking clergy, it is not surprising that immigrants felt uneasy, fearing assimilation into the "French church" or the Latin rite.[93]

Despite the vehement call for Catholicization and Canadianization that resonated from the CCES, the English-speaking Catholic quest for control of the church outside Quebec was thwarted on three fronts by the time of the Great War. In the first instance, the immigrants themselves were wary recipients of the English-speaking Catholic Canadian dream. Although Budka affirmed his support for English-language schools, and some Ukrainian laity established English-language study groups, most immigrants feared the loss of their linguistic and religious traditions at the hand of French- and English-Canadian churchmen.[94] Priests on the frontier still reported hostility from their flocks, and few children clamoured to get into English and Ukrainian colleges.[95] To make matters worse, journalists and detractors had labelled Budka a traitor during the war because of his early support for the Austro-Hungarian Empire, support he withdrew after Britain declared war. These charges, and the bishop's perceived incompetence seriously discredited the home missions and forced some clerics, including George Daly, to entertain the idea of formally abolishing the Eastern rite in Canada.[96] This dissolution never came to pass, although the mere suggestion indicates the despair felt by some English-speaking Catholics after a decade of home-mission work.

The second major problem affecting the society, and with it English-speaking Catholic visions of a Catholic Canada, was the person of Alfred E. Burke. While Burke had been the chief visionary of "Canadianization and Catholicization," his British imperialism, bellicose and opinionated writings, and caustic mannerisms had alienated French Canadians, some anglophone bishops, and the editors of Catholic weeklies competing with the *Register*.[97] When Neil McNeil succeeded Fergus McEvay as archbishop of Toronto and chancellor of the CCES, relations among members of the board soured. Worried that society collections fell far short of similar Protestant efforts, McNeil wanted major reforms in the *Register*, better fund-raising, and more like-minded members on the board of governors. Burke and his allies refused to change, and the society was crippled by internal bickering until Burke resigned in 1915 to assume his duties as a chaplain in the Canadian Expeditionary Force.[98]

Ironically, although McNeil instituted several changes in the society's fund-raising, in the *Register*, and in personnel, the aims of Catholicization and Canadianization remained unaltered. The new president, Father Thomas O'Donnell of St Anne's parish in Toronto, was a better fund-raiser than Burke, although his emphasis on a "crisis" in the church differed little from that of his predecessor. Schools, colleges, and hospitals, designed to offset the Protestant challenge and to introduce the English language, remained fundamental to the CCES.[99] Toronto remained the hub around which other dioceses focused their home-mission activity. McNeil was quick to admit that immigrants wanted to learn English, and that the church would be "foolish" to pursue any other policy with regard to language.[100] The *Register* added that schools and hospitals under English-speaking Catholic auspices would save the newcomers and initiate all concerned in "the customs and manners of the country."[101] Indeed, Burke's zealous and confrontational edge was absent from the *Register*, and perhaps his more blatantly imperialist jargon was dated in the postwar world, yet English-speaking Catholic attempts to ally new Canadians to an English-speaking Catholic Canadianism continued until 1930. At that point, immigrant churches took more formal control of their own funding, and the Depression redirected the focus of society fund-raising.

The third and most serious challenge to the English-speaking Catholic vision of Canada, as embodied by the home-mission movement, came from French-Canadian Catholics. From the inception of the CCES, many French Canadians had regarded it as an anglicizing institution that threatened the French-Canadian sense of *Gestae Dei Per Francos*,[102] the divine mission of French Canadians to spread the Catholic faith in the West and to preserve "the faith" under the auspices of the French language. The society's intrusion into the western missions was viewed by French Canadians as a serious threat to their position of dominance in the Canadian church. Several factors accentuated these French suspicions: the society's base of operations in Toronto, its preference for English-speaking missionaries, the use of St Dunstan's College as its first missionary school, the dominance of anglophones on the board of governors, and the British imperialism and pro-English-language policies of Alfred E. Burke.

When thrust into the vortex of the larger ethno-cultural melée between French- and English-speaking Catholics, the home mission movement was symbolic of further attempts by English-speaking Catholics to take control of the Catholic church outside of Quebec.

Archbishop Adélard Langevin of Saint-Boniface was by far the most vociferous opponent of the CCES and the program of anglicization it represented. Langevin regarded the society as both an insult to his mission program for the Ukrainians, Poles, Hungarians, and other Catholic immigrants and as a serious attempt by the "Irlandais" of Ontario to spread "la rage anti français [sic], francophobie" to the West. He was particularly angry that Fathers Hugh Canning and J.T. Roche of Toronto had entered his diocese in his absence and had promised new aid programs to immigrants.[103] He wrote angrily to McEvay, insinuating that the society had been formed behind his back and was recruiting English-speaking priests who were of no use to his Prairie missions. Langevin added that he preferred clergy from the particular ethnic groups concerned, or those trained at his Collège de Saint-Boniface.[104]

Langevin's image of the insulted bishop was partly a smokescreen for a more fundamental objection to the CCES. Some francophone bishops feared that the society might allow the English-speaking Catholics a foothold in the West from which the French-Canadian ecclesiastical power base could be eroded. Langevin explained to Father Arthur Beliveau:

Les ruthènes seront aidés par la 'Church Extension Society'; mais nous resterons maîtres du terrain et nous leur conservons la foi en leur conservant leur langue qui est le rempart. Les idées ambitieuses des irlandais des Etats-Unis et du Canada, j'allais dire *d'Ontario surtout* ... n'auront guère de réalisation j'espère.

Il faut autre chose que l'or de la 'Church Extension Society' pour sauver la foi des catholiques de l'ouest; il faut de saints prêtres, de saints missionaires remplis de l'esprit de Jésus-Christ; or, il semble que c'est le moindre souci de cette société qui devrait recruiter le clergé d'Ontario avant de songer à celui de l'ouest canadien.

Dieu nous préserve de ce nationalisme étroit et provocateur qui croit tout conquerir avec de l'argent et de beaux discours.[105]

Langevin was also concerned that the CCES ventures in the West would add further support to English-speaking Catholic demands for Irish and Scottish bishops in both Regina and Winnipeg.[106]

This intrusion of Toronto's Extension Society into the ecclesiastical province of Saint-Boniface undermined Langevin's own vision of a Catholic West under the leadership and control of French-Canadian clergy. Langevin's imperial designs were recognized by society members, the English-speaking Catholic hierarchy, and the immigrants themselves. Dr John Schwegel, the Austro-Hungarian consul in the West, openly denounced Langevin for what he termed his efforts "to force French people [priests] upon Ruthenians."[107] Similarly, Archbishop McEvay, the *Catholic Register*, and Michael Fallon saw the hand of "françisation" in Langevin's intentions to settle French-Canadian priests among immigrant groups. The *Register* identified Langevin as an "ardent Frenchman," who "would make Northwestern Canada French if he could."[108] McEvay regarded him as a French-Canadian nationalist who threatened the unity of the church in the West.[109]

These accusations by immigrants and English-speaking Catholics were confirmed by Langevin's own manoeuvres. In 1913 he informed Josaphat Jean, one of the French-Canadian priests who had transferred to the Byzantine rite, of the rights of the archbishop of Saint-Boniface to intervene when Bishop Budka's actions interfered with his own for the West.[110] Jean reported to Langevin that the Ukrainians were inimical to the French-Canadian Byzantine rite priests, a fact not helped by the ardent French-Canadian loyalties announced by these clergymen.[111] The strong influence exerted by the French clergy seriously questions the assumption that French-Canadian priests and bishops were merely attempting to preserve ethnic pluralism in the West,[112] and indicates sharply how unwelcome the CCES vision really was among many francophones.

Langevin's relationship with Burke was tenuous, to say the least. When Burke discovered that Langevin was angry about the Toronto-based society's initiative to establish ten chapels for Ukrainian Catholics, at a price of $5000 each, and to provide $1000 towards the founding of a Ukrainian Catholic newspaper, he called the archbishop's bluff. He graciously apologized to Langevin, withdrew the financial aid, and assured the prelate "we shall never offend again by attempting to impose our services upon you."[113] Burke's syrupy but effective response forced Langevin into a corner and, knowing he needed the money and the assistance, he wrote to Burke attempting to smooth things over. Burke agreed to proceed as scheduled and, in doing so, won a victory in the society's attempt to establish its home-mission efforts in Manitoba.[114]

Within a year the manoeuvring and negotiating by mail soured, and relations between Saint-Boniface and Toronto took another turn for the worse. In 1910 Langevin accused the *Catholic Register* of belittling his work among the immigrants, and Burke retorted that the society's main concern was for the immigrants, not for any narrow selfish ambitions. Shortly thereafter, Langevin issued a circular on the immigration question that was unflattering to the work of the

CCES. Burke's reply in the *Register* was blunt: "let it be understood that we cannot permit our work, so signally blessed by the Holy Father, to be subjected to open or veiled attacks from any quarter."[115] This mutual hostility between Langevin and the Extension Society, however, did not destroy relations with Langevin's French-born suffragans in the West, who were too dependent on society funds and, perhaps, by reason of birth, sufficiently removed from French-Canadian nationalism not to be overly sympathetic to the "seigneur" of Saint-Boniface.[116]

French-Canadian bishops and newspaper editors in the East, however, shared Langevin's view that the Catholic Church Extension Society was a vehicle for the anglicization of the West. As early as 1908 Burke attempted to establish the CCES headquarters in both Ottawa and Montreal, but neither Archbishops Thomas Duhamel nor Paul Bruchési would permit it. The society bore too much of a "made in Ontario" label to be satisfactory to the French-Canadian prelates in two of Canada's largest francophone centres. Likewise, Burke's reputation as a proponent of English-language interests had preceded him and, for the French-Canadian bishops concerned, he was "a Greek bearing gifts."[117] Later, Patrick T. Ryan, the auxiliary bishop of Pembroke, noted that Burke's pleas on behalf of the immigrants fell on deaf ears in Quebec because the society "was regarded as an organized attempt to forward the interest of the English language and English influence ... in the Canadian West," and Burke was simply trying to discredit French-Canadian home-mission efforts among the new Canadians.[118]

French Canadians singled out Toronto's *Catholic Register* as the font of English-speaking Catholic aggression in the West. *Le Droit* and *L'Action Sociale* both took aim at the *Register*, claiming it had ignored the French-Canadian cause in the Ontario bilingual schools question while fostering the anglicization of the Canadian West. The *Register* responded in kind, making it clear that it was the French Canadians, not the CCES, that dwelt in the "narrow provincialism" by exalting language over faith. Toronto's official Catholic paper added that it knew no favourites with regard to language, but facts had to be faced: "There is nobody menacing the French language. We are all glad to speak it and hear it spoken. The 'Gestae Dei per Francos' in the Province of Quebec will be one of our tenderest memories. We cannot neglect business, however, for any language in any circumstances."[119] For the Extension Society, English, by practical necessity, would be the language of conversion and consolidation in the West.[120]

The Extension Society's precarious position with French Canadians was further complicated when CCES leaders and the *Register* became directly involved in several major skirmishes between French- and

English-speaking Catholics. From 1908 to 1915 these linguistic factions struggles for the control of six major Canadian episcopal sees
– Toronto, London, Ottawa, Regina, Calgary, and Winnipeg. Archbishop McEvay was the mastermind behind a concerted effort to
consolidate English-speaking Catholic control over Ontario and to
eradicate French-Canadian nationalism in the West. Aided by the
manoeuvring of agents in the Vatican, and tacitly supported by the
apostolic delegate, McEvay and his fellow anglophone bishops were
largely successful.[121] Michael Fallon was appointed bishop of London
and, during McEvay's recurring illness, became the public voice of
the Ontario bishops. Charles Gauthier, more anglo in his sympathies
than his name might suggest, was appointed to Ottawa, a Franco-
Ontarian bastion. The French Canadians won a temporary victory
with the appointement of Olivier-Elzéar Mathieu in Regina, but this
was offset by the appointment of John McNally in Calgary and Alfred
Sinnott in Winnipeg, and by the eventual succession of James
McGuigan to Regina after Mathieu's death. By 1930 only three Prairie
sees remained in "French" hands.[122]

   The English-speaking Catholic effort to consolidate their control
over the church in Ontario and the West had a spillover effect on the
Extension Society. McEvay's role as head of the "Irish" party seriously
compromised his role as chancellor of the CCES and convinced francophone prelates that the society was merely part of the Toronto
"Irish's" master plan. Similarly, the *Register's* front-page enthusiasm
for Archbishop John Bourne's plea for the spread of Catholicism in
Canada under the auspices of the English language convinced many
French Canadians that the Extension Society's organ was a proponent
of "anglicization" in the church. Although the *Register* provided no
editorial comment on the speech, it was clear from the headline,
"Power, Influence and Prestige of the English Language Must be
Definitely Placed on the Side of the Church – No Religious Division,"
that Bourne's speech to the Eucharistic Congress was warmly received
by the paper.[123]

   The Extension Society's reputation as an agent of anglicization was
confirmed by its indifference to Franco-Ontarian appeals during the
Ontario bilingual schools crisis. Throughout 1909, the English-
speaking bishops of Ontario engaged in serious negotiations with
the provincial government for extended funding of separate schools.
In January 1910 the Whitney government's interest in settling the
long-standing issue of separate-school funding ended abruptly when
the French-Canadian Educational Congress issued a series of
demands for the extension of bilingual schools. Whitney explained
to McEvay that the French-Canadian demands had created so much

stress among his cabinet colleagues over issues of language and religion that the bishops' negotiations had to be shelved.[124] Whitney's subsequent legislation, Regulation 17, limiting the teaching of French to the first two years of school, widened the breach between the principal linguistic groups in Ontario, and ironically made uncomfortable allies of English-speaking Catholics and Protestants.

In August 1910 the bishops from the ecclesiastical provinces of Kingston and Toronto met and decided to oppose the demands of the French-Canadian Educational Congress in Ottawa. Angry that the French-Canadian demands threatened the existence of separate schools in general, and fearful of the growing Protestant backlash against bilingual schools, the bishops delegated Michael Fallon to approach the Ontario government and to reassure Whitney that the English-speaking hierarchy was opposed to the extension of bilingual schools.[125] Fallon fulfilled his errand, but some of his more intemperate personal remarks against bilingual schools in the London diocese were leaked to the press in October 1910. When French-Canadian papers accused Fallon of bigotry, the *Register* rushed to his defence, allowing him the front page. Earlier that year the *Register* itself had noted that bilingual schools were impractical and that their "imposition of another language" on the English-speaking Catholic children of Ontario was "unjust, unwise and injudicious."[126] Such harsh criticism of bilingual schools, Franco-Ontarian tactics, and even the French-Canadian press sucked the *Register* into the linguistic tempest and sealed the fate of the CCES in French Canada.[127]

On 19 November 1910 Archbishop Louis N. Bégin of Quebec and Bishop Joseph-Alfred Archambault, vice-president of the CCES board of governors, resigned from the Extension Society. The resignations were sent by mail, with no explanation, although, given the tone of McEvay's responses to both men, it is reasonable to assume that the bilingual schools controversy, succession questions, and allegations of anglicization had played a dominant role in the Quebec bishops' decisions. Their departure left only the French-born Emile Légal, bishop of St Albert, on the board. Ironically, at that same meeting Bishop Fallon was elected as a new governor of the society.[128]

McEvay answered the resignations in two letters, one written as archbishop of Toronto and the other in his capacity as chancellor of the CCES. As chancellor he chided Bégin and Archambault for leaving the society under a cloud at a most inopportune time. He added that the society was in the business of helping Catholic immigrants, noting that its funds were collected from English-speaking Catholics and then given almost entirely to French-speaking clergy. Despite these charitable intents, McEvay conceded that the English language, by necessity, had to play a role in securing the loyalty of new Canadians, given the fact that English was the language of the West and one that the immigrants would have to learn if they wanted to succeed in their adopted land. He also politely asked all parties concerned to place the good of the faith above all other interests, so that "the main opportunities of the Church may not be compromised to any narrow, national or sectional ambitions, but worked out for the greater ... glory of God, and for the well-being of this blessed Canada."[129] Ironically, by admitting that the society's agenda included the introduction of the English language to the immigrants of the West, McEvay's plea failed to bring back the errant governors, thus confirming the linguistic polarization that had taken place.

Future letters and appeals by Neil McNeil and Thomas O'Donnell for *rapprochement* between the French-Canadian bishops and the CCES failed to repair the damage of the Burke years. After his installation in Toronto, McNeil worked tirelessly to sooth the ill will engendered by the bilingual schools controversy, and in doing so won considerable praise and the respect of many French-Canadian leaders.[130] Despite McNeil's fairness on bilingualism and other cultural issues, the French bishops continued to boycott the CCES, preferring to aid the Catholic immigrants by means of independent diocesan collections.[131] The Extension Society was still regarded as Torontonian and an agent of anglicization by many French-Canadian prelates.[132]

The archdiocesan immigrant-aid program in Toronto, the rise of the Extension Society, and French-Canadian anxiety demonstrate clearly the English-speaking Catholic belief that the extension of Catholicism and the building of a better Canada were two sides of the same coin. Between 1900 and 1930 the English-speaking Catholics of Toronto had begun to identify more readily with certain cultural, social, economic, and patriotic features of English-Canadian life. Better socio-economic conditions, religious change, the patriotic thrust in separate schools, the reorientation of Catholic voluntary associations, the unabashed patriotism of the Catholic press, and the consecration of Catholic loyalty in blood during the Great War collectively provided the impetus for the significant changes undergone by Catholics in Toronto. As the product of a "double minority"[133] situation – a linguistic minority in Canadian Catholicism and a religious minority in English-speaking Canada – they were able to incorporate some of the characteristics of each minority without being fully assimilated into either. In time, they cultivated a national vision that fused zealous Catholicism with many of the social and patriotic traditions of English-speaking Canadians, and in doing so they gained confidence that Catholicism and patriotic citizenship were compatible.

The arrival in Canada of Catholics who spoke neither English nor French prompted anglophone Catholics to re-evaluate their own position in Canadian society and the responsibilities of their Canadian citizenship. Toronto's English-speaking Catholics began to wear their patriotism more openly, equating their religious mission to save the newcomers with a national mission to assimilate Catholic "foreigners" into Canada's anglophone society. Fundamental to their missionary impulse was a new confidence among English-speaking Catholics:[134] they identified themselves more fully with the promised glory awaiting Canada on the world stage, and with the strength offered Canadian Catholicism through the conversion of the immigrants. English-speaking Catholics had imbibed the sweet wine of Canadian citizenship and were now eager to share their cup with new Catholic Canadians. The Catholic Church Extension Society provided Toronto's Catholics with an agency to spread this vision of Catholic Canadianization throughout the dominion. Although the clergy and laity of Toronto became the principal sources of cces policy, resources, and leadership, Catholics in the Maritimes, Prairie cities, and in other parts of Ontario soon joined the Extension Society, and, thereby, shared in its mission and vision.

The Extension Society's religious program and Anglo-Canadian patriotism had serious implications for both the immigrants and the Canadian Catholic church as a whole. The cces agenda and the national vision of the Catholics it represented threatened the *Gestae Dei Per Francos*[135] in the West. French Canadians, for whom Frenchness and Catholicity were almost mutually inclusive, could never support the Extension Society as long as it encouraged the immigrants to learn the English language. Consequently, the society failed to speak with a truly national voice. Similarly, some Catholic immigrant groups feared the loss of their religious and cultural traditions should the influence of the society and its backers loom too large. In both Toronto and the West, immigrant cultures successfully defended their traditions and created a third block of Canadian Catholics, distinct from the power bases of Toronto or Quebec. This rise of an English-speaking Catholic vision as a counterweight to French-Canadian nationalism, and the ensuing development of independent ethnic churches, laid the broad foundations of cultural pluralism in Canadian Catholicism.

NOTES

1 Carl Berger, *The Sense of Power: Studies in the Ideas of Canadian Imperialism, 1867–1914* (Toronto: University of Toronto Press 1972), 9.

2 "Opening Address," in F. C. Kelley, ed., *The First American Catholic Missionary Congress* (Chicago: J.S. Hyland 1909), 4.

3 Mason Wade, *The French Canadians*, 2 vols. (Toronto: Macmillan 1968), I, 580; *Register*, 15 Sept. 1910.

4 George Daly, *Catholic Problems in Western Canada* (Toronto: Macmillan 1921), 85. Similar statements are found in the *Catholic Register* (*Register*), 12 Nov. 1908, 18 Feb. 1909, and 26 Feb. 1920.

5 *Globe*, 11 Feb. 1858. These stereotypes are reinforced in Murray Nicolson, "Irish Tridentine Catholicism in Victorian Toronto: A Vessel for Ethno-religious Persistence," Canadian Catholic Historical Association, *Study Sessions* 50 (1983): 415–36, and Nicolson, "The Irish Experience in Ontario: Rural or Urban?" *Urban History Review* 14 (June 1985): 37–45.

6 Murray W. Nicolson, "The Other Toronto: Irish Catholics in a Victorian City, 1850–1900," in Gilbert Stelter and Allan Artibise, eds., *The Canadian City: Essays in Urban and Social History* (Ottawa: Carleton University Press, revised 1984): 328–59; the best study of Irish nationalism in Toronto is Brian P. Clarke, "Piety, Nationalism and Fraternity: The Rise of Catholic Voluntary Associations in Toronto, 1850–1895" (PhD dissertation, University of Chicago 1986).

7 Mark G. McGowan, "'We Are All Canadians': A Social, Religious and Cultural Portrait of Toronto's English-speaking Roman Catholics, 1890–1920" (PhD dissertation, University of Toronto 1988).

8 *Catholic Register*, 18 May 1893.

9 A sample of 2500 household heads in five city parishes (chosen on the basis of income, age, suburban/inner city location, prestige, and population size, and assessed decennially between 1890 and 1920) reveals that Catholic Torontonians were becoming socially and spatially mobile. In suburban St Helen's parish, clerical household heads jumped from 6.3 per cent in 1890 to 19.4 per cent in 1920, and home ownership rose from 30.7 per cent to 48.3 per cent in the same period. In Holy Name parish, in the eastern suburbs, clerical workers accounted for 27.8 per cent of the parish population in 1920, and 70 per cent of all household heads owned their own homes. In such inner-city parishes as St Paul's (Cabbagetown) and St Mary's the rise was less dramatic, although "labourers" declined from 21.7 per cent to 11.5 per cent in St Paul's over the same thirty-year period. Inner-city parishes became catch basins for new Catholic migrants to the city, while most longer-term residents moved to the suburbs or out of Toronto. City of Toronto Archives, Assessment Rolls, 1891, 1901, 1911, and 1921. See McGowan, "'We are all Canadians,'" chap. 1.

10 *Register*, 28 Feb. 1908.

11 *Catholic Weekly Review* (CWR), 28 Dec. 1889 and 13 Dec. 1890; *Register*, 19 March 1896; *Catholic Record* (*Record*), 15 Feb. 1896 and 27 Oct. 1910; Archives of the Roman Catholic Archdiocese of Toronto (ARCAT), Holograph Collection, 22.79, "Address from the Clergy of the Diocese of Toronto to the Most Reverend Neil McNeil, D.D., Episcopal Silver Jubilee, 20 October 1920"; ARCAT, St Augustine's Seminary Papers, box 2, "The Laying of the Cornerstone at St. Augustine's Seminary, Sunday, 23 October 1910"; Edward Kelly, *The Story of St. Paul's Parish* (Toronto: Private 1922), 305; St Michael's College Rare Book Room, Dean William Harris, "Our Own Land," *Book Reviews*, 3 Sept. 1900.

12 ARCAT, Denis O'Connor Papers, O'Connor to Martin Whalen, 10 June 1901; ARCAT, Neil McNeil Papers, a "Catholic" to McNeil, 31 Oct. 1919; ARCAT, Roman Correspondence, rough draft of letter from O'Connor to Cardinal Gotti, 22 Oct. 1904; Archives of the Archdiocese of Kingston (AAK), James Vincent Cleary Papers, Bishop McQuaid of Rochester to Cleary, 7 July 1895; copy of letter from Cleary to McQuaid, 11 July 1895; *Register*, 4 Feb. 1909 and 24 April 1919.

13 ARCAT, Marriage Registers, Urban Parishes, 1890–1920; Dispensation Stub Books, 1890–1920. In 1890, less than 6 per cent of marriages officiated in the church were mixed. By 1897 this percentage had risen to 20.3. During the episcopate of Archbishop Denis O'Connor (1899–1908) there was a virtual ban on dispensations for mixed marriage. O'Connor's draconian marriage regulations did not have any lasting impact. By 1910, mixed marriages had risen to about 14 per cent, and steadily grew to a level of 31.1 per cent in 1920.

14 Roman Correspondence, John Walsh to the Propaganda Fide, 24 Feb. 1893; Walsh to Pope Leo XIII, 14 March 1898.

15 *Canadian Catholic Readers*, Fourth Book (Toronto: Copp Clark 1899), 257–99.

16 *Register*, 12 April 1900 and 5 June 1919.

17 Neil McNeil, "A Need of the Day," *Cathedral Magazine* 3 (Oct. 1919): 2.

18 Archives of Ontario (AO), *Detailed Report of the Inspector of Insurance and Friendly Societies* (Toronto: Queen's and King's Printers 1895–1920); ARCAT, Knights of Columbus Papers, *Columbiad*, Sept. 1918.

19 National Archives of Canada (NA), Fanny Penfold Coffey Papers, manuscript history of the Catholic Women's League of Canada. See also ARCAT, Holy Name Society Papers, Constitution, By-laws and Pledge; *Register*, 5 Sept. 1919.

20 *Knights of Columbus, Toronto Council 1388, Seventy-Fifth Anniversary, 1909–1984* (Toronto: np 1984); *City of Toronto Directory* (Toronto: Mights 1909).

Occupational Group	Charter Members	
	Number	Per cent
Professional	22	16.8
Private	3	2.3
Business	26	19.8
Clerical	60	45.8
Skilled labour	11	8.4
Semi-skilled	3	2.3
Unskilled	2	1.5
No data	4	3.1
TOTAL	131	100.0
White collar	108	82.4
Suburban dwellers	76	58.0

21 I.J.E. Daniel and D.A. Casey, *For God and Country: A History of the Knights of Columbus Catholic Army Huts* (Toronto 1922), 13.

22 *Irish Canadian* (IC), 4 Dec. 1890 and 29 Dec. 1892. For a more developed chronicle of the transition of the English-speaking Catholic press in Toronto see Gerald J. Stortz, "The Irish Catholic Press in Toronto, 1874–1887," Canadian Catholic Historical Association, *Study Sessions* 47 (1980): 41–56; Stortz, "The Irish Catholic Press in Toronto, 1887–1892," *Canadian Journal of Communications* 10 (1984): 27–46; and McGowan, "'We are all Canadians,'" chap. 5.

23 *Register*, 14 Feb. 1901.

24 Helen Kernahan, "Why Canadians Should Love Canada," *St. Joseph's Lilies* 8 (Dec. 1919): 122–4; M.L. Hart, "Things We Might Have," ibid., 1 (Sept. 1912): 10–11; *Register*, 16 Oct. 1902, 26 March 1903, 13 Feb. 1908, 9 Oct. 1919, and 1 Dec. 1921; and the *Record*, 29 Oct. 1898, 25 March 1899, and 22 Aug. 1914.

25 CWR, 4 June 1892; *Register*, 3 June 1897, 24 Jan. 1901, and 12 May 1910; *Record*, 2 Feb. 1901; and IC, 31 Jan. 1901.

26 *Register*, 31 Dec. 1903. Rejections of annexation and invocations against American society were legion. CWR, 18 May and 17 Aug. 1889, and 25 Oct. 1890; *Record*, 22 Dec. 1900 and 31 Dec. 1904; *Register*, 23 March 1906, 4 April 1912, 25 Jan. and 8 March 1917, and 27 May 1920. The American atrocities in the conquered territories of the Philippines and Cuba, in the wake of the Spanish-American War, were proof to Canadian Catholics that Catholic minorities in the United States could not expect just treatment from the American government and hostile non-Catholic citizens. *Register*, 12, 19, and 26 May, 23 and 30 June, 28 July, and 10 Dec. 1898, 13 and 20 July, 24 Aug., and 26 Oct. 1899, 25 May 1902, and 7 May 1903.

27 *Register*, 10 May 1900, 21 Aug. 1902, 23 and 29 Oct., and 5 Nov. 1903.

28 NA, Charles Murphy Papers, vol. 10, Father James T. Foley to Murphy, 25 March 1913, 4134–5.
29 *Register*, 20 Aug. 1914.
30 McNeil Papers, circular, 25 Aug. 1914; War Box, circular 1917; War Box, John M. Godfrey to McNeil, 17 June 1917; *Register*, 11 Jan., and 8 and 22 Nov. 1917. For references to conscription see *Register*, 21 and 28 June, 24 July, and 2 Aug. 1917.
31 ARCAT, War Box, handbill, 198th Battalion; Parish Records, Our Lady of Lourdes parish, report of Eleanor Moore, secretary, Patriotic Association, 13 Nov. 1917; War Box, Major F.K. Prowse to McNeil, 22 Nov. 1916.
32 For a more elaborate statistical breakdown of Catholic enlistment by class and time of recruitment see McGowan, "'We Are all Canadians,'" chap. 7.
33 *Register*, 22 Aug. 1901 and 16 Jan. 1913; *Sadlier's Catholic Almanac and Ordo* (New York: D.J. Sadlier 1890), 21–2. In 1892 a special Mass was said at St Michael's Cathedral for the small Italian community. The celebrants were Fathers Cruise and Coyle, both of whom could speak Italian. CWR, 9 April 1892.
34 *Register*, 16 Aug. 1894, 14 July 1904, 21 March 1901, 6 Nov. 1902, and 5 March 1908. The paper issued was concerned over the arrival of Asians and Doukhobors, as well as those migrants who might have a criminal background. O'Connor Papers, letter from J. Schweitzer to O'Connor, 12 April 1907, complaining of Anglo-Celtic indifference and naughty altar boys at St Mary's parish.
35 *Register*, 14 May 1908; Nicolson, "The Other Toronto," 341. Nicolson estimates that one-fifth of the Catholics in the city were "foreigners" by 1900. According to appropriate census data, his estimate for 1900 is far too liberal. Robert Harney, however, demonstrates that the Canadian census underestimated the seasonal variations in size of the Italian community. The census was taken in months when many Italian men were sojourning in other areas of Ontario, working on railways or in lumber camps. In the winter months hundreds of these migrant labourers ventured back to their home bases in Toronto. Harney, "Toronto's Little Italy," in Harney and J. Vincenza Scarpaci, eds., *Little Italies in North America* (Toronto: Multicultural History Society 1981), 46. For a statistical profile of declining levels of Irish immigration to Canada see Kerby A. Miller, *Emigrants and Exiles: Ireland and the Irish Exodus to North America* (New York: Oxford University Press 1985), 569.
36 Robert Harney, "Chiaroscuro: Italians in Toronto, 1885–1915," *Italian Americana* 1, 2 (1975): 158. Harney considers the exoticism of the newcomers to both Catholic and Protestants in the city.

37 Harney, "Toronto's Little Italy," 42, 46–7; Zofia Shahrodi, "The Polish
    Community in Toronto in the Twentieth Century," in Robert Harney,
    ed., *Gathering Place: Peoples and Neighbourhoods of Toronto, 1834–1945*
    (Toronto: Multicultural History Society of Ontario 1985), 244; and
    Zoriana Yaworsky-Sokolsky, "The Beginnings of Ukrainian Settlement
    in Toronto, 1891–1939," in Harney, ed., *Gathering Place*, 280–1.
38 ARCAT, Baptismal Registers, St Mary's and St Patrick's parishes, 1890,
    1895, 1900, 1905, 1910, 1915, and 1920.
39 *Christian Guardian*, 13 Oct. 1916. John Zucchi, "Church and Clergy
    and the Religious Life of Toronto's Italian Immigrants, 1900–1940,"
    Canadian Catholic Historical Association, *Study Sessions* 50 (1983): 537;
    see also United Church Archives (UCA), Toronto, Italian Church file;
    Harney, "Chiaroscuro," 158–9; and Harney, "Toronto's Little Italy," 49.
40 *Register*, 11 June 1908.
41 Ibid., 3 Dec. 1908.
42 McNeil Papers, draft of a circular letter, c. 1920.
43 *Ontario Catholic Year Book* (Toronto: Newman Club 1920), 54–5. The Ital-
    ians held Our Lady of Mount Carmel, St Agnes, and St Clement's; the
    Poles worshipped at St Stanislaus Kostka and St Mary's; Ukrainians
    established St Josaphat's; and the Maronite Syrians and others of the
    Melchite rite shared Assumption parish. See also *Register*, 13 April
    1911.
44 Roman Correspondence, James McGuigan to Sacred Congregation of
    the Council, c. 1949; Sacred Congregation of the Council to McGuigan,
    26 March 1949.
45 *Register*, 30 July 1908 and 13 April 1911.
46 Ibid., 26 March 1914.
47 Ibid., 22 Jan. 1914. McNeil addressed 1700 members of the city's Holy
    Name Society, demanding that offensive words regarding Italians be
    stricken from a Catholic's vocabulary.
48 Ibid., 25 May 1911; Harney, "Chiaroscuro," 158. Harney reports that
    some Italians in the city were also eager to learn English.
49 The Holy Name Society was not the only local association engaged in
    attempting to assimilate and "save" the "foreigner." The Knights of
    Columbus and the Catholic Women's League joined forces to ensure
    "the Canadianization of the Newcomer." Knights of Columbus Papers,
    chart, "Canadianization of the Newcomer," 10 Feb. 1923; Coffey
    Papers, typescript, "History of the C.W.L."
50 Holy Name Society Papers, Secretary's Report, minutes of the Annual
    Meeting, 1916.
51 Ibid., Presidential and Executive Committee Report, 10 Feb. 1913; min-
    utes of Fall Quarterly Meeting, 25 Sept. 1916; Secretary's Report,
    Annual Meeting, 1916; Archdiocesan Holy Name Union, Executive
    1918; and *Register*, 19 April 1917.

52 Holy Name Society Papers, Secretary's Report, minutes of Annual Meeting, 1916; and minutes of Fall Quarterly Meeting, 25 Sept. 1916. The executive report of 1918 put the Syrian membership at twenty-one.

53 Zucchi, "Church and Clergy," 545–6.

54 *Register*, 24 July 1919; Holy Name Society Papers, Secretary's Report, 1916; and minutes of Annual Meeting, 16 March 1924. The latter indicated at least one Polish branch had been founded since the end of the war. For numbers of immigrant members see Archdiocesan Holy Name Union, Executive, 1918.

55 Holy Name Society Papers, Fall Quarterly Meeting, 14 Oct. 1920.

56 McNeil Papers, "National Unity and the School," 8 Feb. 1933; see also "Nations and Races, Wars and World Peace, Schools and Religion," 1932. Separate schools became vehicles for promotion of the home mission movement, as children were urged to support Catholic efforts to thwart Protestant proselytism among Ukrainian Catholics. *Separate School Chronicle* 1 (1919).

57 AO, Ministry of Education Papers, Report of Separate School Board Inspector, Toronto 1907.

58 *Separate School Chronicle* 1 (1919).

59 ARCAT, Carl Doglio file, Doglio to McEvay, 23 Sept. 1909; draft of letter from J.T. Kidd to Doglio, nd; Kidd to Doglio, 1 March 1910; draft of letter from Fergus McEvay to bishop of Rochester, 13 and 28 May 1910; Apostolic Delegate Papers, McEvay to Donatus Sbarretti, 28 May 1910; *Register*, 24 Sept. and 15 Oct. 1908; Joseph Longo file, copy of letter from McEvay to unnamed bishop, 5 Nov. 1909; apostolic delegate to McEvay, 8 Nov. 1909; and "private" letter from apostolic delegate to McEvay, 8 Nov. 1909.

60 O'Connor Papers, J. Schweitzer to Denis O'Connor, 12 April 1907.

61 *Register*, 29 June and 7 Sept. 1911; Shahrodi, "The Polish Community in Toronto," 250–1; Shahrodi, "St. Stanislaus' Parish: The Heart of Toronto Polonia," *Polyphony* 6 (fall/winter 1984): 27–8. Brewer Eugene O'Keefe bought Toronto's West Presbyterian Church for $28,000 and donated it to the Poles. The community numbered about 4000 by the time of the Great War. Yaworsky-Sokolsky, "The Beginnings of Ukrainian Settlement in Toronto," 280 and 286.

62 ARCAT, St Stanislaus Parish box, copy, "Rule and Regulations for St. Stanislaus Kostka Parish Church, Toronto, Ont," c. 1920; copy of letter from departing parishioners to Blum, 9 Feb. 1920.

63 Yaworsky-Sokolsky, "The Beginnings of Ukrainian Settlement," 286; ARCAT, St Mary's Parish (Polish) Papers, Father Charles Bonner, St Cecilia's parish, to McNeil, 28 July 1920. Bonner informed the archbishop: "The polish children are taught this polish language and history by a pole under the auspices of some anti catholic organization,

in a protestant hall, where they occasionally hear anti-catholic remarks. Also I heard from one Russian schismatic laity and from one Pole of good character, that this anticatholic organization intends to buy the Russian Schismatic church ... on cor. Royce & Edwin Ave, in the center of the Polish settlement, and which is at present vacant, to be known as 'the Polish independent Church of Canada.'" Bonner added that the Polish clergy gave the people little sympathy or encouragement.

64 In this article the author will refrain from using the term Ruthenian – now considered pejorative – and will use the title "Ukrainian" throughout, except where the other term is used in direct quotations.

65 *Register*, 23 Feb. and 25 May 1911.

66 ARCAT, Catholic Church Extension Society (CCES) Papers, Archbishop Paul Bruchési of Montreal to Fergus McEvay, 13 June 1910; Father Achille Delaere to Paul Bruchési, 7 June 1910.

67 Ibid., memorandum of Leo Sembratowicz, 22 Oct. 1909.

68 *Register*, 29 Feb. 1912; Yaworsky-Sokolsky, "The Beginnings of Ukrainian Settlement," 280; ARCAT, Ruthenian and Ukrainian Papers, John T. Kidd to Bishop Ortynski, 25 Jan. 1912. Kidd's request was answered within the month with the promise of Boyarczuk's transfer to Toronto.

69 Silvano Tomasi, "The Ethnic Church and Integration of Italian Immigrants in the United States," in Tomasi, ed., *The Italian Experience in the United States* (Staten Island: Centre for Migration Studies 1970), 186.

70 Gerald Shaughnessy, *Has the Immigrant Kept the Faith?* (New York: Macmillan 1925), 221 and 267–8; Tomasi, "The Ethnic Church," 185–92; Rudolph Vecoli, "Prelates and Peasants, Italian Immigrants and the Catholic Church," *Journal of Social History* 2 (spring 1969): 220–1, 225, 259, and 263; Victor Greene, "For God and Country: The Origins of Slavic Self-Consciousness in America," *Church History* 35 (Dec. 1966): 255–60. Harney regards immigrant assimilation as the goal behind the establishment of ethnic parishes in Toronto. Robert Harney, *Toronto: Canada's New Cosmopolite* (Toronto: Multicultural History Society of Ontario 1981), 5.

71 Henry J. Morgan, *The Canadian Men and Women of the Time* (Toronto: Briggs 1912); CCES Office, *Meeting Minutes Book*, 2. Members of the board of governors purchased their positions for donations of $5000.

72 CCES Office, *Minutes Book*, 2.

73 Statements regarding the use of anglophone clergy can be found in the *Register*, 31 Dec. 1908 and 20 May and 16 Sept. 1909; and by Archbishop Fergus McEvay in NA, Charles Fitzpatrick Papers, vol. 13, copy of letter from McEvay to Louis N. Bégin, 27 Dec. 1910, 5816, and vol. 82, memorandum from Alfred E. Burke to the Duke of Norfolk, 6

April 1909, 45454. The *Register*, 4 Dec. 1919 and 7 Oct. 1920, hoped that the Ukrainian Catholic students would soon become "genuine" Canadians. George Daly, an ardent supporter of Extension in the interwar period, boldly asserted that "the sooner our Ruthenians will know English well, the better they will be equipped for the struggle of canadian life and for the preservation of their Catholic Faith." *Register*, 19 Feb. and 4 March 1920.

74 Fitzpatrick Papers, vol. 13, copy of letter from McEvay to Archbishop Louis N. Bégin, 27 Dec. 1910, 5816. On a similar note see *Register*, 31 Dec. 1908 and 16 Sept. 1909.

75 *Register*, 18 Nov. 1909. Burke continued, "the other day we heard with amazed satisfaction, a great British Imperialist say: 'I admire the work of the Catholic Church in this grand Canadian member of the Empire. I hope for everything from it in the development of an ideal race and government. I would be delighted to see Canada Catholic and a model member of the Empire.' And may it be so."

76 Ibid., 12 Nov. 1908. When the paper officially reverted to the CCES in 1909, the masthead changed to *Catholic Register and Canadian Extension*.

77 *Register*, 24 June 1915.

78 Daly, *Catholic Problems in Western Canada*, 85; similar statements can be found in *Register*, 12 Nov. 1908, 18 Feb. 1909, and 26 Feb. 1920. Bishop Michael Francis Fallon of London, an ardent society supporter, offered a far wider interpretation of the society's aims when he asserted, "we propose to make this North American Continent Catholic; to bring America to Jesus Christ through the divine doctrines of the Catholic Church." "Sermon by Michael Francis Fallon," *Official Report of Second American Catholic Missionary Congress* (Chicago: J.S. Hyland 1914), 33–4.

79 CCES Papers, *Annual Reports*, 1917–19.

80 The auxiliary founded the St Philip Neri hostel for immigrant working women in Toronto and opened night schools for English-language instruction. *Register*, 12 Sept. 1912, 8 May 19193, and 15 April 1920; for complete inventories of auxiliary activities see *Register*, 3 Nov. 1910, and CCES Office, *Minutes Book*, report of the Women's Auxiliary, April 1915, 47–50. Branches in Edmonton and Calgary were in operation as early as 1910, and St Patrick's parish in Montreal began a branch in 1915. *Register*, 5 May and 10 Nov. 1910, and 2 Dec. 1915.

81 Ruthenian and Ukrainian Papers, "Memorial to the First Plenary Council," 1 Oct. 1909. Burke appealed to the Canadian hierarchy for the building of Ukrainian chapels, the recruitment of missionary priests, the founding of a Ukrainian Catholic paper, and the appointment of a Ukrainian Catholic bishop. Alfred E. Burke, "The Need of a Missionary College," *First American Catholic Missionary Congress*

(Chicago: J.S. Hyland 1909), 83.; R.P.A. Delaere, *Mémoire sur les tentatives de schisme et d'hérésie au milieu des Ruthènes de l'Ouest Canadien* (Quebec: L'Action Sociale 1908). See also *Register*, 15 April 1909.

82 Francis C. Kelley, *The Story of Extension* (Chicago: Extension Society Press 1922), 163; *Register*, 24 Feb. 1910 and 16 Sept. 1909; Delaere, *Mémoire sur le tentatives de schisme*; and Toronto *Telegram*, 20 Sept. 1909.

83 *Register*, 5 Sept. 1912.

84 CCES Papers, "Record of Donations Sent to Dioceses," 1 March 1919 to 1 March 1928.

85 Ibid., "Annual Report of the Church Extension Society of Canada," 1918, 20.

86 *Register*, 23 Feb., 27 April, and 17 Aug. 1911; *Telegram*, 20 Sept. 1909; *Register*, 7 April 1911; other attacks against Protestants, especially Presbyterians, can be found in the *Register*, 15 and 29 April, 20 May, 23 Sept., and 21 Oct. 1909, 13 Jan. 1910, and 10 Aug. 1911.

87 Jules Joseph Pirot, *One Year's Fight for the True Faith in Saskatchewan, or the Hungarian Question in Canada* (Toronto: Catholic Register and Canadian Extension 1911); *Register*, 25 Feb., 11 Nov., and 21 Dec. 1909, 30 June and 22 Sept. 1910, and 6 April, 11 May, and 25 May 1911. For an interesting account of the crisis in Pirot's missions in Saskatchewan see Martin R. Kovacs, "The Hungarian School Question," in Kovacs, ed., *Ethnic Canadians, Culture and Education* (Regina: Canadian Plains Research Center 1978), 333–58.

88 CCES Papers, *Minutes Book*, 29.

89 Prior to the Great War, Hungarians were served by Jule Pirot (Belgian), Father A. Conter (Belgian), Francis Woodcutter (German), Jean T.G. Vorst (Belgian), and Menyhért Érdujhelyi (Hungarian). See Martin Kovacs, "The Saskatchewan Era, 1885–1914," in N.F. Dreisziger, ed., *Struggle and Hope: The Hungarian Canadian Experience* (Toronto: McClelland and Stewart 1982), 61–93; and Pirot, *One Years Fight for the True Faith in Saskatchewan*, 4–6; *Register*, 30 June 1910 and 11 May 1911.

90 CCES Papers, Archbishop Paul Bruchési of Montreal to Fergus McEvay, 13 June 1910; Father Achille Delaere to Paul Bruchési, 7 June 1910.

91 *Register*, 19 March 1914. The newspapers reported that there were fourteen candidates for the Eastern rite under the spiritual direction of the Reverend "Dr. Radkiewicz" at St. Augustine's Seminary in Scarborough.

92 Ibid., 31 May 1917; Ruthenian and Ukrainian Papers, "Fact Sheet Submitted by Archbishop Budka," 1919; *The Official Catholic Directory* (New York: P.J. Kenedy and Sons 1927 and 1930).

93 Ruthenian and Ukrainian Papers, "Fact Sheet Submitted by Archbishop Budka," 1919; Josephat Jean, "S.E. Adelard Langevin, Archévêque de St. Boniface et les Ukrainiens," Canadian Catholic Historical

Association, *Report* (1944–5): 103; Paul Yuzyk, "Religious Life," 149; CCES Papers, Father Boels to Archbishop Fergus McEvay, 13 Oct. 1909.

94 *Register*, 3 Feb. and 28 April 1910. For Budka's comments see *Register*, 25 July 1918 and 23 Jan. 1919; and *Kanadyskyi Rusyn*, 29 Jan. 1919.

95 See Mark G. McGowan, "The Harvesters Were Few: A Study of the Catholic Church Extension Society of Canada, French Canada, and the Ukrainian Question" (unpublished graduate paper, University of Toronto 1983), 110–12; CCES Papers, "One of Our Needs for the Church in Canada," by Neil McNeil, 1926.

96 In 1923 Father George Daly made a detailed report on the Ukrainian missions to the Canadian bishops and recommended "THE GRADUAL, PRUDENT, SYSTEMATIC ABSORPTION OF RUTHENIAN CATHOLICS INTO THE LATIN CHURCH." ARCAT, Eparchy of Toronto Papers, "Confidential Report on the Ruthenian Problem in Canada," 1923. Also see Stella Hryniuk, "The Bishop Budka Controversy: A New Perspective," *Canadian Slavonic Papers* 23 (1981): 162; Ruthenian and Ukrainian Papers, circular, 27 July 1914; copy of letter from a "Canadian Ukrainian" to the editor of *Saturday Night*, 22 Jan. 1919, and Thomas Murray to McNeil, 21 May 1921. For more detail on the treatment of Ukrainians in Canada during the war see John H. Thompson and Frances Swyripa, eds., *Loyalties in Conflict: Ukrainians in Canada during the Great War* (Edmonton: Canadian Institute of Ukrainian Studies 1983).

97 McNeil Papers, Bishop J. Morrison to McNeil, 29 Jan. 1913; Bishop David Scollard to McNeil, 4 Feb. 1913; Bishop Olivier Mathieu to McNeil, Jan. 1913; Auxiliary Bishop J.T. Ryan to McNeil, 26 Feb. 1913. CCES Office, *Minutes Book*, 2 April 1913, 28–30; Fitzpatrick Papers, vol. 15, McNeil to Fitzpatrick, 8 Nov. 1913, 6540.

98 Under the pontifical constitution of the society (1910), the president was appointed directly by the pope for a term of five years. Consequently, as a papal appointee, Burke could not be fired by McNeil. Intimidation left Burke unmoved. McNeil then tried to convince the Vatican to create new ecclesiastical jurisdictions in the Yukon or Prince Rupert and to appoint Burke prefect apostolic. CCES Papers, copy of letter from McNeil to the apostolic delegate, 1 March 1913.

99 *Register*, 4 Jan. 1917. For programs see *Register*, 9 and 11 March 1922, 25 March 1926, and 15 Dec. 1927.

100 McNeil Papers, copy of letter from McNeil to Mr Whalen of *The Casket*, 6 Dec. 1913.

101 *Register*, 5 Feb. 1920; Ruthenian and Ukrainian Papers, circular letter from Neil McNeil to priests of the archdiocese, 1 Oct. 1924.

102 Raymond Huel, "*Gestae Dei Per Francos*: The French Catholic Experience in Western Canada," in Benjamin Smillie, ed., *Visions of the New Jerusalem* (Edmonton: NeWest Press 1983), 39–54.

103 Archdiocesan Archives of Saint-Boniface (AASB), Adélard Langevin
Papers, copy of letter from Adélard Langevin to Archbishop L.N.
Bégin of Quebec, 21 Aug. 1908; Langevin to Bégin, 20 Sept. 1909;
copy of letter from Langevin to Father Thomas Dauson, 24 Oct. 1912;
and Langevin on "le Canadian Catholic Church Extension Society," 13
Jan. 1913.
104 CCES Papers, Adélard Langevin to Fergus Patrick McEvay, 16 Jan. 1909.
105 Langevin Papers, Langevin to Arthur Beliveau, 20 Sept. 1909.
106 Raymond Huel, "The Irish-French Conflict in Catholic Episcopal Nominations: The Western Sees and the Domination within the Church,"
Canadian Catholic Historical Association, *Study Sessions* 42 (1975): 51–
70.
107 Quoted in Pirot, *One Year's Fight for the True Faith*, 9; See also Kovacs,
"The Hungarian School Question," 341 and 350; Huel, *"Gestae Dei Per
Francos,"* 42. Other references to the French-Canadian vision in the
West can be gleaned in Arthur I. Silver, "Some Quebec Attitudes in an
Age of Imperialism," *Canadian Historical Review* 57, 4 (1976): 440–60;
Robert Painchaud, "French-Canadian Historiography and Franco-Cana-
dian Settlement in Western Canada," *Canadian Historical Review* 59, 4
(1978): 447–66; and Raymond Huel, "French-speaking Bishops and the
Cultural Mosaic in Western Canada," in Richard Allen, ed., *Religion
and Society in the Prairie West* (Regina: Canadian Plains Research
Center 1978): 335–58.
108 *Register*, 24 June 1915; Murphy Papers, vol. 9, Michael F. Fallon to
Charles Murphy, 29 April 1909, 3548–51.
109 ARCAT, McEvay Papers, copy of letter from McEvay to Cardinal DeLai
of the Consistorial Congregation, Rome, 30 April 1911.
110 AASB, Josaphat Jean Papers, document 12, Langevin to Father Josaphat
Jean, 4 Aug. 1913.
111 Jean Papers, document 13, Jean to Langevin, 10 Aug. 1913; and Langevin Papers, Father A. Husson, 7 March 1910, L34297.
112 This view contradicts more sympathetic portrayals of Langevin and his
francophone priests in John Herd Thompson, *The Harvests of War: The
Prairie West, 1914–1918* (Toronto: McClelland and Stewart 1978), 93;
and Huel, *"Gestae Dei Per Francos,"* 46–8.
113 Langevin Papers, A.E. Burke to Langevin, 3 Oct. 1909.
114 Langevin Papers, Langevin to Burke, 12 Oct. 1909; and Burke to Langevin, 13 April 1910.
115 *Register*, 1 Sept. 1910; Langevin Papers, copy of letter from Langevin
to Burke, 16 April 1910; Burke to Langevin, 16 July 1910. See also
L.P.A. Langevin, *Mémoire confidentiel sur la situation religieuse et statis-
tique de la population catholique de l'archdiocese de St. Boniface* (Saint-Boniface: np, 18 mai 1911).

116 Of the eight francophone bishops and vicars apostolic serving western
    sees from 1910 to 1920, only Ovid Charlebois (Keewatin) and Olivier-
    Elzéar Mathieu (Regina) were French Canadian by birth. Emile Bunoz
    (Prince George), Gabreil-Joseph Breynat (McKenzie), Emile Légal (St
    Albert [Edmonton]), Emile Grouard (Athabasca), Celestin Joussard
    (Athabasca), and Albert Pascal (Prince Albert) were all born in France.
    André Chapeau et al., *Canadian R.C. Bishops, 1658–1979* (Ottawa:
    Research Centre in Religious History of Canada, St Paul University
    1980). Several of the suffragans expressed reservations when Langevin
    insisted that the Canadian bishops' collection for the Ukrainians be
    sent to Saint-Boniface for distribution throughout the West. Bishop
    Pascal wanted to receive money directly, but was afraid to differ
    openly with Langevin, when McEvay suggested he press the issue.
    Ruthenian and Ukrainian Papers, Fergus McEvay to Bishop Richard
    O'Connor of Peterborough, 22 Nov. 1910. Langevin Papers, Father A.
    Husson to Langevin, 7 March 1910, indicates that Extension Society
    leaders were well aware that French-born bishops were friendly to the
    society, while French Canadians were too preoccupied by nationalism
    to support it.
117 Francis Clement Kelley, *The Bishop Jots it Down: An Autobiographical
    Strain on Memories by Francis C. Kelley* (New York: Harper & Row 1939),
    146–7. Murphy Papers, vol. 4, file 19, copy of letter from Murphy to
    Paul Bruchési, 22 Aug. 1910, 1344–7. In the letter, Murphy implies that
    Bruchési regards "Dr. Burke as a mischief-maker."
118 McNeil Papers, Bishop Ryan to McNeil, 26 Feb. 1913; further evidence
    noted in Fitzpatrick Papers, vol. 82, "Memorandum from A.E. Burke to
    the Duke of Norfolk," 6 April 1909, 45453–4; Burke to Fitzpatrick, 9
    April 1909, 45458.
119 *Register*, 4 July 1912; *Le Droit*, 9 Sept. 1913; and *Register*, 18 Sept. 1913,
    5 March 1914, and 30 March 1916 16 Sept. 1916.
120 *Register*, 24 June 1915 and 15 Sept. 1910. The apostolic delegate, Pelle-
    grino Stagni, demanded an end to the war between English- and
    French- Catholic newspapers. He ordered McNeil to muzzle Burke on
    issues regarding French-Canadian nationalism. ARCAT, Apostolic Dele-
    gate's Correspondence, Pellegrino Stagni to McNeil, 18 Sept. and 16
    Oct. 1913.
121 CCES Papers, Burke to McEvay, 17 July 1909; McEvay Papers, Henry
    O'Leary to McEvay, 4 Nov. 1909; Langevin Papers, A. Husson to Lan-
    gevin. Father Husson revealed that Francis Kelley of the American
    Extension Society boasted that Langevin's aims would be crushed by
    the curia if he complained to Rome about the CCES. Kelley told Husson
    that the CCES and the Anglo-Celtic bishops "are very strong there
    [Rome]." McEvay as mastermind is revealed in Apostolic Delegate's

Correspondence, McEvay to Donatus Sbaretti, 10 March 1909 (copy); McEvay Papers, copy of letter from Cardinal DeLai to Sbarretti, 17 Feb. 1909; and Archives of the Archdiocese of Ottawa (AAO), Toronto Correspondence, McEvay to Gauthier, 15 March 1909. Fallon acknowledged McEvay's role in ARCAT, McEvay Education Papers, Fallon to McEvay, 21 Jan. 1911.

122 Raymond Huel, "The French-Irish Conflict in Catholic Episcopal Nominations: The Western Sees and Domination within the Church," Canadian Catholic Historical Association, *Study Sessions* 42 (1975): 51–70.

123 *Register*, 15 Sept. 1910.

124 AO, James Pliny Whitney Papers, Fergus McEvay to Whitney, 15 Feb. 1910; and Whitney to McEvay, 9 March 1910.

125 McNeil Papers, McNeil to Mr Whalen of *The Casket*, 6 Dec. 1913; *Register*, 14 Sept. 1916.

126 *Register*, 27 Jan. 1910.

127 Whitney Papers, quoted in letter from James Whitney to Alfred Burke, 3 July 1914.

128 CCES Office, *Minutes*, 19 Nov. 1910, 23; Fitzpatrick Papers, vol. 13, copy of letter from Louis Bégin to Burke, 4 Nov. 1910, 5736; and copy of letter from Joseph Archambault to Burke, 2 Nov. 1910, 5735.

129 Fitzpatrick Papers, vol. 13, file 1910, copy of letter from Archbishop McEvay to Bégin, 27 Dec. 1910, 5823; copy of letter from Fergus McEvay, chancellor of extension, to Louis N. Bégin, 27 Dec. 1910, 5814–19. In the former letter he also defended his record of fairness to French Canadians and added that the bilingual schools issue was more the creation of the French-Canadian nationalist press than Ontario's English-speaking Catholics.

130 McNeil Papers, J.E. Cloutier, president of ACFEO to McNeil, 18 Feb. 1920; Archbishop Arthur Beliveau of Saint-Boniface to McNeil, 27 Jan. 1919; Father L.N. Campeau to McNeil, 15 June 1917; and clipping, "The Language Question, by Archbishop McNeil," 14 Feb. 1920; also ARCAT, Father James Athol Murray Papers, Father J.A. Murray to McNeil, 7 June 1916; and AAK, Michael J. Spratt Papers, minutes of the Meeting of the Archbishops of Canada, 27–30 April 1919.

131 Fitzpatrick Papers, vol. 26, Bishop Roy to Fitzpatrick, 20 Jan. 1920, 15197–8.

132 CCES Papers, Thomas O'Donnell to the bishops of the West, Dec. 1917. O'Donnell sent a series of questionnaires to all the western bishops regarding anglicization. Several responded by saying it was the case under Burke, but were not certain about the present. Arthur Beliveau of Saint-Boniface refused to endorse the society. Fitzpatrick Papers, vol. 28, McNeil to Fitzpatrick, 5 Jan. 1920.

133 Moir, "The Problem of a Double Minority: Some Reflections on the Development of the English-Speaking Catholic Church in Canada in the Nineteenth Century," *Histoire sociale/Social History* 4 (April 1971): 53–67.
134 *Register*, 22 Feb. 1912.
135 Huel, *"Gestae Dei Per Francos,"* 39–54.

Index

Acadians: growth of population, 7; and higher education, 9, 20; relations with English-speaking Catholics, xxii, 5, 7–9; and separate schools, 8
anti-Catholicism: British and American background of, 35–6; and Canadian nationalism, xxv, 38–41; decline of, 41–2; and Irish Catholics, 36–8, 206–7; and missions to native peoples, 40; as official policy, xxiv–xxv, 26–31; promoted by Equal Rights Association, 12, 38; and Protestant evangelicalism, 3; successive phases in Canada, 25; theological form of, xxv, 31–8; in Upper Canada, 171–2
Apostleship of Prayer (League of the Sacred Heart), 189–90, 193, 195
Archambault, Joseph-Alfred, 219, 229

Archconfraternity of the Holy Family, xxxiv, 190, 192–3, 195–6
Archeparchy and Metropolitan See of Winnipeg, xxxvii

Bailly de Messein, Charles-François, 5
Basilians, 162, 165
Beck, Nicholas, 219
Bégin, Louis N., 219, 229
Belcourt, Georges, 15
Benediction of the Blessed Sacrament, 192, 196, 198
Benevolent Irish Society, 58, 136–7
Blanchet, Norbert, 15
Bourg, Joseph-Mathurin, 106–8
Bourget, Ignace, 10, 33, 154–5
Bourne, John, xxxvi, 205, 228
British imperialism, xxxvi, 210–11
Brown, George, 37
Browne, Timothy, 139
Bruchési, Paul, 227

Budka, Nicetas, xx, 221–3, 226
Burke, Alfred, 219–27
Burke, Edmund: appointment as vicar apostolic of Nova Scotia, 6, 91–2, 113, 115, 131; candidate for vicar apostolic of Newfoundland, 57; correspondence with Propaganda, 109; and the division of the Diocese of Quebec, 92, 105, 111–12; and French-Canadian priests in the Maritimes, 7; lobbying at Rome, xxx; and trusteeism in Halifax, 130
Burke, Edmund (Dominican priest), 53, 130
Burke, Thomas, 63–4

Campbell, John, 52
Canning, Hugh J., 221, 225
Carroll, John, 101–2, 131, 142
Carroll, Michael, 141
Carson, William, 61, 66–7, 138

Catholic Church Extension Society: financial supporters of, 220–1; governors of, 219; and missions to European Catholic immigrants, xxxvi, 206, 214, 219–24; opposition of French-Canadian bishops to, 224–31

Catholic Emancipation: definition of, xi; in Atlantic Canada, xxv, 5; in the Maritime colonies, 28–9; in Newfoundland, xxvi, 29, 63, 64–6; and lay Catholic leadership, 127, 129

Catholic Institute, 165

Catholic Ladies Aid Society, 163

Catholic Ladies Hospital Visiting Society, 163

Catholic Mutual Benefit Association, 166, 209

Catholic newspapers, 209–10

Catholic Record, 209, 211

Catholic Register: and the assimilation of European Catholic immigrants, 214, 218–19; and bilingual schools in Ontario, 229; and Canadian Catholic identity, 209–10; and the Catholic Church Extension Society, 220; and French-speaking Catholics, 226–8; and Protestant proselytism, 213, 222; reformed by Neil McNeil, 224

Catholic voluntary associations: and the Canadianization of Toronto Catholics, 209; development at Halifax, 132; and lay Catholic leadership, 134; and missions

to European Catholic immigrants, 215; participation of men in, 198; participation of women in, xxxv, 185–6, 190, 193–9; and promotion of sacramental piety, 191–2; and religious observance among the laity, xxxv, 189, 197–8

Catholic Weekly Review, 209

Catholic Women's League, 209

Charbonnel, Armand-François-Marie de: appointment as bishop of Toronto, 10, 18, 159; and Catholic schools, 164; and development of Catholic institutions in Toronto, xxxii, 159–62; and the division of the Diocese of Toronto, 160; relations with Colin McKinnon, 159, foreign prelates, 159, Ignace Bourget, 155, 159; and spiritual and moral reform of the laity in the Diocese of Toronto, 188–9; succeeded by John Joseph Lynch, 172

Charlottetown, Diocese of, xxx

Chiasson, Patrice-Alexandre, xxii, 8

Children of Mary, 189–90

Chiniquy, Charles, 36

Christian Brothers, 155, 162, 165

Christian Guardian, 213

clergy: and Catholic-Protestant relations, 208; and Catholic voluntary associations, 189–90, 196–8; and community leadership, 12, 30–1, 81, 136, 139–40, 145; conduct of 53, 129–30, 135, 140, 157, 160–1, 216;

correspondence with Propaganda, 111; indigenization of, xxxvi, 206, 208; and marriage laws in Newfoundland, 59–63, 136; recruitment and training of: for European Catholic immigrants, xxi, 216–17, 219, 222–3, 225–6, for French-speaking Catholics, 107, for Irish and Scottish Catholics, xxiii–xxx, 81, 90, 92–5, 106, 108–9, 115, 127, 129, 132, 134, 138, 140, 156, 160, 162; and the reform of lay conduct, 165–6, 188–90; regular clergy: in the Diocese of Toronto, xxxiii, 165, in Quebec, 27, in the West, 15–16; relations with civil authorities, xxviii, 5, 53, 55–7, 84, 107, 129; supply of: for the Maritimes, 5, 7–8, for Quebec, xxii, for Upper Canada, 152, 160, for the West, xxxvi, 15, 218, 220–1; and trusteeism, 127–45 passim

Cochrane, Sir Thomas, 51, 57, 63, 65–6

confraternities. *See* Catholic voluntary associations

Connolly, Thomas Louis, xxxiii, 8, 19, 172

Cornell, Edmund, 14

Costigan, John, 175

Daly, George, 223

Davis, Michael P., 219

Dease, Joseph, 132–3

Demers, Modeste, 15

Denault, Pierre, 130–1

d'Esgly, Louis Philippe Mariauchau, 106, 129

devotional Catholicism:
and the cult of domes-
ticity, xxxv, 194–5; definition of, xi; embraced
mainly by women xxxv,
185, 190; practices asso-
ciated with, 190–2; pro-
moted by Armand de
Charbonnel, 188, clergy
of Diocese of Toronto,
188, Catholic voluntary
associations, xxxiv, 190,
Michael Power, 155; and
the transformation of
lay piety in Ireland, 186
Dollard, William, 6, 141–4
Dorrill, Richard, 51
Doyle, Laurence
O'Connor, 132–3
Duckworth, Sir John
Thomas, 60
Duhamel, Thomas-Joseph,
12–13, 227
Dumoulin, Sévère, 15
Dunphy, James, 143

education: bilingual
schools in Ontario, 228–
9; and the Canadianiza-
tion of Catholics in
Toronto, 208–9; Catholic
schools in the Diocese
of Toronto, 158, 164–5;
Catholic seminaries, 94–
5, 162; Catholic separate
schools and the assimi-
lation of European
Catholic immigrants,
215–16; Orphan Asylum
School in St John's, 58,
137
Edwards, Richard, 52
Elliott, John, 53
ethnic parishes, xx, xxxix
n10, 213
ethnic tensions: between
French-speaking and
English-speaking Cath-
olics: in British North
America (Canada),

xxxvi, 3–4, 18–21, 171,
in the Maritimes, xxi–
xxii, 4–9, 129, 140–1, in
Upper Canada
(Ontario), xxiii, 9–14, in
the West, xxiii–xxiv, 14–
17; between Irish and
Scottish Catholics, 7,
84–5, 93, 96, 129, 131,
133, 142; and missions
to European Catholic
immigrants, 206, 222–5,
231
European Catholics: and
anti-Catholicism, 37;
attempts of English-
speaking Catholics to
assimilate them: xxiii–
xxiv, xxxvi–xxxvii, 203–
6, in Toronto, 214–18, in
the West, 218–20, 223–
4, 231; and ethnic par-
ishes, xxxix n10; immi-
gration to Canada, xx,
181, 203–5, 211–12; and
Protestant proselytism,
205, 213, 215, 221. See
also ethnic tensions
Ewer, Thomas, 59

Fallon, Michael: appoint-
ment as bishop of
London, 228; and bilin-
gual schools in Ontario,
229; governor of the
Catholic Church Exten-
sion Society, 229; rela-
tions with French-
speaking Catholics, 14,
18, 20, 226
Faraud, Henri, 15
Farrell, John, 18
Ffrench, Charles, 140–3
First Vatican Council, 32
Fitzpatrick, Charles, 219–
20
Fleming, Michael
Anthony: appointment
as bishop of St John's,
139, coadjutor to

Thomas Scallan, 136,
curate in St John's, 136,
vicar apostolic of New-
foundland, 138; and
Catholic emancipation
in Newfoundland, 66;
and Catholic schools in
St John's, 137; and the
Newfoundland election:
of 1832, 67, 138, of
1833, 138, of 1840, 139;
proceedings against
him at Rome, 139; rela-
tions with civil authori-
ties, 66, 139; and
trusteeism in St John's,
136–40; and Ultramon-
tanism, 140
Foley, James, 211
forty-hours devotion, 192,
198
Franco-Ontarians, 10, 13–
14, 20
Fraser, William: among
the first English-
speaking bishops in
British North America,
xxviii; appointment as
bishop of Arichat (Anti-
gonish), 6, 133, vicar
apostolic of Nova Scotia,
6, 93, 116, 131; and
leadership of the Scot-
tish Catholic commu-
nity, 81, 91; opposition
from Irish Catholics, 96;
and trusteeism in Hal-
ifax, 131–3

Gaulin, Antoine, 89
Gaulin, Rémi, 10, 18, 153–
4
Gauthier, Charles Hugh,
14, 228
Gower, Erasmus, 50, 55–6
Grollier, Henri, 15
Guigues, Joseph, 10, 12

Hamilton, Sir Charles, 57
Haney, Michael J., 219

Hogan, Timothy, 137–8
Holloway, John, 55
Holy Name Society, 208–9, 215
Hubert, Jean-François, 54, 106, 112

Independent Greek church, 221
Irish Canadian, 210
Irish Catholic Benevolent Union, 166
Irish Catholics: and anti-Catholicism, 36–8; immigration to Atlantic Canada, 4–5, 126, to British North America, xviii–xxi, xxv, to Newfoundland, 51, 56, to Toronto, 158, 186, to Upper Canada, 153, 171; place in Toronto society, 206–8; religious background of, xxxiv–xxxv, 186–8. *See also* ethnic tensions
Irish nationalism, xxxvi, 208–9

Jesuit Estates Act, 38
Jones, James: appointment as "superior of the mission" for Nova Scotia, 129; correspondence with Propaganda, 109; missionary at Halifax, 5, 106, 108, 129; and recruitment of clergy, 109; and trusteeism in Halifax, 129–30

Kanadyskyi Rusyn, 222
Keats, Richard, 56
Kelley, Francis Clement, 219
Kent, John, 50, 66–7, 138–9
Kingston, Diocese of, xxx
Knights of Columbus, 208–9

Kough, Patrick, 67, 138

Laflèche, Louis-François, 15
Lafrance, François-Xavier, 9
Lambert, Patrick, 56–7, 135
Lang, George, 219
Langevin, Adélard, 225–6
Larkin, John, 10
Lartigue, Jean-Jacques, 10, 153
League of the Cross, 166
League of the Sacred Heart. *See* Apostleship of Prayer
LeBlanc, Edouard, xxii, 8
Légal, Emile, 229
Little, McLean, 137, 139
London, vicariate apostolic of, 105, 126, 133
Lynch, John Joseph: alliance with Liberal-Conservative party, 174; appointment as bishop of Toronto, 172; and Catholic voluntary associations in the Diocese of Toronto, 190, 197; and development of Catholic institutions in Toronto, xxxiii–xxxiv, 162; and the Diocese of Ottawa, xxiii, 11–12; and Irish Catholic immigration, xxxiii–xxxiv, 172–4, 179–81; and promotion of sacramental piety, 191; and proposal for New Ireland, xxxiii–xxxiv, 172, 174–8

McCarthy, D'Alton, 40
MacDonald, James, 5, 87, 107, 109
McDonald, John, 96
Macdonell, Alexander: among the first English-

speaking bishops in British North America, xxviii; appointment as bishop of Kingston, 9, 93, 106, 113, 116, 153, vicar-general for Upper Canada, 106, 114, 153; consecration as bishop of Resina *in partibus infidelium*, 153; death, 96; and the division of the Diocese of Quebec, 92–3, 112; friendship with John Strachan, 171; and immigration of Scottish Catholics to Glengarry County, 171; and leadership of the Scottish Catholic community, 81, 91; lobbying at Rome, xxx; missionary in Upper Canada, 9, 87, 152; and plan for a seminary at Glengarry, 94; relations with Quebec bishops, 9–10, 19; succeeded by French-speaking bishops, 18
Macdonell, Alexander (of Scothouse), 87
MacEachern, Angus Bernard: among the first English-speaking bishops in British North America, xxviii; appointment as bishop of Charlottetown, 6, 93, 116, 142, vicar-general for Prince Edward Island, Cape Breton, Iles de la Madeleine, and New Brunswick, 114–15; and the division of the Diocese of Quebec, 92–3, 111–12; and the founding of St Andrew's College, 95; and leadership of the Scottish Catholic com-

munity, 81, 91; missionary in Prince Edward Island, 87, 107; and the recruitment of clergy, 89; relations with the Quebec bishops, 91; and trusteeism in Saint John, 142

McEvay, Fergus: and the Catholic Church Extension Society, 219–20, 225; and ethnic parishes in Toronto, 213; and European Catholic immigrants, 212, 218; relations with French-speaking Catholics, 226, 228–30

McGuigan, James, 213, 228

McGuire, Francis, 108

McKinnon, Colin, 159

MacLeod, Alexander, 90

McMahon, Patrick, 141–2

McManus, John, 108

McNally, John Thomas, 17

McNeil, Neil: and Canadian Catholic patriotism, 209, 211; and the Catholic Church Extension Society, 223; and ethnic parishes in Toronto, 213; and European Catholic immigrants, 216, 218; and lay obedience to ethnic clergy, 217; relations with French-speaking Catholics, 14, 230

McQuade, Paul, 140

Magann, George P., 219

Maillard, Pierre A.-S., 5, 28

marriage laws in Newfoundland, 59–63

Mathieu, Olivier-Elzéar, 228

Milbanke, Mark, 53

Montreal, Diocese of, xxxii

Moran, William, 143

Morissette, J.-E., 140–1

Morris, Patrick, 51, 59, 64

Murdoch, John, 153

Newfoundland School Society, 58

Oblates, 15–16

O'Brien, Richard Baptist, 132–4

O'Connor, Denis, 216, 218

O'Donahoe, John, 174

O'Donel, James Louis: appointment as prefect apostolic of Newfoundland, 53, 105, 109, 134–5, vicar apostolic of Newfoundland, 109, 115, 135; attacked by Prince William Henry, 30, 53; missionary at St John's, 106; relations with civil authorities, 54–5

O'Donnell, Thomas, 224, 230

O'Grady, William John, 96

O'Keefe, Eugene, 219

Orphan Asylum School, 58, 137–8

Palliser, Hugh, 52

Panet, Bernard-Claude, 112, 142

parish missions, 189

Phelan, Patrick, 18, 53, 155

Phelan, William, 129–30

Pickmore, Francis, 60

Pinsoneault, Pierre-Adolphe, 10, 18

Plessis, Joseph-Octave: appointment as archbishop of Quebec, 115; and the division of the Diocese of Quebec, 92, 112, 115; lobbying at Rome, xxx; membership of the Executive Council of Lower Canada, 63;

relations with civil authorities, 56; and Scottish Catholics in British North America, 89; and trusteeism in Saint John, 140–2

population statistics: Catholic population of Canada by linguistic affiliation, 5 (table 1); English-speaking Catholics in British North America (Canada), xix; growth of Catholic population in Atlantic Canada, 145, in eighteenth-century British North America, 103–4; and the proportion of Catholics in the Newfoundland population, 68–9 n1, European immigrants among Toronto Catholics, 212, French to English-speaking Catholics in Canada, 3, 6; provincial origins of Irish Catholics in Newfoundland, 78 n129; social mobility among Toronto Catholics, 232 n9

Power, John, 57

Power, Michael: appointment as bishop of Toronto, 10, 18, coadjutor bishop of Kingston, 154; and Catholic schools in the Diocese of Toronto, 158; and the creation of an ecclesiastical province of Quebec, 154; and development of Catholic institutions in the Diocese of Toronto, xxxii, 155–8; and the division of the Diocese of Kingston, 154; and Irish Catholic immigration to

Toronto, 158; relations with Quebec bishops, 155
Power, Patrick, 53
Protestant Laymen's Missionary Movement, 221
Provencher, Joseph-Norbert, 15

Quebec, bishops of, 5, 111–12
Quebec, Diocese of: division of, xxviii, xxxii, 92–3, 105, 111–12, 115; and English-speaking Catholics, xxi–xxii, xxx, 104–5; jurisdiction over the Maritimes, 126; recognition as archdiocese, xxxii, 116
Quiblier, Joseph, 10, 153
Quigley, James, 219

Redemptorists, 162, 166
Reeves, John, 54
Roche, J.T., 221, 225
Rogers, James, 19
rosary, xxxiv, 191
Ryan, Patrick T., 227

Sacred Congregation de Propaganda Fide (Propaganda): and the choice of a successor to Alexander Macdonell, 153; definition of, xiii; and the division of the Diocese of Kingston, 154, of Quebec, 92–3; jurisdiction over North America, 101; policy towards North America, xxix–xxxi, 114–17; reprimand of Bishop Lynch, xxxiii; sources of information on British North America, 107–11
Sacred Heart of Jesus, xxxiv, 192

Saint-Boniface, Archdiocese of, xxxvii
Saint John, Diocese of, xxxii
Saint Joseph's Society, 193–4
St Vincent de Paul Society, xxxiii, 162–6, 190, 196
Sbaretti, Donatus, 219
Scallan, Thomas: appointment as vicar apostolic of Newfoundland, 57, 116, 135; criticized by Michael Anthony Fleming, 137; and marriage laws in Newfoundland, 62; relations with civil authorities, 57–8, 63–4
Schweitzer, J.P., 216
Scottish Catholics: declining influence in British North America, xxix; immigration to Atlantic Canada, 126, British North America, xviii–xxi, xxvii, 79, 85–7, Glengarry County, 171; national customs, 88; relations of Scottish Catholics in British North America to Catholic church in Scotland, xxvii–xxviii, 80–5; relations with Acadians, 87–8, civil authorities, xxviii–xxix, Diocese of Quebec, 89–93, Irish Catholics, 88; and the transformation of British North American Catholicism, xxviii–xxix. See also ethnic tensions
Shaughnessy, Sir Thomas, 219
Signay, Joseph, 154
Sinnott, Alfred, xxi, 219–26, 228
Sisters of Charity of St Vincent de Paul, 162

Sisters of Loretto, 155, 165
Sisters of St Joseph, 162, 165
Sisters of the Good Shepherd, 162
Sisters of the Precious Blood, 162
Skerrett, John, 54
Society of Our Lady of Perpetual Help, 197
Society of the Blessed Virgin Mary, 189–90
Sodality of the Blessed Virgin Mary, xxxiv
Sweeny, John, 19

Taché, Alexandre-Antonin, xxxiv, 15, 175–6
Taschereau, Alexandre, 219
Thibault, Jean-Baptiste, 15
Tobin, Michael, 132–3
Toronto, Diocese of, xxxii
Toronto Savings Bank, 166
Troy, John Thomas, 54, 56, 138–9
trusteeism: in Atlantic Canada, xxxi–xxxii, 126–9, 144–5; and ethnic tensions, 129, 131, 133, 140–2; in Halifax, 129–34; in Saint John, 140–44; in St John's, 134–40; in the United States, xxxi–xxxii, 127–9, 144–5
Tucker, Chieff Justice, 65–6

Ukrainian Catholic Church in Canada. See Budka, Nicetas
Ultramontanism: and centralization of church government, xxxii; and the clergy of the Diocese of Toronto, 188; definition of, xv; and growth of episcopal